SPY CAPITALISM

Jonathan E. Lewis

SPY ITEK AND THE CIA

CAPITALISM

Yale University Press

New Haven & London

FOR LAURA, STEVEN, AND HANNAH

Published with assistance from the Louis Stern Memorial Fund.

Designed by Nancy Ovedovitz and set in Galliard Old Style type by Achorn Graphic Services. Printed in the United States of America by R. R. Donnelley & Sons.

Library of Congress Cataloging-in-Publication Data
Lewis, Jonathan E., 1962–
Spy capitalism : Itek and the CIA / Jonathan E. Lewis.
    p.   cm.
ISBN 0-300-09192-3 (cloth : alk. paper)
1. United States. Central Intelligence Agency. 2. Itek Corporation.
3. Rockefeller, Laurence S., 1910–   I. Title.
JK468.I6 L47 2002
327.1273 — dc21   2001004665

A catalogue record for this book is available from the British Library.

The paper in this book meets the guidelines for permanence and durability of the Committee on Production Guidelines for Book Longevity of the Council on Library Resources.

10 9 8 7 6 5 4 3 2 1

CONTENTS

1

THE BATTLEGREEN INN

Could he save the company? In May 1962 it was a question that must have weighed heavily on Laurance Rockefeller's mind.

It was the most dangerous year of the Cold War. Assassins from the Central Intelligence Agency were stalking Fidel Castro, communist insurgencies in Laos and Vietnam were gaining momentum, and the moment of near Armageddon, the Cuban missile crisis, was just months away. Yet Rockefeller, grandson of the Standard Oil founder, John D., and younger brother of Nelson, was about to make decisions critical to the security of the nation. He didn't hold elected office or serve in a president's cabinet. He was a businessman, a venture capitalist. And he made this contribution to America's national security anonymously.

A venture capitalist is a special breed of investor. Not content with the returns produced by mere stocks or bonds, a venture capitalist seeks investments of a higher order. Greater returns can be attained only by taking bigger risks. Namely, calculated long shots. For the venture capitalist this can mean providing capital to the kind of small, start-up company that often can't get a loan from a bank. But if the company succeeds, the payoff can be huge.

Laurance Rockefeller was a different kind of venture capitalist. He believed that there was a strong link between the quality of American technology and the credibility of U.S. national security. Jets, rockets, and nuclear bombs could make America safe. But only as long as the jets were faster, the rockets stronger, and the bombs more powerful than anything the Soviet Union could build. Rockefeller wanted to achieve a high return on his investments, but his primary goal was to invest in technologies that would strengthen U.S. national security. As an heir to one of America's great fortunes, he had sufficient means to pursue his vision, and the acumen to build a staff that could implement it. Rockefeller invested in jets, rockets, and nuclear research. And along the way he multiplied his millions. Suddenly, one of Rockefeller's best-performing investments was on the verge of collapse. The company was Itek.

In response to the emergency, Rockefeller had just flown up from New York City in his private plane and landed at a small airport outside of Lexington, Massachusetts. A driver in an unmarked car belonging to the Itek Corporation took Rockefeller the short distance to a small Lexington motel. The Battlegreen Inn, as it was aptly called, bordered the historic field where almost two centuries earlier, the minutemen took their stand against the British in the effort to gain America's freedom. That evening Laurance Rockefeller would take a stand of a different kind to preserve it. Rockefeller was scheduled to attend an emergency meeting of Itek's board of directors. Although Rockefeller wasn't on the board, he was Itek's largest shareholder.[1]

Founded in 1957 with seed money from Rockefeller, Itek was the kind of investment that venture capitalists dream about. In the first three months of the company's life, its payroll swelled from a handful of executives to more than one hundred scientists, engineers, and technicians. By the end of the company's first full year of operation, revenues and profits soared from zero into the millions. And when Itek decided to sell its stock to the public after less than two years in operation, investors were eager to buy their share of what the financial world considered a miracle company.[2]

Wall Street analysts, journalists, and investors alike believed that Itek was leading an information revolution that would sweep America into the future. The company's crisp-sounding name was a phonetic contraction of the very words *information technology*. The investment community bought Itek's story and they also bought the stock. Less than eighteen months after the initial offering, the price of a share of Itek's stock had soared from $2 to more than $200 a share.

Itek's tale was more than breathtaking; it was, in part, a cover story.

Wall Street tycoons and main street investors who owned stock from 1958 through 1962 had scarcely an idea about how the company made money. They didn't know the true source of the company's profits or the name of its biggest client.

Laurance Rockefeller knew.

Itek was the most sophisticated manufacturer of reconnaissance cameras in the world, and its products were the crown jewels in the most important CIA program in U.S. history—Project CORONA. CORONA was the code name for America's first spy satellite program. Itek cameras, launched into orbit aboard Lockheed rockets and returned to earth in a General Electric capsule, took photographs of the Soviet Union from more than two hundred miles in space. Analysts at the CIA's National Photo Interpretation Center used the photographs to locate Soviet missile sites and to develop overall assessments of Soviet military strength. Information obtained by Itek cameras was critical to U.S. national security. So was Itek.[3]

Now the company was in a state of crisis. The crisis had been brewing for months. After three years of consecutive record growth in earnings and revenues, the company reported a surprising loss for fiscal 1961. The stock price was down and a painful restructuring was on the drawing board. These were symptoms of troubles far greater than either the investment community or CIA officers at the time would ever know.

A key group of Itek scientists, engineers, and executives wanted the board of directors to fire Richard Leghorn, the company's president. Leghorn was the visionary entrepreneur who had made Itek possible. He had developed the company's original business plan and persuaded Rockefeller to invest in it.

The mutineers, as the scientists termed themselves, demanded a meeting with the board to state their case. Members of the Itek board quickly assembled to hear their story. The mutineers explained that Leghorn was hurting the company. And hurting Itek meant endangering national security. Leghorn, the mutineers insisted, had to go.

Under ordinary circumstances, the men on Rockefeller's handpicked board of directors would keep the president and fire the mutineers. After all, the board was filled with men who had served in high levels of government and the military, or were members of old-money families. In their conservative world, the sanctity of the corporate command structure was unquestioned.

The board faced a difficult problem. The mutineers comprised some of the top scientists and engineers in the country. If the situation at Itek deteriorated any further and affected their work — or worse, if any of them left the company — the single most important national security project in the country would be seriously jeopardized. Would the board back Leghorn or the mutineers? As Laurance Rockefeller arrived at the Battlegreen Inn, it was probably not yet clear in his own mind what course of action he would choose.[4]

The Itek board of directors meeting began that night at about 8:00 P.M. Not long afterward, the mutineers marched in to present their case. The national importance of the decisions to be made that day in Lexington was unquestionable, yet no representative of the CIA, the Department of Defense, or the National Security Council was present. No government officials were aware of the meeting, and no security officials swept the room for listening devices despite the acutely sensitive nature of the meeting.

Albert Pratt, former assistant secretary of the navy and current partner with Paine Webber, was chair of the board's executive committee and ran the meeting that night. Laurance Rockefeller listened quietly as scientists and engineers like Walter Levison, Dow Smith, and John Wolfe presented the case against the man who had founded and built Itek. Wolfe stood up and faced Rockefeller. Where had he been the past year? Why had he allowed the company to nearly disintegrate? Surely, this was not treatment to which a Rockefeller was accustomed, certainly not from an employee of a company that he controlled. As the meeting wore on, Leghorn's supporters waited in the hallway for their turn to speak.[5]

That evening, Frank Lindsay sat at home and considered his future. One of the few American spies to penetrate Hitler's Third Reich, Lindsay was a risk taker. Now he was Itek's executive vice president. He joined the company after leaving a job at the prestigious consulting firm McKinsey and Company. That evening he wondered whether this gamble was a mistake. Technically speaking, he was the number two man at the company. In actuality, he felt like an outcast. When he had left his job as a McKinsey consultant to join Itek, he had had high hopes for his future. Now, almost a year later, he had yet to make his mark at the company. He had no operating responsibilities and spent most of his time on long-range planning documents. Leghorn had effectively shut him out, and Lindsay was thinking of resigning. The idea of leaving the corporate world and becoming a professor at his alma mater, Stanford, seemed attractive.

Yet Frank Lindsay was an unlikely professor. Although Lindsay was a soft-spoken, articulate man, above all else he was a man of action. Given his temperament, it seemed unlikely that Lindsay would spend the Cold War on the sidelines as a professor, or in a corporate staff position — precisely his two career options at that moment.

Late that same night, the telephone rang at Lindsay's house. It was Albie Pratt.[6]

Why should we care what Pratt told Lindsay that night? After all, Itek is a forgotten name and the company itself was dismantled years ago.

But there was a time when Itek was one of the great glamour stocks on Wall Street. At its peak, Itek's fame rivaled the notoriety, and the price-to-earnings ratio, of the top Internet stocks of the great NASDAQ bubble of the late 1990s. Its name was splashed across the front pages of *The Wall Street Journal* and *Business Week*. Its virtues were extolled in the likes of *Barron's* and *Forbes*. Yet the significance of Itek's story goes well beyond its value as a stock market parable for all ages.

In part Itek deserves to be remembered because of its historic contributions to U.S. national security. Without question, Itek's camera technology was critical to the success of the CORONA spy satellite program. When Itek's cameras began clicking in space during the summer and fall of 1960, the photographs they produced tore the Iron Curtain to shreds. The Kremlin's ability to keep great military secrets was destroyed, and the myth that a missile gap existed was shattered. Pictures taken by Itek cameras helped Presidents Eisenhower, Kennedy, Johnson, and Nixon to better understand the nature of the Soviet threat, and to effectively structure America's defense posture in response.

But just as Itek cameras helped secure America's defense, they also paved the way to peace. Technology developed at the company allowed the CIA to monitor the Soviet Union's intercontinental ballistic missile forces. Thanks to Itek's cameras, U.S. diplomats were confident that verifiable arms control agreements could be negotiated with the Soviet Union. When President Nixon signed the Strategic Arms Limitation Treaty (SALT) with Soviet Premier Leonid Brezhnev in 1972, the world became a less dangerous place. It would not have happened without Itek's technology.

Itek's birth in 1957 heralds the rise of the intelligence-industrial complex. In the history of the CIA, the period of the 1950s and early 1960s was a golden age of daring innovation led by the visionary Richard M. Bissell Jr. Manager of the U-2 program, architect of the SR-71 Blackbird, and artificer of CORONA, Bissell ripped government red tape to pieces and pulled the CIA from the era of Mata Hari into the space age. Along the way he built a pioneering partnership between business and the CIA that harnessed the ingenuity of the nation's industrial base to achieve important intelligence objectives. Today, as the CIA again seeks to leverage the best ideas in the private sector, Bissell's management approach remains fresh and relevant.

Unlike many other firms that became key CIA contractors, Itek was a start-up company. During this period Itek had to overcome a series of technical, financial, and managerial problems in order to grow and survive in a world of industrial giants. For the company's executives, the pressure of being a contractor on the most important national security program of the time was magnified by the challenge of managing a new corporation.

In order to build manufacturing facilities and research laboratories, Itek needed capital. At first Laurance Rockefeller provided it. Itek's story, written in large measure from his papers, offers a rare glimpse inside his trendsetting venture capital operations. Later the company turned to the American public for funds. But management could never tell the vast majority of its shareholders about the true nature of Itek's business. During this critical period, which lasted from 1957 to 1965, management made many difficult decisions as it balanced the need to keep secrets, grow a company, and meet shareholders' interests.

Told from documents never before available, Itek's story provides an inside look at a company positioned at the crossroad where business and espionage intersect. As a result, its story helps us to understand the questions raised by the CIA's partnership with business. In working behind a cloak of secrecy, for example, did management work more wisely, or more recklessly? Did company executives guard the best interests of shareholders, the CIA, the nation, or themselves? And when the interests of these constituencies diverged, was it possible to reconcile their differences?

Before these questions can be answered, at least from Itek's perspective, it is important to place the company in the context of its own place and time. The men who founded and managed Itek were all veterans of World War II. Richard Leghorn, Itek's president, flew dangerous reconnaissance missions over Normandy and brought back intelligence that General Eisenhower used to plan for D-Day. Franklin Lindsay, Itek's executive vice president, was among the first American spies to penetrate the Third Reich. The lessons and ideological values men like Leghorn and Lindsay learned during the war shaped the way they looked at the postwar world and influenced how they managed the company as well.

Although World War II was the shared experience that bound Itek's management team together, their operating environment was the early years of the Cold War. It was a time when the Soviet Union loomed large in the minds of all Americans and the very existence of the United States seemed threatened.

In a time of great danger, men who might ordinarily have led quiet lives chose to live with an uncommon purpose. Many of the executives and scientists who worked at Itek and Laurance Rockefeller's venture capital operations were such men. They pursued private-sector careers with a sense of civic duty. Yet even in the best of times it was a difficult balance to achieve.

It was a goal that Franklin Lindsay tirelessly pursued. Long before he was a businessman, Lindsay was a commando. The story of his rise through America's national security establishment in the years immediately after World War II helps to explain why the Soviet Union was such a treacherous enemy and why a company like Itek was necessary. For that story, we must go back in time to 1944, to a plane flying high above Nazi-occupied Europe.

2

"YOU DAMNED FOOL, NOW LOOK
WHAT YOU'VE GONE AND DONE"

May 14, 1944. Maj. Franklin Lindsay, aboard a British Halifax bomber, prepared to jump out of the plane into German-occupied Yugoslavia. Lindsay was a member of the elite Office of Strategic Services. Established in 1942 by Gen. William "Wild Bill" Donovan, the OSS was America's wartime spy service. Lindsay's mission was to join Tito's partisans and fight the Germans from behind their own lines.

The plane descended to a low altitude for the final approach to the drop zone. The time to jump arrived. Lindsay leaped through the small opening in the floor of the plane and into a 120 mph wind. After a few seconds of free fall, the chute opened and Lindsay could see the Halifax flying back to base. "You damned fool," he thought to himself, "now look what you've gone and done." If the Germans captured Lindsay, he would probably be executed as a spy.[1]

It didn't have to be this way. Lindsay grew up in Pasadena, California, an only child. Before he was eleven years old, he turned his ankles while playing baseball. The damage was severe. He completely tore the attachment of the Achilles tendon to the heel in both legs. The next two years of his life were spent in a wheelchair. Unable to climb up the steps that led to his classroom, Lindsay was carried in each day by the school janitor. It was a humiliation he would not forget.

Unable to play baseball or sports of any kind with his friends, Lindsay devoted his energies to his studies. It was a habit that lasted long after his legs healed. When he graduated from high school, Lindsay finished near the top of his class. His next stop was Stanford University.

At college Lindsay was drawn to engineering. He wanted to build, to shape the world around him, but in a practical way. At the same time, he was increasingly concerned about growing tensions in Europe. In the summer of 1938 he traveled to Germany for a firsthand look at Hitler's Third Reich and was appalled by what he saw. After graduation he worked for a year at U.S. Steel as an industrial engineer, but decided to return to Stanford for business school. Then in 1940 France fell to the Germans. Lindsay left school and volunteered for the army; by 1941 he was sent to Washington to work in the U.S. Army Ordnance Department.[2]

Lindsay soon found himself working to solve manufacturing problems for the army. Copper shortages were slowing the production of cartridge cases and small arms. Lindsay, a young second lieutenant, stepped into the breach, and from his office on the south side of Constitution Avenue he wrestled with the laws of supply and demand. Helping American copper producers more efficiently allocate their inventory to industry, Lindsay made sure the factories never had to slow their assembly lines due to a supply shortage again.[3]

Lindsay was transferred overseas in late 1942. He was sent to Iran. By this time a German offensive had forced the Soviets to retreat all the way to the Caucasus. In order to launch an effective counteroffensive, the Red Army needed new supplies, and fast. If the Red Army didn't hold the line, the Germans would break through into the Persian Gulf, gain control of vital oil fields, and obtain a commanding position in the region. Lindsay's mission was to set up a truck assembly plant in Iran, train a local labor force, and then send truck convoys filled with supplies to the Soviet Union. Time was of the essence.

Lindsay's workforce lacked education and technical skills of any kind. And with few army interpreters who spoke Persian, crude sign language was the only way for Lindsay and his sergeants to communicate with the workers. Yet somehow Lindsay's factory was soon reaching its production targets.

After a string of initial successes, Lindsay became fed up with factory life. At the beginning of the operation it was a small command, and Lindsay had independent authority. But as time went on the operation became more bureaucratic. He wanted out. A chance meeting with an officer from the U.S. Command in Cairo led to a transfer there. On several occasions he ran into officers in Cairo who were in the oss. Cairo was the center for Allied military planning for the Balkans, and the oss operatives were beginning to prepare for commando operations there. Lindsay was intrigued by their work and they were intrigued by his engineering knowledge, the kind of skills that might prove handy when a bridge needed to be destroyed. Soon he was a member of the oss.[4]

When Lindsay joined he knew it would be dangerous. But it also offered him a chance to "break out" of the "mass anonymity" of the army. As Lindsay recalled years later in his memoirs, "I sensed in ways that could not be charted it would change my life after the war and it did."[5]

As Lindsay floated toward the ground, he could see the fires marking the drop areas set up by the Partisans. He had succeeded in breaking out of the anonymous life of the army; he was now an elite commando.

Lindsay hit the ground and quickly took off his parachute. He saw flashlights in the distance. They might be Germans. Lindsay had little choice but to signal back with his flashlight and pray.

It was the Partisans. Within days, Lindsay had traveled with them to the border that separated German-occupied Yugoslavia from the Third Reich itself. If he crossed the border successfully, he would be one of the first Americans — perhaps the very first — to infiltrate the Reich since the start of the war. The crossing could be made only at night. When the sun began to set that evening, the Partisan leader outlined his plan. Thirty men would escort Lindsay to the border. There they would find a death zone of double barbed-wire fence, minefields, patrols, and watchtowers. After sunset, an advance party would cut a path through the fences and the mines, and local Partisans would scout the area for enemy patrols.[6]

At the outset of darkness Lindsay and the Partisans began their single-file advance to the German border. After a long walk, they could finally see the barbed wire illuminated by the white glow of moonlight. The leader of the Partisans stopped the column. He declared that each man was to follow the exact path of the man before him. A step in the wrong direction and a mine would be detonated, a body would explode, and the Germans would kill the survivors. That night they crossed the frontier. But the sense of victory was fleeting. They soon made a chilling discovery. One of the men in the column had silently dropped out of sight.

The following day, Lindsay was shaving outside a farmhouse when his group was surprised by a German patrol. The Germans attacked the farmhouse with machine-gun and mortar fire. Lindsay ran back into the house. The Partisans were already gone. He had a bad feeling, but there was no time for fear. He simply had to "get the hell out of there." He quickly located his gun and his pack. Then running out the door, he ran up a steep slope, with bullets hitting the grass all around him, and followed the Partisans into the forest. The Partisans had been penetrated. The man who had dropped out of the column the night before had alerted the Germans that an American spy was in their midst, and now they were coming after Lindsay.

As Lindsay and the Partisans spent the day in the forest, waiting for night before making their next move, a courier reached them with more bad news. A large force of German troops was preparing to encircle them. They had to make an immediate break out of the forest or face capture, or worse. After a dangerous night evading the Germans, they broke out of the forest and reached safety.[7]

Now Lindsay's real mission could begin. His objective — to blow up German railway lines deep in the Third Reich. If he could accomplish his mission, Germany's strategic ability to move troops quickly to and from the eastern and Italian fronts would be seriously compromised. Lindsay and the Partisans embarked on a series of daring attacks against the German rail system, and the Nazi war machine was dealt a damaging blow.[8]

Lindsay's initial experience with the Partisans was exhilarating. Day after day he was alternately fighting, marching, fleeing, sleeping, eating, drinking, and mourning with his Partisan comrades. The bonds that developed between Lindsay and the guerrilla fighters were genuine. But they went only so far.

Over time Lindsay concluded that the Partisans were using him. As Lindsay fed his superiors a stream of positive reports on his commando raids with the Partisans, the Allied Command grew increasingly confident that they were a capable fighting force deserving of increased support. The once-erratic pace of airdrops turned into a steady stream of supplies. Guns, explosives, ammunition, all reached the Partisan army in increased quantities, strengthening their firepower and their ability to fight.

But they didn't. By the fall, Lindsay realized that the Partisans were saving the supplies in "mountain bunkers." They were preparing for their next battle, after the Allies defeated the Nazis. Then the real Partisan campaign would begin, a campaign to create a Communist Yugoslavia led by Marshall Tito. Lindsay tried to get the Allied Command to turn off the supply spigot. Yet the same military bureaucracy that had been slow to respond to Lindsay's requests for aid was equally sluggish in stopping the shipments.

Lindsay's preconceptions about the Partisans had been completely shattered. Before he made his fateful jump to join them, Lindsay had believed that he was teaming up with a guerrilla army fighting for the liberation of their country. Now he saw the Partisans for what they really were: "a nationalist Communist political movement." They used their training camps as "centers of political indoctrination" and to enforce "police control" of the civilians. In order to spread their Communist ideology, almost all the major Partisan units had their own printing presses, which were more closely guarded than their few artillery pieces. And as the Germans withdrew, the Partisans ruthlessly eliminated all potential challenges to their leadership.[9]

By the time Lindsay left Yugoslavia, he had received a complete education on Communist tactics and strategy. Lindsay's expertise made him a valuable man. Before he returned to the United States in late 1945, Lindsay made an appearance at the Council of Foreign Ministers meeting in London that fall. Robert Joyce, head of the OSS mission in Switzerland, arranged for Lindsay to serve as an adviser to the U.S. delegation. The purpose of the meeting was to continue the work begun at Yalta—the creation of a postwar international order. Yugoslavia was likely to be a continued flashpoint, and Lindsay's knowledge and growing reputation earned him a place at the conference.[10]

Lindsay's role at the conference was limited, but through his participation, his contacts and reputation continued to grow. By early 1946, after leaving the OSS, he briefly flirted with the idea of getting a doctorate in economics at Harvard. Instead, he soon found himself working for the famed Wall Street speculator — and presidential adviser — Bernard Baruch.

Barely two weeks after Winston Churchill's famous Iron Curtain speech, President Truman handed Baruch one of the great political footballs of the century — trying to figure out a plan to control the spread of atomic weapons. Baruch, now the U.S. representative at the United Nations Atomic Energy Commission, was widely respected by the American public. And, he had the ability to communicate complex ideas in plain language that the public could understand. If anyone could credibly explain to the nation the vital importance of crafting a policy on the international control of atomic energy, it was Baruch.

Baruch quickly built a staff to support his efforts. In addition to Ferdinand Eberstadt, John Hancock, and Fred Searls, he hired Franklin Lindsay. Negotiations with the Russians would be critical to Baruch's success, and Lindsay had already built a reputation as an expert on Communist tactics.[11]

Much of the work on developing America's atomic energy policy had already been done. A group headed by Dean Acheson, the undersecretary of state, and David Lilienthal, head of the Tennessee Valley Authority, had finished a report on the subject just days before Baruch's appointment. The report recommended that a new international agency, the Atomic Development Authority, be created to "exercise world control over atomic energy." All the world's uranium mines and processing plants would be owned by the agency. As a sign of good faith, America would turn over to it the only atomic bomb factories on earth.[12]

It was an idealistic plan. Though Baruch adopted many of the proposals in the Acheson-Lilienthal report, he made an important revision. The original plan contained no provision to stop a nation from violating the agreement. Such an omission was optimistic at best. In a dramatic radio address Baruch explained, "We must provide the mechanism to assure that atomic energy is used for peaceful purposes. To that end, we must provide immediate, swift, and sure punishment of those who violate" the agreement. The old speculator's proposal, outlined to the American people in stark and simple terms, quickly became known as the Baruch Plan.[13]

America applauded Baruch's speech, but Andrei Gromyko, speaking for the Soviet Union, quickly communicated the Kremlin's lack of enthusiasm for it. If America really wanted to stop the spread of atomic weapons, Gromyko argued, then the United States should destroy its own stock of atomic bombs. As U.S.-Soviet relations deteriorated, and the Cold War began in earnest, Baruch's plan became stalled.[14]

Months passed and Baruch and his team made little headway. Finally, on Saturday evening, October 19, Franklin Lindsay and Ferdinand Eberstadt had dinner with the assistant secretary general of the United Nations, a Soviet bureaucrat named Arkaday Sobolev. Lindsay had always found it difficult to talk with Gromyko. Although Sobolev was essentially an international civil servant, Lindsay was certain that he took instructions from his own government. As Lindsay explained days later in a memorandum of the meeting to Baruch, his goal that evening was to establish a new channel of communications with the Soviet government apart from the official channel with Andrei Gromyko.

Dinner was at the exclusive River Club. Sobolev arrived at the restaurant by himself, his independence an indication of high rank in the Soviet Communist Party. Sobolev bluntly stated that "in the present international situation" the United States' continued atomic bomb production was a destabilizing "force in the world." America's plan, he declared, "was in essence a plan for world government." And, Sobolev assured his dinner companions that the world "was not ready for world government." After some genuine discussion on the subject of world government, Sobolev presented his most important objection to the proposal. Simply put, the Soviet Union wanted "freedom to pursue its own policies in complete freedom and without any interference or control from the outside."

Lindsay was impressed with Sobolev's frankness, and he told Baruch that he believed Sobolev's views represented official Soviet policy on the subject. Lindsay concluded that Sobolev's emphasis on the need for unlimited Soviet freedom "strongly indicate[d] that no general understanding based on mutual trust and cooperation is possible between the two systems of government." Lindsay's conclusion was inauspicious for the future of the Baruch Plan, but his dark analysis began to receive wide attention within foreign policy circles, and his reputation continued to grow. Not long after Lindsay's dinner with Sobolev, the United States ambassador to the Soviet Union, Walter Bedell Smith, was praising his analysis as "eminently sound."[15]

By late 1946 the Baruch Plan had been defeated. It was a personal blow for Lindsay. When Baruch called Lindsay to his home on Fifth Avenue to explain that his job was finished and he was resigning his position, Lindsay chastised the old man. Baruch tolerated Lindsay's outburst but made it clear that he believed Lindsay was "uppity" to question him in such a manner. Later, when Lindsay asked one of his colleagues why he thought Baruch resigned, he was told that Baruch always got out at the top of the market.

Perhaps Lindsay's strong reaction to Baruch's resignation reflected his own deep disappointment over the deterioration in East-West relations. When he signed up to work for Baruch, Lindsay had seen enough war and bloodshed to last a lifetime. He believed that there was still hope for a true peace between the United States and the Soviet Union. Certainly his disillusionment with the Partisans at the end of the war prepared him for the possibility that the Baruch Plan might fail. But the experiences of his early days in Yugoslavia, as a respected comrade fighting shoulder to shoulder with the Partisans against the Nazis, as well as his work in Iran with the Russians, made him equally aware of the promise of genuine cooperation.

In retrospect, Lindsay's meeting with Sobolev was a defining moment. The Soviet Union and its Communist allies would cooperate with the West only when it was in their interest. In late 1946 Lindsay could see that the interests of the United States and the Soviet Union were moving farther apart.[16]

As Lindsay finished his work at the United Nations, Secretary of State George Marshall delivered his historic commencement address at Harvard University, outlining the features of a bold American plan to revive Europe's economy. By the spring of 1947, almost two years after the end of the war, Europe's economic future was dark. Industrial production was low, unemployment was high, and food shortages made famine a genuine possibility. Against this backdrop, Marshall explained the objectives of the plan in purely economic terms. He declared that U.S. policy was "directed not against any country or doctrine, but against hunger, poverty, desperation and chaos." Yet the Marshall Plan was always about more than simply creating jobs and feeding people. Unless Europe regained its economic health, it would be vulnerable to communism and Soviet imperialism. And as long as Europe was weak, the national security of the United States itself was endangered.[17]

Marshall's proposal was hardly destined to succeed. Congress had to approve the funds to finance the plan. Growing isolationist sentiment in the country meant that Truman and Marshall were going to have to fight hard to win congressional support. As opinion in the House of Representatives became the next important battleground in the Cold War, Lindsay found himself working for Congressman Christian Herter, who chaired the House Select Committee on Foreign Aid. Lindsay traveled with the committee to Europe in the fall of 1947, along with another consultant to Herter's committee, Allen Dulles. Their mission was to evaluate the European situation. The committeemen, with Lindsay as their guide, left Europe convinced that the Marshall Plan was "essential to strengthening Western Europe against Communist expansion."[18]

Lindsay's work with Herter brought him into contact with a young Yale-trained economist named Richard M. Bissell Jr. The scion of a prominent Hartford family, Bissell had made a name for himself in the war by developing logistical plans at the War Shipping Administration to support Allied operations around the world. At about the same time Lindsay signed up to work for Herter, Bissell was hired by Averell Harriman to serve as executive secretary of the Harriman Committee, officially known as the President's Committee on Foreign Aid. President Truman had created Harriman's committee to forge a bipartisan consensus on the importance of funding the Marshall Plan. It was Harriman and his team, along with key State Department officials, who were responsible for convincing Congress to support the plan.[19]

Congress passed the Economic Cooperation Act in spring 1948, and Secretary of State Marshall finally had the funding for his plan. The legislation that funded the Marshall Plan also created an agency to oversee its implementation — the Economic Cooperation Administration (ECA). One of the first people hired to run the ECA was Richard Bissell, and it wasn't long before he recruited Lindsay. Bissell remained at ECA headquarters in Washington, but Lindsay was sent to Paris to work on issues critical to Europe's economic revival. Lindsay acted informally as Bissell's liaison with the rest of the ECA's Paris office, and nine months into his new assignment he was deeply involved in his work. But Lindsay's career quickly took an abrupt, if not entirely unlikely, departure. Frank Wisner, a former OSS colleague, had been given the task of forming a new covert action group to fight communism. The group was innocuously called the Office of Policy Coordination (OPC), and Wisner asked Lindsay to stop in at his new office the next time he was in Washington. Although the purpose of the meeting was unstated, recruitment was clearly on Wisner's mind. When Lindsay met with Wisner, he became "intrigued" by the prospect of joining an organization that was just starting out. "I was getting a little frustrated with the Marshall Plan organization that had grown in Paris," he recalled. From Lindsay's perspective, it was fast becoming a bureaucracy. Lindsay explained to Bissell that he was leaving ECA to fight communism in Europe with covert action. Bissell was disappointed but supported Lindsay's decision.[20]

Soon after Bissell gave Lindsay to OPC, he found an even better way to support the organization: money. Bissell's source of capital was a little-known stash of Marshall Plan cash called counterpart funds. Bissell neatly outlined the concept of counterpart funds in his memoirs. "For each dollar in U.S. aid received," he explained, "the recipient had to contribute an equal amount in local currency, 95 percent of which would be used for Marshall Plan programs and 5 percent (counterpart funds) by the U.S. government and, in particular, the ECA to finance administrative and other miscellaneous costs." Nobody in the U.S. government was paying much attention to the counterpart funds, except for Bissell. "Whether anyone anticipated that these miscellaneous costs would include covert activities is difficult to say," Bissell later admitted. "This was most definitely a gray area." Gray area or not, when Frank Wisner approached Bissell seeking a new source of funds to finance his covert operations, Bissell enthusiastically tapped the counterpart funds at his disposal. Like a venture capitalist sprinkling seed money to a start-up company, Bissell was providing OPC with the money needed to get its new programs off the ground.[21]

And Lindsay needed help. When he arrived back in Washington to join Wisner at OPC, he learned that there were only five people in the whole organization. This was a meager beginning for an agency committed to supporting armed resistance behind the Iron Curtain. But with a little help from Bissell, OPC quickly grew. By 1949 OPC had more than three hundred employees, and just three years later that figure had mushroomed to more than five thousand. And along the way OPC had been merged into the newly created CIA.

During OPC's start-up phase, Lindsay was Wisner's "operations chief and second in command." Within months, the organization had grown sufficiently large that Wisner reorganized his management team along more specialized lines, and Lindsay became head of "the all-important Eastern European division." In this role, Lindsay was the CIA's point man for infiltrating spies and covert action operatives behind the Iron Curtain. Soon he had hundreds of operatives and planners reporting to him.

Initially Lindsay was confident he could get the job done. When Gen. Curtis LeMay, father of America's Strategic Air Command, demanded that he set up escape lines through the Soviet Union for his airmen to return home, Lindsay didn't question the order. After all, his own experience in Yugoslavia had taught him that it was possible. But as mission after mission failed, and the months turned into years, Lindsay came to question whether his own experience as a guerrilla fighter had any relevance at all behind the Iron Curtain.

Lindsay searched for an explanation, and he found it in a small village in Bavaria. Lindsay had decided to travel overseas to meet with a group of Russian émigrés who had been recruited to work for the CIA. Lindsay spent three days in the countryside getting to know the members of the group, some of whom he might send one day on missions into the Soviet Union. Lindsay turned to the leader of the group and asked him a hypothetical question. "Imagine," he asked, "that you have in place in the Soviet Union the best possible man you can imagine." Lindsay then assigned to this "best possible man" superlative attributes. He was the perfect political organizer, already well positioned in government, with flawless credentials, and the stature of a young Tito. Once Lindsay had established the qualities of this imaginary agent, and identified his mission — building a resistance organization — he broached the query: "Now, how soon would he be able to make his first approach to the first person to recruit him to an underground network in the Soviet Union?"

"Well," the leader replied, "he'd probably have to work side by side with somebody every day for six months at least, before he felt confident enough to even begin to talk to him about resistance."

"All right," Lindsay said. "Then assume you have such a man and he recruits. How many people do you think he could be able to recruit before he picked up a police penetration or police informer as one of his recruits?" Lindsay waited for an answer he expected would be in the dozens.

The leader replied, "About ten."

Almost half a century later, Lindsay recalled that answer as the revelation that "crystallized" everything for him. Infiltrating spies, organizing resistance, rollback — everything was hopeless. Lindsay returned to Washington with a renewed sense of mission. Now, instead of figuring out how to send men behind the Iron Curtain, he was committed to finding a way to stop the missions. Eisenhower had been elected president, and the inauguration was just weeks away. During the campaign there had been a great deal of talk about rolling back the Iron Curtain, particularly by Ike's chief foreign policy adviser, John Foster Dulles. Unless John Foster Dulles, the incoming secretary of state, or Allen Dulles, who was to be the new CIA director, could be convinced otherwise, more men would be sent on missions to penetrate the Soviet Union and die.

Lindsay outlined the reasons behind his change of heart in a memorandum and brought it to Allen Dulles's home one Saturday morning. For more than two hours, Lindsay explained to Dulles why rollback could never succeed, that penetration missions would always fail. Dulles refused to listen. The more Lindsay tried to bolster his argument, the more upset Dulles became. Dulles repeatedly interrupted Lindsay, objecting at every turn. "Frank, you just can't say that." It was a phrase Dulles used over and over that morning. When Lindsay left Dulles that day, he decided that it was time to leave the CIA.[22]

Although Lindsay may have believed that he was leaving the world of covert action, he could not give up the fight entirely. Lindsay told Dulles to abandon the old policy, but he offered nothing in its place. This was unacceptable. There must be some positive lesson Lindsay could glean from his experience, at least a hint of an active strategy Dulles could pursue. Lindsay outlined his thoughts in an essay, "A Program for the Development of New Cold War Instruments." Reflective and searching, Lindsay devised an approach that held out the promise of new beginnings. His premise was simple: "The Soviet vulnerabilities have not been analyzed with the fundamental precision necessary to devise effective methods of attack." Coming from the man who had been in charge of the CIA's operations against the Russians, this was a stunning admission. Lindsay recommended that a "program of research and development of offensive Cold War techniques must be carried out." This time, however, the CIA could not afford to go it alone. The plan had to be devised "in close association with the military, political, and intelligence agencies of the government in order that the resultant developments are consistent with capabilities." Although Lindsay recommended that "new instruments . . . must be developed," he did "not presume to suggest what these instruments may be." For many of Lindsay's action-oriented colleagues, his conclusion must have been unsatisfying.[23]

Lindsay left the CIA for a job at the Ford Foundation, maintained a consulting relationship with his old employer, and continued to research a new approach to fighting the Cold War. Lindsay's ideas became sharper. His recommendations seemed increasingly practical. "There is much evidence," he wrote, that "while the Soviet leadership would be prepared to accept in conflict heavy human casualties and massive destruction of physical plants, they will never knowingly risk the impairment or destruction of their political control system. But our present weapons for attacking the Soviet internal control system are about non-existent." Lindsay recommended the creation of a RAND-like organization that could support the CIA in developing such weapons. Allen Dulles appreciated Lindsay's work, but Lindsay's thoughtful approach was an imperfect fit with Dulles's activist disposition. His recommendation, and his insight, went nowhere.[24]

By 1955 Lindsay found a patron with the imagination to appreciate his ideas and the prestige to champion them in the corridors of power — his name was Nelson Rockefeller. In late 1954, after serving a stint as undersecretary of health, education, and welfare, Rockefeller became President Eisenhower's special assistant for psychological warfare. Rockefeller was enthusiastic about covert operations and looked to strengthen his ties to the CIA.

Lindsay was a natural choice for Rockefeller. Lindsay's own expertise in psychological warfare was qualification enough to earn a position on Rockefeller's staff. But his friendship with David Rockefeller, which dated back to World War II, probably enhanced his candidacy. David, who served in Army intelligence in North Africa, had stayed in touch with Lindsay in the years after the war and had maintained a close relationship with Allen Dulles as well.

By the summer of 1955 Nelson Rockefeller was in search of a new foreign policy proposal that he hoped would break open the diplomatic logjam of the Cold War. He organized a series of brainstorming sessions at the Quantico Marine base, not far from downtown Washington. It was far enough from the daily grind of government that Rockefeller's advisers could work without interruption, but close enough so that VIPs could join them for dinner to hear the latest ideas the team had developed. Rockefeller hoped that the meetings would yield a concrete proposal.

One of Rockefeller's guests was Richard Bissell, Lindsay's friend from the Economic Cooperation Administration. Bissell had developed a reputation as the brains behind the success of the Marshall Plan and was a rising star in Washington. Just the year before he had been recruited by Allen Dulles to join the CIA. Now he was in charge of a project that was one of the most closely guarded secrets in the nation—development of the U-2 spy plane. Lindsay had learned that human spies couldn't penetrate the Soviet Union. Bissell's job was to make a machine that could. If he succeeded, the United States would have a high-flying spy that could gather more information about Soviet military bases and weapons than a spy ring ever could.

Rockefeller's advisers had conceived a bold idea for President Eisenhower to propose at his upcoming summit in Geneva with the first secretary of the Soviet Communist Party, Nikita Khrushchev. The plan was probably of considerable interest to Bissell, whose U-2 was getting ready for its first test flight. It was an arms control proposal called Open Skies. Under the plan, the United States and the Soviet Union would be allowed to fly reconnaissance planes over each other's territory. The planes would be free to go anywhere and take photographs of any kind of military installation. Ground observers would also be permitted, and even blueprints of key military facilities would be exchanged. Franklin Lindsay worked on some of the preliminary studies that contributed to the proposal, with the help of Teddy Walkowicz, a member of Laurance Rockefeller's venture capital staff who had been loaned to Nelson that summer on a part-time basis. Nelson Rockefeller needed to move quickly if he was going to champion the idea as his own. Harold Stassen, another Eisenhower adviser, was said to be at work on a similar disarmament proposal, thanks to the help of his team of advisers, including Kodak executive Richard Leghorn. Rockefeller sold the idea to Eisenhower, who decided to unveil it at the summit in Geneva. If Khrushchev accepted Open Skies, it would be a great breakthrough for peace. If he said no, Bissell's U-2 would soon be ready to fly. Either way, Ike would get his pictures.

Although Khrushchev turned down the proposal, Open Skies remained a great personal victory for Eisenhower. Despite the lost opportunity for an early détente, Eisenhower was now heralded as an imaginative advocate for peace. Not long after the conference, Ike had a better reason to feel optimistic. In the first days of August 1955 Bissell's U-2 had its first successful test flight.

Despite the propaganda triumph of Open Skies, Nelson Rockefeller's influence in the administration was beginning to wane. In fall 1955 he directed a project designed to better integrate psychological warfare in U.S. foreign policy. Assisted by Lindsay and a team of experts, Rockefeller produced a report filled with concrete proposals. But John Foster Dulles was not about to permit Rockefeller to grab any more of the foreign policy portfolio. Dulles unleashed a withering bureaucratic counterattack that diminished Rockefeller's influence with Eisenhower. Rockefeller resigned from his position, returned to New York, and set about looking for a new enterprise toward which to direct his energies.[25]

It was time for Franklin Lindsay to leave Washington as well. He returned to work at the Ford Foundation, but this time in New York City. Yet he became restless in a world of policy papers. A chance encounter with an acquaintance led to a job offer from the prestigious New York consulting firm McKinsey and Company. If Lindsay accepted the job, he would become an adviser to major U.S. corporations seeking to streamline their management structure or improve their operations. The work at McKinsey would be far removed from the world of policy battles in

Washington. But in many ways it offered Lindsay a rare chance to get back on the career track he had envisioned for himself before the war, when he had enrolled at Stanford's business school.

Lindsay accepted the job. Commuting each morning to McKinsey's office in Manhattan, Lindsay developed his business expertise and maintained his relationship with Nelson Rockefeller. In June 1956, months after they both left Washington for New York, Lindsay pitched a proposal to his old boss. A Council on Foreign Relations study group, under the leadership of John McCloy, had just released its conclusions regarding the state of relations between the United States and the Soviet Union. Although Lindsay found the study interesting, he doubted that it would be "particularly effective in influencing policy decisions." The report's "diffuse organization and presentation" was unlikely to make key policy makers "face unpleasant facts" and take sufficient "strong action" to strengthen America's position versus the Soviets "soon enough." Lindsay proposed that Rockefeller organize a new kind of study, one that presented genuine "solutions" and "practical action programs" that could be implemented by both Congress and the president.[26]

Nelson Rockefeller loved the idea. Along with his brothers Laurance and David, Nelson decided to fund a study on the tough foreign policy and domestic issues facing America. It would be called the Rockefeller Brothers Fund Special Study Project. Lindsay was an active member of the study group, debating the issues of the day with young Henry Kissinger, Polaroid founder Edwin Land, hydrogen bomb developer Edward Teller, *Time* magazine's Henry Luce, and Laurance Rockefeller's assistant Teddy Walkowicz.[27]

By the summer of 1957 Lindsay was maintaining a difficult balancing act: his job at McKinsey, his commitment to the Rockefeller project, and the growing demands of his work on a committee chaired by H. Rowen Gaither, head of the Ford Foundation, and commissioned by President Eisenhower to study the question of America's "survival in the atomic age."

The Gaither Committee's conclusions were bleak. America's civilian population was vulnerable, and so were its defenses. William Foster, who was coordinating the panel's work, felt as though he was spending "ten hours a day staring straight into hell." Lindsay felt little better. In his meeting with General LeMay, Lindsay discovered that the United States had no retaliatory strike capability. In the event of a Soviet surprise attack, LeMay declared, none of his bombers would make it off the ground. Presenting these conclusions to President Eisenhower would not be easy. Yet the due date for the report was fast approaching. For Frank Lindsay, the next weeks would be very busy.[28]

It had been more than a year since Lindsay left Washington to start a new career in New York. He may have tried to return to the career plan of his youth by joining McKinsey, but he quickly gravitated back to the world of policy discussions and position papers. It is ironic, then, that Lindsay was to make his greatest contribution to U.S. national security, and to espionage, as a businessman.

3

CORPORATION X

The trajectory of Lindsay's career, from commando to corporate consultant, was not unique. Just as the war redirected Lindsay's life in unexpected ways, it had the same impact on others. Laurance Rockefeller, Richard Leghorn, and Teddy Walkowicz were all veterans who made essential contributions to the birth of Itek. Although they served their country individually, they reached a shared conclusion — technology and national security were now inseparable.

Dwight D. Eisenhower had the same realization. For him, the Battle of the Bulge was the moment of epiphany. In late 1944 heavy cloud cover prevented Allied reconnaissance operations from gathering any intelligence on German activities. The German army, cloaked by clouds, concealed its preparations for a winter attack. The Germans launched their attack, caught the Allied forces completely by surprise, and came close to reversing the course of the war. Eisenhower, the supreme Allied commander, learned an important lesson — in a dangerous world a steady stream of good intelligence was essential for survival. And good intelligence required advanced technology.[1]

As president, Eisenhower sought to apply advanced technical solutions to important national security challenges. But the technology of the 1950s, though often promising, also had severe limitations.

In 1957, for example, the computer was just a child beginning to test its limbs. The most powerful machines of the age were sensitive creatures that filled entire buildings with flashing lights, push-button consoles, and temperamental scientists scurrying about. For all of the computer's impressive physical attributes, the miles of wire, the thousands of vacuum tubes, the teams of technicians who attended the unruly child with twenty-four-hour-a-day feeding and care, in the age of Eisenhower a computer could do little more than basic math.

Addition, subtraction, multiplication, and division. Arrange those four words in a variety of patterns, and you have the stuff of mathematical formulas. Throw the letter X into the recipe and you have algebra—the search for an unknown. The United States Department of Defense was a key funding source for computer research in the 1950s. It wasn't because generals, or admirals for that matter, have an innate curiosity about the mystery of numbers. But ask a general how to stop a Soviet bomber from dropping a load of nuclear bombs on an American city? That's a mystery that commands attention. It also requires lots of basic math, more than an army of people can handle; in short, it requires computers. The computers, by analyzing data from radar stations, could help figure out the location of the bomber. That information, combined with exceptionally brave fighter pilots, would give a 1950s superpower the chance to save its people from nuclear Armageddon. Unfortunately, the bomber first had to get close enough to the continental United States to be seen on radar.[2]

There had to be a better solution. President Eisenhower *demanded* a better solution. In the nuclear age, there could be no more Pearl Harbors.

What if the top brass at the Pentagon could constantly monitor Soviet bomber forces? They would know when an attack was being planned. And they would be able to present the president of the United States with his military options hours before a plane came anywhere near an American city and perhaps in time to stop the attack on the ground. But how could this be done?

Eisenhower knew that better intelligence was his only option. Yet the CIA had failed to successfully develop even a handful of spies within the Soviet Union. Using people to monitor bases was simply not possible. In desperation, Ike approved a stopgap measure. It was a spy plane called the U-2, and it penetrated Soviet air space for the first time on July 4, 1956. The plane flew at such high altitudes that it was supposed to be invisible to Soviet radar, yet it was detected on the first mission.

By September 1957 the U-2 had flown only a handful of missions over the Soviet Union. Each was an invasion of Soviet territory, a hostile act with the potential to cause war. The Soviets had yet to shoot down a plane, but it wasn't for lack of trying. Eisenhower knew that it was only time before the Soviets destroyed a U-2, or worse.

Eisenhower was willing to take great risks in the interests of defending America, but with the stakes this high he maintained tight control over the program. After the U-2's maiden voyage, he reviewed the proposed intelligence objectives and flight path of every mission before giving his personal approval. And he gave it sparingly.

Intelligence brought back by the U-2 increased U.S. knowledge of Soviet military capabilities, but it was hardly a steady stream. Infrequent missions meant that the Soviets could still mount a surprise attack. Eisenhower needed almost daily information about Soviet military activities, and top civilian scientists, military leaders, and intelligence officials were pushing to develop a capability to deliver it to him in near real time.

By late 1957 the top secret espionage program Project SAMOS was Ike's best hope for more frequent intelligence. SAMOS was a science fiction fantasy wedded to 1950s state-of-the-art technology. Rockets, yet to be successfully tested, would carry yet-to-be-built satellites into space. Inside each satellite was a TV camera. The satellite would fly over the Soviet Union, well out of harm's way, while the TV camera took close-up pictures of the country's most important military installations. The pictures could be beamed back to the United States in near real time, or if there was any fear of Soviet interception, the pictures could be stored on videotape and beamed back to earth just a short while later over friendly territory.[3]

If the American people had known about SAMOS in the summer of 1957, they probably would have been shocked. How could the golf-loving president they thought of as a kindly grandfather back such a futuristic long shot? Although few realized it, behind Ike's benevolent smile was the calculating mind of a high-stakes gambler. His decision to send the largest armada ever into a storm and on a collision course with the Normandy coast in June 1944 was one of the riskiest military decisions in history. When he ordered the U-2 spy plane to penetrate the defense of the Soviet Union, an enemy bristling with nuclear weapons, he chanced bringing the world to the brink of war. Approving a plan to build the world's first spy satellite was bold, but definitely Eisenhower's way of doing business. He was quietly supporting an intelligence revolution that would catapult the CIA and the rest of the U.S. intelligence establishment into the space age. And almost nobody knew it.

Except for key government insiders — and Richard Leghorn.

Leghorn was a businessman with vision, connections at the highest levels of government, and a desire to become rich. He knew about SAMOS and he understood that the program would unleash a flood of information that threatened to wash away the CIA in a torrent of photographs — unless new technologies were developed to process and manage them. Computers couldn't do the job. Storing, organizing, and managing a database of photographic intelligence was simply beyond the mathematical capabilities of the best 1957 computer, and beyond its memory and storage capabilities as well. But Leghorn was very close to getting his hands on the technology that could make sense out of satellite photography. All he had to do was pry it away from a slumbering industrial giant that didn't understand what it was sitting on, and then obtain financing. With those two ingredients, technology and money, he could have a company positioned at the intersection of national security and business. The contracts were sure to be big, and Leghorn would be on his way to great wealth.[4]

But where does a colonel in the air force reserves go to get financial backing? For the kind of business Leghorn wanted to open, his local bank or credit union was out of the question. He couldn't even explain to them what he was working on. He needed a source of funding that was wealthy, discreet, and cleared by the United States government for national security secrets. He turned to his old air force buddy Teddy Walkowicz, who was cleared. Walkowicz turned to his boss, Laurance Rockefeller, who was rich and discreet. With a positive recommendation from Walkowicz, Rockefeller was willing to consider Leghorn's proposal.[5]

In some ways, the roots of Leghorn's business proposal, and the series of chance events that led to its arrival at Laurance Rockefeller's office, can be traced back to a historic conversation in a car parked at the end of an isolated runway at La Guardia Airport. That conversation set in motion a series of events that connected the lives of strangers and drew them into a web of relationships that intersect at Itek's incorporation.

It was September 1944, and in the back seat of the car was its sole passenger, Gen. Henry "Hap" Arnold. Commander of the army air forces, Arnold was on his way from Washington to an important conference in Quebec. He waited patiently in the car for an aid to summon Theodore von Karman, a Hungarian émigré and one of America's leading scientists. Ill from cancer, von Karman left the New York City clinic where he was recuperating, accompanied by an air force escort, to make the secret rendezvous with Arnold. When his air force aid finally brought von Karman to the car, Arnold dismissed both the aid and his chauffeur. Arnold and von Karman were at last alone, and the tired general could finally explain the purpose of the meeting.

"We have won this war," Arnold declared. "I am no longer interested in it."

Arnold's blunt statement, made as Allied forces continued to fight their way across Europe, was only the opening salvo in a barrage of astounding announcements.

"Only one thing should concern us," he continued. "What is the future of air power and aerial warfare? What is the bearing of the new inventions, such as jet propulsion, rockets, radar, and other electronic devices?" Hitler was waging a vicious fight for survival, the Battle of the Bulge had yet to occur, but Arnold was already looking beyond the dangers of the current war to the challenge of maintaining America's military supremacy in the next one.

"What do you wish me to do, General?" asked von Karman.

"I want you to come to the Pentagon," he replied, "and gather a group of scientists who will work out a blueprint for air research for the next twenty, thirty, perhaps fifty years."[6]

Arnold's assignment was a tall order. But when von Karman left Arnold's car that day, he was already thinking about how to proceed. By December, von Karman had been discharged from the hospital and was back at work in Washington. Undaunted by the enormity of his task, von Karman responded by organizing the best scientific and military minds in the country for the effort. He chose as one of his assistants a young air force major, and Massachusetts Institute of Technology doctorate,

Maj. Teddy Walkowicz. In the years to follow, Walkowicz became one of von Karman's closest associates and friends. The final product of von Karman's effort, a seminal work called "Toward New Horizons," was a classified blueprint of air force developments for the foreseeable future, and Walkowicz knew the plan.[7]

In fall 1945 General Arnold called Col. Bernard "Bennie" Schriever into his office for a talk. "Bennie, we have just completed a war which had a large number of major technological breakthroughs," he began. "All of the scientists who came out of academe and the laboratories around the country are going back to their schools. We need to maintain a close and cooperative working relationship with the scientific community." With that brief overview, Arnold gave Schriever responsibility for developing a lasting and effective liaison with the American scientific community, and building an infrastructure in the air force to support development of new technologies.[8]

As Schriever took up his new assignment, von Karman organized his committee of scientists. The new group, which would be called the Air Force Scientific Advisory Board (SAB), became the civilian interface for Schriever's new Pentagon office. Working together, the SAB and Schriever's office were to identify and develop new technologies that would allow the United States to dominate the air in any future conflicts.[9]

One of those technologies was the spy satellite. Early on, General Arnold asked von Karman about the possibility of obtaining strategic reconnaissance from space. As a result of Arnold's prodding, both von Karman and Schriever began to investigate the subject. Their efforts contributed directly to the creation of RAND, the research and development think tank for the air force. RAND's first study, a "crash" research project on satellite reconnaissance, was completed in spring 1946 and was only the first in a series of projects related to gathering intelligence from space. Only a handful of Americans were aware of these secret studies. Among them were von Karman's top aid, Teddy Walkowicz, and a young air force reserve officer named Richard Leghorn.[10]

By the early 1950s the United States was in the midst of fighting the Korean War, and Schriever was in a new, more powerful Pentagon position, where both his ties to the scientific community and his friendship with Walkowicz deepened. Schriever was head of the air force development planning office, and in this position he was in charge of managing long-range studies about areas critical to the future success of the air force. Together, Schriever and Walkowicz fought to bring new technologies off the drawing board, into production, and onto the battlefield. According to Schriever, these were "Teddy's golden days," a booming period of creativity when a close peacetime relationship between the air force and the scientific community was finally forged. It was also during this period that Teddy Walkowicz, through his friend Bennie Schriever, first met Richard Leghorn and Jack Carter.[11]

Schriever's mandate was now broader than purely scientific concerns. He established long-range study projects — in air force parlance DPOs — for tactical and strategic issues, logistics, intelligence, and reconnaissance. Schriever's group was "sowing seeds" for the future. He used his limited budget to support studies, meetings, and papers that would leverage the small size of his forty-person office. Schriever assigned one staff person to chair each DPO study. He multiplied the efforts of his staff many times over by augmenting their ranks with consultants from organizations like RAND. Managing his rapidly expanding world of research studies required assistance and he recruited a top administrator to help him, Jack Carter. Over time, Schriever gave Carter responsibility for the entire administration of his office.[12]

Schriever had first met Jack Carter before World War II. During their early friendship, he came to know Carter as a competent technical person and a good manager, though not a farsighted thinker. Carter had been an air force project officer for the P-80, an early contract with Lockheed's Kelly Johnson. As a result, Carter and Johnson became friends. Carter's contacts at Lockheed eventually led to a job offer from the company, and later to work on SAMOS.[13]

Richard Leghorn first came to Schriever's attention when he was beginning work on a DPO covering reconnaissance and intelligence. Schriever was searching for someone to head the study, and he recalled meeting Leghorn at Wright Field. Leghorn was exactly the sort of person Schriever needed. He knew Leghorn was interested in developing the tools that could make sure that an enemy could never again launch a surprise attack on the United States. He also recognized not only that Leghorn was intelligent and enthusiastic — essential qualities for moving ideas through the labyrinth of the Pentagon's bureaucracy—but that he was looking at the broader dimensions of intelligence in relation to the challenges presented by conflict with the Soviet Union.

Leghorn possessed another quality Schriever admired. He was looking at how technology was forming in the private sector and projecting those developments far into the future. Schriever realized that Leghorn's visionary qualities, combined with his World War II reconnaissance experience, made him uniquely qualified to head the intelligence DPO. Schriever quickly ordered Leghorn transferred from Wright Field to Washington to work for him in 1951. In his new position, Leghorn reported to Schriever on the content of his work, and to Carter on administrative matters.

Leghorn was responsible for developing new ideas about intelligence collection. Namely, how to penetrate a closed society like the Soviet Union and successfully return home with solid information about the enemy's military strength. Leghorn recruited leading members of the scientific community to help him on a top secret study group called Beacon Hill. The ideas in the study group's final report led directly to the creation of the U-2.[14]

By the end of the Korean War, Walkowicz, Schriever, Carter, and Leghorn had all become good friends, but they soon went their separate ways. Richard Leghorn returned to his job at Eastman Kodak, Jack Carter left for a new position at Lockheed, and Teddy Walkowicz left the air force to work for Laurance Rockefeller.[15]

Walkowicz didn't want to leave the service, but his family had financial problems. His mother and father were dependent on him, and he felt that he needed more money to take care of his responsibilities. Schriever tried to talk him out of leaving the service, but Walkowicz had made up his mind. Working for Rockefeller was a once-in-a-lifetime opportunity.

Rockefeller first heard about Walkowicz from Courtland Perkins of Princeton University. Perkins was head of Princeton's aeronautics department, and Rockefeller, a trustee of the university, was a big supporter of the department. Rockefeller's interest in the discipline was both intellectual and economic. He appreciated that technological advances in propeller planes, jets, and rockets would have a great impact on the U.S. economy and its defense establishment. As the largest investor in Eastern

Airlines, a company he had personally rescued from near bankruptcy, he had a big stake in the future of flight. When Rockefeller mentioned to Perkins that he wanted to expand his staff and focus more on companies related to aeronautics and national security, Perkins knew just the man to help him: Teddy Walkowicz.[16]

After his departure from the air force, Walkowicz continued to hold his security clearances and he continued to work with the air force SAB. Perhaps equally important, he continued to be good friends with Bennie Schriever.[17] By 1954 Schriever was given a new assignment. He was now in command of the newly created Western Development Division (WDD) of the air force, and with it, responsible for developing the nation's first intercontinental ballistic missile (ICBM). Schriever, who played an early role in sponsoring RAND's initial research on reconnaissance satellites, was also put in charge of developing an intelligence satellite for the air force. Schriever asked for more than $100 million to fund the project, later called WS-117L, but he was given only seed money. Nevertheless, Schriever kept the satellite project moving forward, even as he became increasingly occupied with building the ICBM.[18]

As Schriever pressed the ICBM effort — a monumental crash program to catch up to the Soviets — Walkowicz focused Rockefeller's interest on rocketry and intelligence systems. But Rockefeller's interest in aviation was sparked long before Teddy Walkowicz joined his staff. In fact, it began before the war.[19]

In 1938 Rockefeller's investment in Eastern Airlines helped to rescue the firm from bankruptcy. He made the investment in part because he admired Eddie Rickenbacker, head of the airline. His chief motivation, however, was his belief that commercial air travel would revolutionize the world by bringing people and markets closer together. Rockefeller also appreciated that changes in aviation technology had the capacity to alter warfare. Just before the start of World War II, he decided to support James S. McDonnell. McDonnell's plans for a pursuit plane intrigued Rockefeller, but he was equally taken by the engineer's fascination with jet propulsion. With war clearly on the horizon, Rockefeller was confident that the nation would need a firm like McDonnell's. By the end of World War II, McDonnell Aircraft Corporation had become a major contractor for the Pentagon.[20]

In 1940 Rockefeller's investments in the aviation industry attracted the attention of Assistant Secretary of the Navy James Forrestal. Up to this point, Rockefeller had only made a few direct investments in the aviation industry. Yet Forrestal asked Rockefeller to organize a company that could assist the navy in "managing and financing certain companies." Although Pearl Harbor, and Rockefeller's own service in the navy, interrupted these plans, the seeds of Rockefeller's postwar career as a venture capitalist had been planted.[21]

Rockefeller's knowledge of the aviation industry, combined with his friendship with Forrestal, led to naval assignments that sharpened his appreciation of the relation between industry, technology, and national security. For most of the war, Rockefeller's job was to monitor the production and development of patrol planes and fighter aircraft. His knowledge of the aviation industry grew, and so did his list of contacts. But most important, he witnessed firsthand the creation of new technologies that transformed the face of warfare, and he became captivated by them. He realized that many of these same technologies, converted to civilian purposes, could have an equally powerful impact "on the way people live in the postwar world." His insight was a powerful one.[22]

After the war, Rockefeller returned to work at the family's office at 30 Rockefeller Center with a new sense of purpose. He assembled a small staff of colleagues to commercialize in the private sector the breakthroughs in aviation, radar, communications, and nuclear energy that had been developed in the war. He needed a seasoned financial professional to review business proposals, and he recruited Randolph Marston, who had been a banker at Chase Manhattan and had known David Rockefeller when he worked there. He also wanted someone familiar with the key technologies developed during the war. Harper Woodward, who had been Gen. Hap Arnold's assistant for procurement in the Pentagon, was soon hired.[23]

By 1946 Rockefeller's Washington connections began to pay off. Now Rockefeller's friend James Forrestal was secretary of the navy, and his department looked to Rockefeller to help an ailing company important to U.S. national security. Piasecki Helicopter was going bankrupt. Unless the company received financial assistance, the country would lose an important manufacturer. Rockefeller responded decisively. He organized a syndicate that included Douglas Dillon and Felix Dupont and took the role of lead investor, raising $500,000 to take control of the company. Over the next few years, Piasecki's financial position improved and it won new contracts. In the Korean War, Piasecki helicopters played an important role in ferrying troops to the battlefield. The company's recovery was complete, and a strategic asset had been saved.[24]

Lewis Strauss, who chaired the Atomic Energy Commission under Presidents Truman and Eisenhower, joined Rockefeller's staff during this period. Strauss, whose career on Wall Street led to a partnership in Kuhn, Loeb in the 1920s, was closely connected with Forrestal. Near the end of the war, Strauss played an important role in getting Forrestal to push Congress for postwar defense appropriations. By the time he left in 1953 to return to government service, Strauss had convinced Rockefeller that the future of the nuclear industry in the United States was promising. Rockefeller's investment in Nuclear Development Corporation was a direct result of Strauss's influence and interests.[25]

Word spread that Rockefeller was willing to invest in young companies, even struggling companies. Soon unsolicited business proposals began to flood the office. By the mid-1950s his office was fully staffed and his informal organization had become more specialized. Proposals would generally arrive on the desk of Woodward or Marston. If it was linked to the military, it was then passed to Walkowicz; if it was related to civil aviation, it was passed to Najeeb Halaby.

Rockefeller recruited Halaby, who was a successful test pilot and aviation industry expert, after a chance meeting in 1953. At a naval reserve officers' meeting at the Navy Yard in Washington, Halaby found himself sitting next to Rockefeller, who was then serving as an adviser to the secretary of the navy. Halaby was exactly the kind of man that appealed to Rockefeller's values. Halaby catapulted from success to success in government and collected useful connections along the way. After the war he served as the State Department's civil aviation adviser to King Ibn Saud Abdul Aziz, helping the king develop Saudi Arabian Airlines. Next he worked as an aid to Secretary of Defense James Forrestal in the late 1940s, then helped Paul Nitze write NSC 68. Rockefeller was impressed with Halaby and invited him to visit his offices in New York. When Halaby finally paid him a visit, Rockefeller explained that Halaby's aviation background would be very useful to him in monitoring his investments in not only McDonnell Aircraft but also Eastern Airlines. It wasn't long before Halaby joined Rockefeller's staff.[26]

According to Halaby, the process of identifying and evaluating companies for investment in Rockefeller's office during this period was surprisingly informal. No elaborate investment analysis was performed, no investment policy committee met to discuss proposals. Hunches, intuition, and telephone calls to friends were central to the process. Because many of Rockefeller's investments in this period were in some way related to government civil and military activities, more often than not the telephone call was made to a friend or contact in the government. "Is this project going anywhere? Will you buy the system?"[27]

And Rockefeller, who often blurred the distinction between business and public service in his own activities, expected his staff to balance the same combination of savvy deal making and social commitment. At various times, Halaby found himself loaned out by Rockefeller to New York Mayor Robert Wagner—to "survey" the city's civil defense program—and later to President Eisenhower's Aviation Facilities Study Group. Halaby wasn't the only Rockefeller employee assigned to assist the study group. Teddy Walkowicz was also there to provide a helping hand.

The study group was concerned with safe air travel in America and was created by Eisenhower at Rockefeller's urging. After World War II, civil aviation in the United States experienced an enormous period of growth. In Laurance Rockefeller's opinion, much of it was haphazard, leading to an increased number of air safety problems, and even crashes. Rockefeller's concern went beyond his own investments in the field. He understood the importance of aviation to the country's economic health and security. As a result, the study group was charged with finding a solution to the problem before it became a national crisis. Its recommendations were to lead to an important breakthrough in the government's role in civil aviation, and to safer skies.

Rockefeller supported flight safety solutions wherever good ones could be found. He favored prudent government policies and nonprofit initiatives, and used his own venture capital operations to fund private sector research and development. In addition to his role in creating the study group, he was a major supporter of the Flight Safety Foundation, a nonprofit group devoted to reducing accidents in the sky and on the ground at airports. He was also an investor, along with his brother David, in Laboratory for Electronics, a fledgling manufacturer of light, portable radar equipment that could be used to improve landing safety at small civilian or military airstrips.[28]

Rockefeller was considering an investment in Richard Leghorn's venture. By the middle of 1957 Leghorn's proposal for an information-processing company had reached Rockefeller's staff—thanks to Teddy Walkowicz. The twenty-page proposal was a clear-eyed appraisal of a new market opportunity, as well as a vision of a world transformed by an information revolution. Leghorn realized that there was a rapidly growing demand for both data processing and information processing. Data processing, the rapid manipulation of numbers and letters, relied on digital technologies being developed by major computer companies like IBM. The digital computer market was young, but the competitive landscape was already taking shape. Information processing—defined by Leghorn as the fast and efficient processing of such graphic information as photographs, maps, drawings, and articles—was an open field. Leghorn's company would harness miniaturized photographs to the Minicard System to lead an information revolution. His first customers, all of which had urgent intelligence needs, would be the Central Intelligence Agency, the U.S. Air Force, the U.S. Navy, and the super-secret National Security Agency. Later, once his company's technology was perfected with the support of government research and development contracts, Leghorn would target the private sector.

Leghorn estimated that in ten years information processing could be a billion-dollar market. His company could capture up to 30 percent of it: $300 million in annual sales. Banks, insurance companies, and law firms would all be using his products to better manage and sort information ranging from property titles to legal articles. Large corporations would manage personnel records better, hospitals would handle medical records with greater efficiency, and the U.S. Treasury would have a powerful tool to process savings bonds and checks.

Early financing would give Leghorn's company a competitive advantage that would be difficult to overtake. There was a limited number of scientists in the field. Leghorn knew them, and he was prepared to hire them. All Leghorn needed to get his company off the ground was $2 million. Then, as operations expanded from government contracting to developing commercial products, he needed another $10 million. In exchange for this financing, Leghorn offered Rockefeller the opportunity to participate in the birth of a new industry and ownership of 49 percent of the company. Leghorn and his partners would retain control.[29]

Now Rockefeller put Leghorn to the test. His business plan was impressive, but Rockefeller and his staff needed further convincing. If Leghorn was willing to resign his position at Kodak, Rockefeller would pay him two months' salary plus expenses to further develop his ideas. There was an important caveat: Rockefeller was not committed to investing in Leghorn's company once the plan was developed. If Leghorn believed in his idea, he would quit his job and throw his future to the winds. If not, no deal.

Meanwhile, Walkowicz had begun to hammer out the details for a preliminary agreement with Leghorn. The company's capital requirement had to be brought below $1 million, not the $2 million that Leghorn originally required. And Rockefeller would be the majority owner, not Leghorn. In order to get financing, Leghorn would have to trade away control of his company. He agreed, and it was a decision he would regret for the rest of his life.[30]

Many executives dream of jumping off the corporate ladder to start their own companies, but few have the courage to take the plunge. In June, Leghorn resigned from his job as manager of the European Division of Eastman Kodak to devote full time to developing a business plan. At Kodak, Leghorn had been responsible for operations with total sales of more than $20 million. He directed seven subsidiaries in Europe and handled distribution arrangements for Kodak products on the Continent. For many executives, this was the kind of job to cap a long, successful career.[31] Instead of savoring his position, Leghorn traded away a top rung on the corporate ladder to become a consultant with a two-month contract, facing certain unemployment unless he could close a deal with Laurance Rockefeller. Richard Sully Leghorn, just thirty-eight years old, had just crossed the chasm that separates dreamers from doers.

And Leghorn had big dreams. Like Laurance Rockefeller, he wanted to have a positive impact on the world. Leghorn saw that rapid changes in society were creating new demands for information and document processing. Yet few products were designed to meet this demand, and no companies focused exclusively on the problem. Leghorn's company would fill this gap in the market. For lack of a better name, he now called it Corporation X.

Leghorn's business proposals, the basis for any investment Laurance Rockefeller might make, were both honest and incomplete. The proposals for Corporation X made it clear that in its early stages the company would build equipment that would process intelligence. It was also apparent that early customers would include the air force and the CIA. But nowhere in the proposal was there any suggestion that Corporation X would process intelligence about Soviet military capabilities obtained from spy satellites. Did this matter? Would this information in any way affect an investor's decision to finance the company?

The success or failure of Leghorn's company was entirely dependent on factors beyond his control and not discussed in his business proposal, or considered in his financial projections. As of fall 1957, the United States had yet to build a rocket that could successfully carry a satellite into space, let alone a satellite that could send pictures from space to earth. If these technical barriers were not broken in the immediate future, Leghorn's business contracts might never materialize. This made investing in his plan speculation of the highest order.

Was it wrong that Leghorn didn't disclose these risks in his business plan? As an adviser to the U.S. government on a variety of national security issues, Colonel Leghorn could hardly be expected to disclose the existence and purpose of classified programs. That's where Teddy Walkowicz came in. He had the clearances and connections to have a complete understanding of the risks of Leghorn's plan. He also understood the opportunity. If the technology worked, and the satellites were successfully launched, Leghorn's company would turn into a gold mine. No documentary evidence exists to suggest that Walkowicz shared these insights with either his colleagues or Laurance Rockefeller. But we do know that Walkowicz was hired specifically for his background in national security issues. And in these matters, his opinion was held in high esteem.

Walkowicz knew that Corporation X would develop equipment whose purpose went beyond the bland description of information processing;

its products would allow the CIA to identify and catalogue the Soviet Union's most sensitive military installations, both for intelligence evaluation, and later for missile targeting. Walkowicz was a hard-line anticommunist. If he could play a role in financing Corporation X, he probably viewed it as a patriotic act of the highest order. But Corporation X had to be formed quickly if it was going to win important secret contracts from the CIA and the military for processing SAMOS intelligence.[32] And without a contract for Project SAMOS, the company might never get off the ground.

There was one potential problem with Leghorn's plan. The technology he intended to use was still owned by the Eastman Kodak Corporation. Undaunted, Leghorn moved forward, secure in his knowledge that Arthur Tyler, a top scientist at Kodak, would join him at the right moment. Tyler was the inventor and developer of the Minicard System. This system, built around miniaturized photographs that were attached to old-fashioned computer punch cards, made it possible to expand the limited memory of a computer into a vast database. Any piece of information that could be captured in a photograph could also be reduced to a microchip of film. Books, engineering drawings, encyclopedias, all could be photographed, miniaturized, attached to computer cards, and organized. So could photographs of military bases, bombers, and even missiles. But Kodak wasn't seriously interested in developing the Minicard System; the company was interested in selling cameras and film. If Leghorn could get Rockefeller to finance Corporation X, Tyler would leave Kodak and join him. Getting Kodak to give them the Minicard System would be the easy part. Obtaining the financing from Rockefeller remained elusive.[33]

At the end of June, Leghorn resigned from Kodak and began to work full-time on his plan. He spent the early part of the first week of July working at suite 5600 Rockefeller Center. Then he flew to Rochester to meet with his former employer and discuss licensing agreements for the Minicard System. He began discussions with IBM about possible business relationships. In Boston he met with prospective personnel working at an air force think tank at Boston University. In Rome, New York, he met with senior representatives of the Air Force Development Command about contract possibilities.

In the middle of July, Leghorn flew to the West Coast. One of his first stops was Palo Alto, where he met with his old air force buddy Jack Carter. When Leghorn had worked for Colonel Schriever at the Pentagon on intelligence issues, Carter had been Schriever's deputy. Now Carter was an influential executive at Lockheed Missiles Division, and he was plugged into many of the nation's most important defense contracts — including SAMOS. Carter's knowledge of the defense business would make him an ideal recruit for Corporation X, and Leghorn wanted him on board as a partner. After talking to Carter, Leghorn's tour of personal reunions continued. He drove to Los Angeles to meet with his old air force commander Bernard Schriever, now a general and head of the Western Development Division. Everyone knew that Schriever was in charge of a crash program to develop the nation's first intercontinental ballistic missiles. The secret was that he was also head of Project SAMOS, and Leghorn and his mentor discussed contract possibilities for ground handling equipment, which would process photointelligence once it was transmitted back to Earth. By the end of the month Leghorn was back in New York and ready to start working on financial projections for his business plan.[34]

On August 7 Leghorn prepared another draft proposal for Corporation X. The billion-dollar market that Leghorn foresaw for information processing by the late 1960s was now projected for the early 1970s. He estimated that sales would be $1.5 million in 1958 and $3.8 million in 1959, the year the company would first turn a profit. By the end of that year it would employ 450 workers. Leghorn would need $1 million to fund the company, but it could be provided in two installments of $500,000 — the first installment to get the company off the ground, the second to be provided once the company proved itself viable. In Leghorn's notes to the financial estimates, he made it clear that about 75 percent of the company's sales in the first year would come from two contracts. Clearly, if Rockefeller was to invest in Corporation X, it was essential that he have an understanding of these contracts. But they were classified, and neither Rockefeller nor anyone else on his staff was cleared to know about them, or had the means to learn about them. Except for Teddy Walkowicz.[35]

Just days after finishing his latest proposal, Leghorn was pushing again for financing. On August 13 he wrote to Walkowicz and reminded him that the company had to be formed quickly if he was going to have any chance at winning key contracts. He needed incorporation to occur as soon as possible so that he could turn his efforts to writing proposals. If Walkowicz could arrange for just $30,000 in financing, Leghorn could incorporate, rent office space, get Art Tyler on board, and hire a secretary.[36]

Rockefeller was impressed with Leghorn's ideas, but he still wasn't ready to finance the project. Perhaps he was reluctant to invest in a company whose first projects were shrouded in secrecy. The documentary evidence provides no answer. We do know that he gave his staff at Rockefeller Center permission to continue to help Leghorn with his plan. By September the business professionals at suite 5600, the home of the Rockefeller family office, were working hard on developing sales, earnings, and cash flow projections for Corporation X. It was looking good. The handwritten spreadsheets included a best estimate, a worst-case scenario, and a most probable estimate. The most likely scenario projected sales of about $1 million in 1958 and $2.5 million in 1959. The best-case scenario showed sales approximately 50 percent higher for each year, and the worst-case scenario showed them 50 percent lower. Using the most probable scenario, the company would be profitable by 1959 and employ three hundred workers.[37]

On September 6 Harper Woodward wrote to Rockefeller in Jackson Hole, Wyoming, to give him an update on Leghorn's progress. He said that the staff at 5600 were now largely in agreement with Leghorn on how to proceed. Woodward made clear it was time for Rockefeller to make a decision whether or not to go ahead with the venture. The company still didn't have a name, Woodward acknowledged, but the staff was working on it.[38]

On the same day Rockefeller's lawyers at the prestigious New York firm of Dewey, Ballantine sent Leghorn a draft of the agreement he and Laurance Rockefeller would sign if the deal went forward. An earlier draft had already been reviewed by Marston and Woodward and the new one reflected their comments. Stuart Scott, the lawyer working on the draft, had a few questions for Leghorn before he began work on a new draft of the agreement. All of the questions were related to financial or tax issues except for one. Even though Laurance Rockefeller was on the verge of investing almost $100,000 in Itek to start, none of his advisers, including his lawyer, was certain how to describe the company's business either in the agreement or in the articles of incorporation. Certainly, Leghorn would be able to help.[39]

While Rockefeller reviewed the briefing materials in Jackson Hole, Harper Woodward began to refine Rockefeller's financing options should he decide to back the firm. Woodward was working to reduce Rockefeller's financial exposure to Corporation X. Leghorn had already reduced his initial financing requirements from $2 million to $1 million. As Woodward saw it, Corporation X could probably begin operations successfully with $650,000.

Although large classified contracts with the air force and the CIA seemed likely to materialize, Woodward's job was to protect Rockefeller, and his plan reflected this. In order to minimize Rockefeller's financial risk, Woodward persuaded Leghorn to accept initial financing of about $100,000, with another $550,000 as part of a second phase about six months later. In the first financing Rockefeller would buy $50,000 in stock, $48,000 in company bonds, and $2,000 in warrants. In the second phase his investment would be about half stock, half convertible bonds. But he would be under no obligation to go beyond the first financing. If Leghorn wanted to proceed and Rockefeller didn't, he could buy Rockefeller's share at original cost. This would let Leghorn regain control of the company and allow Rockefeller to exit the investment without a loss.[40]

Walkowicz summarized Woodward's proposal and presented it to Rockefeller for his approval, along with an update on Leghorn's progress. He informed Rockefeller that his brother David was preoccupied with one of his other investments, Laboratory for Electronics, and was not likely to participate in this deal. Leghorn and his associates were committed. Jesse Cousins had been designated the financial officer for the firm, and business proposals were already looking promising. Walkowicz also mentioned that a name for the company had finally been chosen, just in time for formal incorporation. Several names had been considered: Informatics, Minisec, Informac, Microsec, even Merconics. The name finally chosen was Itek, a contraction based on the words *information* and *technology*.

The news Walkowicz reported next was astonishing. He announced that both the air force and the Ramo-Wooldridge Corporation were ready to negotiate large contracts as soon as Itek was open for business. The contracts were all in the field of processing intelligence information, which, as Walkowicz reminded Rockefeller, was a growing market. Yet Itek was not incorporated, had no established offices, no employees, nor the Minicard System technology from Kodak. Walkowicz offered no further explanation and there is no record that Rockefeller required one.

There was another piece of cryptically reported news. Leghorn had landed a small contract that would cover some of the overhead from the day the company opened its doors for business. The client—unnamed in the documents—was Scientific Engineering Institute and it was a front company for the CIA. It is not clear what product, if any, it purchased from Itek. It is clear that even before the Itek Corporation officially opened its doors for business, the CIA was playing a role in getting it established.[41]

As was standard practice on many of Laurance Rockefeller's transactions, he gave his siblings a chance to participate in his investments. Walkowicz wrote to both Nelson and David Rockefeller to assess their interest in participating in Itek's initial financing. Walkowicz told them, somewhat disingenuously, that the company was being formed to exploit the emerging field of document processing. There was no mention of intelligence, satellites, defense contracts, or the CIA. Both Nelson and David Rockefeller declined to participate.[42]

By late September the details had been ironed out and a letter of agreement had been prepared for Rockefeller and Leghorn to sign. With big business contracts waiting to be executed, Walkowicz was pushing hard to close the deal by month's end. The company had to be incorporated, a board of directors appointed, executives hired, office space located, and bank accounts opened. A special board of directors meeting needed to be held immediately to authorize the financing and to issue stock, bonds, and warrants to Rockefeller and any other investors. But Leghorn decided to change some of the wording in his agreement, and the closing date was pushed back to early October.[43]

Meanwhile, Leghorn started to act with confidence. He began to push Kodak to license the Minicard System to Itek.[44] He started formal discussions with Ramo-Wooldridge to explore submitting a joint proposal to the air force to develop ground equipment for processing SAMOS intelligence. Ramo-Wooldridge, already well established in the field of systems engineering, would take the role of primary contractor. Itek would be a subcontractor.[45]

By the first days of October, Leghorn was rapidly picking up momentum. Major business contracts were falling into place, and Itek's financing was now taken for granted. Yet nobody seemed disturbed that Itek had virtually no employees or any manufacturing facilities. What members of Itek's staff would serve on the systems design group with Ramo-Wooldridge? What Itek factories would build the equipment? Why did Laurance Rockefeller, Ramo-Wooldridge, and the United States Air Force have so much confidence in Itek?

There was one skeptic — Randy Marston, Rockefeller's most trusted adviser. Marston understood that Itek's initial success was highly dependent on getting large research and development contracts. But the Department of Defense was cutting costs dramatically, and research and development programs were being especially hard hit. To compound Marston's misgivings, the stock market was hitting new lows every day. In this environment, he was not willing to bet on a new start-up.[46]

His dissenting voice was soon overwhelmed by national panic.

4

SPUTNIK

On October 4, 1957, just days before Richard Leghorn closed his deal with Laurance Rockefeller, the Soviet Union launched the world's first satellite into space. Sputnik weighed 185 pounds, measured about twenty-three inches in diameter, and did little more than go "beep." Yet that lonely beep from outer space was enough to shatter America's confidence.

Within hours of Sputnik's launch, a political uproar began. Republicans and Democrats alike were furious.[1] The national security of the United States, which appeared so impregnable, now seemed disturbingly fragile. The only solution, many concluded, was to spend more money on satellites, rockets, missiles, and any other program that might make America stronger. President Eisenhower, who had been striving to balance the nation's budget by keeping a lid on defense spending, would have tough decisions to make in the days and weeks ahead. Would he hold the line against a big increase in spending, or would he give in to a growing call for a shift in policy?

Investors knew exactly what course of action to take. When the stock market opened on Monday, October 7, they called their brokers and ordered them to sell. The Dow Jones Industrial Average, which was already in the midst of a correction, opened poorly. Some investors assumed that Sputnik would spur U.S. defense spending, and that defense-related stocks would rally. And that is what happened, for a while, anyway. Aircraft and missiles stocks opened the day strong, but many of those issues were soon overwhelmed by sell orders along with the rest of the market.[2]

It was an inauspicious time to start a new company. Yet there is no evidence that Richard Leghorn, or anyone on Rockefeller's staff, ever became seriously unnerved during that turbulent period. Certainly, Randolph Marston voiced concerns from time to time, but Teddy Walkowicz remained focused and unflappable. In the weeks ahead, as other investors panicked, Rockefeller and company grabbed the opportunities that came their way.

So that Monday morning, as the stock market swooned, Teddy Walkowicz went about his business and called Rockefeller's lawyers at Herrick, Smith in Boston. Because Itek was going to be a Massachusetts corporation, Herrick, Smith had been brought in as part of the Rockefeller legal team to help Dewey, Ballantine in New York. Walkowicz wanted to move Itek's first board meeting to Thursday, and he proposed completing the financing for the company then as well.[3]

That day, Malcolm Perkins, a lawyer at Herrick, Smith drafted an agenda for Itek's first board of directors meeting. Three items on Perkins's draft agenda were out of the ordinary. Item 18 was a special resolution on security issues. No director would be permitted access to classified information unless he had the appropriate security clearance. Item 17 authorized Itek officers to sign cost-plus-fixed-fee contracts (CPFF), the type of contracts the company would have with the air force and the CIA.[4]

Item 16 was noteworthy in ways Perkins could never understand. It authorized Leghorn to sign a consulting agreement with Scientific Engineering Institute (SEI). Leghorn would serve as an adviser to SEI, and Itek would be paid for his services. SEI was a front company for the CIA. Based in Cambridge, an area rich in scientific talent, SEI provided the CIA with access to some of the best technical minds in the country. Some scientists signed up to work for the CIA without even knowing it. Even when scientists realized that the ultimate customer was the Agency, their contract with SEI allowed them to plausibly deny any connection. Using a front company gave the intelligence community access to a broader range of consultants than might otherwise have been possible. It also allowed the Agency to pay them better.

Leghorn's assignment with SEI was an ace in the hole for the fledgling Itek. His job was to serve as a personal adviser to Richard Bissell. Bissell had a problem. The supposedly undetectable U-2 had been tracked by Soviet radar on its very first mission. The Soviets hadn't been able to shoot down a U-2 yet, but they were trying. Bissell turned to the scientific community for help. Could America's leading experts find a way to make the U-2 invisible? The search for stealth technology was on, and Bissell wanted Leghorn to help develop a scientific team that could provide an answer.

Leghorn had first come to Bissell's attention in 1955, just as Bissell was getting ready for the first test flight of the U-2. Leghorn had published an article under the headline "U.S. Can Photograph Russia from the Air Now: Planes Available, Equipment on Hand, Techniques Set." Leghorn boldly stated, "Aerial spying on the Soviet Union—done covertly and without Soviet permission—can be carried out with very, very small probability of loss and with great gains for the West." Bissell was furious. He was working on one of the nation's most classified projects, and now the very concepts behind his effort were trumpeted across the pages of *U.S. News and World Report*. Yet Leghorn was unaware of the U-2 program. As he had demonstrated so many times before in his career, he had merely taken his knowledge of existing technology, drawn the logical conclusions, and projected their strategic consequences into the immediate future. Bissell contacted Leghorn, brought him to Washington, and briefed him on the program. He gained a respect for Leghorn's abilities and asked him to keep his ideas quiet.[5]

In fall 1957 Leghorn met with Bissell at SEI's office, which became Bissell's base of operations when he was in the Cambridge area. At about this time, Leghorn had a conversation with Bissell about Itek's business prospects. Bissell told Leghorn to forget about SAMOS; the television technology behind the concept wasn't moving ahead fast enough. The future, Bissell explained, was with a film recovery satellite. His advice was priceless.[6]

When Perkins wrote the agenda and drafted item 16, he had no idea that SEI was a front company for the CIA, or that Leghorn's job was to serve as an adviser to Richard Bissell. Then again, neither did Harper

Woodward, Randolph Marston, or Laurance Rockefeller. As a result, none of them could have appreciated the value of Leghorn's connection with Bissell. Had they known, it probably would have increased their confidence in Leghorn. Nevertheless, they could rely on the connections and good judgment of Teddy Walkowicz.

As Perkins pushed the legal paperwork forward, Leghorn hustled to build Itek's fledgling business. He wrote to Gen. Gordon Saville, his contact at Ramo-Wooldridge. It was clear that Leghorn's optimism had grown, and Sputnik was the cause. Leghorn confirmed with Saville their plans to meet with the air force the following week in Washington and expressed his desire to build a strong partnership between Itek and Ramo-Wooldridge.[7] Not everyone was as optimistic as Leghorn. By the end of October 7, the Dow had fallen more than nine points, or 2 percent, to close the day at 452.

By the time *The Wall Street Journal* hit the streets on Tuesday, October 8, it was clear to its editors that the United States had reached an important turning point. Sputnik was "proof that a future war will use, perhaps in addition to conventional arms, the weird weapons of the atomic-rocket age," wrote the journal's editors. "So if war comes in twenty years we will be saved not by the bombers being built today but by the research being done today."[8]

Richard Leghorn — or Teddy Walkowicz, for that matter — couldn't have said it better. Sputnik clarified everything. If Randolph Marston was skeptical about investing in Itek before, there is no documentary evidence that he retained any concerns after Sputnik. After all, Itek's business was all research and development. And it was directly tied to the future of America's satellite program. Could there be any doubt now that getting a satellite in space was America's top priority? If a flood of funding was about to be directed to satellites, Itek would be a beneficiary.

On October 8 the stock market opened weak again. What began as a bad week for investors was rapidly getting worse. Yet there is no sign that Leghorn, Walkowicz, or any of Rockefeller's other advisers at 30 Rockefeller Center were growing concerned about the broader economic situation. They remained focused on Itek. Walkowicz spent part of the day going over his checklist to make sure that nothing would delay the closing of the Itek deal on Thursday. He spoke with the lawyers at Dewey, Ballantine and at Herrick, Smith. He was assured there were "no snags" that could interfere with Thursday morning's transaction.

The final copies of the agreement between Rockefeller and Leghorn were ready to be signed. Neil Borman, another Rockefeller lieutenant, had all the other papers and was "going over them with a fine-tooth comb" that afternoon. Borman would finish his review before the end of the day so that Harper Woodward could read them on his train ride home that evening.[9]

Randolph Marston handled the arrangements with Rockefeller's accountants. He explained that the closing was scheduled for Thursday at 9:00 A.M. A check for $90,000 should be made out to the order of the Itek Corporation and given to Teddy Walkowicz to bring to the meeting. In exchange for his initial investment Rockefeller would receive 22,500 shares of Itek common stock (giving him control of the company), warrants to purchase an additional 7,200 shares, and Itek bonds with a face value of $43,200.[10] As everything was falling into place at 30 Rockefeller Center, the Dow staged a late afternoon rally. By the end of the day the stock market closed with modest losses, off barely two points.[11]

Thursday, October 10, finally arrived, and at about 9:00 A.M. the first Itek Board of Directors meeting was called to order. The meeting took place at the Rockefeller family offices at 30 Rockefeller Center, and Richard Leghorn chaired the meeting. Harper Woodward and Teddy Walkowicz, Itek's other directors, representing the interests of Laurance Rockefeller, were also present. The meeting had few surprises. The nominated officers were elected, the sale of stock, bonds and warrants to Laurance Rockefeller was approved, and authorization to sign the expected cost-plus-fixed-fee contracts was given. Laurance Rockefeller even stopped by to say hello.

Then the topic of security clearances came up. It was evident that Itek's business would include government contracts having to do with classified material. So the board authorized Itek's new officers to apply for any security clearances from the government needed to conduct its business. Harper Woodward said that he was not cleared for the kind of classified materials that Itek might process. The board next approved a motion to deny Harper Woodward access to all classified information, unless he was cleared at a later date by the U.S. government.

Soon the meeting was over and Richard Leghorn had his company. Whatever flush of victory Leghorn felt must have been fleeting. The agreement he signed with Rockefeller provided only enough money to get the company through the first six months of business. After that period, there was no guarantee Rockefeller would support the company further.[12] For Leghorn, who had just moved his family from upstate New York to the suburbs of Boston, his excitement was tempered with a heavy dose of anxiety.[13]

As Itek's first board meeting proceeded that Thursday, the New York Stock Exchange opened for business. With the ring of the opening bell, it soon became clear that something was wrong. After Monday's horrible performance it seemed as though the market had stabilized, but by Thursday the bears had again regained control. As on Monday, the Dow fell by nine points.[14]

On Friday, Harper Woodward did something unusual. He telephoned E. S. Farrow, a vice president and assistant general manager of Kodak. He called to check out Richard Leghorn's background and to ask whether Kodak would license the Minicard System to Itek. Considering that both Leghorn and the Minicard System were critical to Itek's future, Woodward's decision to call the day after the Itek closing, and not before it, is puzzling. Maybe the behavior of the stock market made Woodward uncomfortable, or perhaps the news of additional defense cutbacks disturbed him.

Woodward's telephone call was important enough for him to report it to Laurance Rockefeller. In his memo, Woodward relayed information that must have been largely reassuring. Farrow had known Leghorn since he was a small boy. Along with the other executives at Kodak, Farrow had "the warmest and highest regard" for him. While everyone was disappointed that Leghorn had decided to leave the company, they all wished him the best. And yes, Leghorn could have the Minicard System. After all, Kodak had already licensed it to Magnavox.[15]

Licensed the Minicard System to Magnavox? If Magnavox had the Minicard System already, what was Itek's competitive advantage? Leghorn's business proposal clearly stated that a critical factor in determining Itek's success would be the company's ability to gain an early lead in the information-processing business. The Minicard System, and Itek's ability to exploit it to full advantage, was at the center of that plan. Yet there is no evidence that this information concerned either Woodward or Rockefeller. Perhaps the absence of concern — documented concern, anyway — is understandable. They understood, above all else, the importance of personal relations in business. It was clear that with regard to the CIA and the air force, Leghorn was connected. Here is where Itek would have its advantage.

While Harper Woodward was making his calls that Friday and wrapping up business for the weekend, the stock market was again misbehaving. At one point the Dow was down almost eight points to 434. Then the market staged a late rally on heavy volume and finished at 441, down less than a point for the day. In spite of that rebound, the mood on Wall Street was increasingly grim. The loss for the week of October 7 was more than twenty points, or nearly 5 percent. It was the worst single week for the stock market in almost a year and a half. When the closing bell sounded at the New York Stock Exchange that day, the Dow Jones Industrial Average had fallen to its lowest level in two years. The mild stock market correction that had begun just three months ago had turned into a serious bear market.

Sputnik, it turned out, was just one reason for the decline of the market that week. The other key reason was a new Pentagon policy that had been announced weeks before the launch of the Soviet satellite. The Pentagon had ordered a freeze on defense spending. Unfortunately, prices on certain items, like major weapons systems, kept going up anyway. Confronted with the choice of cutting back on weapons systems or on research and development, the armed services kept the weapons. For companies whose primary business was research and development, or the manufacture of more mundane defense items like spare parts or ordinary transportation equipment, the policy was devastating. Layoffs were announced, plants were closed, and defense-related research and development was hit hard. In another money-saving move, the U.S. Department of Defense announced that in addition to the cutbacks, it was going to stretch out its cash payments to contractors. Payments for work in progress were being cut 20–30 percent. This was on top of cuts in progress payments that had been announced just months earlier.[16] Lower cash payments meant lower earnings. For companies that were marginally viable, this created a liquidity squeeze that threatened their very existence. That's not the kind of news investors like to hear.

Neither is confusion. At a time when it seemed clear to many that the United States was falling behind the Soviet Union in military technology, the Pentagon's policy just didn't make sense. The Department of Defense was taking actions that would in the long term weaken America's defense industrial base. In spite of the obvious ramifications of Sputnik, expressed profanely by politicians and politely by *The Wall Street Journal,* the bureaucracy of the U.S. defense establishment was simply incapable of quickly reversing a policy that had been overtaken by events. Levelheaded thinkers knew that this situation couldn't last. In confusion, there is opportunity. Richard Leghorn smelled opportunity.

So did Nelson Rockefeller. Although Nelson had declined the chance to join brother Laurance as an investor in Itek, he had been quite busy with his own major investment that fall—the Rockefeller Special Studies Project. The Special Studies Project was organized into subpanels, and one of them focused on defense matters. The members of that subpanel had reached their conclusions, and the documents for their final report were nearly finished. The group called for a higher level of defense spending, especially on advanced-technology weapon systems. They believed that U.S. defense technology had fallen behind the Soviets, and Sputnik seemed to confirm their worst fears. Now that all of America was focused on this issue, Nelson Rockefeller wanted to strike. He ordered a young academic, hired to steer the project to its completion, to accelerate work on the report for a quick release. If the youthful historian, Henry Kissinger, could move fast enough, publicity for the group's work would be maximized, Nelson Rockefeller's agenda would be promoted, and the defense of the United States would, he hoped, be strengthened.[17]

There was a problem. Kissinger couldn't release the report until he had all of the final papers. Most of the group's experts submitted their papers promptly to Kissinger. Frank Lindsay, for example, had finished his report over the summer, and Kissinger felt that it showed Lindsay's "imaginativeness at its very best." One outstanding paper, on the relation between technology and national security, was central to the work of the subpanel and the final report. Other commitments had kept the report's author too busy to complete it. Kissinger had watched deadlines come and go before, but now he would probably have to put the pressure on. Teddy Walkowicz had to be persuaded to finish his work.[18]

On Monday, October 14, Itek opened for its first full week in business. It was a treacherous week for stock market investors. After a modest two-point rally on Monday and a more impressive four-point rally on Tuesday, the Dow began to nosedive on Wednesday. When the market opened on Thursday, it continued to fall.

Against the backdrop of a national crisis, defense cutbacks, and a falling stock market, Richard Leghorn issued his first press release from Itek's new offices. He announced that Itek had been formed as a research and engineering group. Its mission, he explained, was to develop informa- tion- and document-processing equipment. There was no mention of sat- ellites, the air force, or the CIA. There was almost no clue that the com- pany's entire future rested on successfully serving the intelligence and defense communities — except for the last sentence. In simple words Leg- horn proudly noted that Laurance Rockefeller was behind the company and that Itek was "in line with his interest in furthering creative research by privately financed companies, thus contributing to the nation's secu- rity and its technological lead." A hint of Itek's real interest, but nothing more.[19]

By the end of the day the Dow Jones Industrial Average had fallen another seven points, or almost 2 percent, and on Friday it fell to its lowest level since June 1955. In little more than three months, from the time Richard Leghorn had quit his job at Kodak to the end of his com- pany's first full week in business, the stock market had fallen by nearly 20 percent.[20] Richard Leghorn had picked a fine time to gamble with his career. Laurance Rockefeller had chosen what seemed to be an inauspi- cious moment to make so speculative an investment.

On Monday, October 21, as Itek opened for its second week of busi- ness, the stock market had its worst single day in two years. The Dow Jones Industrial Average fell by more than ten points on extremely heavy volume. Many investors, severely hurt by the stock market carnage the previous week, now faced margin calls from their brokers. Forced to sell their stocks at any price, they drove the market lower, and it slumped again on Tuesday. Then, on Wednesday, the Dow jumped by more than seventeen points, or 4 percent. Whatever exhilaration investors felt was likely short-lived. Journalists were quick to point out that the last time the stock market had such a big rally was fall 1929.[21]

The same day, October 23, Teddy Walkowicz brought exciting news to Laurance Rockefeller. The president of Boston University, Harold Case, had just approached Itek with an intriguing proposition. Would Itek be willing to take over the university's physical research laboratory? If Case couldn't find a new home for the laboratory, more than one hundred scientists would lose their jobs. If Itek took over the laboratory, overnight it would have a research and development capability that might otherwise take years to build. To accomplish this, however, would require more money.

Yet there was no guarantee Leghorn could build his business fast enough to support such a drastic expansion. Itek had one contract — Leghorn's consulting assignment with SEI — and it barely covered his own salary. And it wasn't clear from the proposal how this group of scientists would further Itek's business plan. Rockefeller needed more information before he decided his next move.

Walkowicz neglected to mention one key point to Rockefeller. This was no ordinary group of scientists. The official name of the lab was sleep inducing, the Boston University Physical Research Laboratory (BUPRL). But its actual purpose was anything but boring. These scientists were experts in collecting and analyzing intelligence. Not only were they regarded by defense community insiders as a national treasure, they were the best possible fit with Itek's future plans.

Before negotiations with Boston University became serious, Laurance Rockefeller would have to be more fully briefed. He would then be confronted with a major decision. Would he accelerate the phase two financing and invest another $550,000 in Itek? Would he gamble that Leghorn's dream could support such a cost structure?[22] As in the past, Rockefeller would probably rely heavily on his advisers for counsel, and not all of them were convinced that acquiring the lab was a wise idea. To Randolph

Marston it looked like an intriguing proposition, but could it pay off in a "tight economy on a non-university basis"? That was the great unknown.[23]

Over the next few days, Richard Leghorn and Duncan MacDonald began talks with Dow Smith, director of the laboratory, and several of his top scientists. In their discussions, the most important goal that emerged was to maintain the integrity of the group's defense work. The key challenge was to find a way that Itek could take over the laboratory without suffering too great a financial loss. Could income and expenses be brought in line? Would they be able to retain the remaining research contracts with the air force, or would those be cut as well?

In spite of all the uncertainty, Leghorn saw an opportunity, and he quickly moved to seize it. Earlier he had learned from Richard Bissell of a major shift in government thinking on spy satellites. Specifically, emphasis would now be placed on developing a film-recovery satellite instead of a near-real-time one. This new approach meant that the field was now wide open. Leghorn realized that taking pictures of the Soviet Union from space required a sophisticated reconnaissance camera—the specialty of Boston University's lab. It also required a satellite design that would allow the camera to take the sharpest, clearest pictures possible. Because motion can blur pictures, the trick was to design a satellite that would minimize the effects of motion.

Through his contacts and long experience in reconnaissance, Leghorn already knew what the competition was likely to propose and the key concepts that would shape those proposals. Accepted thinking on the subject was that spin stabilization was the best way to ensure that a satellite maintained a controlled orbit. A spin-stabilized satellite travels through space like a spiraling football pass. Just as the rotation stabilizes the football as it travels straight through air, the motion of a spin-stabilized satellite would keep it in a stable orbit as it traveled around Earth. But spinning would inevitably lead to blurs. Leghorn knew that there had to be a better way. By fall 1957 he had made up his mind that Itek would develop a proposal to build a film-recovery spy satellite for Bissell. Itek's proposal would trump the competition because by defying conventional thinking about the need for spin stabilization it would produce clearer pictures. Still, Leghorn lacked the expertise to develop this better way. He needed help.

He thought of Jack Herther.[24] In the mid 1950s, while Herther was still in the air force, he was sent to the Massachusetts Institute of Technology to study under Charles Stark Draper, who was known as the father of inertial guidance. Draper was head of a lab at MIT that was conducting classified research for the air force. His mission was to develop inertial guidance systems for intercontinental ballistic missiles, and to research how to stabilize satellites in orbit. Herther worked under Draper for twenty-one months and not only earned his master's degree but gained important knowledge about the most advanced concepts in satellite stabilization.[25]

After Herther received his master's degree, the air force sent him to Wright Patterson Field to work on WS-117L, or SAMOS. He became one of the first program team members for the air force reconnaissance satellite project. He was working at the leading edge of space-based research, and he traveled frequently to Washington to brief top members of the Air Force Science Advisory Board, like Richard Leghorn and Duncan MacDonald. In spite of the importance of Herther's work, defense-spending cuts were squeezing his group out of existence.[26]

Now Herther needed a job. In fall 1957 he retired from the air force. He drove to Boston to meet with Richard Leghorn, who had told him about a new company he had just founded. Leghorn took Herther to lunch at a diner across the street from the B.U. labs. Leghorn explained to Herther his plans to take over the lab. He also told him that Itek would propose to develop a spy satellite camera for the CIA. But he needed a more effective stabilization concept than spin stabilization. Herther thought he had the answer — an unproven concept called three-axis stabilization. Leghorn hired Herther, who almost immediately found himself working on the proposal with Duncan MacDonald and John Watson, a scientist who was still officially working at the B.U. lab.[27]

On October 28 Leghorn drafted a letter to Harold Case and sent it to the Rockefeller office for review. In his letter, Leghorn offered to employ all current laboratory personnel. They would terminate their employment with Boston University on November 30 and become Itek employees on

December 1. Itek would continue to use B.U. facilities until suitable quarters could be found, which he hoped would occur by July 1959.

The proposed transfer date was little more than a month away, but Leghorn knew that Case wanted to resolve this issue before the end of the year. If Case hadn't found a new home for the lab by then, he would have to close it down. The greatest collection of scientists devoted to reconnaissance and intelligence systems in America would be thrown to the winds, and the Pentagon's cost-cutting policy would claim another victim. Harper Woodward reviewed Leghorn's draft, and he wasn't pleased with what he saw. Squeezed in the margins of the letter, Woodward scribbled a stern note to Walkowicz. First and foremost, Woodward felt that the memo contained absolutely no facts upon which an intelligent business decision could be made. What are the lab's contracts? Are they profitable? Who are the customers? How much working capital was required? Does the lab have a good fit with Itek's basic objectives? Woodward was intrigued by the opportunity, but he was hardly sold. Yet by November 4, Richard Leghorn was given the green light to send his letter. It was virtually unchanged from the original draft. The letter soon arrived on the desk of Harold Case.[28]

The same day, Teddy Walkowicz finally finished his paper for the Rockefeller Special Studies Project and sent it to Henry Kissinger. "Survival in an Age of Technological Contest" expressed Walkowicz's deep pessimism about America's ability to regain its lead against the Soviets.[29] And if the United States could not regain the advantage, Walkowicz foresaw an apocalypse. "Either the U.S. promptly gets ahead in the technological war and stays there, or human freedom will eventually go by default to Communist tyranny." Part of the problem was bad government. Walkowicz believed that "American science" had been "slowly bogged down by a bureaucracy which places major emphasis on administrative tidiness, and insufficient emphasis on producing results." Walkowicz, former military staff secretary and current member of the Air Force Science Advisory Board, former aid to the chief scientist of the air force, knew what he was talking about—and it scared him.

Walkowicz proposed a solution—or perhaps revolution is a more apt word. He wanted nothing less than a complete restructuring in the way that America's national security establishment did business. His analysis was clear, cutting, and arrogant. From his perspective, the National Security Council and its staff, the State Department Policy Planning Group, as well as the top echelons of the Department of Defense, were institutionally incapable of "understanding the impact of science on national policy." The same was true of the president's cabinet, where most "discussions of problems which have a high technological content are conducted by technically uninformed people." This state of affairs was dangerous.

The only way to stem America's decline, Walkowicz argued, was to streamline the nation's defense establishment and redesign it as a science-driven organization. Walkowicz wanted to integrate the scientific community with the policy-making community. To accomplish this, he wanted a top scientist appointed to the cabinet, perhaps with the title of special assistant to the president for science. Other leading scientists would be recruited and placed in newly created positions throughout the government. In these new positions they could influence national research and development policy and weapons systems planning. The result, Walkowicz believed, would be a defense establishment that measured success in terms of technological innovation, not armaments production.

Redesigning the structure and staffing of the defense establishment was just a first step. America's technological renaissance also required a vast investment in research and development. The Pentagon's research and development budget, except during the Korean War, had been "inadequate every year since the end of World War Two," according to Walkowicz. It wasn't just a matter of spending more money, he insisted; it was essential to direct that money to the right places.

The most important area for Walkowicz was aeronautics. "The race for the conquest of space is today's major engagement in the technological war" with the Soviet Union, he stated. The nation that dominated the air and space "will be in a position to dominate the world." America's survival would be determined by its ability to produce better rockets, missiles, jets, and satellites than the Soviet Union.

Walkowicz had left the government in part because he had decided it wasn't capable of properly developing these technologies. Now, working for Laurance Rockefeller, Walkowicz was stepping into the breach. He was identifying new companies and technologies that needed financial support and that might develop the products that would strengthen America. One of these companies was Itek.

About the time that Walkowicz finished his paper, Richard Leghorn and his team went to work on obtaining their first major contract. Itek and Ramo-Wooldridge were now jointly bidding on a classified contract for the Ballistic Missiles Divisions of the Air Force Research and Development Command (ARDC), run by Bennie Schriever, Leghorn's old air force buddy. The total value of the contract was $2 million, and Itek's share might be as high as $750,000. The deal, which was to develop the ground-handling equipment for the SAMOS spy satellite program, was important to Itek, and Leghorn flew to the West Coast to work on it. If he succeeded, Itek would play a critical role in designing equipment used to store, handle, and analyze intelligence about the Soviet Union and its military forces obtained from U.S. satellites.

On November 11 Teddy Walkowicz gave Harper Woodward an update on Itek's negotiations with Boston University. Initial contacts suggested that the university was in favor of the Itek proposal. Walkowicz, however, had just heard a disturbing piece of news: an unexpected competitor had emerged, Hycon. The president and founder of Hycon, Trevor Gardner, had been an assistant secretary of the air force a few years earlier. Gardner had contacts at the highest levels in the U.S. government. His company, which made the cameras for the U-2 spy plane, was a serious competitor. It was hard to imagine how Itek, which had just six employees and virtually no business, would be able to compete.

Walkowicz had more bad news. Jack Carter, who was supposed to become part of Itek's management team, was not coming aboard. Carter was a senior executive at Lockheed, with extensive experience managing large, classified defense projects. His current project was SAMOS, and his contacts would have been a huge asset to Itek. But Lockheed asked Carter to stay, at least until SAMOS was off the ground. Carter's reunion with his old air force buddies Leghorn and Walkowicz would have to wait. If Walkowicz was worried, he didn't let it show.[30]

By November 15 Harold Case was ready to reply to Leghorn's proposal. He accepted the "spirit and terms" of the letter as the basis for "formal discussions," but a number of details needed to be worked out. Because most of the lab's current contracts were with the U.S. Air Force, and because they were largely classified, Case needed to get the approval of Lt. Gen. Donald Putt for the transaction. If that issue could be resolved, Case was ready to close the deal, but the offer would have to be sweetened. He wanted Leghorn to give the university Itek stock. If it was good enough for Laurance Rockefeller, Case probably felt that it was a wise investment for Boston University. But was Case sincere, or was he now using negotiations with Itek to strengthen his bargaining position with Hycon?[31]

Case made it clear when he wrote his letter to General Putt on November 18 that his responsibility to the nation weighed heavily on his mind. He noted that the research conducted at the lab was important to the national defense. He carefully explained that because of the cuts in air force support for the program, the university could no longer afford to maintain it. Perhaps.[32]

In a follow-up telegram, dated November 22, Case declared that he was leaning toward Itek. Itek was sensitive to Boston University's needs and appreciated the problems connected with the transfer of the lab. It was the university's opinion "that the Itek management does possess the breadth" to manage the transition in a manner consistent with the university's interests and views. "I would therefore request USAF concurrence in the course of action now contemplated by the University in transferring the facility and USAF contracts to Itek Corporation."[33]

A week later Case received disappointing news. The air force was not ready to allow the transaction to proceed. A conference between Boston University, Itek, and the air force was needed to iron out all the details. It would take place on December 10 at the headquarters of the Air Force Research and Development Command in Maryland.

Now Case must have begun to worry. Government funding for the lab would run out on December 31. Case had accepted Itek's proposal with the understanding that the transfer would occur on December 1. Would Case receive air force approval for the transaction before year's end, or would he have to close down the lab on January 1? It was crucial that the conference on December 10 resolve matters.[34]

Leghorn wrote to Case and summarized the state of the negotiations.

The target date for the transfer was now January 1. Both Leghorn and Case must have realized that this had to be the final deadline. If the transfer was postponed again, the lab would officially cease to exist.

The same day that Leghorn met with Case, Jesse Cousins, treasurer of Itek, developed a new set of financial projections for the company. If Itek was able to take over the lab, maintain its current contracts with the air force, and land a couple of new ones, like the ground-handling equipment for SAMOS, it would turn profitable by March 1958, far ahead of schedule. Cousins sent his worksheets to the team at 30 Rockefeller Center. They must have been warmly received.[35]

Within days, Case received another jolt of bad news. In a small revolt at the air force, two senior officers evidently objected to the plan and had asked to postpone the meeting from December 10 to the seventeenth. When Jesse Cousins learned this news, he wrote to Teddy Walkowicz that "getting affirmative action accomplished by January 1st is remote." On December 13 Case wrote to General Putt. He was incensed by Putt's apparent indifference to the fast-approaching deadline. The lab was a national resource and Boston University had done everything possible to hold it together, despite declining air force support. The last set of cutbacks had been enough to force Case to shut down the lab on financial grounds. He had not because "the Itek Corporation expressed a willingness to take over the payroll expense as of January 1st, and because of your expressed view that in the national interest the people in the Laboratory should somehow be kept together as a group." Had Putt already forgotten what he had said? Did he understand that the university was at the end of its rope? Case closed his letter on an ominous note. Unless the air force agreed to the January 1 transfer date, it would be difficult for Case to avoid sending out dismissal notices. He concluded, "It would be most unfortunate if the present staff should now be allowed to break up piecemeal."[36]

On Christmas Eve, Case issued a press release announcing that on January 1, the staff of the Boston University Physical Research Laboratories would become employees of the Itek Corporation. Thanks to this transaction, Case explained, the "internationally known talents of the staff" of more than one hundred people would not "be lost to the nation."[37] The air force had blinked, the transaction had been approved, and just seven days before Case would have been required to fire the entire staff, he was sending them off to new jobs at Itek. For many lab employees that year, Harold Case was truly their Santa.

When Case went to sleep that Christmas Eve, he must have rested a little easier. After all, he had saved a national treasure from destruction and preserved the jobs of many loyal employees. Although Case must have felt a calming sense of accomplishment that night, we now know that it was ill-founded. The employees of the laboratory were still in jeopardy. An undated and unsigned memorandum, written on Itek stationery, outlines the company's plan for the lab and its personnel. The memorandum, sent to Laurance Rockefeller's staff, was probably written late that December. It describes Itek's need to accelerate the phase two financing so that the company could take over the lab on January 1. With the lab under its corporate umbrella, Itek's credibility would be enhanced and its chance of winning contracts would increase. Certainly the plan was a gamble, but "if Itek does not assume this risk, it will have passed up a unique, though speculative, opportunity to accelerate its growth." If control of the laboratory did not result in increased business—and that could be judged fairly quickly—then its "carrying costs [could] be pared down appreciably at the end of January 1958." The lab's main cost was people. If contracts didn't materialize soon, people would be fired. In spite of his hard work, and totally unknown to him, Case had done nothing more than supply Leghorn with chips for his gamble. Case's hard-fought victory—and his gift to his old employees—was perhaps just a brief stay of execution.[38]

5

THE COFFEE SLURPERS AND THE
FRONT-OFFICE PROS

Opportunity and little downside risk—certainly, that is how Richard Leghorn must have viewed Itek's acquisition of the lab at Boston University. The opportunity was clear, the short-term risks seemed manageable, yet long-term dangers remained. The threats, hidden within the culture of the lab itself, were also the very qualities that Duncan MacDonald had worked so hard to cultivate over the years—unconventional thinking, willful self-determination, and independent thought. These characteristics, prized in a nonprofit research organization, would lead to unexpected outcomes within Itek's corporate structure. If Leghorn failed to recognize these threats, his error was understandable. His focus was on business risk, but the real danger was to himself.

By Christmas 1953 the contours of the lab's culture could already be observed. The employees organized holiday parties, sang carols, and produced a show. The only threat to the usual holiday cheer that year was a five-way fight for the lab's bowling league championship. For Dr. Duncan MacDonald, director of the lab, the outcome didn't matter. Not because his team was out of the competition, despite the fact that he was one of the league's best bowlers. That was the price he paid for having Walt Levison on his team, one of the worst. MacDonald had already achieved an important victory—creating a casual, friendly environment where every employee could find a constructive way to let off a little steam. So MacDonald encouraged bowling and softball leagues, golf competitions, game nights, and parties for every holiday on the calendar.

The lab even had its own newspaper, the *700 News,* named after the lab's street address on 700 Commonwealth Avenue. MacDonald supported these activities because it was his nature, and because he was a very good manager.[1]

The lab's specialty, designing, producing, and analyzing high-performance aerial reconnaissance and intelligence systems, was an obscure but critical theater of the Cold War. The exacting nature of the lab's work, the frequent tight deadlines, and the unspoken moral questions had the potential to create a pressure-cooker environment. If the lab accomplished its goal, and the air force or the CIA could do a better job gathering intelligence about potential enemies, the national security of the United States was enhanced. A job finished on time did not necessarily relieve the pressure, though the workload might briefly lighten. The moral ambiguities remained, new deadlines appeared, and the pressure grew.

MacDonald created an environment that helped his team to better handle these pressures, but he was more than a good manager—he was also a visionary. Quite simply, when it came to intelligence systems, aerial reconnaissance, and spy cameras, MacDonald was both an innovator and a perceptive integrator of other people's ideas. Until he founded BUPRL, military photointelligence relied on a few very basic concepts. Put a camera in a plane, fly it around, take pictures, develop the pictures, look for stuff. MacDonald, trained as a physicist, brought a new discipline to the field. He was one of the first scientists to see the intelligence cycle as a whole. This appreciation for all the links in the intelligence process gave him a powerful insight into how to improve it.[2]

Under MacDonald's leadership, the lab became the first research group to develop a systems approach to analyzing the performance of intelligence and reconnaissance systems. The lab pioneered the use of communications theory in the field, performed groundbreaking research on the effects of atmospheric turbulence on aerial spy photographs, and was the first institution to evaluate how psychological factors influence photointerpretation and lens analysis. The lab became an incubator for new technologies and set new standards for excellence in the development of the world's largest cameras and photographic lenses. These camera systems, flown in planes and pointed at enemy targets from just outside hostile borders, were the kinds of tools the U.S. needed if it was going to spy on countries that were difficult to penetrate using human spies.[3]

The lab produced a series of technical papers related to all aspects of the aerial reconnaissance and intelligence cycle. During BUPRL's eleven-year history, more than 130 of these papers, called technical notes, were published. These reports could be incredibly dry reading, but the arid prose concealed a revolutionary agenda—a scientific transformation of U.S. aerial reconnaissance. Spying from a plane would never be the same.

Because spy cameras often took pictures of their targets through aircraft windows, the lab studied how this basic relation between camera and window affected the intelligence-gathering process. The lab produced papers with such titles as "Pressure and Temperature Influences on Aircraft Camera Windows," "The Deterioration of Image Quality Caused by a Heated Air Window Defrosting System," and "Photographic Window Design In Supersonic Aircraft." Committed readers might even work their way through "An Experimental Study of the Thermal Endurance of Plate Glass."

Although the lab studied windows and glass extensively, that was hardly the only area of concern. Because a lens, or combination of lenses, is at the heart of any camera system, the lab did exhaustive research in lens design. Recognizing that a lens cannot take a picture by itself, the scientists at BUPRL also performed in-depth studies on camera and shutter design, as well as film processing. In all of these efforts, the goal was to improve the amount of photographic intelligence that could be extracted from a camera system.[4]

But good spy cameras didn't guarantee good intelligence. Ultimately, a human photointerpreter had to examine the photograph. MacDonald believed that of all the elements of the reconnaissance system, "the interpreter, as a tool, or as a human being, has been subjected to the least study." So the scientists at the lab studied the photointerpretation process, and how to improve it, from all possible angles. How do you choose the right people to be photointerpreters? The lab's paper "A Study of Two Tests for Discrimination of Proficient Photo-Interpretation Students" sought to answer that question. When pilots flew reconnaissance missions over hostile targets, they often had to take photographs at unusual angles, especially when trying to avoid being shot down by enemy planes. "The Effect of Visual Angle and Degree of Imperfection Upon the Recognition of Objects," published by the lab in 1953, addressed that challenge. Finally, the lab developed photointerpretation keys that could help the interpreters more easily identify tanks, planes, and even missiles from pictures taken at extremely high altitudes.[5]

By the mid-1950s Duncan MacDonald and his team of scientists had won a small but important place for themselves as members of the military-industrial complex. Yet scientists in Cold War America, despite their important contributions to national security, were also seen as potential enemies from within. The same men who were admired for the technical marvels they created were feared for the secrets they might share with the Soviet Union.

By spring 1954 Senator Joseph McCarthy was near the peak of his power. Robert Oppenheimer, the moving force behind the development of the atomic bomb at Los Alamos, stood accused of treason. In BUPRL's own in-house newspaper the big story in April 1954, right after the "Duffers League" update and the "Game Night" bulletin, was the paper's editorial. And Harry Keelan, editor of the *700 News*, was angry. He was disgusted by McCarthy and by what be believed was Eisenhower's tacit approval of McCarthyism. He was outraged by the unscientific attitude of administration officials who persecuted Oppenheimer. "The President has 'ordered a wall' between Oppenheimer and all classified information. A wall between the classified information and the man who gave it to them! Do they imagine that once the material is committed to paper the scientist immediately forgets it?"[6]

Not everyone at the lab agreed with Harry Keelan. Ward Low, in a letter to the editor that appeared in the next addition of the *700 News*, saw the Oppenheimer case differently. Although Ward didn't defend the charges against Oppenheimer, he defended the process. The law required the Atomic Energy Commission to investigate the accusations against Oppenheimer, and as senseless as the process seemed, the Eisenhower administration had no choice but to work within the context of the laws.[7]

Dr. Dow Smith, second in command at the lab under Duncan MacDonald, grabbed his copy of the *700 News* and rushed off to catch a train.

Smith, a Canadian by birth, had joined the lab in 1951. He probably hoped to relax on his way home that night by reading about the latest sporting event and the usual gossip.

But Ward Low's remarks disturbed Smith so much that he spent the rest of his train ride "sitting up trying to compete with the rough road bed" to get some ideas on paper. He was angry not because Low's ideas were particularly wrong but because they overlooked the important issue. "In all of this, let us remember that this issue involves intellectual freedom in the broadest sense and not primarily matters of clearance." Smith agreed with Low that "current security regulations made the investigation mandatory. But this does not, as Ward Low implies, absolve those who administer the regulations. On the contrary, they are open to criticism whenever they allow fear and hysteria to take the place of good judgement."[8]

Smith's logic was clear and his moral argument was strong, but his words were growing dangerous. In the age of McCarthy, no American scientist working on a classified defense project was safe from persecution. If Oppenheimer could be ruined, so could anyone else. Many were too scared to speak, let alone write what they really thought. Not Smith. "The concept of guilt by mere association and guilt from unsubstantiated accusation are techniques of Fascism and Communism, not of democracy," he wrote. "They appeal to the emotions, not to reason, and they are built on fear and hatred." The danger, argued Smith, was that when these issues are "fought on an emotional basis, we end up by attacking ourselves. And this attack is against freedom of thought and expression. We do not want communism, but book-burners are equally evil." Was the Eisenhower administration no better than the men who ran the Kremlin? Smith didn't say that, but he was certainly leaving himself open to the charge. In the tense political climate that gripped America that spring, Smith was a braver man than he probably realized.

Life at the lab returned to normal, but Harry Keelan soon found another way to stir up trouble. A restless agitator, Keelan moved on to his next target. He settled on the United World Federalists and their leading activist at the lab, Walt Levison. The World Federalists believed that world peace could be achieved through world government. The goal may have been noble, but Keelan found what he believed was a fatal flaw in the organization's charter. No communists or fascists would be admitted to the group as members. "You cannot have a world organization and leave out half of the world!" Keelan mocked the World Federalists and challenged Levison to defend the group on the editorial page of the *Zoo News*.[9]

Two weeks later Levison's defense of the World Federalists appeared. In a letter to the editor, he explained that the purpose of the group was to inform the American people of the value and practicality of a limited world government. Levison defended the decision to exclude communists and observed that "aside from a few indigenous Marxists," communists in America suffered from "divided loyalties." Levison noted that the American Communist Party always followed "the Kremlin line." "Would you say that an American party member would make a good advocate of world government to the American public? The answer," Levison emphatically stated, "is clearly no!" If the World Federalists admitted a communist to its membership it would "alienate Mr. Average Citizen, and since the aim of the U.S.S.R. is also a world government run from Moscow, we could never be sure which one he is working for — ours or his. Does this clarify our position a little[?]"[10] Levison's idealism, his hope for world peace, was lost in the manner of his message.

Levison believed in his cause enough to swallow his pride and to try again. This time Levison's work appeared as a guest editorial and it was called "The Dream of Peace." The anger, the arrogance, the defensiveness were gone. All that remained was Levison's hope for a better future and a simple explanation of his faith. "Through all its history," Levison began, "mankind has hugged the dream of permanent peace, only to find itself again at the edge of disaster." Levison wrote simply and directly. Most important, he wrote from the heart: "It may be a dream that nations can live in harmony, but without the dream there is no possibility that they can."

Levison explained, "Five years ago when I first joined the United World Federalists, it was a dream. The objective of the organization was to create a world government but that was all. There were no firm ideas as to how this could be accomplished." Yet it was clear to Levison that the goal had to be accomplished if the world was to survive. In the age of the atom bomb, there could be no more wars. But what concrete program did his group advocate? The World Federalists "are dedicated to the support of the United Nations" and "to a definite campaign" to change and strengthen its constitution, and thus its powers. The World Federalists had identified several areas where the United Nations' power needed to be reconsidered, strengthened, or expanded. The ability to regulate armaments and atomic power, the prevention of aggression, the maintenance of a U.N. inspection and police force were all concerns.

Yet it was clear from Levison's editorial, perhaps in a way he never intended, that he was also concerned about the future of the individual, the ability of any single person to make a difference in the world. Melancholy and a little uncertain, he suggested there were probably "few thoughtful persons today who have not been troubled by the fact that in a time of national and international stress the individual as such can make so little a contribution to solving" the world's problems. As Levison worked through the problem, he also revealed his solace. "The voice of any one person may be too weak to reach those charged with the stupendous responsibility for peace and war," he acknowledged. But individuals working together, through an organization, could preserve society. And Levison believed that the "United World Federalists [was] such an organization." Over the years, Levison would continue to fight for world peace and disarmament. He would work on study groups, testify before Congress, and contribute scholarly papers on the subject.[11]

Levison, like many of his colleagues, saw no contradiction in fighting for world peace while working on classified defense contracts. After all, the Soviet Union wanted nothing less than world domination. There could be no real peace with such an enemy. Americans like Levison who had given the best years of their lives to fighting fascism in World War II knew that the nation's defense had to be strong. Its leaders needed the best intelligence possible to make difficult decisions in war, and ideally, to avoid it. In the nuclear age the cost of war was simply too great.

In 1946 Levison witnessed firsthand the destructive power of the atomic bomb. From that point on, he feared and respected it. In October 1945 President Harry S. Truman approved the Pentagon's request to conduct atomic bomb tests. Under the aegis of Project CROSSROADS, the tests would be the first postwar examination of the bomb's military effectiveness. Testing would take place in July 1946 at a peaceful collection of islands in the South Pacific called Bikini Atoll and would be photographed for posterity.

Project CROSSROADS was going to be different from any other nuclear detonation. The tests of the atomic bomb conducted at Los Alamos in 1945 had shown that the bomb worked. Hiroshima and Nagasaki had demonstrated that the bomb could kill large numbers of people and devastate cities. The purpose of Project CROSSROADS was to evaluate in detail how the bomb could be used against military targets such as battleships.

Col. Paul T. Cullen, who was in charge of the reconnaissance unit that would photograph the tests, was given little time to recruit his team. Cullen's photoreconnaissance experience was largely administrative, so it was essential that he select a deputy with broad experience in the field. His choice was Richard Leghorn, who was preparing to leave the service to rejoin his old employer, Eastman Kodak. Walter Levison, along with Duncan MacDonald, and Richard Philbrick, were recruited to photograph the tests. More than a decade before Itek was founded, Cullen had assembled some of the key figures that would play fateful roles in the company's destiny. Cullen and Leghorn, relying on the advice of Amrom Katz, chose an F-13 — a modified version of the B-29 Superfortress — for their mission. It would have to fly well enough for them to take good pictures of the test, and high enough to keep them out of harm's way.[12]

Cullen's photographic unit spent several weeks preparing for the tests on a beautiful tropical island called Kwajalein. In the hours they had to themselves, they tried to relax, but it was difficult. The atomic bomb had just been used the previous year against Japan. There was no reason to believe that it wouldn't be used again. If Project CROSSROADS was a success and the photographic unit accomplished its mission, the Pentagon would have a textbook complete with pictures that would allow military strategists to analyze the bomb's effectiveness against military objectives. The textbook would be studied, the pictures would be examined and reexamined, and the bomb would likely be used again, only the next time with greater destructive effect — thanks to the lessons learned at Bikini Atoll.[13]

By the time Richard Leghorn arrived at Kwajalein, he had done a lot of thinking about war — the comrades lost in the previous one and the lives that could be saved by avoiding, or minimizing the costs of, the next one. He developed an idea called pre-D-day reconnaissance. If the United States was to survive in the nuclear age, there could be no more surprise attacks. America needed advanced warning of an enemy's military preparations, and then it would have the opportunity to use diplomacy to avoid war, or preemptive military action to destroy the enemy's own war fighting capabilities. In 1946 the only way to obtain advanced warning was by flying high-altitude photoreconnaissance missions, and Leghorn focused his intellectual powers on designing a strategy that would allow him to sell his ideas to the Pentagon. He described his ideas to his colleagues at all times of the day. Duncan Mac-Donald and Walter Levison listened to Leghorn. They were influenced by the passion of his argument and the power of his logic.[14]

When Duncan MacDonald opened the doors at Boston University's Optical Research Laboratory (later renamed the Physical Research Laboratory) in December 1946, he had invited Richard Leghorn to give one of the keynote addresses at the dedication ceremony. The nation's top military brass concerned with aerial reconnaissance filled the audience, and representatives from major defense contractors mingled in the crowd. After months of thought, and of testing his ideas in conversations with his friends, Leghorn was ready to formally unveil his strategy.

Leghorn knew that if he was going to sell his ideas to his audience, he needed to begin slowly, and pace himself. Only after he had fully established his credentials with the audience, and mentally prepared them to accept the logic of his conclusions, could he dare present them with a strategy that represented a new departure in military thinking.

So he began with the basics and talked about the principles of military aerial reconnaissance. He talked about aircraft and camera systems, intelligence collection and intelligence dissemination. Carefully, he worked his way through forty pages of double-spaced text, until he was at last ready to unveil the ideas that were closest to his heart. In the atomic age, he explained, "military intelligence becomes the most important guardian of our national security. The nature of atomic warfare is such that once attacks are launched against us, it will be extremely difficult, if not impossible, to recover from them and counterattack successfully. Therefore, it obviously becomes essential that we have prior knowledge of the possibility of an attack, for defensive action against it must be taken before it is launched. Military intelligence is the agency for providing this information, and our national security rests upon its effectiveness next to a sound international political structure."[15]

Leghorn's speech, nine years before President Eisenhower made his Open Skies proposal at Geneva, articulated both the challenges Ike's own proposal would face and the very same solution the president would choose. "It is unfortunate that whereas peacetime spying is considered a normal function between nation states, military aerial reconnaissance—which is simply another method of spying—is given more weight as an act of military aggression," Leghorn observed. "Unless thinking on this subject is changed, reconnaissance flights will not be able to be performed in peace without the permission of the nation states over which the flight is made." Recognizing that the Soviet Union was not likely in the near future to allow the United States to fly reconnaissance missions over its territory, Leghorn recommended a covert solution. "It is extraordinarily important that a means of long-range aerial reconnaissance be devised which cannot be detected."[16]

MacDonald founded BUPRL in 1946 just as the Iron Curtain was beginning to fall across Eastern Europe. Leghorn's speech had made it clear that in order to prepare for a possible war with the Soviet Union—or to avoid it—America needed good intelligence. Spies couldn't penetrate the Communist Bloc, let alone bring back useful military intelligence. Airplanes, carrying long-range spy cameras, became the Pentagon's best hope—just as Leghorn predicted. In the years that followed Leghorn's speech, he continued to campaign for his cause. His ideas about pre-D-day reconnaissance, which later become known as strategic reconnaissance, were adopted slowly by policy makers and Pentagon officials alike. For Duncan MacDonald, this meant a steady increase in the demand for his lab's products, services, and advice.[17]

By 1956, when Duncan MacDonald left the lab to become dean of Boston University's graduate school and Dow Smith replaced him as director, BUPRL had become the free world's largest and most prestigious group working on aerial reconnaissance and intelligence systems. The fun-loving scientists at BUPRL, without realizing it, had grown up. In 1946 they were a bunch of patriot professors, scientists, and technicians bound together by Duncan MacDonald's vision. Now they were a small but essential part of the military-industrial complex. The Department of

Defense and the CIA depended on them to develop better reconnaissance systems and to explore new ways to improve the process of gathering and reporting intelligence.

The guys at the lab still sang, bowled, and played golf, but their research was helping to shape a new industry built on the intelligence needs of America. This influence gave the lab prestige and a deep knowledge of the industrial landscape. Corporations like Eastman Kodak, Bausch and Lomb, and Lockheed repeatedly turned to the laboratory's scientists for solutions to a whole host of problems related to their defense businesses. Kodak looked to the lab for assistance in film processing and evaluation. Lockheed, Martin, CBS, Philco, and RCA all wanted advice from the lab on technical issues. Good spy cameras require quality glass and properly made lens systems. Not surprisingly, Corning and Bausch and Lomb repeatedly sought information from the lab on optical glass evaluation. And the lab wasn't just a think tank. It had state-of-the-art machine shops staffed by highly skilled technicians and craftsmen. When companies like Bulova, Perkins-Elmer, and Convair needed help making tight deadlines for defense contracts, they paid BUPRL to manufacture the special optical components that their own firms could not produce.[18]

Although the lab was at Boston University, its understanding of companies like Fairchild Camera and Instrument Corporation and Chicago Aerial helped it to better meet the needs of industry and to satisfy its ultimate client, the Department of Defense. When BUPRL became part of Itek, this knowledge of the competition, built up over years when the lab and its personnel were viewed as a noncompetitive threat, helped Itek to beat the competition.[19]

In the last months before the lab's acquisition by Itek, its scientists were hard at work on a highly classified if improbable scheme to send spy cameras deep into the Soviet Union and bring them back successfully. The program, called Project GENETRIX, relied on high-altitude hot-air balloons to carry custom-made spy cameras, designed at BUPRL, across the Russian land mass.

The balloon programs were a simple solution to a vexing problem. Although the U-2 had first been sent into the Soviet Union in July 1956, Ike had severely limited its use after the spy plane was tracked on its first mission. Just as Leghorn predicted, the Soviets were enraged that a manned aircraft had been ordered, as they correctly assumed, to penetrate its airspace. Ike and his advisers must have believed that even the Soviets would have a much harder time getting worked up over a balloon. At least a spy balloon, as opposed to a spy plane, had a more plausible cover story for getting repeatedly lost over the Soviet Union. What possible excuse could be given for repeated U-2 flights through Soviet air space? Had the United States simply run out of pilots with a good sense of direction? But everyone could agree that balloons have a mind of their own.

The spy balloons were supposed to follow a basic script. Released on one side of the Soviet Union, they would gently drift across the country—carried in whatever direction the winds blew. Floating peacefully at high altitudes, they were supposed to be beyond the range of Soviet fighters and ground-to-air missiles. Retrieving the balloons and cameras as they scattered across the sky and exited Soviet air space was a daunting task, but that was the air force's problem. Once the balloons were retrieved, their cameras would be brought back to the United States, where the film would be developed and new intelligence about the Soviet Union revealed. The task for BUPRL was to design cameras that could accomplish the mission.

Walt Levison had a bad back. In early 1957, under doctor's orders, he rested motionless in a hospital bed. The doctors hoped, and Levison prayed, that supervised bed rest alone might cure his back and help him avoid an operation. Levison was bored and his mind was restless. So he did what came naturally—he designed new camera systems in his head to pass the time. It was during this period of convalescence that Levison's camera design for Project GENETRIX, also called WS-461L, took shape. This design, the second he had created for the program, was to have historic implications for BUPRL, the future of Itek, and the birth of spy satellites.

Balloons, like most things in life, have both positive and negative attributes. A camera designer like Levison had to be well aware of both. The balloons in the late phases of the GENETRIX program were supposed to be able to fly as high as 100,000 feet. From that height, whatever camera these balloons carried was going to be able to photograph a broad expanse of land with every shot. High-altitude balloons, often maligned for being slow, had another positive feature. Precisely because balloons were lumbering, relatively stable transportation vehicles, they provided an ideal platform for carrying a camera through the sky. The photographs taken from slow balloons would be free from the blurring that marred photographs taken from fast-moving planes. But there was a trade-off. To get very high, these balloons had to carry as little weight as possible. That meant that the camera and its film had to be extraordinarily light. Levison's initial design for the balloon program, called the Duplex, used two cameras. It was a good solution, but he could do better.

The next camera Levison designed, while lying on his back, was nothing short of revolutionary. During World War II the best reconnaissance cameras could resolve no more than fifteen lines per millimeter. The camera Levison designed produced one hundred lines per millimeter. The camera was called the HYAC, for high acuity. Rather than design a high-altitude frame camera, a bigger version of a regular "point and click," in which the film advances frame by frame after every shot, Levison took a different route. The frame camera had limitations in reconnaissance applications. In order to capture a broad swath of land while the balloon passed overhead, a frame camera requires a wide-angle lens. Unfortunately, getting high resolution from a wide-angle lens was very difficult. Thus much detail on the ground would be lost.

Levison's solution was to reach back in history to the age of the early portrait photographers of the nineteenth century. According to his new design, the lens would pivot as the camera slowly drifted over the ground, so that "it swung like a pendulum through a 120-degree arc. During each pass, it 'painted' the image across a strip of film 2 inches wide and about 25 inches long. As the lens swung back, the film advanced, and the next picture could then be taken." Levison's design was described as "elegant," the camera "beautiful" and years ahead of its time. Unfortunately, Levison and his camera were running out of time. By late 1957 BUPRL was about to be shut down, and only a few of the cameras had actually been made.[20] The only thing that would save Levison and his camera design was the pending acquisition of the lab by Itek.

Would the acquisition work? Could the lab be saved? Would Leghorn get the contracts he needed to keep the lab going? Or, just one month after acquiring the lab, would Leghorn be forced to cut costs and fire employees?

On December 18, 1957, Leghorn gave an important speech on strategic reconnaissance at the Franklin Institute in Philadelphia. The timing of the event, just as Itek was about to acquire BUPRL, could not have been more inconvenient. Yet he had to give the speech. In many ways it was a summation for Leghorn, a statement of the ideals that had driven his life up to this point, and the values that would drive the Itek Corporation and Leghorn's activities as its president.

Speaking before one of the country's oldest and most prestigious scientific organizations, Leghorn asked the question, "Can science help to create a rational world security system?" The answer, of course, was yes. Leghorn's faith in science, and in the cool, analytical prowess of scientists, had long bolstered his belief that the world's problems could be overcome, that nuclear war could be avoided. But scientists needed to become engaged in the broader world around them; they needed to fully participate in the great debates of the atomic age. "Until we address ourselves to the problems of enlisting a substantial scientific effort in the construction of a rational world security system, the arms race in all its madness will continue to enslave science throughout the world."

Leghorn explained that a rational world security system had to be built on arms control agreements and the technical means for verifying them. He observed that "the physical sciences" could contribute greatly to "providing the tools for inspection."

And Leghorn knew how the scientists should direct their energies. "Of the many possibilities," he asserted, "one merits specific consideration tonight, as it might provide the key to unlock the entire 'disarmament' deadlock." Leghorn was speaking of satellites—in particular, satellites armed with cameras. He believed that Sputnik had established the "right of large peaceful satellites" to orbit the earth, and that inspection satellites, in the spirit of Eisenhower's Open Skies proposal, constituted a logical next step. "Perhaps a United Nations arms control agency could compile and disseminate the information to all nations. What better contribution could science make to peace!"[21]

Leghorn might very well have been asking, What better contribution could Itek make to U.S. national security, and ultimately to peace? Itek's original business plan, the one that Laurance Rockefeller and his associates agreed to finance just weeks earlier, was for a start-up that would use the Minicard System to build a company at the forefront of information processing. By December, as Leghorn was giving his speech, he already intended to take the company in a completely different direction.

Information processing would be Itek's cover story. The company's real business mission, if Leghorn could win the contract, would be to build the spy cameras for America's first reconnaissance satellite. If the Soviet Union wouldn't join a rational world security system, the United States would take the information it needed to become secure. And Leghorn's company would create the technology central to that effort.

Itek was a long shot to win the spy satellite contract, but Leghorn knew enough about the program to realize that he had a chance. The company, just a few months old, essentially had no products or business. Typical government officials, especially those who value their careers, would never award a major contract to such a company. But Leghorn perceived several factors that gave Itek a shot at the contract. On January 1 Itek would acquire BUPRL, giving it control of the nation's largest institution devoted to reconnaissance, spy cameras, and intelligence systems. This meant that Itek owned the designs for Walter Levison's revolutionary HYAC. And Leghorn understood that many of the operating lessons of the balloon program could be applied to space reconnaissance.[22]

There was a catch. In order to use the HYAC design in outer space, the spy satellite would have to be stable, like a balloon. The problem was that the technology to stabilize a satellite like a balloon didn't exist. So if Leghorn wanted to get Itek in the space reconnaissance business, he had to design and promote a new technology for stabilizing a satellite; gain enough business in the next month to support his scientific base at BUPRL; persuade Laurance Rockefeller to provide additional financing to support the costs of a new business venture that was so highly classified Leghorn couldn't tell him about it; and persuade high-level government officials to gamble their careers on a company that hadn't even existed until a few months ago. Amazingly, Leghorn believed he could do it.

6

INTO THE BLACK

There was no holiday cheer for Henry Kissinger. During the 1957 Christmas season, while most New Yorkers were enjoying the city's wintry beauty, Kissinger was hard at work carrying out Nelson Rockefeller's orders. Kissinger's mission was clear—complete the military report of the Rockefeller Special Studies Project as soon as possible. By New Year's Eve, Kissinger's job was finished, and the report was at long last ready to be released to the press.[1]

The Rockefeller Report, as it quickly became known, made headlines across America. The report was a call to arms. Its grim portrayal of America's military establishment—mismanaged, poorly organized, and improperly equipped—captured the country's imagination. At a time when Laurance Rockefeller's staff was hard at work to help Itek get off the ground, the report demonstrated the close link between his public policy and his business interests.

For Nelson and Laurance Rockefeller, both of whom directed the study and participated in its discussions at various times, the report was a great triumph. Their pictures were splashed across the pages of America's leading newspapers and magazines. The report generated congressional concern and instigated public debate.

Immediately after the report's release Nelson Rockefeller appeared on NBC's *Today Show* with David Garroway. On behalf of Rockefeller, Garroway offered to send free copies to anyone who requested it. The demand for the report, a policy wonk's delight but hardly a popular page-turner, was incredible. More than 400,000 viewers sent in requests. Copies were sent as quickly as they could be printed at a cost entirely underwritten by the Rockefeller family.[2]

The Rockefeller Report was sobering reading. "The world is living through a period of swift and far-reaching upheavals," its authors declared. Unfortunately, the world was changing for the worse, not the better. Empires were collapsing, institutions were breaking down. Certainly, much of the world was "clamoring for a new and more worthy existence," but the communist danger threatened to extinguish any hopes for nations, new or old, to realize their aspirations, or to secure their freedom. The communists would exploit any dissatisfaction "to magnify all tensions," and they would use weapons "capable of obliterating civilization" to achieve their ends.[3]

If the United States was going to lead the free world to victory against the communist threat, its military would have to succeed in facing down the enemy. Unfortunately, the members of the Rockefeller military panel concluded that the readiness of America's defense establishment was suspect. The report's authors saw "the real armaments race . . . in the laboratories" and asserted that America needed a growing pool of scientific talent and an increased commitment to scientific research. Henry Kissinger may have edited and polished the report, but the voice of Teddy Walkowicz could be clearly heard in its concerns and recommendations.

Pure science alone was not a solution. The United States needed to develop the ability to translate new advances "into operational weapons." The report identified two critical parts of the weapons development cycle that had to be drastically improved. The first was the "interval between the drawing board and operational weapon," and the second was the "rapidity with which weapons are manufactured." The report concluded with clinical detachment that "a lag in either category is certain to create a strategic weakness."

The authors bluntly proposed that improving America's scientific-industrial base and providing the Pentagon with better weapons, more quickly developed, would by no means assure the country's survival. The Pentagon itself was gravely in need of reform. "This technological race places an extraordinary premium on the ability to assess developing trends correctly," the project participants flatly stated, "to make and back decisions firmly, and to be able to change plans when necessary." Quite simply, in the view of the authors of the Rockefeller Report, the Pentagon's management track record failed on all counts.[4]

The report offered a way to reform the Pentagon, strengthen America's defenses, and as a result achieve nothing less than the preservation, if not the expansion, of the free world. Goals that big could be reached only by spending big—something Rockefellers intuitively understood. The price tag was a $3 billion a year increase in defense spending and similar increases every year well into the following decade. Spending more money on defense systems was a starting point. Making sure the Pentagon used the money wisely, identifying the right technologies and weapons that would shape the battlefield of the future, was even more important. Massive surgery had to be performed on the management structure of the Defense Department to accomplish that goal.[5]

Meanwhile, under Richard Bissell's leadership at the CIA, the kind of procurement revolution needed at the Pentagon was already well under way. Over the weeks ahead, Bissell continued to make important decisions about CORONA with a minimum of red tape and a maximum emphasis on obtaining results. Bissell's work demonstrated that the ideas promoted in the Rockefeller Report could be achieved in a government agency.

But the public and the press were unaware of Bissell's efforts. Perhaps if Bissell's success had been more widely known, the firestorm that followed would have been less severe. Military and congressional leaders alike attacked the plan. Major newspapers like *The Wall Street Journal* also blasted the report. Yet for all the criticism, the Rockefeller Report remained a huge success. It achieved exactly what the Rockefeller brothers had hoped for when they decided to finance the project. All of America was now talking about the great national security issues of the day. In the aftermath of Sputnik, America's political debate had already increasingly focused on defense issues, but the discussion had yet to lead to any meaningful action. Now the entire country was arguing the pros and cons of a specific reform agenda, and even President Eisenhower was forced to take notice.[6]

James Reston, columnist for *The New York Times,* was deeply impressed by the Rockefeller Report. He called it "one of the most thorough and solemn analyses of the West's security problems produced since the war." Yet the report's greatest significance, he believed, rested not on any one recommendation, but in the process that led to its creation. Reston argued there was a "crisis" in America's public policy establishment. The State Department, the Pentagon, and the National Security Council, handicapped by politics and hamstrung by an obligation to defend prior policies, had lost their objectivity and their ability to contribute in a meaningful fashion to public debate. The Rockefeller Report demonstrated that private citizens were acting "the way responsible citizens of a democracy are expected to act. They are not waiting for Government to lead, but are analyzing and recommending on their own." At a time when American society was "being charged with lacking the vitality necessary to lead the free world," it was especially important that private citizens fill the gap left open by government inaction. Reston concluded that a "free society, when aroused, can call on resources and private initiative unknown in totalitarian states."[7]

Clearly, James Reston believed that one of those resources was the Rockefeller family. In all likelihood, he was right in more ways than he realized. In the first days of January 1958, as Laurance and Nelson Rockefeller basked in the glow of the Rockefeller Special Studies Project, another Rockefeller investment was getting ready to bloom. At the start of the year Itek took over the operations of the Boston University Physical Research Laboratory. Suddenly, Itek's payroll leaped from fewer than a dozen employees to more than one hundred. But Richard Leghorn had little time to savor his victory. Leghorn's dream was both within his grasp and on the verge of collapse. Payroll and general overhead for the lab was running at $80,000 a month, and Itek's phase one financing had raised only $110,000. Although the lab had a valuable backlog of defense contracts, payment from the government was months away. The same cash squeeze that forced Boston University's Case to divest the lab was now beginning to strangle Itek. If Richard Leghorn didn't get money soon to make his payroll and keep his company afloat, he would have to begin firing his staff. He turned, as always, to Laurance Rockefeller for help.

On January 13 Leghorn wrote to Rockefeller and asked for more money. Specifically, it was time to move forward with the phase two financing outlined in their October letter of agreement. Leghorn explained that the acquisition of the lab, plus Itek's own efforts, had created virtually overnight "a very sizeable backlog" of cost plus fixed fee contracts. Leghorn estimated the value of the contracts at $2.6 million. He added "we expect favorable action during the next eight weeks on at least some of our other proposals." Which proposals? Leghorn didn't say. Rather, he couldn't say. If Leghorn named either the project, or the customer, he would endanger the secrecy of one of the most important national security projects in the country.

Leghorn needed at least 25 percent of the phase two money by January 31. He said that Itek's "period of highest risk" was over and that the funds would be used to finance the firm's current projects, and to build for growth. Leghorn admitted that the next few months might not be smooth "as we shake down our organization and customer relationships."[8]

Fortunately for Leghorn, Laurance Rockefeller agreed. Compared with the first round of financing, which raised a modest sum to get the company started, this round of financing was the mother lode. Rockefeller and his associates would invest more than $550,000 in Itek by purchasing both stock and convertible bonds in the company.[9]

The size of the investment wasn't the only difference between the phase one and phase two financings. In the first phase, Laurance Rockefeller had been the only significant investor. This time, Laurance decided to share the risk more broadly. On January 17 he wrote to his brothers Nelson and David. He reminded them that they had declined to participate in Itek's initial financing and that in just a few months the company had made great strides in building its business. "In light of these circumstances," he explained, "you may wish to consider a participation in the further financing, which will be approximately evenly divided" between stock and bonds. He pointed out that this time around the stock was more expensive, priced at $8 a share compared with $2 on the initial offering. The difference, he explained, was "intended to compensate the original investors for the risks undertaken." Rockefeller's letter to his brothers, written in dry business prose, was hardly a marketing piece, yet in its own way it was a highly effective selling document. After all, it didn't take a financial genius to calculate that if Itek's stock, valued initially at

$2 a share, was now worth $8, then the firm's original investors had earned a 300 percent return in less than four months. Even a Rockefeller had to be impressed. If that wasn't enough to convince his brothers to invest, Laurance made it clear they had little time to make a decision. "I intend to take part in this financing and desire to offer participation to three or four outside private investors, but hesitate to allocate any dollar amounts . . . until I know what your wishes are in this matter." In other words, make your decision to invest now, or miss the boat.

Attached to the letter was a brief description of Itek, a summary of its first months in business, and an explanation of the need for the financing. Written by a member of Laurance Rockefeller's staff, William Masson, the memo was brief and forthright—up to a point. Masson's description of Itek, neatly encapsulated in one lumbering, circuitous sentence, has the sound of specificity, but on second reading is extremely vague. Masson wrote: "Itek was organized last September to engage in the research, engineering and manufacture of information handling systems and equipment with particular emphasis on systems and equipment for handling mass graphic material such as documents, maps, charts, and photos."

Masson's description of Itek's commercial focus, while consistent with Leghorn's original plan, omits any reference to Art Tyler's Minicard System, which initially had been at the heart of the company's future. There was no discussion of the company's negotiations with Kodak for a license to the Minicard technology, nor was there any mention that other firms were already using this technology to develop other products. Either Masson overlooked these details or, more likely, they were no longer relevant to Itek's rapidly changing business plan. How this information or change of emphasis had been communicated to Masson is uncertain.

Itek's bold acquisition of Boston University Physical Research Laboratory had turned out to be a good business decision that gave the corporation a strong competitive position in a new and important market, making spy cameras for the world's first reconnaissance satellite. The real reason for the acquisition, and the details of the acquisition itself, are not discussed—even though it was the single most important event in the company's short existence. Masson was not cleared to know about Itek's business aspirations in classified areas, and neither were Rockefeller's prospective investors, but the laboratory itself was not classified and the acquisition certainly could have been discussed.

Thus, although Itek was quickly moving away from its original plan and in a new direction, there is no indication in the letter or the memo that a change had occurred. The documents give the impression that the company was achieving rapid success in executing its plan. The memo notes that Itek was now projected to have $1.6 million in revenue in 1958, yet almost all of it was related to classified projects at BUPRL. Virtually none of Itek's revenue was from selling the kind of information-processing equipment described in the company's original plan.

Masson closed the memo on a high note. "Our impressions of the management group and its capabilities in a business and technical way are most favorable," he stated. The letter and the memo, despite their occasional vagueness, were good enough to persuade Nelson and David Rockefeller to invest.[10]

On January 17, the same day that Laurance wrote to his brothers, Harper Woodward was busy getting commitments from other venture capital investors. Bob Barker, who represented William A. M. Burden, called Woodward that day and said that his firm would provide $100,000 of the proposed phase two Itek financing. Louis Walker, whose family managed its wealth through a corporation called the Long Island Company, also wanted to invest $100,000. The Itek deal was now hot. During Itek's phase one financing, nobody, not even his brothers, wanted to join Rockefeller in the deal. Now, everybody wanted in.

As Richard Leghorn moved forward with Itek's financing, Walter Levison quietly traveled to Washington. He had been on Itek's payroll for less than a month, but he was about to make a major contribution to the corporation's success. Levison had designed the HYAC, the revolutionary spy camera used in the GENETRIX balloon program. Now he had an appointment with Richard Bissell to persuade him to continue to support the balloon program and to buy new HYAC cameras from the fledgling Itek. In the meeting Levison had to sell Bissell on the camera, on the advantages of panoramic photography, and on Itek's capabilities. By the time Levison left Bissell's office, he had an order for forty HYAC cameras.

Itek would manufacture the lenses for the camera, but because it lacked facilities to manufacture the camera body itself, it would have to subcontract production to another company. That other company was Trevor Gardner's Hycon. Gardner may have lost to Itek in his bid to buy the laboratory from Boston University, but at least it now had a production order. In the world of Bissell's intelligence-industrial complex, every company under the classified umbrella had its chance.[11]

By the time the dust settled on January 30, Itek's phase two financing was complete, Richard Leghorn had another $550,000 to keep his company afloat, and Laurance Rockefeller had brought a new group of investors in on the deal to share the risks of investing in a start-up. But now the demand for Itek securities exceeded the supply. Laurance's brothers, not to mention Bill Burden and Louis Walker, received allocations far less than their original requests. Although all these investors later took larger positions in the company, Itek's sudden popularity proved both a blessing and a curse as they tried to get their initial allocations filled.[12]

The happiest investor was Albert Pratt. An alumnus of Harvard College and Harvard Law, former assistant secretary of the navy, and onetime schoolmate of Harper Woodward, he was an early believer in both venture capital and high technology. Pratt — Albie to his friends — was now a partner in Paine, Webber, Jackson and Curtis. Since his recent departure from the Navy Department and his return to normal life as an investment banker, Pratt had focused much of his attention on the high-technology start-up companies that were sprouting along Route 128 in Massachusetts. Pratt was hardly a scientist, but from his career in the navy he had developed a healthy appreciation for the power of technology. If it could transform warfare, it could equally transform civilian life. Pratt realized that companies that developed new products capable of improving people's lives and changing the way they lived and worked could make a fortune in the process.

Itek, which Pratt believed to be at the forefront of a new information revolution, looked like just that kind of company. As a result, Pratt was pleased with his firm's modest allocation of stocks and bonds. Perhaps even more important, the deal offered him the chance to renew his old relationship with Harper Woodward, or Woody, as Pratt called him. If Pratt could strengthen his ties to Woodward, his chances of participating in other Rockefeller deals would improve significantly. On the last day of January, after the Itek deal had closed, Pratt wrote Woodward a brief letter. He mentioned that he would be in New York the following week. "Is there any chance that we could get together for a few minutes?" he politely inquired. "I have nothing specific on my mind except to renew old friendships."[13]

In early February, Richard Leghorn, like Albie Pratt, was also working hard to breathe new life into an old relationship. On February 3 Leghorn wrote to James Killian, special assistant to the president for science and technology, and, incidentally, Leghorn's former fraternity adviser at MIT. Leghorn was preoccupied not with Itek's looming security offering but with the deteriorating state of America's national security. It seemed "imperative" to Leghorn that "we put our reconnaissance satellite projects in the context of 'open skies' and announce immediately that we are building space inspection vehicles whose results will be made available to the U.N." He speculated that "we might even build and operate a space inspection system for the U.N." Unless these actions were taken quickly, Leghorn feared, the Soviets would beat the United States again, create a reconnaissance satellite, offer it to the United Nations, and proclaim that "open skies" had been achieved. The result, he worried, would be another propaganda victory for the Russians, and a weakened environment for real security. A genuine inspection system, Leghorn wrote, required "a proper balance of ground, aerial, and space inspection."[14]

Not long after Killian received his letter from Leghorn, Pratt returned to Boston and wrote Woodward a short, friendly note. "It was good fun seeing you last week." Although it is difficult to imagine an abbreviated business meeting in an office as "fun," Pratt was, after all, an investment banker. "When you come to Boston give me a couple of days notice so that we can have lunch." Woodward, who frequently was at the receiving end of a salesman's pitch, must have anticipated that the punch line was just a word or two away. "I am enclosing a recent statement and description of our sales organization, which may give you a little better concept of our geographical distribution and distributing power." It couldn't have taken Woody long to figure out what old Albie had in mind. For Albert Pratt, partner at Paine Webber, his role in Itek's phase two financing was the start of a beautiful investment banking friendship.[15]

While friends might come and go, brothers are forever. David Rocke-feller probably regretted having missed out on Itek's initial financing, when the stock could be had for only $2 a share. In early February he informed Harper Woodward that "his intention" at the time of the initial financing was "to undertake a participation of 10% of the total involved." Woodward wrote to Laurance on February 6 and pointed out that at "the closing last October the investment taken for your account aggregated $85,000, of which $11,000 would have been allocated to David had we been aware of his intention." But because Woodward and the rest of the staff had been unaware of David's "intention," no such allocation had been made. "In keeping with his desires and if acceptable to you," Wood-ward proposed, "arrangements could be made to transfer $11,000 in ag-gregate amount of the securities which you received in the original fi-nancing to his account." Laurance, in a gesture of filial understanding, approved Woodward's proposal. The securities were transferred at the $2-per-share cost, and younger brother David had a tidy instant profit.[16]

The same day that Woodward wrote to Rockefeller, CIA Director Allen Dulles met with Secretary of Defense Neil McElroy, Undersecretary of Defense Donald Quarles, and the president's top science advisers, Edwin Land (founder of the Polaroid Corporation) and James Killian. Their discussion that day was a watershed both for America's spy satellite pro-gram, and for Itek. The air force satellite program, WS-117L, had become compromised. WS-117L was a technologically ambitious reconnaissance program that encompassed a "family" of satellite systems. The major part of the program, SAMOS, was an attempt to develop a near-real-time recon-naissance capability. Not only had this aspect of the program become mired in technical problems, but security had been broken, and the press was now openly describing it as "Big Brother" and "Spy in the Sky."

Another part of the project, Program IIA, though technically less ambi-tious, had the virtue of being an achievable interim reconnaissance solu-tion. The designers of Program IIA envisioned sending a satellite in space armed with a camera that would take high-resolution photographs of Russia. Then, after the mission was completed, the capsule would return to Earth with the film to be developed upon retrieval. There were a num-ber of technical challenges to be overcome in this aspect of the program, including how to safely return the film to Earth, but the president's scientists believed that they could solve the problems in the immediate future and provide a good interim solution to real-time-reconnaissance. By the time the discussion concluded, all the meeting participants agreed that the film-recovery satellite program would be taken away from the air force and given to the CIA to manage. The decision was based on the CIA's proven ability to keep matters secret, and on confidence in Richard Bissell. It was Bissell, after all, who had been so effective managing a joint CIA–air force team during the U-2 program. He would be put in charge of the new team.[17]

President Eisenhower met the next day with Killian and Land to review the new plan. Land had good news and bad news to report. The film-recovery satellite would not provide the level of resolution or quality of detail that Eisenhower had become accustomed to from U-2 flights. But there was an upside to this type of satellite. Unlike the spy plane, which could be detected by radar, or even SAMOS, whose electronic signals could be intercepted, Eisenhower's advisers believed that the film-recovery satellite was a stealthy spy that could not be tracked. Most important, the film-recovery satellite could be developed quickly. So Ike approved the new plan. Given how rapidly the CIA had been able to develop and deploy the U-2, it was an easy decision for Eisenhower to turn authority for the program to the nation's preeminent spy agency. He took Program IIA away from the air force and gave it to Bissell to manage, and at the same time authorized the air force to continue its effort to develop a real-time capability.

Eisenhower's decision reflected his confidence in Bissell to move the project forward quickly and his belief in "civilian control of national intelligence." There may have been another reason why Ike liked Bissell. Back when Eisenhower had been army chief of staff, he wrote a position paper on the relation between technology and the future of the army. "Scientists and industrialists must be given the greatest possible freedom to carry out their research," he wrote. Keep instructions to a minimum, he explained, and the creativity of America's scientific and industrial community would be unleashed. Eisenhower's position paper was an apt description of Bissell's own philosophy. On the subject of program management, Ike and Bissell were nothing short of soul mates. Within days, Edwin Land met with Bissell at his CIA office to let him know the president had put him in charge of an intelligence project even more revolutionary than the U-2.[18]

Bissell immediately began work on building a project team. Select members of his development projects staff, who had successfully built and managed the U-2, were chosen by Bissell to form the nucleus of the new team. Air force Brig. Gen. Osmond J. Ritland, who had been Bissell's first deputy at the start of the U-2 program and now worked for General Schriever at the Air Force Ballistic Missile Division, was recruited for a second tour of duty as Bissell's deputy. Ritland again was to play a critical role as Bissell's ambassador to the Pentagon, working with the air force to ensure that the proper launch, command, and control infrastructure was in place to support the project. Soon Bissell ordered John Parangosky back to Washington from an overseas assignment at a U-2 base in Turkey. Parangosky, who had worked with top technicians from Lockheed, Eastman Kodak, and Hycon to support the U-2 program in the field, was needed to help manage contractor relations for CORONA. Parangosky's specialty was "obfuscation." His job was to teach American companies to act covertly.[19]

In the middle of February, as Bissell was building his project team, he received an unsolicited proposal from Itek to build the camera for CORONA. Bissell may have been taken aback. His project was a closely guarded national security secret. The contractors had already been chosen, including Fairchild for the camera. Yet a fledgling company, Itek, was essentially proposing that he change his plans, revise the structure of the program, and take the contract away from Fairchild—a long-established company.[20]

But in many ways Bissell also played the role of midwife to the successful birth of Itek. In fall 1957 he gave Itek its first contract when he hired Leghorn as a consultant to SEI. Then he told Leghorn to shift his focus from building ground equipment for SAMOS to looking at opportunities related to a film recovery satellite. In January 1958 he personally gave Walter Levison Itek's first big camera order when he purchased forty HYACs—a piece of business that helped get Itek though its first difficult months. So while Itek's proposal may have been unsolicited, it could hardly have been a surprise.

Before Itek's proposal arrived on Bissell's desk, he was moving forward with essentially the same contractor team that he had inherited from the air force program. Now he had the opportunity to put his personal stamp on the program. Itek's proposal gave him the opportunity to revisit the structure of the program. After all, the entire purpose of it was to get a camera in space to take great photographs of the Soviet Union. Was the Fairchild camera proposal the best design for the job, or was there a better alternative?

Trevor Gardner believed that Bissell should consider Hycon. Gardner had learned that Bissell was now in charge of the spy satellite program and that Itek was suddenly in the running to win the camera contract. Gardner felt that Hycon, which had designed the cameras for the U-2 program and worked closely with the CIA to provide field support services to U-2 bases around the world, should be given a chance. He went to visit Bissell in Washington and brought along Bernie Marcus, a top executive at the company. Meeting in Bissell's office, Gardner and Marcus lobbied hard for their proposal. During the discussion, Gardner excused himself to use the men's room. Bissell told Marcus that he had already made up his mind; the program would not go to Hycon. The U-2 program would continue, and Hycon would retain that business. Bissell assured Marcus that he would let Gardner down easily. Then, before Gardner returned, Bissell gave Marcus a proposal to consider. He asked him to leave Hycon and get a job at Itek. The next time Marcus met with Bissell on business for Hycon, Walter Levison was waiting outside the office. Within weeks, Marcus was working at Itek.[21]

Before Bissell could make a final decision about the contractor team for the program, he had to resolve a big problem. Spies are supposed to work in secrecy. Yet the film-recovery satellite, Project IIA, had been exposed by the press along with the rest of the program. The Soviets might already have been tipped off to the fact that the United States was working on a spy satellite, but they still didn't know the satellite's capabilities, or its launch date. So many details remained unresolved at this early stage that Bissell didn't know those details either — no one did. Bissell would push his project team and the contractors hard, and if he didn't have all the facts yet, he would soon. But he couldn't let the Soviets know any more than they already did. He had to throw them off his track.[22]

On February 28 a campaign began to trick the Soviets. On that day the air force announced the cancelation of Project IIA. Would the deception work? Would the Russians really believe that the project had been canceled, or would they see through the ruse? The first test case was promising. At about the same time that the air force made its announcement, Jack Carter, the Lockheed manager in charge of WS-117L—the same Jack Carter who had nearly left his job to join Leghorn as a founding partner of Itek—held a meeting with the program's contractors. He announced, without warning, that Program IIA was canceled. Present at the meeting were two key advisers to the program, Amrom Katz and Merton Davies of the RAND Corporation. When they heard the news, they "jumped out of their chairs" and "went ballistic." If Katz and Davies could be tricked, so could the Soviets.[23]

Out of the public eye, Program IIA moved forward covertly. One of the few new persons brought into the program at this stage was James Plummer, a Lockheed engineer who had worked on WS-117L. His superiors at Lockheed gave him a new set of orders. He was told to "disappear" from Lockheed and to "set up a totally covert program" to build a film-recovery satellite on a "high-risk . . . short-timetable basis." Plummer was given a few sketches to guide him and immediately set up shop in a hotel room to consider his next steps. Working with a few other Lockheed engineers, Plummer evaluated satellite designs ranging from one shaped like a cigar, to one that looked like a football. The football-shaped satellite was selected. Its mission was to carry a Fairchild camera, still on the drawing board, through space as it took photographs of the Soviet Union. The satellite was shaped like a football because it was supposed to spin like one as it traveled through space. This rotation, it was hoped, would stabilize the satellite as it orbited Earth and prevent it from tumbling out of control and falling out of the proper orbit. As the satellite rotated, according to the designers, the camera would rotate as well. The camera was designed to take pictures only during that part of the satellite's rotation that pointed it toward Earth. As the camera pointed toward space, the film would reload.[24]

As Plummer moved forward, Bissell turned his attention to the capsule's payload—the camera. On March 18 Bissell and his deputy, General Ritland, met in the ornate Old Executive Office Building, next to the White House, with James Killian, Edwin Land, and some of the best brains in science and national security issues. The purpose of the meeting was to take another look at the type of camera payload the CORONA satellite would carry into space and to select a backup design to the original Fairchild proposal. Word had clearly spread within the contracting community that the film recovery system, not the real-time-photography system, was now the government's highest priority. In addition to Itek's unsolicited offer, General Electric, Eastman Kodak, and even Fairchild were submitting new designs. Perhaps in deference to its industrial might, General Electric was first to present its proposal. As Richard Raymond made G.E.'s proposal, the other companies' representatives waited their turns in separate meeting rooms. Fairchild was next and the company presented a refined version of the camera system that had already been selected for the program. Kodak, which held the contract for the WS-117L real-time-photography system that had just been put on the back burner due to technical difficulties, made the next presentation.[25]

It must have struck Bissell, and the other experts assembled that day, that General Electric, Fairchild, and Kodak, the blue-chip names of American industry, had lost their spark — at least as far as camera systems were concerned. The three corporations offered similar camera designs: a panoramic camera system wedded to a spin-stabilized satellite — Plummer's spinning football. Certainly, the three proposals appeared to constitute a validation of Fairchild's initial concept, but did that mean that the best approach had been found?[26]

The last presentation made that day was by Itek's Duncan MacDonald and Jack Herther. MacDonald and Herther offered a camera based on the successful HYAC design that the Boston University team had developed for the air force balloon reconnaissance programs. In technical terms, it was a "reciprocating 70-degree field panoramic camera with an f/5 Tessar-type 24-inch focal length lens." What made this camera system distinctive, even revolutionary, was that it required "a satellite horizontally stabilized on all three axes" — not spin-stabilized like a football. MacDonald explained the camera design and turned the presentation over to Herther to explain the need for three-axis stabilization.

Herther pointed out that by stabilizing the satellite using small jets, the design ensured that the capsule would act in space the way a balloon acts in air. Instead of spinning around the earth like a football, the spin-stabilization concept incorporated in the other camera designs, the Itek camera would orbit the earth on a stable platform — its camera always pointed at Earth. To achieve this capability, Herther explained, the satellite required horizon sensors to determine the capsule's orientation, and gas jets to adjust its position. The design would allow the satellite to control the effects of "pitch, roll, and yaw." A stable satellite system reduced the risk of image blurs caused by a spinning satellite. Itek's camera system, Herther claimed, would produce better, clearer pictures, with a resolution on the earth's surface of twenty feet, far superior to the sixty-foot resolution of the Fairchild design. At the end of the day, Bissell and his advisers decided that Itek would supply a backup camera for the program. If anything went wrong at Fairchild, Bissell would have an ambitious alternate system waiting in the wings.[27]

On March 24 the CIA's Richard Bissell arrived at the Flamingo Motel, a garishly decorated roadside inn, to meet with the key contractors who would develop the CORONA spy satellite. Located in San Mateo, California, the motel was cheap and tacky — the perfect place to disguise a high-level spy meeting. For Bissell, raised to enjoy the finer things in life, the Flamingo was a far cry from his usual accommodations.

At the meeting it was announced that Lockheed's James W. Plummer would be responsible for systems integration for the project. Bissell also told the other contractors that Itek would supply a backup camera for the program. With Bissell's announcement, Itek was anointed. The company was now an official member of the nation's inner circle of defense contractors, and it was working on the most important intelligence project in the Western world.[28]

Two days later, the contractors assembled again, but this time at the Villa Hotel. The meeting was held in the hotel's Pacifica "A" Conference Room. Changing locations frequently for security purposes was standard operating procedure in the intelligence world, but security at the Villa Hotel was "far from desirable." Everyone at the meeting was cautioned to speak only in a low voice and to remain constantly on alert. Lockheed's James Plummer discussed the schedule and planning "of the covert phase of the program," and he essentially directed the meeting, as Bissell either approved or overruled proposals. During the meeting, the subject of contracts came up. Bissell explained that his contracting officer, George

Kucera, would visit with each of the companies individually over the next week to discuss arrangements. But Bissell had another announcement to make — he was broke. The program had moved forward so rapidly in the past several weeks, including the change in program responsibility from the air force to CIA, that somehow the issue of funding had been overlooked. Bissell told the contractors that he would obtain the needed financing as soon as possible, but that in order to be effective he needed hard cost estimates from each contractor. The contractors readily agreed to give him the cost estimates by the following week. Bissell warned that knowledge of the program had to be restricted to "as few people as possible." At the end of the meeting a copy of the "CORONA roster" was given to Bissell.[29]

On March 31, as Bissell was beginning to collect his cost estimates, Laurance Rockefeller was relaxing in the sun at the Caribe Hilton Hotel in San Juan, Puerto Rico. While vacationing, he received a letter from Teddy Walkowicz. It was an update on Itek. "One of your newest ventures, Itek Corporation, is just about six months old," Walkowicz noted with paternal pride, "and you will be interested in the enclosed summary of its rather fast-moving activities." Itek was indeed precocious. Walkowicz reminded Rockefeller that in late 1957 the company had begun business with four employees and no revenues. "It now appears that the company's first year will result in nominal earnings on sales of $1.8 million." The company would begin its second fiscal year in late 1958 with "about 300 people on the payroll and a backlog of well over $3 million." Amazingly, Itek had already broken into the black, turning a small profit during the first two weeks of March.

Walkowicz had even more astounding news to report — Itek was on the verge of making its first acquisition. On March 28 Itek had signed a premerger agreement with the Vectron Corporation. Vectron was a production company "whose capabilities nicely complement[ed] the research and development activities of Itek." Vectron had a 43,000-square-foot factory, located near Itek headquarters. Now when the guys from the lab came up with a great idea, there would be a manufacturing facility to convert concepts into products.

There was only one problem with Vectron. It was losing a fortune. The same defense cutbacks that were hurting the rest of the industry in

1957 had hit Vectron especially hard. To make matters worse, the company was struggling under the weight of several poorly considered fixed-price development contracts. A fixed-price contract is a great inflation fighter for the government: a company guarantees that it will deliver its product, on time, at a specific price. If the cost of the raw materials, labor, or any other factor of production increases during the development process, the company still has to deliver the goods—no matter how much money it loses in the process. As a result, Vectron was on the verge of going out of business.

So why buy Vectron? Certainly, Itek had other options if it wanted to develop a manufacturing capability. In his letter to Rockefeller, Walkowicz attached a one-page review of Itek's operations. Half the page was devoted to Vectron. Walkowicz gave only one reason for the merger—the synergies between Itek's brains and Vectron's manufacturing brawn. In the most general terms this was sound reasoning, but if this was the only purpose behind the merger, then buying a money-losing company, with few apparent short-term prospects of a turnaround, was not necessarily the best decision. Was there another reason, an agenda that Walkowicz could not share with the company's largest shareholder?

Even though Itek had just been selected to produce the backup camera for Project CORONA, Leghorn and Walkowicz probably had bigger ideas. Itek needed Vectron because Leghorn and Walkowicz wanted to push Fairchild out of the CORONA program and take its place as the CIA's chief manufacturer of satellite spy cameras. In order to get rid of Fairchild quickly, Itek needed a manufacturing plant as soon as possible. Buying Vectron was the fastest way to accomplish that goal. With a little bit of luck and negotiating skill, the executives at Itek might be able to convince the air force to eliminate Itek's financial liability for the fixed-cost contracts. If they could accomplish that goal—and with their air force connections it seemed possible—the deal could be closed and the merger completed by May 1. The consolidated company would have combined sales of about $4.8 million and a modest projected operating profit of $200,000 a year. Itek was barely six months old, young for a company on the acquisition trail. But the numbers were impressive and the team at the Rockefeller office was pleased.[30]

7

PUGWASH

The same day that Walkowicz wrote to Laurance Rockefeller at the Caribe Hilton, Richard Leghorn arrived in Canada as U.S. delegate to the Second Pugwash Conference of Nuclear Scientists. Pugwash was a peace movement with a highbrow pedigree. Bertrand Russell, an early advocate of conference meetings between Western and Soviet scientists to reduce world tensions, was the inspiration for the cause. For nearly a decade after the atomic explosions at Hiroshima and Nagasaki, he had warned the world about the cataclysmic consequences of nuclear war.

By 1955 Russell had drafted a manifesto that was nothing less than a call to arms to the world's great scientists. Nobel Prize winners like Max Born and Linus Pauling were signatories. When Albert Einstein signed the manifesto, just two days before his death, its influence grew, and it quickly became known as the Russell-Einstein Manifesto. The language of the manifesto became a clarion call to the world's citizens to wake up and acknowledge the possibility of their destruction. "People scarcely realize that the danger is to themselves and their children and their grandchildren. They can scarcely bring themselves to grasp that they, individually, and those whom they love are in imminent danger of perishing agonizingly." East and West, capitalists and communists, had to put aside their differences. "We appeal, as human beings, to human beings: remember your humanity and forget the rest. If you can do so, the way lies open to a new Paradise; if you cannot, there lies before you the risk of universal death."

The international press praised the Russell-Einstein Manifesto. Its idealistic call for an international meeting of scientists in the pursuit of peace captured the imaginations of many, including Richard Leghorn, who made a similar appeal in his 1957 speech to the Franklin Institute. The first Pugwash conference, which took place in July 1957 in a small fishing village in Nova Scotia, was designed to break down barriers between the Soviets and their Western counterparts. When the delegates weren't in meetings together, they were eating together, or sleeping in shared facilities. There was no opportunity for escape, and that was exactly the point. Sooner or later, the delegates would be forced to see each other as individuals, and that, at the very least, would be the beginning of a common understanding.[1]

The first conference ended after a few short days, but it set precedents for the future. The scientists discussed important issues of concern to all the world's citizens — the hazards of nuclear weapons, and ways to control them. But the value of the conference was not only the issues discussed or the statement of purpose released at its end. The significance of Pugwash, in an age when the world was edging ever closer to the abyss of nuclear annihilation, was that it took place at all.

When Richard Leghorn arrived in Lac Beauport for the second Pugwash conference, he was one of twenty-two scientists who had been invited from around the world to participate. Leghorn was now widely recognized as a leading arms control expert. If Pugwash was going to lead to practical results, it needed participants who understood the realities of the negotiating table. Leghorn, as a close adviser to Eisenhower's own recent arms control counselor, Harold Stassen, knew both the possibilities and limitations of the current administration's thinking.[2]

At a time when his young company was struggling to get off the ground, Leghorn's decision to attend the conference seems unusual at first. But there was a correlation between Leghorn's business goals and his personal beliefs. And Pugwash, though a peace conference, was more than an opportunity for him to promote his own views on foreign policy. Over the next several days, as Leghorn pushed his policy agenda, he simultaneously promoted his business interests and cultivated valuable connections.

The conference began like most — an opening speech, announcements about meeting arrangements. But breaking news from the Soviet Union must have been on everyone's mind. Nikita Khrushchev stunned the world that day by declaring that the Soviet Union was unilaterally ceasing all nuclear weapons testing. President Eisenhower, considering Khrushchev's announcement to be little more than a propaganda ploy, was furious. Khrushchev's proposal set the tone for the rest of the conference, and the delegates from the Soviet Union worked to use it to their advantage.[3] Richard Leghorn, periodic arms control adviser to the Eisenhower administration, worked equally hard over the next few days to bring reason to the discussion of nuclear weapons.[4]

On April 2 the delegates heard a paper presented by Jerome Wiesner of the United States. Wiesner, who later served as President Kennedy's science adviser, argued that the best way to reduce nuclear tensions was to forget politics and focus on the technical details. He admitted that this was a "brash" approach, but nevertheless he felt that it was the most sensible way to proceed. "Every proposal by either side is scanned for the hidden purpose. . . . There has been a reluctance to accept the fact that such proposals are put forward with good intentions." For Wiesner the historical conclusion was inescapable. "The problem," he explained, "is to create an environment . . . in which experiments in reducing the tensions, normalizing relations, and directing our energies and resources for useful peaceful purposes can be carried forward."

Progress could occur, Wiesner declared, only when both the Soviet Union and the United States possessed the technical means to verify compliance with a disarmament treaty. Pugwash, he proposed, could best serve the world by pointing the way to these technical solutions. "If one starts with the premise that it is in fact in the interest of the parties involved in the Cold War to find relief from the burdens and threats which its continuation assures," he said, "then it is appropriate to explore at this meeting means of building the security system which all the people of the world deserve."

Wiesner knew that his proposal was ambitious. He also realized that he risked being criticized as naïve for suggesting that it was possible. Yet he was convinced that a technical solution, properly integrated into a well-considered strategic approach, could lead to a genuine disarmament breakthrough. To accomplish this, Wiesner suggested that the Pugwash delegates begin with a reexamination of the facts that could be applied "to the solution" and then develop a "bold new attack on the problem."

For Wiesner, the key facts at the root of the problem were fear and mistrust. He asked his fellow scientists to consider all the fears that were the cause for mistrust. Once the source of fear had been catalogued in a rational manner, a technical system could be considered that would directly address each level of insecurity. But even a scientific approach had its limitations. "In the problem with which we are grappling, the dissipation of mistrust, imagined fears may be more difficult to deal with than fears based on real threats." For scientists used to dealing with the physical principles of the real world, the challenge of examining imaginary fears was substantial. "Missiles and bombs which do not exist outperform the real ones and exist in greater numbers." These fears and imaginary threats could not be realistically evaluated, yet Wiesner remained confident that a rational approach would yield genuine success.[5]

The next day, April 3, was Leghorn's day. It was time to discuss Leghorn's proposal to establish a U.N. Arms Information and Research Agency. According to Leghorn, this agency would "openly collect, process, and distribute data on world armaments." But collecting and distributing data was a technical means to achieve a lofty goal—world peace. Leghorn, like Jerome Wiesner, believed that the arms race was built on fear and misunderstanding. "Truth alone," he believed, "has the power to break the cycle and bring sanity out of the present madness of the arms race." Leghorn proposed a variety of measures that a new U.N. agency could immediately take to gather information on the state of the U.S. and Soviet armed forces. Certainly ground inspectors, as well as aerial inspections from high-flying reconnaissance airplanes, should be at the agency's disposal. But its most promising tool, which was still on the drawing board, was a space satellite armed with a camera. Leghorn explained in his paper that either "the U.S. or Russia could operate fairly soon an inspection satellite on behalf of the U.N., turning the results over to the proposed Agency. Or the Agency could develop its own capability, with cooperative help from both countries." Leghorn's proposal was technically sound and potentially lucrative for Itek. After all, if the United Nations was permitted to operate its own satellite, a new client for Itek's products and services would be created.

But was Leghorn's proposal workable? In spring 1958 it seemed unlikely that the Soviet Union or the United States would just hand over satellite technology to the United Nations. Yet Leghorn predicted not only that the chief antagonists in the Cold War would take these steps but that as a result the "loyalty of the world's people" would shift toward the United Nations. If his proposed U.N. agency was created and arms control agreements were violated by government officials, Leghorn said, the world's citizens, because of their new loyalty, would report these violations to the agency. Perhaps citizens living in a free United States might be able to report on their government, but citizens living in the Soviet Union, even brave ones, stood little chance of betraying their government's violations and staying alive. Yet Richard Leghorn, his vision gazing far into a distant and better future, failed to grasp, or accept, just how brutally ugly the world around him really was. He concluded that his proposed agency would "become a symbol and focus of an enforceable world peace."[6] Leghorn must have been disappointed by the discussion that followed. His ideas were greeted by skepticism and indifference.[7]

Over the next few days the meetings continued much as they had begun. Papers were presented — including one by Leghorn on nuclear testing and the danger of accidental war. Polite discussions were regularly punctuated by heated exchanges, and some of the best minds in the world tried to find a way to save the human race.

April 8 was Leghorn's last day at the conference, and he presented his final paper on the design of a world security system. Leghorn's presentation was wistful. He readily accepted that conflict was an ever-present part of human existence, and he conceded that disarmament was an ephemeral goal. "And when one says, 'Let us disarm,' what does he mean?" Leghorn asked. "To rid the world of nuclear weapons? Rocket missiles? Aircraft, tanks, and submarines? Pistols and machine guns? Bows and arrows? Sticks and stones?" Leghorn was struggling for an answer, attempting to reconcile the world as it was with the world as he wanted it to be. "And yet man desperately needs protection from organized violence by his fellow men." Leghorn was determined to find a solution, an instrument that would protect mankind from the worst attributes of human nature.

Leghorn detested nuclear weapons, yet he also saw them as tools to achieve his dream of an effective world security system. As a starting point, this system had to deter both small and large aggressions and deal with the "valid security fears of all nations." But it also had to minimize the dangers from "accidental, fanatical, or catalytic" wars. Most important, for mankind's sake, it had to "liberate a substantial percent of the vast economic and technological resources of the world now enslaved by the arms race."

In Leghorn's world security system the atomic bomb was the guarantor of peace. The entire system hinged on the willingness of the United States and the Soviet Union to cooperate and jointly use the threat of their nuclear weapons to stop war. Leghorn believed the nations would work together because their desire for peace could overcome their fear of each other. In a time when many eagerly joined the clamor for conflict, Leghorn worked for a solution. In the midst of the most dangerous moments in mankind's history, he still invoked the best of man.[8]

Leghorn left the conference the next day. Although his idea for a new world security system had no lasting impact, the conference itself marked an important turning point in East-West relations. Wiesner's proposal—that peace could be better achieved by focusing on the technical details of disarmament rather than on politics—was embraced by Washington and Moscow as a fresh approach to the arms race. Within months Eisenhower and Khrushchev agreed to send delegates to an international conference to discuss this topic. Wiesner would serve as a U.S. delegate to the conference, and Leghorn would work as an adviser to the State Department's delegation. Over the next twenty-four months Leghorn's relationship with Wiesner expanded from a friendship into a business relationship as well. But the deal that transformed their relationship was a disaster for Itek.

8

BISSELL FOR VICE PRESIDENT

On April 9 Richard Leghorn was back in the office after "ten days of 'negotiations' with the Russians in Quebec." Over the next few weeks Leghorn had a lot of work to get accomplished. Once the Vectron merger was out of the way, he was going to have to focus on building a new board of directors. Now that Laurance Rockefeller was no longer the only major investor, the other major shareholders would require board representation. Leghorn proposed that Elisha Walker Jr. represent the Long Island Company on the board, that James T. Hill sit in for William A. M. Burden and Company, Albert Pratt for Paine, Webber, and Harold Case for Boston University, which had received stock in Itek as part of the agreement regarding the lab.[1]

Meanwhile, the same scientists and technicians who had published the *700 News* at the lab had regrouped under a new masthead — the *Itek Intelligence*. The newspaper's name demonstrated that the same wry humor that characterized the lab's newsletter would carry over into the new company. The editorial staff also made it clear that although the outside world may have thought that Itek had acquired the lab, from their perspective it was really the other way around. "The 700 Club wishes to extend a hearty welcome to our new employees. We want you to know that all Itek corporation personnel automatically become members of the 700 Club." The newsletter closed with the long-awaited announcement that the annual bowling banquet would still take place and that all were expected to attend — "Don't be Spare. Be there!"[2]

On the same day that Richard Leghorn returned to Itek, the CIA's Richard Bissell was hard at work completing the CORONA project proposal for Eisenhower's approval. Bissell's proposal seemed a judicious solution to a vexing problem. By this point he had decided that Itek's camera design promised better resolution and greater potential for improvement than Fairchild's proposal. Yet Fairchild, a long-established company with strong ties to the defense community, had been involved with the spy satellite program from the start. It would be politically difficult to abruptly push Fairchild out of the program, and besides, Fairchild had a proven track record. Itek was just a start-up. So Bissell's proposal recommended the purchase of both camera systems. Fairchild's system would be developed first, and Itek's design could function as both a backup and potential follow-on system. Fairchild would be kept happy, and Bissell would keep his options open a little longer. If Itek's design lived up to its promise, Bissell could simply thank Fairchild for its work but send Itek's camera into space.[3]

Forty-eight hours later Bissell changed his mind. The reasons for his change of heart are unclear. It may be that presidential adviser Edwin Land, founder of the Polaroid Corporation, urged him to reconsider. Land's views on science carried great weight with President Eisenhower, and the strength of his argument and his influence would not have been lost on Bissell. At the same time, Bissell had a searching, powerful mind; he may simply have recognized that funding two camera systems had the potential to slow down the program's overall development, or at the very least would be an inefficient use of limited program resources. Fairchild's camera required a spin-stabilized capsule. Itek's camera needed a capsule with three-axis stabilization. Funding both cameras would inevitably mean funding two types of capsules to support them. If rapid progress was going to be made, it was best to make a clean decision at the start and pour all of the resources possible into the best design choice.

Bissell agonized over the decision, but he finally decided to risk everything on Itek's design and the untested concept of three-axis stabilization. In his final draft, which requested $7 million for "covert procurement" of satellite capsules, reconnaissance equipment, and recoverable film cassettes, Bissell justified his decision on the basis of cost effectiveness, better resolution, and the high potential of long-term program improvements.

His proposal also requested funds for the procurement of twelve rockets to launch the satellite into space — essentially a combination of a Thor booster, manufactured by Douglas, and a Lockheed-built second-stage vehicle called Agena. On April 16 President Eisenhower approved Bissell's proposal. The decision and the discussion around it remain shrouded in secrecy. The only documentation of Ike's approval that exists is a brief note handwritten on the back of an envelope by Gen. C. P. Cabell, the CIA's deputy director.[4]

Once Eisenhower gave his approval, Bissell developed a "formal plan" for the program. Because the concept of a film-recovery satellite was viewed as nothing more than an interim solution, a technical device to fill the gap between limited U-2 missions and the deployment of a satellite like SAMOS with real-time capabilities, time was of the essence. The final plan was simple. Project CORONA's mission was to develop a reconnaissance satellite that after its mission would eject a recoverable capsule containing exposed film. This capsule, manufactured by General Electric, would safely bring the film, manufactured by Eastman Kodak, and the camera, designed by Itek, back to Earth. If Itek's camera design, combined with the stability provided by a three-axis design, could be successfully developed and integrated, the photographs could achieve a ground resolution of twenty feet. This level of clarity would allow photointerpreters at the CIA to identify specific buildings, as well as targets such as missile sites and bombers. Despite the fact that CORONA would be a major breakthrough, only twelve launchings were envisioned. From the time of the first anticipated launch in June 1959 to the last one in the middle of 1960, little more than a year would pass. By that time, Bissell hoped, the next generation of spy satellites would be developed and CORONA could be retired.[5]

Bissell had broad backing at the highest levels of government to take whatever actions were needed to make CORONA a success. Yet at the same time he was highly dependent on a confederation of private-sector contractors and government agencies to achieve his mission. In addition to his own small staff at the CIA, Bissell needed the support of Advanced Research Projects Agency (ARPA), a newly created Defense Department agency. ARPA would provide Bissell with scientific resources and technical support so that oversight over the satellite's development could be more effectively performed. Bissell and his staff would "supervise technical development and covert procurement of the reconnaissance equipment," and would provide cover and security for the program, but the satellite could not get into space without a rocket. Bissell turned to Gen. Bernard Schriever, head of the Air Force Ballistic Missile Division, for procurement of launch vehicles, and for managing overall launching, tracking, and capsule recovery capabilities. Schriever, an old buddy of Richard Leghorn, Teddy Walkowicz, and Jack Carter, would provide an important connection between Itek executives and the inner working of the program.[6]

Now Bissell had a thorny problem to resolve. What should he do about Fairchild? Bissell was committed to maintaining a cloak of secrecy around the program. Yet if Fairchild was unceremoniously ejected from the program, hurt feelings (not to mention lost profits) might easily lead to a security leak. Bissell's solution was Solomonic. In order to "soften the financial blow to Fairchild," Itek was put in charge of the camera's design and development, but Fairchild was made responsible for manufacturing the camera "under subcontract to Itek." Everyone would make money, and everyone would be happy, or so Bissell thought.

CORONA moved forward, and on April 25 Bissell issued a work statement to Lockheed that finalized the program's structure and contractor relationships. Lockheed, as prime contractor, was officially in charge of the program. Itek and General Electric, which was in charge of manufacturing the space capsule, were two of the key program subcontractors, with Fairchild working as a subcontractor to Itek. Within days the contractors began work on preliminary systems designs, and on May 14 the designs were submitted for a first review. There was little time to spare. Initially, Bissell wanted all equipment "assembled, tested, and the first vehicle launched" in little more than three months. This meant that all the individual systems components had to be manufactured by July 1, 1958. Bissell quickly recognized that this schedule was untenable, but he still insisted that the first launch occur no later than mid-1959, and in order for this to occur all systems designs had to be "frozen" by July 26. For Bissell, this was a significant concession; for the development of a system that stretched existing capabilities beyond state of the art, it was little more than a modest extension of what likely seemed to many as an unattainable deadline.[7]

On May 19 Itek's board of directors met in the Rockefeller family offices at 30 Rockefeller Plaza. It was the first board meeting since the Vectron acquisition, and the mood was upbeat and expansive. Leghorn declared that Itek, after barely six months in business, had already broken into "the very top echelon" of the military business. Surely, the company still faced many challenges — not the least of which was anemic profitability. For the fiscal year ended September 30, the combined operations of Itek and Vectron were now projected to show a $150,000 profit. That was good news for a start-up company but still a meager profit margin. Part of the problem was that the firm's business was still slanted heavily to research and development projects. Unless those projects could quickly be converted to production contracts, Itek would remain saddled with the carrying costs of Vectron's production facilities, without the business to support it. The solution was obvious. Leghorn explained that management would now focus its resources on "internal organization and building up production."

Itek's management team had its work cut out for it, and Leghorn recognized the need for outside help. He proposed that the company's expanded board of directors should be a working board. Each company director was expected to closely monitor the company's affairs and assist in the business "in every possible way." As Leghorn demonstrated moments later, that was easier said than done.

When the time arrived to discuss new business, Leghorn asked the board to approve a new contract. At a previous meeting, the board had approved a resolution that prevented the company from accepting fixed-price contracts — the kind that nearly ruined Vectron. Now Leghorn was in the uncomfortable position of asking the board to approve a fixed-price contract in "the Special Intelligence Field" that, "although fixed price, would be subject to periodic adjustment based on cost." The contract was "in the field which he could not discuss, but he did say that it would be in connection with Lockheed Aircraft and involved funds which did not come from the Department of Defense." Leghorn concluded by stating that it was "very important" for Itek "to take this contract because of its extremely high priority." That was all the information Leghorn gave the board. It had to approve the contract without knowing the name of the customer, or what Itek was selling the mysterious buyer.

Leghorn's description of the contract placed the Itek directors in a very difficult situation. None of the directors, except for Teddy Walkowicz, was cleared to know what Leghorn was talking about. We now know that he was referring to Itek's contract for the CORONA spy satellite, the unknown customer was the CIA, and the unmentioned product was a spy camera powerful enough to take pictures of the Soviet Union from outer space. But Leghorn couldn't tell the directors any of this, and neither could Walkowicz. And the directors, knowing that the matter was related to an important national security project, were probably too respectful to ask.

We don't know how much time elapsed after Leghorn finished his presentation and the board was asked to vote. However long the moment, it must have been an awkward one for any corporate director who took his responsibilities seriously. Charged with the duty to exercise great care and diligence in the management of company assets, the directors couldn't possibly discharge that responsibility properly with the information at their disposal. They would have to either vote the contract down or take a leap of faith. When the vote was called, the directors approved the contract and crossed the Rubicon. From that point on, it would be easier and easier to vote for unknown projects for mystery customers. As long as the business was in the national interest, and revenues kept growing, and the stock price kept rising, approving mystery contracts probably seemed patriotic—and good business.

There was another unusual moment during the meeting. Leghorn announced that the company had just lost a $2 million manufacturing order to Fairchild. This represented Fairchild's contract to manufacture Itek's camera design. Although "Itek was the prime contractor for the product," the company had lost the business, Leghorn explained, "due to Vectron's past history." As a result, Itek's management was "fully aware that they must establish, at the earliest possible time, a reputation for reliability, quality, and meeting time schedules." This was a golden opportunity for Itek's new investors, present at their first board meeting, to question the logic behind the Vectron acquisition. After all, they had just learned two important facts about Vectron during the meeting: Vectron's costly production facility was underutilized, and thanks to its reputation, Itek had lost a big contract. Had Itek's management failed to learn about Vectron's reputation before the acquisition?

The records that exist from the May 19 board meeting reveal that the opportunity to question the reasoning behind the Vectron acquisition passed without discussion. Had one occurred, it would have revealed that Vectron's troubled reputation had been known before the acquisition, but management had overlooked it in a rush to obtain a manufacturing capability. Leghorn and his management team hadn't just wanted the contract to design the CORONA spy camera and build the lenses, using the expertise of the Boston University crew, they had wanted to win the manufacturing contract as well. They had wanted to push Fairchild out of the picture, and to accomplish that end they bought Vectron. The gambit failed, Fairchild had the manufacturing contract, and Itek was stuck with Vectron. If the full board were to learn the true reasons behind the acquisition, the members would appreciate that a major miscalculation had occurred. But the decisions were cloaked behind the veil of national security, and the entire board would never know the complete set of facts.[8]

By the beginning of June, the Vectron acquisition had closed, and Itek completed work on its first major contract, a special spy camera for the air force. Duncan MacDonald, vice president of Itek and one of the company's founders, must have been satisfied with the company's rapid progress, but his aspirations for Itek went beyond the bottom line. He explained his vision for the company in an issue of the *Itek Intelligence*. "Itek must assume a position of leadership," he declared, "in recognition of industry's social responsibilities; these include responsibilities to staff, to [the] local community, to education, to the nation, and to the international community." MacDonald had high hopes for what Itek could achieve, but more than anyone else, he appreciated the capacity for Itek's products to change the world. If Itek could maintain "leadership in both social responsibilities and technological development," he said, then the company could contribute both to arms control and to building a business. MacDonald's message was clear: Itek's purpose was more than just business, it was "the full breadth of the problems of mankind."[9]

Just as Leghorn was the entrepreneurial visionary who made Itek possible, and MacDonald was the scientific prophet whose technical innovations promoted peace, Jesse Cousins was the financial manager who liberated talent. Cousins, treasurer of Itek and one of its founders, had a long and varied business career before Rockefeller's staff recruited him for the company's top financial position. Cousins brought to Itek a "wealth of experience in administration and finance," as well as practical knowledge of "research-based" businesses. He also gave Itek a credible face to present to the financial community. When Dun and Bradstreet issued its first Itek report on July 3, Cousins's previous experience as vice president and treasurer of both the Chase Aircraft Company and the Strouckoff Corporation figured prominently in the report. In his role at those companies Cousins had helped to finance and develop the "first American built jet transport" and "the only medium transport in quantity production" in the United States at the time.

Yet Cousins was a different breed from the typical financial officer. In many ways his habits and appetite seemed consistent with the image of the well-heeled businessman of his era. At first glance, his elegant attire and demeanor reminded many of his colleagues of *Esquire* magazine's mascot—a tuxedoed cartoon character named Esqy. Cousins relished a good steak, a fine cigar, and the arts. But in a time when corporate position was often linked to social status, Cousins earned his position on the corporate ladder rung by rung. He grew up poor in the farm country of eastern Long Island. He went to Cornell University on a four-year scholarship but dropped out after just one year to return home and help support the family, which, he decided, "needed income, not scholars." Along the way he learned the value of hard work, grew to love the arts, married an actress, and gained an important appreciation for the relation between freedom and creativity. Only when Cousins wore his beret to work was there a hint to those around him that the well-mannered businessman was something quite different. In his own way—perhaps not understood by the Rockefeller office when he was hired—Cousins was just as much a visionary as Leghorn and MacDonald.

Cousins believed that in a research and development firm like Itek, the best management was the least management. It was a philosophy that he expressed simply and directly: "In an era of breathtaking technological progress, business forms will change to match the dynamics of the times. Organizations that fail to grasp this dominant factor for growth and survival will inevitably fall behind in the race for leadership." For Cousins the form of organization that best suited Itek must promote "an environment of freedom and creative thinking that is not shackled by the rigid hand of orthodox business standards." Cousins would do his best to create this environment, and in some ways, his efforts would prove his undoing.[10]

On June 10 Richard Bissell sent a CIA officer to Itek to find out what was happening. The agent, whose name remains classified to this day, learned that the film-transport system — the mechanical part of the camera that moved the film from the supply spool, through the camera lens for exposure, and into the take-up spool — was "a major problem." The U.S. government was spending a considerable fortune to launch an Itek camera into space. No matter how successful the launch, or the capsule recovery, the entire mission would be a loss if any part of the camera system failed while in orbit. Basic to the successful operation of any camera is the ability to move film forward after a picture has been taken so that fresh film can be exposed for the next shot. If the film jams, the camera — no matter how sophisticated it is — just doesn't work. By early June, Itek's space-age spy camera had a problem with film jams. On Earth a film jam could easily be fixed, but once the satellite was in orbit, a jam would ruin an entire mission.

Ordinarily, building a film-transport system might not seem a major technical challenge, but Itek faced design hurdles that went beyond the ordinary. Not only did the film-transport system have to operate in the vacuum of space, but the entire camera had to be squeezed into the irregular shape of a space capsule. And every object in the capsule had to be as light as possible if the satellite was going to reach and maintain orbit for the entire length of a mission.

The design and engineering of the film transport system fell to Itek's Frank Madden. His design, loosely based on the conveyer belt layout of an early-nineteenth-century water-powered textile mill, used three rollers between the supply and take-up spools. To move the film effectively through the system, tension on the film must be even and "well controlled," but not so strong that the rollers caused pressure streaks on the film. Pressure streaks would not only damage the film but degrade the image on the final photograph, causing a loss of intelligence. While Bissell's ambassador was visiting Itek, word arrived from Fairchild that pressure streaks and mistracking had occurred in the test model film transport system. To compound difficulties, various parts of the film transport system were plagued by "film sag" and alignment problems. All these problems would be aggravated by the initial shocks of takeoff.

Yet Bissell's representative to Itek concluded that the company's camera design remained "the best available" for the program. In meetings with Walter Levison, he received a briefing on Itek's design concept and discussed the assignment of Bernard Marcus as Itek's first CORONA Project Officer. Marcus, who had been recruited to Itek from Hycon, the manufacturer of the U-2 program's spy cameras, was given the assignment because he could be "easily cleared" by CIA security, and because "Mr. Bissell highly recommended him." Finally Levison said that he needed help in obtaining enough special film for testing. Going through ordinary commercial channels in order to protect the program's cover, Levison was having trouble obtaining the quantity and type of film he needed. Evidently the film was still considered experimental, and Kodak was "reluctant" to supply the film because "its performance [was] not known." Within days, the CIA had taken care of Itek's supply problem.[11]

While the CIA worked with Itek to resolve technical problems in the camera design, Jesse Cousins was hard at work preparing for another Itek stock offering. Itek needed more capital to support the growth of the company. Leghorn and his management team wanted at least a quarter of a million dollars in capital to build a new test facility at its Waltham, Mass., plant, and to buy property in Lexington to build a factory.[12]

On at least two occasions that summer, Jesse Cousins corresponded with William Mason in Laurance Rockefeller's office. Mason was gathering information for the Rockefeller office as part of the preparations for Itek's stock offering. Cousins outlined the transformation that had occurred that year in Itek's business plan. The company was "organized to exploit the field of information and data handling." With the acquisition of the Boston University Physical Research Laboratory, Itek had entered new markets. These included markets for "the development of both airborne and ground handling equipment for aerial photography" and for "systems studies in the problem of aerial reconnaissance." Cousins made it clear that these reconnaissance markets were primarily military and that Vectron had been acquired to strengthen Itek's military business, not its initial commercial target market. He concluded on an apologetic note. "Much of the work done by the company is highly classified for security reasons and it is therefore difficult to be more specific."[13]

Although there had been no initial public offering to broadly distribute the stock, a small over-the-counter market had already developed in Itek securities. On September 8 Cornelius Borman in Laurance Rockefeller's office gave Teddy Walkowicz an update on how Rockefeller's investment in Itek had performed. The total cost of Rockefeller's investment as of September 5 was $252,667. The total value of his investment, based on a market price of $37 per share and full conversion of Rockefeller's notes and stock warrants, was $1,562,720. Rockefeller's return was about 500 percent in less than a year.[14]

In early September, Rockefeller transferred modest positions in Itek's stocks and bonds to his key employees. He didn't give it away; they had to pay for these investments at the market price prevailing in the small over-the-counter market. Yet Randolph Marston, Harper Woodward, and Teddy Walkowicz were able to obtain larger stakes more economically than might otherwise have been possible. At the same time they were increasing their positions in Itek stock, they were also increasing their exposure to another Rockefeller investment, Scantlin. For Rockefeller, this was a smart move. If his employees' personal wealth was tied to one of his own substantial investments, they certainly were likely to pay attention to developments at the company.[15]

By the beginning of October, Itek's stock offering was ready to move forward. On October 10 Leghorn wrote all Itek shareholders and offered them the chance to purchase more shares in the company. Essentially, for every twelve shares of Itek stock a shareholder currently owned, he had the opportunity to purchase one additional share. Leghorn enclosed with his letter an offering circular that explained the transaction.[16]

Itek's offering circular made many of the same points about the company's development that Jesse Cousins had in his letter to William Masson just a couple of months earlier. But in the circular the story underwent a subtle transformation. The circular explained that Itek's ac-

quisition of the Boston University Physical Research Laboratory, its acquisition of Vectron, and its recent creation of an electronics laboratory
"have been consistent with its long range plans." As a result, the company
had "developed a strong capability in the field of military reconnaissance."
But Itek's only known long-range plan up to that date — its original business plan — had made no mention of becoming a military contractor, nor
did Itek's business plan mention making such significant acquisitions in
its first year. Now Itek's sales were almost entirely military. It seems difficult to reconcile these statements with Itek's business plan, but in the
press of business, when opportunities present themselves, sometimes they
are taken. Justification to shareholders is left for later on.[17]

Less than two weeks later, as Itek shareholders were still considering
whether to increase their positions in the company, Itek's board met to
review operations. The agenda sent out to directors before the meeting
was an unadorned list of corporate nuts and bolts. Board members expected presentations on Itek's preliminary year-end results, financing options for the new factory, and the usual progress reports. The meeting
began as expected: Leghorn discussed the need for a new corporate staff
position, and the board approved the proposal. Then he reported on current operations, and the prospects for new business. Finishing his reports
on these topics, he broached the subject of hiring key technical personnel.
The official board minutes are silent on the subject of what names Leghorn considered, but handwritten notes, written in the margins of Teddy
Walkowicz's copy of the meeting agenda, suggest that the conversation
veered into unexpected territory. Notes written on another copy of the
agenda, most likely Harper Woodward's copy, confirm what happened
next.

Leghorn's proposal was audacious — Dick Bissell for Itek executive vice
president. As the CIA's top executive in charge of developing CORONA
and the SR-71, and of managing the ongoing operations of the U-2 program, Bissell was more than a high-level spook. He was the leading expert
in the U.S. government — and thus in the free world — on developing
cutting-edge reconnaissance systems. If Bissell could be persuaded to join
Itek, he would bring unparalleled expertise and insider knowledge of future programs, not to mention connections, to the fledgling company.
Leghorn knew Bissell's attributes and the programs that he managed, but

did he tell the rest of the board? There is no evidence that Leghorn shared Bissell's secret with the board; it would have been a severe breach of U.S. national security for him to do so. After all, the U-2 remained one of the country's most important national security secrets. CORONA and the SR-71 were equally cloaked in deep secrecy. All we know about the discussion is a cryptic comment. Bissell was "not a delegator."

Then another candidate — Jack Carter — was discussed. In the early stages of Itek's formation, Carter had been on the inside track, along with Leghorn, to be a member of the founding executive team. Carter's role at Lockheed, where he was a key member of the development team working on the SAMOS spy satellite, was so critical to that project's future development that in the interest of national security, at the request of his company, he stayed at Lockheed. Now that CORONA was the top priority, and SAMOS was not, Carter was free to move. Carter was no Richard Bissell, but he was a heavyweight in the defense-contracting world, and like Leghorn, he had connections. Considering that Lockheed was the prime contractor for CORONA, and that Carter was highly respected by his colleagues, this was another obvious plus for Itek.

Then Leghorn dropped another bombshell. Just months after acquiring Vectron, he was ready to make another acquisition. His target was Vidya, a small research and development group working on "problems of space satellites and optical instrumentation for space exploration." Vidya was not a company. It was a team of six scientists who had research contracts with companies like Boeing and Douglas. The group had outstanding orders of about $100,000, but more important, it was located on the West Coast, in Palo Alto — close to Lockheed and in the heart of where the main contracting work on the CORONA project was taking place. If Itek could acquire the team, the company would have a base of operations closer to its most important contracting relationships, and it could provide a field headquarters for Jack Carter.[18]

Leghorn's proposals may have been bold and the acquisition program risky, but Itek directors didn't question him. And given Itek's stock performance, why should they? The next day the asking price on Itek stock rose to $58 a share, up from $37 barely a month earlier. For Itek's largest investors, who were also its board members, everything was smooth sailing.[19]

There was one problem. Itek's directors still did not know that Itek's most important customer was the CIA, and that its most important product was a spy camera for the CORONA satellite. At the company's November board meeting, Leghorn distributed a sales analysis for the directors to review. Sales were divided into four categories, and each line on the report listed not only the Itek project number for a product but the customer as well. Leghorn was probably pleased to report that at that point Itek had a sales backlog of more than $3 million. That was nearly equal to total sales for the company's first fiscal year ended that October and augured well for a strong fiscal 1959. The largest sales category in the report was for defense-systems projects. Backlog for this category was nearly $2 million and was clearly Itek's most significant market. Walkowicz, Leghorn, and the other Itek founders held important security clearance, but the other directors interested in learning more about company sales in this area immediately ran up against a roadblock—national security. One project, with a sales backlog of $1.6 million, represented most of the defense backlog, and half the company's total backlog. The project was obviously critical to the company's future—and off-limits to discussion. Every other line on the sales report listed the project's customer. This project's customer was identified only as "Confidential."[20]

If Itek's other directors, like Pratt and Hill, were curious about the project, there was little they could do to satisfy their curiosity. But Leghorn's increasing interest in acquisitions gave them plenty of other activities to occupy their interest. On December 9 Leghorn sent a memorandum to the board outlining the agenda for the next meeting on December 17. The agenda for the meeting, which would take place in the offices of William A. M. Burden at 630 Fifth Avenue, may have shocked at least a few of the company's directors. In addition to considering a stock split and a new issue of company stock, the directors would discuss Leghorn's proposal to acquire Vidya. But the surprise item on the agenda was number six—the proposed acquisition of the Photostat Corporation.

Photostat, an old-line blue-chip company, was the pioneer in photocopy products. Its brand name was recognized around the world and was synonymous with photocopying. Founded in 1911, it had annual sales of more than $20 million a year. Itek, barely a year old, had sales of little more than $3 million. Leghorn's plan to take over the company seemed improbable except for one powerful fact — the value of Itek's stock was jumping higher at an astonishing rate. This gave the company a huge war chest. All the company had to do was issue new stock at sky-high prices, pocket the money, and go on a shopping spree. And Richard Leghorn was planning to do exactly that.

Photostat and Vidya weren't the only companies Leghorn wanted to purchase. By early December he and his staff had already identified at least eight other companies for possible acquisition. The companies that caught Leghorn's wandering eye supposedly had some strategic fit with the company's long-term business goals. Some, like Vidya, provided the company with research and development talent compatible with Itek's own interests. Hycon, designer of the top secret cameras on the U-2 spy plane, was also on this list, as was a small computer start-up company destined for success — and independence from Itek — called Digital Equipment Corporation (DEC). Others, like Photostat, could provide Itek with a marketing organization. Yet aside from Hycon, Vidya, and DEC, it was difficult to argue that these companies would be good matches for Itek.[21]

In preparation for the meeting, Jesse Cousins sent Leghorn an artful memo bristling with financial data and company information. Sales for the next year were expected to triple to more than $9 million and rise at least another 50 percent the following year to more than $14 million. Over the same two-year period expenditures on capital equipment would be at least $1.2 million.

In order to build a suitable factory at its Lexington site, the company would have to spend $2 million, of which $1.5 million could be financed with a mortgage on the building. In order to support "a larger volume of operations," the company needed working capital of $750,000. To finance the capital spending program and the development of the Lexington site, the company needed another $1.25 million. Itek's total financial requirements (exclusive of the mortgage): $2.5 million. Yet for all the company's ambitious plans, spending on research and development, the heart of Itek, would be held to an average of $180,000 a year for the next two years. It was an ominous sign.

Cousins's memo included a simple, but effective plan for financing these activities. First, Itek would split its stock to four shares for every one share of stock outstanding. At the same time, the company would offer an additional 100,000 shares of new stock at $25 per share in a fully registered public offering. There were risks to this approach. Itek's stock was hot, but it was highly speculative. There was no guarantee that by the time of the offering the company's stock price would remain high. If the stock fell sharply, raising the money needed would be much harder.

So Cousins proposed an alternative approach. If Itek could combine an acquisition of Photostat with a simultaneous stock offering, the chances of a successful financing would be greatly improved. Cousins suggested that "a combined Itek-Photostat financing might have good appeal — Photostat had history and earnings; it is a leader in its field; the trade name is almost generic in the language of copying systems; the relationship between offering price and 'book values' would be greatly improved; and finally there would be investor interest in an opportunity to participate for the first time in an old and respected name company, locked for fifty years in family control." This transaction would raise money both for Itek's expansion, as outlined by Cousins earlier in his memo, and for the acquisition of Photostat. It was a brilliant idea.[22]

If Leghorn was ever going to pursue his dream of building a company at the forefront of the information revolution, this was his moment. Itek's overvalued stock gave him the currency to fund an ambitious acquisition program. National security, which required that Itek's most important product and its customer remain secret, meant that no one would figure out for a long time that 50 percent of the company's backlog was with one customer, the CIA. This was a huge concentration of business risk that was greatly magnified by the political and technical hazards of the CORONA program itself.[23] The longer investors remained in the dark about the risks they were taking, the better for Itek's stock price and Leghorn's acquisition campaign.

Itek's December 17 board meeting was a pivotal moment in the company's short history. Key decisions made at this meeting would set the stage for the next act in Itek's history, its meteoric public rise. The meeting was held at James T. Hill's office at 630 Fifth Avenue. Leghorn and Cousins were at the meeting, and so were Walkowicz, Woodward, Pratt, and Walker. Leghorn, who chaired the meeting, presented his proposal to acquire Photostat. The board approved the proposal, appointed a negotiating committee with Leghorn, Cousins, and Pratt as members, and also appointed a financing committee to select the best way to finance the acquisition and accomplish a public offering of company stock.

The board made another critical decision that day—to hire Jack Carter. Carter's recruitment had been discussed just weeks earlier, and now his election as a company vice president made his employment official. Leghorn, increasingly involved with acquisitions and his personal disarmament campaign, needed a strong second in command to manage company affairs on a daily basis. He believed Carter was that man.[24] And Carter was to do an excellent job—until the day he betrayed Leghorn.

At that December meeting the board also approved a draft of Itek's first annual report. Released just a few weeks later, it was an alluring description of a successful young company poised at the cutting edge of technology. In his letter to stockholders, which appeared in the first pages of the report, Leghorn proudly stated, "the company's business has been marked by accomplishments that go beyond your management's more optimistic expectations." Revenues for the company were $3.6 million, net income was $169,000. Company employment, less than a dozen at the end of 1957, now stood at more than five hundred. Certainly, the basic facts sounded impressive.

Leghorn declared that the company was started to produce new information-management technologies that would allow companies to better manage the way graphic information was handled. He observed, perhaps in a Freudian slip, that graphic information "is the 'intelligence' of modern business and industry. It ranges from simple written or typed communications" to "enormous volumes of printed material, maps, drawings, photographic material, directories, files and technical literature." Then Leghorn attempted to reconcile the acquisition of both the Boston University Physical Research Laboratory and Vectron with this strategy. These organizations, he stated, "have together put us in a position where we can render an exceptional service in aero-space reconnaissance, a specialized activity in the general field of information technology." Leghorn offered no further definition of aerospace reconnaissance, nor any additional description of Itek's business activities in this field. At a time when the United States had yet to successfully orbit a satellite in space, and the existence of the U-2 remained unknown to all Americans except a select few, it would have been very difficult for anyone to imagine the true meaning behind this phrase.

Leghorn's statement, though accurate in its broadest sense, was a slight stretch. The capabilities of the B.U. lab were exceptional, and the team from the lab possessed unique strengths in reconnaissance, which at its most basic level is information gathering. But it is difficult to justify the acquisition of the lab, or Vectron, as a necessary step toward realizing Itek's commercial ambitions in graphic handling. Nor is it completely appropriate to characterize their capabilities as a field within information technology as defined by Leghorn earlier in his letter to stockholders. The lab had no real experience developing equipment to facilitate massive handling of documents, directories, maps, or whatever else Leghorn envisioned. The lab's experience was in developing and using spy cameras, certainly a type of information technology, but a type probably far from the minds of prospective shareholders.

Leghorn saved the most important piece of information for the end of his letter. More than 90 percent of Itek's "gross income," a phrase with no corresponding line on Itek's income statement, "came from military contracts." Any serious investor who had made it through Leghorn's management letter now understood that despite all the talk about commercial products to revolutionize the business community, Itek's real success, nearly all of it, came from providing products and services to the military. Nowhere in the annual report were these products and services better defined. Like the phrase "aerospace reconnaissance," the definition of these products and services would be left up to the imagination of the reader.

At a time in the Cold War when it was clear that U.S. defense spending was on the rise, a successful, mysterious start-up company that had achieved great success as a military contractor must have fired the imagination of investors. They may not have known what Itek made, but they knew from reading the annual report that Laurance Rockefeller had two representatives on the company's seven-member board. Certainly he must have known what Itek did, they may have reasoned, and if the business was good enough for a Rockefeller it was good enough for them. There was a catch. Itek's annual report may have made it clear that the company had an extremely high concentration of business in the military sector, but there was no way that a prospective investor could determine that a single customer, the CIA, accounted for more than half of the company's backlog. Nor could any investor know that if the CORONA spy satellite failed to make it into space—or if another spy satellite program was funded that promised superior results—the company would probably collapse. These risks were not disclosed in the annual report. They could not be disclosed in the annual report. The reason: national security.

So investors intrigued by Itek had only one choice. Until the company issued stock broadly to the public, shares could be acquired only through the narrow over-the-counter market that had developed in Boston. Surging demand for the stock and limited supply led to the inevitable—Itek stock was going through the roof.

9

GOING PUBLIC

In the first days of 1959 Richard Leghorn and the Itek management team put the finishing touches on a letter to the company's shareholders. Nineteen fifty-eight had been a breathtaking year for the company, but as Leghorn's letter made clear, 1959 was going to be even better.

Leghorn's plan for the New Year was confident, if not brash. First, he asked shareholders to approve a five-for-one stock split, a slight revision to the plan recommended just weeks earlier to the company's board of directors. Then Leghorn explained that if the increase in authorized capital was approved, shareholders would be asked to give the board of directors further authority to issue stock through a public offering of securities managed by Paine, Webber, Jackson and Curtis, Albie Pratt's firm. "The most important single purpose" of the offering, Leghorn flatly stated, "was the purchase of all the outstanding stock of Photostat Corporation." This must have been startling news for investors. Itek, a fledgling company, was now preparing to acquire the oldest and most trusted name in photocopying in the world.

Richard Leghorn, barely thirty-nine years old, was reaching for the corporate brass ring. If Itek could successfully acquire Photostat, Leghorn would be propelled into the top ranks of America's captains of industry, and perhaps most important, he could at last find some relief from the strain he was under. For more than a year now, he had been walking a tightrope. Itek's success had pushed Leghorn into the spotlight, but with the attention came inquiry. Who were Itek's customers? Which products accounted for most of Itek's earnings? What was the biggest risk the company faced? If Leghorn answered the questions truthfully, he would compromise national security, and both his career and his company would be mortally wounded. In the absence of the truth, just what could Leghorn say? Years later, Leghorn acknowledged that the Photostat acquisition was done in part to provide a "cover story" for Itek's classified operations. Before the acquisition, he explained, it took "a lot of energy trying to portray to the world that we were a legitimate business."[1]

Leghorn gave shareholders ample reasons to vote for the Photostat acquisition. The most compelling was the potential strategic fit Leghorn described as existing between the two companies. Itek had spent its first full year in business "on building up research, development, and manufacturing" capabilities, including "technical competence in photo-physics and the field of information technology." Like the annual report that was enclosed with Leghorn's letter, this description of Itek's activities, true in the broadest sense, was as tangible as vapor.

Yet it was an intoxicating haze. If Itek's technical ingenuity, apparently confirmed by the company's phenomenal growth and stock performance, could be combined with Photostat's "nation-wide established sales and marketing organization," were there any limits to what Itek could achieve?

There was more. Itek would use the funds from the offering to invest in a new California subsidiary called Vidya Corporation. Leghorn correctly noted that "Vidya is staffed by a group of scientists and engineers who specialize in problems encountered by vehicles in space and the upper atmosphere, and whose abilities could effectively complement" Itek's capabilities. But Itek's shareholders could never know the true story behind Vidya, because they could never know about CORONA.

The veil of secrecy that cloaked Itek's relationship with the CIA began to affect management's judgment in unexpected ways. Management had increasing difficulty distinguishing between secrecy in the interests of national security and secrecy to shield management from unpleasant questions — perhaps because, at least initially, the two appeared to be the same.

Nowhere in Leghorn's letter to shareholders does he mention that as recently as early 1959 Vidya didn't even exist as a corporation. Vidya is simply presented as a promising acquisition target — as if it were a typical operating company with a strong strategic fit with Itek's core business. In all likelihood, had Leghorn stated the truth about Vidya, he would have exposed himself to serious questioning from shareholders. Such questions could have placed Leghorn in an extremely awkward situation, and might have raised doubts about his judgment in acquiring Photostat. From Leghorn's perspective it probably seemed far better to avoid disclosing the truth about Vidya and thus to evade the scrutiny that would endanger security for CORONA.

Yet Vidya was little more than a name, simply a business proposal on paper. Specifically, it was five well respected scientists — Wallace Davis, Jack Nielsen, Morris Rubesin, Karl Spangenberg, and Jackson Stalder — and a former high-octane jet pilot and near Itek founder, Jack Carter. Vidya's cadre of scientists came with high-level credentials, clearances, and contacts that enhanced Itek's credibility. Financed by a $110,000 venture capital investment from Itek, and the promise of an additional investment as long as the company met its goals, Vidya was less a company than a dream.

If Vidya demonstrated that it could meet Itek's corporate objectives, Itek would invest more capital in the company during a second phase of financing. At this time Itek would purchase additional Vidya stock at $4 a share. Not only would this transaction inject capital into the company, but it would establish a market value for the founders' shares. Within months they would all have a potential 300 percent return.[2] Little more than a year earlier, national security had stopped Jack Carter from leaving Lockheed to become a founder of Itek. Now he would have a second chance at great wealth.

Leghorn asked shareholders to approve his proposals in person at a special shareholders meeting at Boston's Somerset Hotel later that month, or by proxy. At 3:30 P.M. on January 28, Itek's special stockholders meeting was called to order. By the time the meeting was over, all of Leghorn's proposals had been approved.[3]

The preliminary prospectus for Itek's stock offering was published in early March. Itek's prospectus, written in the staid legal prose typical of such documents, nevertheless conveyed to prospective shareholders a sense of unlimited promise for the young company. The risks were great, and the stock was "highly speculative," but Itek was also a company that in barely eighteen months had gone from fewer than ten employees to more than five hundred, and whose revenues, profits, and stock price were shooting to the stars. For 1958, the prospectus reported, Itek had sales of more than $6 million and net income of more than $250,000. The company's stock, which was as low as $11 a share in October 1958 (adjusted for the five-for-one split in January 1959), reached a high of $63 in February. This incredible performance occurred at a time when the Dow Jones Industrial Average essentially remained flat.

Investors, drawn to Itek by its fantastic growth and the phenomenal performance of its stock, found plenty of other information in the prospectus to confirm that in Itek they had found their El Dorado. The prospectus explained that Itek had been formed to "undertake research and development in the field of information technology." The focus of the company's research was the "gathering, handling, storage and retrieval of all types of graphic information." Yet buried deeper in the prospectus was a warning. Although Itek specialized in information-management systems, it had yet to market "any information handling systems." Furthermore, the prospectus made clear, there was no guarantee that Itek would ever market these systems commercially.

The understated, overcrowded legal prose was cautionary and dry, but the message remained exciting: Itek was developing technology at the cutting edge of an information revolution. It must have been easy for investors to overlook the blinking yellow lights in the prospectus. Not only did Itek's sales seem to prove that it had promising products, but the business risks that faced Itek, delicately revealed in the prospectus, probably only intensified investor interest. The prospectus stated that virtually all of Itek's sales and profits came from highly classified government research and development contracts: "The subject matter of these contracts includes work on gathering, storing, filing, indexing and sorting information, particularly graphic information, and presenting it in convenient form." Only an imaginative mind could conclude from that meandering sentence that Itek made space-age spy cameras. The fact that Itek's business was highly concentrated with one customer, the U.S. government, was clearly a significant risk. But at the height of the Cold War, when most people still had great faith in their government, the fact that these products were important enough to be classified, and ambiguously described, probably confirmed in the minds of many that their commercial promise must be great.

The clincher, for any wary investor participating in Itek's securities offering, was probably the company's acquisition of Photostat. The capital raised by the stock sale would be used not only to invest in Itek's futuristic technology but to finance the acquisition of Photostat. Whatever business uncertainties surrounded Itek's classified government business would presumably be offset by Photostat's blue-chip operations. Photostat had been in business since 1911, and its photocopying machines dominated the market. Photostat's sales, which were less than $11 million in 1949, were nearly $20 million by the end of 1958. The company's sales had been stagnant for the past three years, and its moderate losses in 1957 and 1958 must have concerned at least some investors. The combined operations of Itek and Photostat had sales in 1958 of more than $25 million and net income of nearly $100,000. Itek's small but profitable business could carry Photostat's larger but unprofitable operations until Leghorn and his team had implemented their turnaround strategy. Many surely reasoned that in the hands of Itek's savvy management team, Photostat would rapidly return to growth and profitability.[4]

Yet for all the disclosures in Itek's prospectus, no prospective investor would ever know that Itek's entire future rested on a spy camera, untested, that would take photographs of the Soviet Union from space. Nor could investors evaluate the risks to the company if the rocket designed to place the camera in space continued to fail—or even worse, a better camera system was developed at another company.[5]

The same week that Itek's prospectus began to circulate, Richard Leghorn sent his board of directors a copy of a letter he had received from Arthur Young and Company a month earlier. Leghorn had decided to engage the well-known firm of accountants and auditors to help management strengthen its internal controls and management practices. Before beginning work at Itek, the accounting firm had conducted a preliminary survey of the company's operations. What the accountants discovered and communicated to Leghorn was disturbing news.

Prospective Itek shareholders, eager to add the high-flying growth stock to their portfolios, might have thought twice if they had seen the letter from Arthur Young. The white shoe accountants flatly told Leghorn that a "major obstacle" in strengthening the company's financial controls was its uncertain organizational structure. Without "a firmly established organization plan," successful management reforms would be difficult to make.

But the problem was deeper than resolving Itek's structure. Unless basic accounting systems and procedures were in place at the company, at all levels, information would never flow to senior management regardless of how the boxes on the organizational chart were rearranged. For a company to function properly, information must flow not only up to senior management, through an effective "accounting reporting system," but back down to the company through a "formalized budget program." At Itek, the accountants observed, there "has been little opportunity to plan and forecast during this period of extremely rapid growth." Their conclusion, unambiguous and unqualified, was a warning: "If this growth is to be directed properly," they cautioned, "a budget program must be developed and installed."[6]

Inadequate financial controls constituted just one unknown risk that faced prospective shareholders. Itek's deteriorating relations with Fairchild were another. When Fairchild became the subcontractor to Itek, part of the agreement required Fairchild to ship the cameras to Itek for environmental testing, which included shaking the camera and testing it under the vacuum conditions the camera would experience in space. If the camera passed all of Itek's tests, it would be shipped out to the West Coast to a classified facility at Lockheed for installation in a space capsule.[7]

Fairchild decided to build its own environmental testing facility and stopped shipping the cameras to Itek. It was nothing less than an attempt to regain the top position in the program. When Walt Levison first heard the news, he was enraged. But he quickly channeled his anger into action. Levison flew to Fairchild's Syosset facilities on Long Island, where manufacture and testing of the camera took place. His mission was to foil Fairchild's plan and force compliance with the agreement. He spent his entire day there working his way up through various levels of Fairchild's corporate bureaucracy until he found himself waiting outside the office of Charlie O'Donnell, who ran Fairchild's Syosset operation. O'Donnell kept Levison waiting for two hours. When O'Donnell finally agreed to see Levison, his position was inflexible: Fairchild would no longer ship cameras to Itek for testing. Levison announced to O'Donnell that he was taking the next plane back to Boston. He declared that when he arrived back at Itek's headquarters, the first thing he would do is issue an order to stop work. "You wouldn't dare," O'Donnell responded.

Itek, as prime subcontractor to Fairchild, had the power to stop all work on the camera program, if needed, to resolve a work dispute. If Levison chose this route, he would be delaying the timetable for the most important national security program of the time. He had another option. Instead of issuing the order and delaying the program, Levison could appeal to Lockheed as prime contractor for the program to adjudicate the dispute. Work on the program would move forward, memos would be sent back and forth, but there was no guarantee that Lockheed would support Itek. Fairchild might over time demonstrate that its environmental testing facilities were completely capable of doing the job. It took extra time to ship the cameras from Fairchild to Itek for testing. Perhaps Lockheed would agree that it was a step that could be safely eliminated.

O'Donnell was betting that time was on his side and that Levison would never threaten the program's timetable. He bet wrong. Levison returned to Itek and decided that Fairchild's plan had to be halted. He issued his stop-work order and sent copies to the appropriate parties at Lockheed and CIA. That weekend the entire system stood down.

A meeting was hastily scheduled for Monday morning. Representatives of Itek, Lockheed, Fairchild, and the CIA would meet to resolve the issue. After Fairchild's O'Donnell presented his case, Lockheed's Irving Jaffe resolved the issue decisively. Fairchild had a contractual obligation to ship the cameras to Itek for testing. Period. In retrospect, Levison considered the stop-work order "an outrageous thing to have done." After all, "this was the most secretive project in the country at the time," but the stop-work order got results — and fast. Until Itek could successfully push Fairchild out of the program, relations between the two companies remained tense.[8]

Meanwhile, Leghorn turned his attention to the next deal — even though the Photostat acquisition had barely closed and the company's new accounting controls had yet to be fully implemented. By late April, Leghorn had a list of nine potential acquisition targets that he presented to the board for discussion. The possibilities on the list included the microfilm division of Remington Rand, a potential joint venture with McKinsey and Company to apply "advanced techniques of systems analysis to management and information control systems," and Photon, Inc.[9]

In retrospect, Leghorn's analysis of the potential Remington Rand acquisition, and the others farther down this list, is ominous. He explained that Remington Rand's microfilm division, a subsidiary of Sperry Rand, was "being offered for sale" in line with Sperry's policy to "spin off marginal operations." The divisions operations "were not profitable," but Leghorn dismissed this problem because "no real effort appears to have been made toward making it . . . profitable."

Leghorn, whose assessment of the division's problems was extremely candid, ignored his own analysis and focused instead on the promise of the future. He used the same argument to defend this acquisition that he had used to support Itek's proposed purchase of Photostat — distribution. "Through the Remington Rand sales organization," he proposed, Itek would obtain "a method of entry to the office systems field and its customers." Itek could sell these customers Remington Rand's products, as well as Itek's own internally developed "graphic files and related equipment."

Certainly, Leghorn's optimistic view of the future painted a failing microfilm division with the veneer of strategic promise. But the holes in his argument were just too big. Not only had Itek yet to complete a study of the microfilm field, a fact that Leghorn properly disclosed to his directors, but the company's proprietary commercial products, the ones that would be sold through the division, were still on the drawing board. How would Itek leverage this new distribution channel without new products?[10]

The Remington Rand acquisition never occurred; it was an idea that simply dried up on the vine. But it was only the first company on Leghorn's acquisition list. As Leghorn worked his way down that list, he wasted valuable management time on acquisitions that would never occur.[11]

As Leghorn pushed new acquisitions, board member Albie Pratt was content to peddle Itek's stock. In a memo to his Paine Webber colleagues, Pratt reported "encouraging" progress "at the Board of Directors' meeting last week." According to Pratt, "The Photostat acquisition was consummated April 9th, but Itek management" was "moving fast to improve their profit picture." He baldly stated that Photostat was likely to "break even this month and be in the black from here on out." Pratt's confidence in Itek's ability to implement effective cost controls at Photostat, in light of the Arthur Young memo on Itek's own nonexistent internal accounting procedures, was either extraordinarily optimistic or shamelessly opportunistic.

And that was just the start of Pratt's memorandum. Next he turned to the subject of Itek's earnings. "Earnings of Itek alone are running about the same as for the first quarter," he noted. Consolidated earnings for the fiscal year, he predicted, would be about fifty to seventy-five cents per share. For the next fiscal year, however, Pratt forecast a dramatic acceleration in earnings growth. Earnings per share "should be at least $1.50 and perhaps as high as $2.25, based on normal growth of present activities and product lines." In a rare demonstration of understatement, Pratt drily observed, "Itek is still open to further acquisitions that will enhance its earnings picture and future prospects." Soon enough, he was back to old form, concluding his report with an evaluation of Itek's research and development efforts: "From what I hear about this activity," he wrote, "it should pay off in the end."[12]

As Pratt pushed Itek's stock, Richard Leghorn waited for Arthur D. Little, a highly respected consulting firm, to present him with a report on the firm's organizational structure. Early in 1959, at about the same time Leghorn had engaged Arthur Young to review Itek's accounting deficiencies, he retained Arthur D. Little. Leghorn gave the consultants at Little challenging marching orders. He told them to recommend an organizational structure that would accommodate future expansion yet retain the informality that contributed to the company's early success.

On June 12 the consultants from Arthur D. Little submitted their report to Leghorn. To prepare Leghorn for the bitter pill that would follow, the cover letter was flattering. "As outsiders we very quickly caught the enthusiasm of all Itek people and came to believe in the aspirations of the individuals and in the prospects for Itek's future," wrote Little's Philip Donham. He observed that Jack Carter, who had moved from the West Coast to become Itek Boston's general manager, had already accepted the report's conclusions and had begun to implement them with modest modifications. "His realignment of our plans . . . carried out with thoughtful deliberation, was practical and realistic." Donham practically squealed with praise, noting, "Since then we have followed with admiration the progress of the reorganization."

But once Leghorn turned to the first page of the report, he was confronted with a litany of management failures. The conclusions were harsh and ominous. Itek's "explosive growth threatened to get out of control." The current organization was failing because "organizational lines were more often circumvented than followed." Complicating matters, "several self-contained cells had developed, performing in many instances duplicate, competing, or conflicting functions." Financial controls were in horrible shape. Little's consulting team found that "the formal accounting system and record keeping had fallen far behind the day-to-day activities. Budgeting was virtually impossible because the plans of different groups within the company did not fall together into an integrated whole." That was just the beginning.

The pressure to grow the company was immense. The consultants found that Itek's key technical people had turned their efforts away from research and development, the heart of the company, to sales. It was a vicious circle. The company's "startling success in the sales of military projects led to a somewhat indiscriminate hiring program." As a result, "pressure to obtain income for the support of what had grown to a roster of about 500 people had forced all of the officers and most of the key technical people to focus their primary attention on sales activities." Leghorn's strategic vision—that Itek would leverage its military research acumen and develop commercial products to be sold through Photostat—was threatened. "The objectives of using military projects as a means of realizing commercially salable products had fallen between the chairs."[13]

Fortunately for Leghorn, the bad news ended by the bottom of page two of the report, exactly where the recommendations for the future began. Over the next nine pages, Arthur D. Little's consulting team outlined a major restructuring of Itek's operations. "Recognizing that Itek planned to pursue an aggressive program of expansion through acquisitions," the team separated responsibility for corporate finance from internal accounting and control. Under the plan, Itek's vice president and treasurer would be given responsibility for "external contacts," with "the expectation that he would devote a considerable share of his time to the evaluation of possible acquisitions." A new corporate controller position, located in Boston, would be created to implement and manage the company's new accounting procedures.

The report's most important recommendation was the creation of a new matrix organization at Itek's Boston research and development branch — the heart of its classified operations. A matrix organization is a tricky affair. A traditional line organization, akin to the direct top-down flow of command that occurs in a military organization, creates a clear hierarchy of authority. A matrix organization has multiple sources of authority. As a result, power doesn't necessary flow from the top to the bottom of the company, but radiates from competing centers of influence. In a line organization, a senior manager has direct authority over the human, financial, and physical resources that have been assigned to him. In a matrix structure, a senior manager must compete with other managers for those resources. While a line organization's structure is intended to be static, a matrix organization is fluid by design. In 1959, when Itek optimistically adopted this matrix structure, it seemed to ensure that classified and commercial projects would thrive side by side, and that the creative tensions of a growth-driven organization could be successfully resolved.[14] By 1962 it was to become painfully clear that a new structure, however ingenious, could not by itself solve Itek's problems.

In early July, Richard Leghorn and Harper Woodward held extensive talks on the future of Itek. Their discussions were wide-ranging — corporate mission, internal management, mergers, and acquisitions. Following a year of explosive growth, Woodward wanted to make absolutely sure that Leghorn had a firm grip on how to lead Itek into the future. No doubt Leghorn was pleased to report that he had already begun to implement Arthur D. Little's recommendations.

Leghorn took the opportunity to explain his vision to Woodward: Itek was an information management company. Future earnings growth would result from new products and markets in office equipment, printing and publishing, communications, and education. Leghorn's target list for mergers and acquisitions was long. It was filled with company names both obscure and famous: Photon, Diebold, Remington Rand, Hermes, Bell and Howell, and Western Union.[15]

Most of the targets on the list were Leghorn's idea, but one, Bell and Howell, had been promoted by Laurance Rockefeller's staff. The idea of a merger with Bell and Howell had been considered as early as February 1958, just a few months after Itek's incorporation. The source for this idea was Laurance Rockefeller himself. That month, Harper Woodward wrote to Rockefeller and summarized the action to date that had been taken. "I took up with Dick Leghorn your suggestion that he consider at some appropriate time an affiliation with Bell & Howell. . . . He appeared completely open minded on the subject and I think we can perhaps follow-up with him in the future."

Leghorn may have seemed open-minded, but he dragged his feet on the Bell and Howell merger plan. By spring 1959 the Rockefeller staff was still talking about the possibility. Randolph Marston, writing to Woodward and Walkowicz, observed, "Market appraises Bell & Howell at $68,000,000 — 2.25 times net worth; Itek at $42,000,000 — 7 times net worth; B&H at 24 times earnings; and Itek???" Later that summer Harper Woodward again gave Laurance Rockefeller an update on the possible merger. His language was familiar. "Leghorn is completely open-minded on this subject," Woodward wrote, "and it has occurred to me that David [Rockefeller] might possibly be able to set up some sort of a meeting for him with Mr. Percy [Charles Percy, president of Bell and Howell]." But Leghorn would never accept a merger with a company as large as Bell and Howell; it would mean losing his company, and his position as president. Instead, perhaps in part to protect his own position, in part to achieve his corporate vision, he pursued an acquisition campaign of a completely different sort. It would lead to his undoing.[16]

Mergers and acquisitions were the easy part; crafting a corporate structure and management team that could actually run Itek's fast-growing operations was an entirely different matter. The consultants at Arthur D. Little may have conceived a new organizational chart, but were the right people in the boxes? Woodward was concerned that Leghorn was stretching himself too thin. Leghorn, now president of a large, complex organization, was still focusing on making the deal, not on making the company work. In handwritten notes, evidently kept by Woodward as minutes of his talks with Leghorn, he observed that "Leghorn needs an assistant to the Pres. and some additional staff help. Dick does not have his job in hand." Woodward made a note to himself to help Leghorn get the support staff he needed. Woodward had another concern about Leghorn—his lack of corporate focus. Leghorn was passionate about public policy issues, especially the cause of world peace and disarmament. Leghorn's values were noble, but it was far from certain that he could reconcile his corporate responsibilities with his civic commitments. Woodward wrote himself a cryptic note in the margins of his meeting agenda with Leghorn: "RSL—At home or abroad: Save the World or Itek."

Woodward had concerns about Itek's other founding managers as well. He thought that Cousins was "not only not doing the job assigned him, but disturbing Leghorn and the rest of management." He "should either be fired, or retired." And Art Tyler, the man at the core of Itek's original business plan and the Minicard System, was floundering. Tyler, who now reported to Jack Carter, had no operating responsibilities. His only role was as an inventor. Woodward wrote, "Dick thinks 50% probability this will work out. Recommend we give it 6–12 [months] trial—then reassess."[17]

On July 13, the day after Woodward and Leghorn finished their talks, the lead story in *The Wall Street Journal* was about Laurance Rockefeller's venture capital operations and, as the headline proclaimed, "The Case of Fabulous Itek." Whatever problems Woodward discussed with Leghorn were nowhere to be found in Richard Cooke's story. The reporter clearly swallowed the Itek story hook, line, and sinker. "Not long ago a company with the cryptic name of Itek Corp. quietly announced it had purchased Photostat Corp.," Cooke began. Reeling his readers in further, just as, perhaps, he had been reeled in, Cooke continued. "The announcement went on to say that Itek was organized only 21 months ago to 'develop and produce new systems and specialized equipment in the field of information technology,' a statement hardly more enlightening to the general public than the company's name."

The mystery that surrounded Itek, now well established by Cooke, was likely a magnet to investors looking for an exciting new company—and Cooke didn't disappoint them. "What the modestly worded news release didn't mention was that the fledgling firm already is well along into a $20 million sales year, compared with $3,464,000 volume last year. . . . Unmentioned, too, was the meteoric rise Itek's stock has enjoyed: From

$2 initially to more than $345 last winter. Split five-for-one last January, Itek's shares now sell around $46 each over the counter." But Cooke's glowing portrayal of Itek's sales explosion failed to tell the whole story. Most of the increase in sales was not because of internal growth but because Itek's high-flying stock had enabled management to acquire Photostat, an organization with nearly $20 million in sales itself.

Then, after retelling the story of Laurance Rockefeller's role in financing the company, Cooke returned to the mysterious side of Itek. "Itek at present has about $10 million of highly secret Government contracts," Cooke reported. "These are believed to cover the handling of data from missiles and space vehicles." What kind of data did Itek handle? *The Wall Street Journal* didn't know and couldn't say. Its readers probably concluded that if the business was growing fast, classified, and backed by a Rockefeller, it was a smart investment.

Then Cooke described, as accurately as he could, Itek's products. "The company," he wrote, "has developed its own methods of storing information and putting a finger on it very quickly by electronic or optical means." Although Cooke didn't state that the government used these techniques, the implication was clear. "Scanning devices," he stated with assurance, "are expected to have commercial applications at a later date" and "reportedly can select information" much faster "than other presently known devices." Reading between the lines, the paper's savvy readership would draw the right investment conclusion. When Itek was in a position to sell its classified technology to the public, shareholders would make a fortune. There was just one problem with this conclusion: it was based on information that was incomplete at best, and incorrect at worst. Itek's government sales consisted largely of spy satellite cameras. These instruments might broadly be called scanning devices, but they were hardly the information management tools described by Cooke.[18]

The Wall Street Journal wasn't the only publication entranced by Itek's story. Just days later a big photo of Richard Leghorn adorned the cover of *Business Week*. "Prodigy with a Flair for Profit," the title of the article proclaimed. The feature on Itek was the centerpiece of that issue of *Business Week,* and like its counterpart in *The Wall Street Journal,* it was a disturbing mix of fact and fiction. The article began innocently enough. It described a futuristic technology called "memex," which Vannevar

Bush had predicted would one day revolutionize information management. Bush was no crackpot. At the end of World War II he was director of the United States Office of Scientific Research and Development, and he wrote about his idea in 1945. Memex was a "wondrous device" that was "no bigger than a desk." It could store "books, pictures, maps, letters, and memoranda at the rate of thousands of pages a day for hundreds of years." While memex was wonderful in concept, it was little more than an idea.

The story of memex was *Business Week*'s way of introducing its readers to Itek. "Memex isn't available yet," the author of the article seriously intoned, "but a number of companies and research laboratories are working to make it a reality." One of these, the reporter wrote, was Itek. "It's uncanny how close what we're working on is to memex," Richard Leghorn told *Business Week*. Uncanny? Certainly Itek's original business plan focused on information management, but the company's resources were now being poured into spy satellite cameras and Photostat. As the consultants at Arthur D. Little had discovered just weeks earlier, little research was being carried out at Itek. Information management akin to memex was only a dream built on Kodak's old Minicard technology. And Art Tyler, inventor of the Minicard System, was on the verge of being fired. A small part of Itek's operations was still directed toward that original plan, but now it was inconsequential to the company's future—though that would be impossible to discern by reading the *Business Week* article.

Investors who read about Itek in *Business Week* would have been impressed not just with its technology but with the quality of its management team. "In its brief corporate career [Itek] has performed some feats almost as remarkable" as memex, the reporter proclaimed. Not only had Itek been profitable from its founding, according to the article, but it had successfully executed an acquisition strategy. "It acquired three outfits, all in the red, and not only meshed them together into a profitable whole, but put each one of them separately into the black." And that was just a start. "In doing these things, Itek has jumped in two years from nothing to a current sales volume at the rate of $30 million a year. Starting business with four second hand pieces of furniture and a telephone, it now employs nearly 700 people." *Business Week* concluded that "Itek has put together a whole that is greater than the sum of its parts" and as a result "turned red ink into black." A prospective Itek investor might reasonably conclude that only a talented management team could execute its business plan so swiftly and successfully. Then again, a prospective investor couldn't read Arthur Young's report, or Arthur D. Little's.

After describing Itek's information management aspirations and its recent operational successes, the *Business Week* reporter turned to the inevitable: the mystery that surrounded the company. "Itek's reticence about specific commercial work is nothing compared to its deathly silence in military matters." But Leghorn was willing to publicly discuss enough of the company's business to make sure that readers knew it was very important, and highly classified. "All Leghorn will say about Itek's defense business is that it is in these areas: Various intelligence systems including the handling of data, military reconnaissance, and satellite tracking." Leghorn may have been reticent, but *Business Week* — either on its own, or with inside help — reached a more precise conclusion. "The fact of the matter is, however, that Itek is hard at work in the R&D stages of a reconnaissance satellite."[19] If *Business Week* had any readers on Richard Bissell's staff, they couldn't have been pleased with this disclosure.

Days later, as Itek was bathing in the glow of its national media coverage, Albie Pratt sent his Paine, Webber colleagues a new update on the company. *The Wall Street Journal* and *Business Week* may have fallen in love with Itek, but Pratt was getting cold feet. Pratt had been photographed by *Business Week* as part of its story on the company, but his views on Itek diverged widely from what was published in the magazine. Pratt may have smiled for the camera, but he kept his mouth closed for the reporter.

Pratt's bulletin, sent to his colleagues on July 21, must have been disturbing reading to anyone who had bought shares in the company based on the recent articles. Pratt warned his colleagues that earnings would be weak due to a write-off of research expenses. Just a few months earlier, he had told his colleagues to expect fiscal 1959 earnings to be between fifty and seventy-five cents a share. Now he doubted that earnings would exceed fifty cents. Although the Photostat acquisition was going well, Pratt did not expect that company to make a meaningful contribution to Itek earnings until the introduction of new products the following year.

Investors could expect Itek to make at least one or two small acquisitions to strengthen the company's commercial lines of business. Pratt concluded on a positive note. "I remain a strong believer in a brite [*sic*] future for Itek," he said, but investors would have "to be patient" until these prospects were "reflected in earnings." Pratt may not have told his colleagues to sell, but seasoned investors must have realized that all the good press was an excellent opportunity to lighten up on their positions.[20]

And they did. Within days of Pratt's bulletin to his colleagues, Itek's stock had sold off sharply. It didn't take long before word of Pratt's bulletin reached Richard Leghorn, and he was furious. So was Harper Woodward. In a terse note to Randolph Marston, Woodward summarized the situation. "Itek['s] recent sell-off due to another recent letter sent by A. Pratt to all Paine Webber and other dealers using info gotten by him at last Itek Bd. Mtg. and without prior clearance with the company. Leghorn wants Pratt to resign from Itek Bd. and I feel he should do so. This is second time Pratt has done this. After first occasion, he agreed he would not repeat."[21]

Woodward's attitude was understandable but surprisingly naïve, given his long exposure to the harsh climate of investment banking. Pratt's lifeblood was making deals, and information—shared properly or inappropriately—greased the wheels of commerce. Expecting Pratt to honor his word, though admirably idealistic, was unrealistic. Although Pratt's future on Itek's board was jeopardized in the short term, he was to remain active in company affairs, immune to the controversy that swirled about him. In the crisis that occurred in less than two years, Pratt was to redeem himself and secure his spot for years to come.

Pratt's behavior wasn't the only personnel problem Itek faced that summer. Jesse Cousins, the company's treasurer, who believed that his laissez-faire attitude toward control fostered innovation, was on the verge of being dismissed. Richard Leghorn, in a charged memorandum to company directors Harper Woodward, Teddy Walkowicz, Elisha Walker, and James Hill, defended Cousins's performance and acknowledged his failings at the same time. Cousins, Leghorn explained, "has been relieved of all operating responsibilities for control functions, including the preparation of data on operations for Management and for the Board of Directors." Duncan Bruce, controller of Itek's Boston operations, would be given responsibility for corporate control functions. "In analyzing all of the criticisms which have been made to me, and in analyzing my own criticisms and enervating frustrations with [Cousins's] performance," Leghorn reflected, "I estimate that 80% relate to his inability and lack of interest in the control function."

Leghorn was not quite ready to bow to pressure from the board and fire Cousins. "In assessing whether or not other members of the Board have lost so much confidence in [Cousins] that the Corporation will suffer," he wrote, "I have, as you know, been unable to obtain any collective view, other than 'The decision is yours and we will back you.'" Having firmly established that he had the board's backing to make the final decision, Leghorn proceeded to dissect their complaints to arrive at the root cause of the problem. "Over the past several months," he observed, "individual comments, with one exception, have also indicated that the problem . . . is one of his operating performance (and therefore my problem) rather than a loss of confidence in his financial and business judgement." Leghorn, the squadron leader who had taken personal responsibility for the well-being of his men during war, was not about to leave Cousins wounded and exposed to enemy fire on the boardroom battlefield.

Leghorn's solution successfully addressed the board's chief criticisms of Cousins—namely, that his accounting skills were weak, and that as a result he was unable to fulfill the board's need for timely and accurate information. Leghorn's decision to assign Duncan Bruce the role of corporate controller satisfied that problem. "I do believe," Leghorn confidently stated, "I have now solved this operating problem. . . . I consider this matter settled." But this solution planted the seeds for a much greater crisis firmly in Itek's corporate structure. Leghorn gave Cousins a new set of responsibilities. Chief among these was as Leghorn's "principal aide in the investigation and negotiation of mergers, acquisitions and related operations."[22]

Leghorn was probably weary of restructuring. Dwelling on past mistakes, correcting errors, was the melancholy job of a corporate mechanic. Leghorn by nature was forward-looking and optimistic. In a July report to the board of directors he stated, "Although our organizational and control programs have not been completely put into effect, they have been sufficiently well thought-out and are sufficiently in motion to enable us to move ahead with confidence." Never mind that the Arthur D. Little report was just weeks old, and that the same accounting problems that Arthur Young found in winter had yet to be corrected by late spring. The future was what mattered to Leghorn, and bad memories could be dealt with. Buried deep in his memorandum, almost as a sidenote, was Leghorn's revelation that he had decided to replace Arthur Young as Itek's auditors with Arthur Anderson and Co. He offered no real explanation, and the board probably reasoned that one Arthur was as good as another one. Leghorn concluded on a positive note: "Our consolidation program is well into execution, and I believe we need have no undue apprehensions as we once again begin to step firmly forward."[23]

Looking for brighter tomorrows, Leghorn returned to the acquisition trail. His next target was Flofilm, a division of Diebold, Inc., which manufactured microfilm cameras, readers, and processors. Diebold, a respected manufacturer of bank safes, safe-deposit vaults, and steel file cabinets, acquired Flofilm in 1946. Leghorn's case for the acquisition was essentially the same rationale he used to sell his proposals to acquire Remington Rand, Photon, and Kalvar — namely, that Flofilm would have a strong strategic fit with Photostat, providing Itek with additional products to broaden its product lines.[24]

After all the memos and board meeting discussions, Flofilm was simply another acquisition idea that never got off the drawing board. Itek had little to show for all Leghorn's efforts. Yet the cost was incalculable. It was the price of an executive who refused to focus on the problems of the present, in search of an ever-better tomorrow. Perhaps Leghorn believed that the problems would take care of themselves, that his trusted subordinates would address them once pointed in the right direction. But managing a corporation, and the people who make it run, requires constant attention and focus. And Leghorn's focus was elsewhere. During the spring and summer of 1959 profit margins at Itek's Boston operations slipped, management problems remained incompletely resolved, and the pressure to develop commercial products to revive Photostat's aging product line was mounting.

In the months ahead, a great deal would depend on the man Leghorn chose to become Photostat's new president. The executive Leghorn hand-picked for this assignment was a World War II veteran, who like himself, had been a pilot. His business record seemed impeccable. A former president of Sun Tube Corporation, a division of Bristol-Myers, he had managed an operation with several manufacturing plants in the United States, Canada, and Mexico. And not only did Photostat's new president share Leghorn's optimism about the future, but he was a person who enjoyed his complete trust and backing. He was Kenneth Leghorn, Richard's older brother.[25]

10

"AN EXCUSE TO SELL"

In July, while Itek bathed in the glow of national press attention and Leghorn worked on plans for his next acquisition, the entire CORONA project team continued its effort to get a spy satellite into space. Meanwhile, unknown to any of them, Eisenhower's peace gambit began.

In summer 1959 the press was filled with stories about the "new" Eisenhower. The aging general, fully recovered from both a stroke and a heart attack, displayed renewed vigor and enthusiasm for his job. Ike was getting ready for one last battle, one final campaign. His objective — secure the peace. In secret he invited Nikita Khrushchev, leader of the Soviet Union, to visit the United States. Khrushchev, replying through secure channels, agreed.

On Wednesday, August 5, Eisenhower announced Khrushchev's visit. His plans for peace hit Wall Street like a bombshell. Startled investors rapidly concluded that peace was bad for business. Acting as if in unison, they called their brokers and told them to sell. Defense stocks were especially hard hit. The case for defense stocks, based on promising forecasts for rising earnings, was completely dependent on a lengthy Cold War. If President Eisenhower could achieve a breakthrough in his meetings with Khrushchev, the game would be over. Stocks dropped sharply that day — the steepest market decline in three weeks.

On Thursday the selling pressure intensified. Defense and electronics stocks again led the market's decline. Raytheon and Thiokol were both down more than two dollars a share. High-profile glamour stocks like

Litton Industries and Texas Instruments were hit even harder. In over-the-counter trading, the bid for Itek stock, which had been as high as $54 a share just two days earlier, closed Thursday's trading at $48. On Friday the selling continued, and the bid for Itek stock finished the day at $43 a share.[1]

The worst stock market decline in almost four years occurred on Monday, August 10. The Dow Jones Industrial Average fell by nearly fifteen points to 653.79, a drop of more than 2 percent. Volume was extremely heavy on the New York Stock Exchange as investors continued to view the prospect of peace as a reason to sell. Every industry group was down for the day, but electronics and defense stocks again dominated the action. Thiokol was the most active stock on the NYSE that day, closing with a loss of nearly 2 points. Over on the American Stock Exchange, the carnage was even worse: Fairchild Camera and Instrument plunged more than 24 points. Itek, in over-the-counter trading, finished the trading session unchanged from Friday's close. But Itek's comparative stability that day was deceiving. Since the Dow had begun its drop on August 4, it had fallen 24 points, or less than 4 percent. Itek, on the other hand, had plummeted 20 percent.[2]

The last time the stock market had experienced such a bad day was when news of Eisenhower's heart attack was announced to the world in 1955. Stock market analysts offered investors meager insight into the reasons behind the sell-off. Sidney Lurie, a partner of Josephthal and Co., observed that "on fundamentals, the market was vulnerable. . . . You needed something to tip over the scales and Khrushchev tipped the scales. I don't think it's major." Louis Stone, of Hayden, Stone and Co. explained, "The current weakness is an adjustment rather than a major reversal of the trend." An unidentified official at E. F. Hutton joined the parade of platitudes and simply stated that "Khrushchev's visit and the possibility of reductions in defense spending provided an excuse to sell." It seemed that Khrushchev's willingness to consider peace was more unsettling to American capitalism than his threats of war.[3]

On August 13 the world learned that the United States had successfully launched a Discoverer satellite. The two previous Discoverer capsules may have failed to attain orbit, but this launch was a winner. As Discoverer orbited Earth, trading on the New York Stock Exchange slowed dramatically. After all the uncertainty and volatility of the past weeks, the high-volume slump in the market finally appeared to be over.[4]

But was it? The market may have stabilized for the moment, but the fundamentals of the market, especially the outlook for future earnings in the defense and electronics sector, continued to deteriorate. Suddenly the Defense Department announced the cancelation of an experimental program for developing a new high-energy aircraft fuel. Then the Pentagon announced that it would save more than $200 million by cutting eight aircraft from its original purchase order for the new supersonic B-58 bomber. Wall Street was hit with additional bad news at the end of the week when Boeing, General Dynamics, and United Aircraft all reported disappointing earnings.[5] The defense and electronics sectors, which had driven the market's recent rally, looked as if they were beginning to sputter out.

Late Monday, August 17, stock market bears found new reasons to sell. United Fruit, a venerable blue-chip company—not to mention a beneficiary of the CIA-sponsored coup against Guatemalan president Jacobo Arbenz Guzmán in 1954—didn't pay its usual dividend. It was the first time in decades that the company had failed to make a dividend payment. On Tuesday morning the NYSE was hit with a flood of sell orders for United Fruit. By the end of the day, the stock was down 3 points to $29 a share; it was the most actively traded stock on the exchange. If misery loves company, United Fruit found plenty of comfort in the performance of the rest of the market. Of the 1,183 stocks that traded that day, 745 issues declined and the Dow finished the day with a loss of more than 1 percent to close at about 650.[6]

The news out of the Pentagon that week continued to hurt the market. Secretary of Defense McElroy made it clear that he was going to tighten the belt in defense spending and that there were no easy solutions. Ripe targets for spending cuts included the air force's B-70 supersonic bomber and the F-108 interceptor plane, both made by North American Aviation. The Nike-Zeus antimissile missile, the space-age weapon of choice for the army, was also a prime candidate. This was very bad news for the prime contractors on the program, Western Electric and Douglas Aircraft. So for the third consecutive week, stocks fell as the "disarmament scare" continued to unnerve investors and rattle the markets.[7]

As a new week began, Secretary of the Air Force James Douglas decided to throw investors a bone. Douglas announced that he might be able to protect all of the major air force aircraft and missile programs from further cutbacks in defense spending. He acknowledged that moving forward with the development of a variety of missiles, bombers, and fighters would be "hard to do," but Douglas appeared to feel up to the challenge. The stock market applauded his bravery with a rally, and on August 27 it surged to its highest level since the steep drop that occurred on August 10.[8]

While the Dow rose and fell that summer with the shifting prospects for war and peace, Richard Leghorn remained focused and unflappable. He continued to look for new ways to expand Itek's commercial business and to reduce its reliance on government contracts. Perhaps the market's volatility, the exaggerated swings in Itek's stock price — not to mention the effect of those swings on Leghorn's personal fortune — persuaded him of the desirability of a more diversified revenue base for the firm.

Itek stock, which in the summer and early fall was trading at an extremely high price-to-earnings ratio, appeared to discount an unusually favorable view regarding the firm's future earnings growth — despite the recent correction in the stock's price. In light of a possible slowdown in defense spending, investors might easily conclude that paying a premium for Itek's earnings, by assigning Itek a higher price-to-earnings ratio than the market's, was not sensible. If Itek's P/E simply fell to the level of the Dow Jones Industrial Average, the stock price would decline.

The only way Itek could avoid this fate, Leghorn probably reasoned, was to accelerate his acquisition campaign and demonstrate that investors were justified in placing such a high P/E on Itek stock. One internal planning document from the period clearly demonstrates that senior management believed that the firm's stock price was "vulnerable." As a result, Leghorn and his management team were under great pressure to take dramatic action to support the stock price. "There is a forward momentum in Itek as a 'growth situation' that derives in part from the fact that it is alert and on the move," according to the memorandum. "This is an intangible, not reflected in balance sheet figures, that is enhanced by logical acquisition. This is a good value that could be dissipated *if not used right now*." In other words, unless acquisitions were concluded in the immediate future, while Itek stock was high, the opportunity to take action might be lost.[9]

"Logical" acquisitions meant purchasing companies with strong current earnings and promising futures. After buying these companies, Itek's own earnings would be higher, and the P/E of the company, even if the stock price remained unchanged, would by definition be lower. A lower price-to-earnings ratio, especially one that came closer to a market P/E, would make the stock price less vulnerable to changes in investor sentiment.

In a presentation to Itek's board of directors, Leghorn identified four companies in the printing industry for possible acquisition. Leghorn wanted to acquire them simultaneously and consolidate them into one Itek printing division. The names of the companies and their products ranged from the mundane, Robertson Photo-Mechanix and Lanston Industries, to the futuristic sounding Photon and International Photon. But whether these companies made typecasting machines or photocomposition equipment, it was an inescapable fact that printing was a mature industry. By the late 1950s the printing industry was growing at a slower rate than the rest of the economy. The companies Leghorn wanted to acquire seemed unlikely to sustain Itek's image as a "growth situation."

Leghorn's plan had even bigger problems. Three of the four acquisition targets were losing money. And the only company making money, Robertson Photo-Mechanix, was clearly in decline. Company sales, which peaked in 1957 at $2.2 million, had fallen to an annual rate of $2 million by 1959. The decline in profits was even worse. Income before taxes, which peaked at $346,600 in 1957, had slumped to $261,400 in 1959. Yet Itek's internal research study on the company concluded, without any explanation, that it was "well run by an alert and aggressive management. The prospects for the continued growth in sales and earnings are good."

When Leghorn tried to sell this acquisition plan to the board, he made his case based on earnings estimates for these companies that showed all the firms making money in 1960. There was no indication how Itek would turn these companies around or how Itek would accomplish this financial wizardry at a time when its own internal controls had yet to be strengthened. Harper Woodward, looking after Laurance Rockefeller's investment, immediately recognized the weakness in Leghorn's proposal and put a halt to his buying spree. Writing his comments in the margins of an Itek memorandum entitled "Highlights of the Acquisition Program," Woodward was brutally candid. "These things need to be thoroughly examined and analyzed before they are presented to us," he told Leghorn. "This has only been partially done." In case Leghorn missed the point, Woodward wrote elsewhere in the margin that the plan was "not sound or thought through."[10]

At about the same time that Leghorn presented his new acquisition program to Itek's board, he accepted an important part-time position as an adviser to a new disarmament committee created by the U.S. Department of State. Appointed by Secretary of State Christian Herter, Leghorn was to serve as a technical adviser to the group. Informally called the Coolidge Committee after its chairman, Charles A. Coolidge, the panel was charged with designing a new disarmament strategy that could be used in talks with the Soviet Union in 1960. Leghorn was to identify the technical tools that could provide both parties with greater confidence in the inspection system needed to make disarmament and arms control effective.

On the same day that he was appointed to the committee, Leghorn informed his board of directors of the news. In a memorandum to the board Leghorn cheerfully observed, "You will be interested, and I trust delighted, to learn that of the seven responsibilities with which I am charged by Mr. Coolidge, the first priority item reads as follows: 'Find available full-time replacement.'"

But Leghorn enjoyed his recurring cameo appearances in Washington, and it is unlikely that he genuinely wanted to find his own replacement. He believed in his cause, trusted in his abilities to advance it, and understood that at the same time he could make connections that might advance his business interests. The same day that Leghorn wrote to his board, he also wrote a brief letter to James Killian, who had recently resigned his White House position as President Eisenhower's science adviser. Leghorn had offered him a position on Itek's board of directors and had just learned that Killian had declined the offer. "Although it will not be possible to enjoy the stimulation of working with you in the Itek context," he said, "I am looking forward with major anticipation to at least some working contacts in the Arms Control area."[11]

Laurance Rockefeller, who generally took a hands-off approach to his venture capital investments, was growing concerned. The same week that Leghorn wrote to his board of directors — the note having been signed for Leghorn by his secretary because he was away from the office traveling — Laurance Rockefeller encountered him by chance in Washington, D.C. Rockefeller, who believed strongly in civic duty, approved of Leghorn's activity. Yet he was apprehensive. He asked Leghorn to consider how the firm's board of directors could assist him over the next few months. Next Rockefeller called Harper Woodward and encouraged him to consider ways to support Leghorn. Woodward gingerly broached the subject of Leghorn's civic commitments in a letter. "Since we will be reviewing Itek's progress, plans and problems with Laurance and David this next Friday," he explained to Leghorn, "perhaps we can also review this question at an appropriate time during the day."[12]

Woodward was troubled by Leghorn's actions. He unloaded his concerns on Laurance Rockefeller in a memorandum that was unusual both in its length and in its anxious tone. "All of us are aware of the importance of people of experience and ability being made available for work such as that which Leghorn has undertaken for the Coolidge Committee," Woodward stated with earnestness. Woodward also acknowledged "both the basic importance to the nation of Leghorn's work on disarmament and the Itek-business implications of this work."

Despite the obvious case for supporting Leghorn, Woodward was worried. "The amount of time which the chief executive of a young and rapidly growing company can spend on assignments of this kind," he explained, "is a matter for the collective judgement of the chief executive and his Board of Directors." Leghorn's decision to accept the Coolidge Committee assignment had been made without consulting the company's board. As far as Woodward was concerned, Leghorn's decision should "have been discussed with all of his Directors before rather than after the fact."

That was just the tip of the iceberg. "Itek is a publicly owned company," Woodward bluntly reminded Rockefeller. "It is now a little more than two years and still, since early 1958 until the first part of this month, the Directors had been furnished very, very little reliable financial data." Woodward told Rockefeller that Itek's management control systems had yet to be put into effect, and as a result, the company had "very few of the management tools needed for the effective operation of a corporation."

In spite of these serious problems, Woodward had grudging admiration for what Leghorn had accomplished. But the growing risks, in Woodward's estimation, were beginning to endanger all that had been accomplished. "Leghorn and his associates appear to have done a marvelous job, so far, in bringing Itek from nothing to its present size and status," he admitted.

But Leghorn's acquisition strategy, Woodward cautioned, could prove to be Itek's undoing. "In looking ahead," Woodward warned Rockefeller, "Leghorn's attitude is that Itek must 'keep up its momentum' by further acquisitions and mergers. On the other hand," he explained, "Itek's Directors feel that Leghorn has a tendency to underestimate the seriousness of his internal problems and may inadvertently risk marring Itek's record and financial success." To make matters worse, "our apprehensions on this subject are reinforced each time there is a merger proposal, since the basic data furnished Directors . . . have rarely been adequate."

Now Woodward's ruminations on Itek darkened. "We have pressed the management to put their house in order; none of us really knew either where we were financially, where we had been, or where we were going." Woodward was trying to find a way out of Itek's financial quagmire.

"This situation is not in the best interest of Itek's shareholders," he declared, "particularly in cases such as your own, where you have indicated on several occasions an interest in disposing of a portion of your holdings." Woodward's next sentence was extremely unusual. In language plain and simple, he told his boss that selling his shares now was just not proper. It would be "virtually impossible," he explained, for Rockefeller to sell his Itek holdings "until the 'company house' is more in order."[13]

Woodward's choice of the phrase "virtually impossible" deserves closer inspection. Of course Rockefeller could sell his shares. There was an active market in Itek stock. So the reason for not selling had nothing to do with any genuine barriers to executing the trades. The reason, it seems, was Woodward's sense of responsibility to Itek's other shareholders and his belief that Rockefeller shared that concern. If Rockefeller began to sell his substantial holdings, not only would that put constant selling pressure on the market for Itek stock, but news of his disposition would raise concerns about the firm's future. At a time when the firm faced serious problems, this would be improper, not only because the firm needed Rockefeller's support, and the continued guidance of his staff, but for another reason unstated in Woodward's memorandum: fairness. All the press on Itek was extremely positive, and no one, including Woodward, had sought to correct that impression.

Woodward wasn't the only Itek board member writing letters and memos those last days of October 1959. Albie Pratt had all kinds of news to report; he shared some of it with Richard Leghorn, and the rest with his partners at Paine Webber and the syndicate of firms that had helped to underwrite Itek's recent stock offering. In his letter to Leghorn, Pratt told of a thirty-minute meeting he had had with Art Tyler, one of Itek's founders. It was Tyler, the former Kodak inventor, whose Minicard System was at the heart of Itek's original business plan. Tyler had just been fired, and he wanted an explanation. He told Pratt that he had done a good job and couldn't see how the board members could believe that they had reason to dismiss him. "I told him," Pratt related to Leghorn, "that . . . in any business concern every employee took the risk of being asked to leave if he didn't 'fit.'" Tyler, who had shared Leghorn's dream of leading a revolution in information management, was gone.[14]

Tyler's dismissal, just two years after the company's founding, was an important turning point. Investors still viewed Itek as an information management company, albeit one with significant classified sales to the U.S. government. When Itek was founded, the phrase "information management" had a clear and distinct meaning. But the phrase was getting stretched in ways that would make it unrecognizable to readers of Itek's original business plan.

In summer 1957, when Itek's business plan was written, the phrase didn't mean building cameras for spy satellites, selling photocopy machines, or manufacturing and distributing tools for the printing industry. It meant the integration of advanced photo-optics with state-of-the-art computer technology to create a system that extended the limited memory of computers reliant on punch cards. Now Photostat copiers, typesetting machines, and tools for the printing industry were all considered information management. The phrase had been extended to cover and rationalize ventures so far afield from its original meaning that it had lost any real meaning. The general public, which lacked any real information about Itek's classified business, still believed that it had to do with information management.

Albert Pratt's memorandum to his partners and to his fellow underwriters was extraordinarily upbeat. Written on the day after his meeting with Tyler, it is an unqualified endorsement of the company's prospects. Pratt, who cleared the memorandum with Jesse Cousins, told his colleagues to expect Itek to report earnings "somewhat better" than fifty cents a share for the 1959 fiscal year. When Itek reported its earnings at fifty-seven cents a share just weeks later, Pratt's reputation as a reliable source of company information was enhanced. He concluded, "Itek offers the best medium for investment in the field of information technology due to the company's excellent business management and unique combination of scientific talent."[15] Certainly Itek's scientists were gifted, but Pratt's public praise of Itek's management was questionable.

On October 30, 1959, Laurance and David Rockefeller decided to take a close look at their investment in Itek. Accompanied by Harper Woodward and Teddy Walkowicz, they spent the day on an inspection tour of Itek's operations. The genesis for the trip could be found in a July memorandum from Harper Woodward to both Rockefeller brothers. He suggested that a one-day field trip would give them "a first-hand impression of the company and its outlook — and people — which would be impossible to convey to you" through typical reports. Woodward pointed out that the value of their combined investment in the firm now exceeded $15 million, a fantastic return on their original stake. In the weeks since Woodward had made his original suggestion, his increasingly dark reports about Itek probably underscored in Laurance Rockefeller's mind the importance of making a personal visit.

Flying from La Guardia Airport in New York aboard Rockefeller's private plane, *The Wayfarer's Ketch,* Laurance and David Rockefeller traveled first to Rochester to visit Photostat's operations and then to Boston to inspect the core of Itek's classified business. Heading to Massachusetts, the Rockefeller brothers had a special guest on the plane with them. Dow Smith, head of Itek's optical research group, was on the plane to brief the brothers about the wonders of Itek's optical capabilities. After sitting at a small table with Laurance and David Rockefeller, Smith carefully placed a special mahogany box on it. He opened it and unveiled a hand-crafted jewel of glass, honed to space-age tolerances. It was one of the lens elements used to manufacture Itek's C Camera, the heart of Project CORONA. Although the word CORONA was never uttered in conversation, and spying from space was never discussed, Smith was certain that his hosts had been completely briefed about Itek's most important mission.

It seems likely that by this time at least Laurance Rockefeller had indeed been briefed. Richard Bissell, eager to ensure that Itek remained on secure financial footing, arranged a special briefing for Rockefeller at his offices at Rockefeller Center. Bissell wanted to accomplish more than to merely educate Rockefeller about espionage; he wanted Rockefeller's commitment to support the firm over the immediate future. Walter Levison, present at the meeting, watched as Bissell's representatives explained the basics of Project CORONA and Itek's role in the program. Rockefeller listened intently as the CIA officers noted that only the film returned to Earth; the camera, purchased by the CIA for about $500,000, remained in space, never to be used again. It seemed obvious to Levison that Rockefeller appreciated the significance of the program's structure. More missions meant more camera sales and bigger profits for Itek. By the end of the briefing Rockefeller happily announced that Itek would continue to have his financial backing. And over the years Rockefeller, as well as his brother David, would continue to receive briefings from the CIA.

Harper Woodward, whose views on Itek had turned gloomy in the fall, considered the Rockefeller brothers' Itek tour an unqualified success. In a note to David Rockefeller, he observed that the visit had "improved group morale by at least 50%!" Woodward displayed a wry humor that had been absent from his recent reports on the company. "You and Laurance were good to devote a long and strenuous day to our flying circus visits," he quipped. Woodward characterized Itek's executives as "a dynamic group of people moving at trans-sonic speed," but he quickly added they were flying with a "somewhat limited set of flight instruments in the cockpit." Although the language was buoyant, Woodward still delivered a message of concern: "Without dampening the dynamics, we have been trying to emphasize to management the need for orderly internal controls."[16]

Richard Leghorn also considered the day a success. In a letter of thanks to Laurance Rockefeller, in fact, Leghorn's enthusiasm was a bit overdone. He thought that it was "marvelous" that the Rockefeller brothers had been able to make the trip. The reaction from Itek's employees was "practically electric." Perhaps the hyperbole was an unconscious attempt to mask his disappointment. Laurance Rockefeller had at about the same time declined Leghorn's invitation to sit on Itek's board. "My continuing review of various commitments does not appear to result in eliminating very many of them," Rockefeller had explained, "and I must regretfully put off any further thought of joining you more actively in the near future."[17] Certainly, Rockefeller was a busy man with many demands on his time. But he also made his decision with full knowledge of the serious problems that existed at Itek and at a time when he was hoping to further reduce his exposure in the company. His decision may have had less to do with a hectic schedule than he was willing to admit.

Now that the Rockefeller brothers' visit was behind him, Leghorn returned to the acquisition trail. He demonstrated the same relentless zeal as before. Even though Itek's management controls had yet to be completely implemented, and the board had resisted his last proposals, he was ready to pursue his next target. The company was called Hermes Electronics.

Hermes, originally called Hycon Eastern, was a spinoff from Trevor Gardner's Hycon Corporation and a complete departure from Leghorn's attempt to acquire a strategic presence in the printing industry. Hermes was a space-age company whose future was intrinsically linked with the future of America's defense. From missile programs to radar to navigation equipment, Hermes proprietary crystal filters played an important role in sending and receiving the signals that made those systems work. Before Hermes' work in the field, crystal filters, exceedingly difficult to manufacture to the government's exacting standards, were unavailable in sufficient quantities or frequency ranges to meet the Pentagon's needs. Hermes, which sold 80 percent of its products to the government, had achieved a technical breakthrough that allowed it to meet the Pentagon's demand. As a result, it had become the market leader in the field.

Leghorn's interest in Hermes was no doubt its proprietary technology, but the company's Washington connections and its technical advisory committee could not have escaped his notice. Three Nobel Prize winners sat on its panel of scientific advisers, including I. I. Rabi of Columbia University and E. M. Purcell of Harvard. Jerome Wiesner, well connected in Washington policy circles and a friend of Leghorn's from their joint appearances at disarmament conferences like Pugwash, was both a scientific adviser to the company and a founder with a large stake in it. The Hermes management team included men who had served in key roles at MIT's Lincoln Laboratory and senior positions in the U.S. Air Force.

Hermes was impressive, and compared with many of Leghorn's acquisition targets, it had a far more credible future as a growth vehicle. Yet for all of Hermes' positive attributes, it remained a problematic acquisition target. Acquiring Hermes would increase Itek's dependence on government sales, not reduce it. The firm's technology seemed impressive, and its rapid conquest of market share was genuinely remarkable. Yet for a firm with these qualities, sales were stagnant and earnings remained elusive. Sales had declined from a high of $3 million for fiscal 1957 to $2.6 million in fiscal 1959.

On the earnings front, the news was better, but still not as impressive as the firm's reputation might suggest. After Hermes lost more than $500,000 in 1957, profitability had improved sharply. In both fiscal 1958 and 1959, the company earned slightly more than $70,000. Hermes could make a meaningful contribution to Itek's sales and earnings, and thus support Leghorn's goal of maintaining Itek's "growth story," only if its own sales and earnings turned up sharply in the next few years. Perhaps not surprisingly, that's exactly what Itek's internal financial projections for Hermes showed. According to Itek's projections, sales would more than double to $6 million in less than two years, while earnings would leap from $70,000 to $400,000 in the same period. If Hermes could achieve these results, it would make a genuine contribution to Itek's financial objectives.[18]

On December 7, the anniversary of the attack on Pearl Harbor, Itek was back in the news in a feature article filled with surprises. *Aviation Week,* which seemed to specialize in pulling the veil at least partially off secret government programs, published a lengthy article on a new breed of high-technology companies. "Some companies," the article reported, "are beginning to orient themselves toward defense business in the 1960's on the premise that a new kind of system built on gathering and processing of intelligence will be a major factor in maintaining national security." Itek was cited as one of the key pioneers in this field. So was Thompson Ramo Wooldridge. But what set Itek apart from the rest of the pack was Leghorn's spin on the company's mission. Leghorn, perhaps keeping in mind the stock market's reaction to Eisenhower's peace initiative, firmly declared that Itek would be a major beneficiary of better relations between the U.S. and the U.S.S.R. *Aviation Week* explained to its readers that Leghorn was a key member of the President's Joint Committee for Disarmament Study, headed by Charles Coolidge. It noted that Leghorn "feels his company will be on the right side of the curve if disarmament does come." In the article Leghorn observed that high-technology intelligence systems would be essential to maintaining the peace, providing both major powers with information on each other's military capabilities and deployment strategies. Leghorn was proud of how he positioned the company in the article. In a note attached to copies of the article that he sent to his directors, Leghorn explained that the piece was "very helpful in positioning Itek on the 'right' side of the disarmament issue." It must have been clear to Itek's directors that in the mind of the investment community Leghorn was a vocal advocate for peace, and in the public's mind, so was Itek.

Leghorn made an unusual confession in the article. The need to maintain Itek's image as a growth stock and address its high price-to-earnings ratio had been weighing on his mind in recent weeks. He shared his feelings with both the Boston Society of Security Analysts and with *Aviation Week*. Commenting on the meteoric rise of Itek's stock price in barely two years, his comments were honest and confused. "Let me say that we have been surprised, disturbed, proud, and concerned." He felt immense pressure to keep the company growing quickly, and the strain showed — to *Aviation Week* and to its readers, including anyone at the CIA who took notice of the article.[19]

Yet the company continued to attract favorable attention from the investment community. Although the veil on Itek's core business was less secure than before, few seemed to suspect yet that the company's entire future rested on whether the CIA's Richard Bissell could make the CORONA spy satellite program a success. Unless Bissell could pull off that feat, there would be no further orders of Itek spy cameras for the program, and the company's core business, its entire research and development effort, would be endangered.

On December 18 the Wall Street investment firm Carl M. Loeb, Rhoades and Company recommended that its clients add Itek stock to their portfolios. The company's analysts said that Itek, "although a young company, has become one of the nation's leading scientific and technological concerns working with newly developed concepts in the field of information technology." Information technology did not mean espionage; it meant "miniaturization, indexing and storing of documents by means which permit their rapid retrieval and easy presentation." The final recommendation of the report was an unqualified vote of confidence in Itek's future: "While Itek is very much in its infancy and its operations in information technology are still mainly in the research and development stages, the wide range of its research effort and the vast potential of the field make Itek an unusually interesting long term speculation."[20]

When Itek published its fiscal 1959 annual report just a few weeks later, investor confidence in the company seemed immensely justified. On the surface, the acquisition strategy appeared to be paying off. Revenues had leaped from about $3.5 million in 1958 to more than $25 million in 1959. Earnings, while growing at a slower rate from thirty cents a share to fifty-seven cents a share, were strong.[21] Investors probably reasoned that if Itek's heavy investment in research and development, which held back earnings in the present, paid off in the future, the company's stock would surely continue its upward climb. Yet investors who read Itek's 1959 annual report, whether they were partners of Wall Street firms or individual investors, would still have no way of knowing the full risks associated with buying the company's stock. They would fully appreciate those risks only much later.

11

"FRIENDLY IN THE EXTREME"

Nikita Khrushchev wanted to be good host. In the first weeks of 1960 he put the finishing touches on the agenda for Eisenhower's trip to the Soviet Union in June. Certainly, there was still the Paris summit in May to be successfully negotiated, but after his own triumphal trip to the United States in 1959, this probably seemed just a formality. In a January meeting with America's ambassador to Russia, Khrushchev said that Eisenhower was free to go "anyplace in the Soviet Union," even restricted areas. Ike's welcome would be "friendly in the extreme." Khrushchev would take Eisenhower and his family on a whirlwind tour of the country. Eisenhower would receive an honorary degree from Moscow University and even be allowed to address the Soviet people on radio and television. Hopes for peace were high—even in the Soviet Union.[1]

By the middle of January, Richard Leghorn had completed his own peace assignment with the Coolidge Committee and was back to work at Itek on a full-time basis. His absence had been noticed. Itek's directors felt that they had lost touch with developments at the company, and there was renewed pressure on Leghorn to focus on the operating issues that could make or break Itek.

Harper Woodward, speaking for the board, wanted an update on the implementation of improved financial and management controls. He demanded definitive information—not generalities—on the status of the firm's contracts by the next board meeting in February. Woodward was frustrated with management's inability to supply the board with timely information, financial, or otherwise. Itek's classified contracts no doubt contributed to the problem. Woodward didn't care. He wanted a "detailed report on *all* contracts," and he wanted the backlog "broken down by customers." Woodward predicted that the next year would be "of critical importance to the company," and he did not want to be blindsided because of lack of information.[2]

Leghorn began to collect information in preparation for his meeting and the news was not good. Ken Leghorn, president of Photostat, sent his brother a blunt critique of emerging problems at his division. Sales at Photostat, Itek's largest commercial operation and the biggest contributor to the firm's total revenues, were "considerably under forecast." Evidently branch managers had been overoptimistic in their projections, perhaps to impress their new president, and had relied on incomplete data to develop their budgets. The sales of Diebold products, a subsidiary recently purchased by Itek, were "running approximately 50% under forecast." Richard Leghorn may not have liked the message, but there was little he could do to the messenger.[3]

As Leghorn prepared for his board meeting, President Eisenhower's thoughts were increasingly occupied with his upcoming summit with Khrushchev in May. The president was deeply committed to achieving a breakthrough at the Paris meeting that would contribute to a genuine peace. A nuclear test ban treaty and real disarmament were now the goals of his last year in office. Yet just as peace seemed within Eisenhower's grasp, he found himself drawn by the inexorable pull of presidential politics into a spirited debate on the nation's defense policy. Eisenhower wanted to reduce world tensions, but politics was forcing him to declare that the nation was prepared for war.

Governor Nelson Rockefeller, challenging Richard Nixon for the presidential nomination in the Republican primaries, charged that Eisenhower's defense policy had compromised America's security. Rockefeller argued that the government should be spending more money on defense, and Pentagon potentates sanctimoniously agreed. Meanwhile, congressional Democrats were also pushing for a bigger defense budget. Democratic presidential hopefuls like John F. Kennedy and Stuart Symington were scoring debating points with the American people by accusing Eisenhower of endangering America's welfare with a weak defense policy.

They even charged that a missile gap existed — that the Soviet Union was better prepared for nuclear war than the United States. The balance of power, they argued, had shifted to Moscow.

Eisenhower had few defenders. The military wanted new weapons systems, the White House press corps hounded him with questions, and even many Republican leaders turned their back on him.

Yet Eisenhower stood up to the pressure. He was determined to fight any increase in defense expenditures that would saddle the economy with bigger government deficits. His confidence was in part the result of his conviction that America's security was more than the sum of its military weapons. He understood that a vibrant economy, unfettered by ballooning deficits, was perhaps the most important legacy he could leave behind — not a bevy of new weapon systems and a country mortgaged to the breaking point to pay for them. Eisenhower's confidence was also based in part on the U-2 program. He knew that the United States was militarily far superior to the Soviet Union, and that the unfavorable missile gap was a myth. But he could not share that information with the American people without revealing the existence of the U-2 program and America's ability to fly over the Soviet Union with impunity. Khrushchev was doubtless already embarrassed that his Kremlin colleagues knew that he was powerless to stop U-2 flights over Russia. If this weakness was brandished before the whole world, who knew what belligerent action Khrushchev might take to prove his strength? Eisenhower stayed the course, said nothing about the U-2, and bravely defended his policy. "I don't believe we should pay one cent for defense more than we have to," he declared. "Our defense is not only strong, it is awesome."[4]

The agenda for Itek's February board meeting was ambitious. Over the course of two days at Boston's Somerset Hotel, the board was to receive briefings on all the firm's major divisions, review a proposal to build both a major corporate headquarters and a research and development facility, and hear the latest news on Leghorn's acquisition program. Leghorn's printing industry targets were still on the agenda, but so now was Hermes.

Handwritten notes from the meeting reveal that Laurance Rockefeller's staff was disappointed in the presentation on Itek's own operations. In addition to the bad news at Photostat, it now appeared that Itek Boston would not make its sales targets for the year. It looked as if "Itek has been coasting," and more attention needed to be given to generating future sales. Earnings for the first quarter of fiscal 1960 originally had been forecast to be about $276,000 on sales of $8.7 million. Instead, the actual earnings were approximately $163,000 on $7.6 million in sales. The forecast for total 1960 earnings and sales were now revised down from about $1 million and $35.9 million, respectively, to $750,000 and $32.9 million. Implicit in this forecast was not only that sales volume would improve modestly over the rest of the year but that profitability would improve as well.[5]

Two days after Itek's board meeting concluded, Laurance Rockefeller appeared before the United States Senate. In 1958 Congress had created the Outdoor Recreation Resources Review Commission (ORRRC). Rockefeller, long an advocate of conservationism, was appointed as chairman. He was charged with developing a national blueprint that would guide America's park strategy to the bicentennial in 1976 and beyond.[6] Rockefeller's testimony before the Senate, essentially an update on his progress since appointment, was also a declaration of the personal values that guided him in his work. Although the senators in the audience no doubt assumed that Rockefeller was referring to his job as chairman of the commission, his statement could have applied equally to how he led his life, or directed his investment in Itek.

Rockefeller sought to "discover how both private and public interests can best work together" to accomplish his mission. Certainly these were soothing words to senators who may have been hopeful that a large Rockefeller check might underwrite some of the costs of his strategy. But Rockefeller had not traveled to Washington to dispense platitudes. He had a higher purpose. If the assembled senators did not consider a national parks and recreation strategy a pressing concern in an age of nuclear confrontation, Rockefeller's statement served notice that they were mistaken: "In this mechanized, depersonalized, and urbanized twentieth century, man cannot long afford to ignore or fail to experience the inner identity between himself and the world of nature." Laurance Rockefeller, venture capitalist, artificer of Eastern Airlines, McDonnell Douglas and Itek, declared that "technology has freed us from much physical effort, but nature has not." He explained: "Physical indolence may be as detrimental to our general well-being as mental sluggishness and spiritual indifference." His ideas were intellectually challenging, maybe in a way to which some senators were unaccustomed. But his message was clear—humankind's well-being was inextricably linked with a vital interaction with the physical world.[7] Promoting that activity through an energetic parks policy and protecting Americans' freedom to explore that world—by backing companies like Itek—were twin pillars of Rockefeller's mission.

Meanwhile, Leghorn's ambitions to expand Itek's presence in the printing industry began to fade. Instead, Hermes Electronics became the focus of his attention. Carl M. Loeb, Rhoades and Co., the same Wall Street firm that had turned bullish on Itek, was pounding the table for investors to buy Hermes while they still had the chance. George Edgar, director of research at Loeb, Rhoades, qualified his recommendation by noting that the high-risk profile of Hermes might make it "[un]suitable for average accounts." Nevertheless, Hermes, along with a few other "small specialties," were "potentially explosive." He meant that in a positive way. Edgar stated with enthusiasm that Hermes' technical staff included three Nobel Prize winners, who, based on the company's stock price of $10 a share, "can be bought for $3.33 a piece! For those who like low-priced speculations, this stock has real validity."

Harper Woodward, who maintained close ties with Loeb, Rhoades, was excited by the prospect of an Itek-Hermes merger. The day after the February board of directors meetings, Woodward accompanied an Itek negotiating team to meet with Hermes representatives. Among those joining him were Itek's treasurer, Jesse Cousins; the firm's controller, Duncan Bruce; and the general manager of Itek Boston, Jack Carter. Representing Hermes were its three top executives and Jerome Wiesner. The Hermes team forecast a glowing future for their company. Sales for Hermes crystal filters, used in "almost all missiles presently manufactured" and in "four out of five radars now being built," would continue to grow sharply from $730,000 in 1959 to $1.5 million in 1961. But the strongest growth engine for Hermes was its engineering division, which had sales of $1.4 million in 1959 but was projected to achieve $2.5 million by 1961. If these growth targets could be achieved, and if projected profit margins held firm, profits would surge from $66,000 in 1959 to $700,000 just two years later. After the financial briefing from the Hermes team, the Itek group was treated to a tour of the firm's facilities.[8]

Harper Woodward liked what he saw, and he wanted to keep the process moving forward. "Who has the ball on Hermes and where do we go from here?" he asked Jesse Cousins. Cousins and Leghorn picked up the ball at this point and continued negotiations. Hermes' president, Mac Hubbard, resisted the idea of a merger. He believed that Hermes "had a lot more velocity" and that his firm's sales and profits would grow at a faster rate than Itek's over the next several years. This potential, he believed, commanded a premium. As a result, Hubbard and the Hermes team would accept only a merger based on a stock swap of one share of Itek for every two shares of Hermes, even though the ratio was closer to five to one in trading on the open market. This was based on Itek's recent high of $45 per share and Hermes' high of slightly more than $9. The Itek team decided to hold out for a ratio closer to five to one, and talks soon broke down. Weisner and some of the other science advisers were more favorable to the merger, but the divide in Hermes ranks made closing a deal in the short term difficult. "Thus, as it now appears," Leghorn wrote to Woodward, "we had all the elements of a good merger except for that vital one—the stock ratio."[9] Woodward was disappointed, but at the same time he didn't believe in acquiring Hermes at all costs. Woodward was ready to move on. "I have reluctantly reached the conclusion," he told Leghorn, "that we should mark this merger possibility as a closed item and do nothing further about it."[10]

With the February board meeting out of the way and the Hermes merger stalled, Leghorn could again focus on what was closest to his heart—peace. He wrote to tell his directors that he would soon be leaving for the Soviet Union. "[The] Soviet Academy of Sciences has for the third time invited me to spend some time in Russia," he informed them. Leghorn, who had turned down the previous invitations, worried "that if I do not accept the invitation this time, it will not be extended a fourth time." It was "now or never" for Leghorn to make this kind of trip, and he decided to go, for two weeks, at the end of March.[11]

As Leghorn dealt with board meetings and prepared for his trip to Russia, Richard Bissell's team at the CIA prepared for a new round of CORONA launches. The program had been suspended since the failure of

Discoverer VIII in late 1959. It was a difficult time for Bissell. Evidence was mounting that the Russians had made "considerable improvements in their air defense system," and as a result "the possibility of losing a U-2" was growing. Pressure was building for Bissell and his team to get CORONA operational before a U-2 was finally shot down by the Russians. But technology could not be pushed. Finally, after several weeks of research, CORONA engineers believed that they solved the problems, and launches were ready to resume. Discoverer IX, armed with its covert CORONA payload, was scheduled to be launched on February 4. It was the first time that Itek's camera was loaded with Kodak's new "polyester-based film," and hopes must have been high for a successful mission. As the rocket lifted off the launch pad, the engines inexplicably shut down early. The rocket failed to achieve orbit, and the new system was never tested.

About two weeks later, on February 19, another CORONA mission was launched aboard Discover X. The rocket lifted off at 12:16 P.M., but it quickly became apparent that all was not well. The rocket began to wobble back and forth, and at an altitude of "several hundred feet" it "trembled" as it began to head toward populated areas. Less than a minute after the launch, the CORONA team was forced to send the destruct signal. The rocket exploded in a "huge orange fireball," and "chunks of steel the size of automobiles" fell to the ground. The men at the base scattered for safety as the wreckage rained down. People within the intelligence community and the executive branch began to have doubts whether CORONA would ever succeed. They began to talk about canceling the program. Bissell, the brains behind the Marshall Plan and mastermind of the U-2, used his influence and prestige to quell the talk of cancellation.[12]

In March the Soviets responded favorably to Eisenhower's nuclear test ban proposal. Khrushchev and his national security advisers were willing to accept all requirements for an agreement, as long as the United States froze certain underground nuclear tests. The Soviets were "making considerable concessions." It looked as though Eisenhower's hope for a lasting peace was within his grasp.[13]

Meanwhile, Leghorn departed for the Soviet Union. He was not the only American invited by the Soviets to tour their research facilities. Accompanying him was fellow scientist, champion of arms control, and entrepreneur Jerome Weisner. Leghorn spent a lot of time with Weisner that March, and their talks ranged from improving relations with the Russians to revisiting the price for Itek's acquisition of Hermes Electronics. Weisner, one of Hermes' founders and largest shareholders, had more than a passing interest in the subject. But Weisner was not softened by Leghorn's well-known charm or the camaraderie of their shared interests. Returning from the Soviet Union at the end of March, Leghorn gave Woodward an update on his discussions. "From my long talks with Jerry Wiesner during our trip to Russia, I don't think the Hermes deal is closed permanently," he said. "However, it is certainly out for the next few months, and whether or not it will ever become an opportunity again is something we'll just have to wait to see."[14]

While Leghorn waited, Bissell and the CORONA team were getting ready for another launch. As preparations were under way, Eisenhower summoned Bissell to the White House to discuss additional U-2 flights over Russia. The Pentagon and the CIA had been putting pressure on Eisenhower to give a green light to another series of flights. More information was needed on the state of the Soviets' missile program, and in the absence of CORONA, the U-2 was the only way to get it. Eisenhower was ambivalent, but he approved Bissell's request for a mission. Although photography from the early April flight showed that the Russians were moving fast to deploy intercontinental ballistic missiles near Plesetsk, about six hundred miles north of Moscow, it was difficult to draw any clear conclusions about the size of the Soviet missile force. The air force "still insisted that the Soviets had deployed as many as 100 missiles." The other armed services and the CIA disagreed. If Eisenhower was going to resist pressure for increased defense spending, it was essential that the myth of the missile gap be put completely to rest. And it was critical to examine the area around Plesetsk again. Time, however, was quickly slipping away. Unless photographs could be taken in the next several weeks, when the sun's angle in the northern latitudes was favorable for the mission, the flight would have to wait for nearly a year.[15]

As Eisenhower and Bissell considered whether or not to send one last U-2 mission over Russia before the summit, the countdown for the launch of Discoverer XI began. No doubt a great deal of nervousness prevailed in the moments immediately after the April 15 launch, but this time all went well and the capsule successfully reached orbit. Inside the capsule was Itek's C camera, loaded with sixteen pounds of film. Each time it traveled over the Soviet Union, the camera took pictures. It operated successfully throughout the flight. After the capsule's seventeenth orbit around Earth, the "reentry sequence began." As the satellite finished its final orbit and prepared for its descent to Earth, expectations at the CIA must have been high. Finally, after ten failures, Bissell and his team were on the verge of success. Perhaps another U-2 mission over Russia would be unnecessary after all. Then, when the ground control initiated the reentry sequence and the rockets fired, something went wrong. The spin rockets, designed to send the capsule back to Earth, misfired. Instead, the capsule was launched farther out into space. It was never recovered. The intelligence captured by Itek's camera was gone, and with it any possibility that another U-2 flight could be avoided. Bissell made preparations to send one last U-2 flight over the Soviet Union before Eisenhower's summit with Khrushchev, as the CORONA team fell into "despair."[16]

On May 1 Francis Gary Powers took off from Pakistan on the most ambitious mission in the history of the U-2 program. Until this time, no U-2 pilot had ever dared to fly more than midway across the Soviet Union. Powers's mission, given the code name Operation Grand Slam, was to fly from a base in Pakistan, across the Soviet Union, all the way to Norway. Along the way, Powers would photograph key military installations and gather intelligence that could verify the concerns raised by the early April mission. Powers never made it to Norway. Shot down during his mission, he was captured by the Soviets and quickly put on trial as a spy. Khrushchev scolded America for its "aggressive provocation" and the untimely "bandit flight." Although Khrushchev flew to Paris to meet with Eisenhower, the mood was dark, and he ultimately used Powers's flight to torpedo Eisenhower's peace agenda at the summit. An early opportunity for détente was lost. The summit died and "with it the best chance to slow the arms race of the sixties and seventies and eighties."[17]

Negotiations may have broken down in Paris, but suddenly the Hermes management team was willing to return to the bargaining table — two months after it had rejected Itek's first offer. This time Hermes was willing to virtually meet Itek's terms. Hermes' first-quarter earnings were weaker than expected, and as a result its executives "had shifted their view on a fair exchange ratio." Negotiations moved swiftly, and by May 12 Itek and Hermes announced that the companies had agreed in principle to merge. Less than a month later the boards of directors of both firms approved the transaction.[18]

Meanwhile, Bissell and the CORONA team were ready to try another launch. With Gary Powers a prisoner in the Soviet Union and the U-2 program grounded, CORONA was the United States' only hope to obtain intelligence on Soviet military capabilities. In the weeks since the failure of Discoverer XI, program engineers pored over data from the "limited amount of telemetry" from the flight. The data were inconclusive; it was impossible to determine with certainty the cause of the mission's failure. Finally, the decision was made to launch Discoverer XII in June. The mission would be a "heavily instrumented diagnostic flight" and would not carry a camera. If something went wrong with this flight, the instruments were ready to record in detail what happened. Launched on June 29, Discoverer XII failed to reach orbit because of a malfunction in the Agena upper-stage rocket. The instruments that had been set up to record any problems encountered during reentry never got a chance.[19]

CORONA may have stalled, but Itek's acquisition of Hermes moved swiftly forward. There was just one last obstacle to complete the Itek-Hermes merger: approval from Itek's shareholders. In late June an explanatory statement and proxy were sent to Itek's shareholders. The reasons for the merger given to shareholders were as compelling as they were vague: "Itek and Hermes, both research-based organizations, are concerned with the broad field of information technology." Itek's specialty was "optically oriented" and focused on the "design and development of systems and equipment for handling aerial reconnaissance." Hermes' strength was electronics, especially in "telecommunications, radio wave propagation," and "electronic and digital data devices." Concerned shareholders who couldn't quite figure out what Hermes actually did after reading those phrases were assured that the merger would create a company "unusually well adapted to designing today's complex information processing systems." That was good enough for the shareholders, and the merger was approved in July.[20]

Even before the Hermes acquisition was completed, Leghorn was focusing on his next acquisition targets. He was looking at Dalto Corporation, a money-losing manufacturer of flight simulators and color television projecters, and Seeburg Corporation, "the world's largest maker of coin-operated phonographs." It was hard to understand how Seeburg, whose sales had been in a slow decline since 1957, would enhance Itek's growth story, let alone its information-management capability, yet it was added to the acquisition list.[21]

By the middle of the summer, Leghorn's acquisition train had picked up new momentum. Dalto and Seeburg had yet to be acquired, but Leghorn was already moving ahead. Ditto, Inc., was his new prospect, and the reasoning behind the acquisition sounded a familiar refrain. Ditto, an old and trusted name in office products and copying materials, would benefit from Itek's research and development capabilities. New products developed for Ditto would help to revive sales, while Ditto would provide Itek with additional marketing capabilities. Redundancies between the Itek and Ditto organizations would be eliminated, and costs savings would flow to Itek's bottom line.[22]

Like the Hermes transaction, the Ditto acquisition broke down over price. Ditto management wanted more than Leghorn was willing to pay. So Leghorn moved on. Dictaphone was his next infatuation. It was a mature company, like Photostat, with a well-known brand name. Dictaphone had been one of the pioneers in voice recording, tracing its roots back to 1906, when the Columbia Graphaphone Manufacturing Company decided to copyright the name Dictaphone for its emerging dictation and office equipment business. By the end of 1959 company sales had grown to almost $39 million a year, and net income, at 4.6 percent of sales, was healthy. Sales had grown at a faster pace than the economy for nearly a decade, and, with a market share of about 50 percent, the future seemed bright for Dictaphone. IBM and foreign competitors were beginning to enter Dictaphone's markets, but surely Dictaphone would be able to fight them off. Or so Leghorn argued.[23]

Dictaphone's management team was elderly, and the company had no clear plan of succession. Surely, an attractive acquisition by Itek, paid for in company stock, would relieve them of the decision and enrich them at the same time. Leghorn probably thought that he was in a good position to strike a deal. But after extended talks with Leghorn, Dictaphone management just wasn't interested.[24]

Leghorn rarely asked Laurance Rockefeller for help, but he wanted Dictaphone badly enough to ask for it now. On August 1 Leghorn sent Teddy Walkowicz a short note. He wanted Laurance Rockefeller to have lunch with Dictaphone's management team. If Leghorn hadn't been able to persuade them of the wisdom of a merger, certainly a lunch with a Rockefeller would signal that they would be in good company at Itek. Leghorn was in a hurry and Rockefeller wouldn't be back in the office for another two days. "Could something be arranged with Laurance's secretary," Leghorn implored, "even prior to his return on August 3?" The answer was no.

If all good things come to those who wait, in Leghorn's case, they sometimes came to the impatient. On August 4, after Rockefeller returned to his office, he agreed to have lunch with Dictaphone's management team. Nothing would be left to chance. Rockefeller's secretary would make the seating arrangements and the place cards, and Walkowicz would review the seating arrangement. The lunch may have gone well, and all the guests were probably impressed with their host. But in the end Dictaphone's management team decided that they preferred regular currency, not Itek stock.[25]

Leghorn didn't give up on his acquisition strategy, and Bissell never stopped pushing the CORONA program forward. On August 10 Discoverer XIII was launched into orbit. Like its predecessor several weeks earlier, this launch contained no camera but was laden with instruments that could carefully monitor the performance of all essential systems. The only payload in the capsule was an American flag. Finally a mission was a success, and the flag returned to Earth, where it was presented to President Eisenhower. Now Bissell and his team confidently prepared to send a camera in space to spy on the Soviet Union.[26]

On August 18 the Soviet Union sentenced Gary Powers to ten years in prison for espionage. The same day Bissell's team launched Discoverer XIV into space. Hopes must have been high after the success achieved just days earlier. The rocket lifted off, the Agena separated from the Thor booster rocket carrying the capsule into orbit, and the capsule in turn circled Earth, taking photographs of the Soviet Union.

That day the CORONA capsule traveled seventeen times around Earth in a north-south polar orbit. During the first couple of orbits the capsule was off balance, but by the third orbit it had stabilized and was taking pictures over the Soviet Far East. With each orbit, the capsule moved westward, and by the last orbit it was taking pictures over Eastern Europe. Itek's C Camera had performed successfully, and all twenty pounds of film had been used during the voyage. Now the moment of truth arrived. The capsule's rockets successfully fired for reentry. After the release of its parachute, the capsule floated down toward Earth and was snatched from midair by a specially equipped air force plane. The film was developed at Kodak and the results rushed to the CIA's photointerpretation center (PIC) for analysis.

Art Lundahl, director of PIC, gathered his staff for a briefing about the wondrous accomplishment of Discoverer XIV. Many would learn about the CORONA program for the first time at this meeting. A great curtain opened over a map of the Soviet Union, and the audience broke out into a cheer as PIC staffers realized that something special had occurred. During the days of the U-2 program, they had become accustomed to such briefings. Then, when the curtain was drawn, they would generally see a single line representing the flight path of a U-2 flight. This time, the map was covered with lines, and the mood turned joyous as Lundahl explained the true purpose behind Discoverer XIV and CORONA. Itek's camera had taken pictures covering more than 1.6 million square miles, more area than all the previous U-2 missions combined. By the time Lundahl's team finished examining the photographs taken by Itek's C Camera, sixty-four new Soviet airfields and twenty-six new surface-to-air missile (SAM) sites had been found. The Cold War would never be the same. The U-2 had pierced the Iron Curtain; CORONA tore it to shreds. Now the U.S.S.R.'s ICBM sites could finally be located, and America would at last have the intelligence it needed. It was a grand accomplishment.[27]

Yet President Eisenhower, the man who initiated this revolution in intelligence collection, was soon pushing Itek to develop an even better camera system. Not long after the mission, Eisenhower sat through his own "private showing" of Itek's photography. Edwin Land, president of Polaroid and one of the president's key intelligence advisers, was at the meeting. He told Eisenhower that Itek could do even better. Walter Levison had briefed Land on a new design Itek was developing, and Land was sufficiently impressed to bring up the topic with the president. Land explained that Itek needed support from the highest levels in government. Fairchild Camera and Instrument, still hoping to push Itek out of the program, had convinced Lockheed that it finally had a winning design. Lockheed concluded that Itek's design was "too advanced to be reliable" and was leaning toward Fairchild's safer approach. Land told Eisenhower that Itek's design could lead to a "100 percent improvement in the quality of CORONA photography." Fairchild's design would yield only a 15 percent improvement. Eisenhower decided to take the chance on Itek and personally gave Land approval to authorize Itek to develop its design. Land traveled to Itek, Frank Madden and his team of scientists and engineers received the green light to begin work, and Itek's classified laboratories were busier than ever. The camera they began to build, called the C‴ (C triple prime), was indeed to prove to be another great leap forward. But first it had to be built.[28]

As Madden and his team moved forward, more CORONA launches occurred. But the follow-ups to the successful August mission were failures. A capsule was lost, a rocket fell into the Pacific, and broken film ruined an otherwise successful mission. America's vital window on Soviet military activity was again shuttered.

As engineers worked feverishly to fix these problems, John F. Kennedy and Richard Nixon fought each other for the presidency. Americans were increasingly concerned about national security issues. Fidel Castro's recent rise to power in Cuba, just ninety miles off the coast of Florida, meant that communism was taking root in America's own backyard. Kennedy exploited that concern and reprimanded Republicans for allowing "a communist menace" to flower "only eight minutes from Florida." Then, in broad attacks on Eisenhower's defense policy, Kennedy charged that the United States badly lagged behind the Soviet Union in missile production and that the missile gap was dangerously growing. He "warned that the risk of a Soviet surprise attack would grow as their missile lead increased" and called for an increase in U.S. ICBM production. Nixon charged Kennedy with trying to scare the American people. There was no missile gap, he argued, and there was no need for a huge defense buildup. Nixon, who had access to recent U-2 and CORONA intelligence, knew that Kennedy was wrong and that he was correct, but he was unable to divulge the source of his information, and his arguments failed to convince the American public. When election day arrived, Nixon lost by a narrow margin.[29]

Shortly after Thanksgiving, Richard Bissell flew to Palm Beach, along with Allen Dulles, to brief president-elect Kennedy on a secret plan to overthrow Castro. Bissell, now the CIA's deputy director of covert operations (in addition to his U-2 and CORONA responsibilities), was in charge of the plan. Meeting with Kennedy at his family's compound, Bissell outlined the operation with maps spread across a large table next to the family's swimming pool. Under Eisenhower's orders, Bissell had been actively working to overthrow Castro since the start of the year, but Cuba's Communist government was proving to be stronger than he had realized.

Initially, Bissell ordered commandos and guerrilla teams to infiltrate Cuba. Their objective was to create a broad organization "along the lines of the underground organizations of World War II." It didn't work. Castro's police state was already too powerful. The infiltrators were captured, the guerrilla organization was stillborn, and Castro's power grew.

Now Bissell's plan took on an entirely new character. It would be a military operation, allegedly financed and planned by Cuban refugees, but run entirely by Bissell. Kennedy "listened attentively" to Bissell but was "careful not to say much." Whatever Kennedy's true feelings about the operation, he kept them to himself that day.[30]

As Bissell's time was increasingly torn between the U-2 program, CORONA, and military plans to overthrow Castro, Richard Leghorn remained focused on his acquisition campaign. His next targets were Dialaphone, manufacturer of an automatic phone dialing machine, and Space Recovery Systems, a high technology parachute maker. Both companies were losing money, with few prospects of a turnaround. In an age when rotary phones were still the norm, dialing a phone could take a long time. Dialaphone offered business professionals, who used the phone often and called the same people frequently, a time-saving automated dialing device. But the product was expensive and took up desk space, and few people bought it. The Dialaphone acquisition died on the vine.[31]

As an acquisition target, Space Recovery Systems (SRS) wasn't any better. The company, based on the West Coast, was hard at work developing a complete product line of parachutes for bringing objects back from space. Leghorn believed that he had negotiated a great purchase price for the company. "We are only paying two dollars for all the stock (negotiated down from the $200,000 originally asked)," he proudly told Itek's directors. "We will have to put in $150,000 in working capital," he acknowledged, but this was a small price considering the company's sales potential of $1 million for 1961. Amazingly, the deal was approved by the board, and srs became part of Itek.[32]

Leghorn disclosed the acquisition with great fanfare on December 7. His announcement, filled with the usual hyperbole reserved for such occasions, contained a few other surprises. "SRS will add another dimension," he said, "to Itek's broad activities in building information handling systems for aero-space reconnaissance and exploration." Exploration? Although Itek had no space exploration contracts in 1960 — in fact, John Glenn had yet to orbit Earth — space exploration was a sexy realm that probably appealed to Leghorn's imagination and his desire to position Itek as a company on the cutting edge. Leghorn's next statement was not only unusual but potentially explosive. "SRS is joining Itek just at a time when techniques for the physical recovery of objects from space — which are concerned essentially with the recovery of the *information* they contain — are assuming new importance in America's space programs." Leghorn's choice of words, just months after the CORONA team had finally recovered a space capsule filled with photographs of the Soviet Union, seemed unnecessarily provocative.[33]

When Itek's William Sheppard was assigned the task of making sense of the srs acquisition, he shared his dismay and frustration with Teddy Walkowicz. "It turns out that I have the additional duty of helping to turn the srs sow's ear into a silk purse," he wrote. "The only serious problems they have," he wrote facetiously, "are concerned with sales, finances, public relations, personnel, and real estate."[34]

Now nearly all of Leghorn's management time must have been focused on acquisitions — identification of attractive companies, meetings with management teams, board presentations, negotiations. Leghorn wanted to maintain Itek's growth rate, and he wanted to keep the stock price high. It seemed that he was now so intent on growing Itek that he had lost sight of the fact that his scientists were working on one of the country's most important national security projects. That wasn't big enough for Leghorn's dreams; he wanted more.

Itek's classified business, its work on CORONA, had become a cash cow to Leghorn. It was a way to make enough money to finance further acquisitions, or to fund the development of commercial products, but little more. Itek's Information Technology Laboratories, which housed the firm's classified operations, produced more than a third of the firm's sales and accounted for more than half of Itek's income before taxes. Yet barely a quarter of Itek's research and development funds were allocated to the division. Instead, Itek was pouring money into commercial product developments that could be marketed through Photostat.[35]

Leghorn may have led the charge in these matters, but he was hardly alone. In 1959, when Leghorn reorganized Itek's management team, he institutionalized a culture of acquisition by giving Jesse Cousins a new job description that was essentially a mandate to shop. In the case of Ditto, Leghorn's initial meeting with its president, Scott Harrod, was arranged by Albie Pratt. Pratt, Itek's prodigal director and partner at Paine Webber, always stood ready to help the firm with the needed investment banking work to consummate a transaction. Harper Woodward, who most of the time played the role of the clear-eyed realist on the board, was a member of the Itek negotiating team for both the Hermes and Ditto transactions and actively supported his share of acquisitions — as did the other board members.[36] In fact, none of Leghorn's plans could be accomplished without board approval. So although the board may have put the brakes on Leghorn's plans from time to time, although it may have voted down the weakest acquisition prospects, it never told Leghorn to stop the campaign. As long as revenues, earnings, and the stock price kept rising, the strategy seemed to be paying off.

Toward the end of 1960 Harper Woodward wrote Leghorn to thank him and his staff for their fine presentations at the board of directors meeting held at the exclusive Wiano Club on Cape Cod. "As you know," he confessed with guilt, "we sometimes appear to be focusing all of our attention on the things that are wrong, without giving you the credit you deserve for the progress that is being made."[37]

Woodward's letter was kind, and graciousness was his hallmark. But at Itek's last board of directors meeting of the year, he received an update on the company's operations that must have been disturbing. The sales and earnings figures for October, the first month in Itek's fiscal 1961 year, had just been released. Not only were sales down by more than 10 percent compared with the previous year, but earnings for the company were barely 33 percent of the previous year's levels. Meanwhile, the development of one of Itek's most promising commercial products, a special thermographic paper for use in copying machines, was falling farther behind schedule. The company had made a significant investment in the paper, and now that sales and earnings had fallen below budget, a successful new product launch was more important than ever.

The last item discussed at the board meeting didn't appear on the original agenda. The subject was revolutionary, the commercialization of space. Only Harper Woodward's handwritten notes from this part of the meeting exist. Barely fifty words in length, and in a sometimes-cryptic bullet-point form, Woodward's notes are clear on two key points: the board had had an extended discussion about the commercial opportunities in space, and Itek was aiming for an early and significant piece of whatever market appeared.[38]

Yet seemingly oblivious to Leghorn's expansion plans or the board's fleeting dreams of profits from the commercialization of space, Frank Madden, the project manager for the C''', soldiered on, along with Dow Smith, Bill Britton, and the rest of Itek's anonymous team of scientists and engineers. For all of the space-age hype surrounding Itek's stock, Madden, Smith, Britton, and all the rest were in some ways more like artisans than computer-age whiz kids. And the C''' camera was an exacting taskmaster. The camera design — the one personally supported by President Eisenhower and Edwin Land — utilized a lens concept invented for portraiture by Josef Petzval in the nineteenth century. Long forgotten, the bulky Petzval lens had properties ideally suited to Itek's panoramic approach to space photography. But the large lens elements at the heart of the camera had to be crafted by hand and positioned by hand in the lens cell, which held the glass. All these tasks had to be accomplished within incredibly precise standards. Itek's artisans, ignoring Leghorn's acquisition campaign, overcame daunting technical challenges and kept their minds focused on one goal—making a better spy camera. They knew that if they did their jobs well, the president of the United States would have better intelligence about the Soviet threat, and the nation, and their families, would be safer.[39]

Meanwhile, Richard Leghorn was off to Moscow. It was another mission for peace, a Pugwash Conference just steps away from the Kremlin, to promote international understanding.

12

"THIS IS NO GROUP OF LONG-HAIRED SCIENTISTS"

The annual meeting of the National Federation of Science Abstracting Indexing Services was not the typical venue for an important speech. Nor was the location of its 1961 conference, Cleveland, usually associated with futuristic themes. Yet when Richard Leghorn rose to speak at the podium to deliver the keynote address, both unlikely scenarios materialized. Leghorn regaled his audience with tales of his trip to Moscow. He explained how freedom of information was linked with the future of disarmament. Then Leghorn turned to a new subject, the emerging information industry. Leghorn had written and spoken on this theme in the past. But this time he delivered a broad synthesis of his views and ideals that was sharper and more carefully reasoned than before.

"A new industry is taking form," Leghorn proclaimed, "whether we like it, or not — by the needs and creations of a scientifically oriented society." He spoke with confidence, like a voyager from the age of discovery. "We have discovered new techniques," he declared, "which I shall call the 'information technologies.'"

Leghorn's journey must have begun during World War II. While flying his daring reconnaissance missions, speeding through the sky at a rate and height unimaginable to his spiritual forebears, he must have realized that valuable information captured from high above, via aerial reconnaissance, could shape events on the battlefield below. For Leghorn it was the beginning of an idea. Information influenced how war was waged, and information could shape the peace.

That winter day in Cleveland, all of Leghorn's actions, his past, his present, his future—everything made sense. His feverish acquisition activities of the past two years, his unwavering commitment to disarmament, his confidence in what business and the free market system could accomplish fit together like the highly polished pieces of an exquisite mosaic. And his ideas gleamed.

Information technology was forcing a reorganization of publishing, data processing, communications, military and arms inspection intelligence, education, and entertainment into one cohesive information industry. "The gradually forming . . . information systems of our modern society are cutting across these older industrial subdivisions," Leghorn explained. "This new industry," he boldly predicted in 1961, "will become the largest in modern society."

Leghorn was predicting more than an industry of new scope and size. He envisioned a reordering of society, a reinvention of how people and organizations interacted, all as part of an information revolution. He dreamed of a new information industry "possessing a collective power to supply the maximum useful information . . . to the most people at the least cost." Leghorn, the reconnaissance pilot, had surveyed the industrial landscape in his high-velocity acquisition campaign. Now he shared his intelligence report with his audience. "Today's fragmented, duplicating, and gap-ridden network of organizations now concerned with acquiring, publishing, processing, storing, retrieving, exchanging, and transmitting information cannot escape unification," he warned. Yet unification was for a nobler goal than mere industrial efficiency. It was to better mankind, to make the world safer, and more productive, through shared information. Now Leghorn's acquisition strategy made complete sense. He would be the unifier. He would create order out of chaos.[1]

Less than a week after Leghorn's speech, Richard Bissell walked into the White House to brief President Kennedy on the CIA's plan to overthrow Castro. Plans had changed since Bissell had met with Kennedy at his family home in Palm Beach. There was no more talk about a guerrilla operation. Now Bissell recommended a World War II–style invasion.

The Cuban freedom fighters, financed secretly by the CIA, would storm the island in a combined amphibious and airborne attack. They would land near the city of Trinidad, not far from the Escambray Mountains on the southern coast of Cuba. If all went well, Bissell predicted, Castro's militia would be demoralized and defect in large numbers to join the invaders. Widespread rebellion would ensue, and Castro would be overthrown. If the invasion failed, the brigade could retreat to the mountains and continue the fight.

"Too noisy," said Kennedy. He wanted the invasion plans scaled back. No one could ever know that the United States was behind the plan. Kennedy told Bissell to rework the plan and devise a "less spectacular" alternative — in four days. Bissell presented the new plan on March 15. In this version the troops would land at a swampy, isolated area called the Bay of Pigs. Far from any major population centers, or even the Escambray Mountains, the Bay of Pigs seemed to meet Kennedy's requirement for a quieter invasion. The only "noisy" part that remained was the air strike against Castro's air force.[2]

On the morning of April 12 Pierre Salinger, Kennedy's press secretary, barged into the president's bedroom to report bad news. He handed Kennedy an Associated Press bulletin: "The Soviet Union announced today that it had won the race to put a man into space." It was true. At a time when Bissell's CORONA team was still confronted with periodic mission failures, the Soviet Union had launched the first man into orbit — cosmonaut Yuri Gagarin. Later that day, Kennedy held a press conference. The questions were tough. A reporter asked, "The communists seem to be putting us on the defensive on a number of fronts — now, again, in space. Wars aside, do you think that there is a danger that their system is going to prove more durable than ours?" Kennedy waxed philosophical on the comparative strengths of communist dictatorships and democracies. His answer, unsatisfying, left open a dire possibility. With Russia's victory in space, and communist forces on the offensive in Southeast Asia, the tide of history might be moving away from the United States.[3] The pressure for a U.S. success was greater than ever. Perhaps Bissell could achieve it at the Bay of Pigs.

Sunday night, April 16, was bad for Bissell. It was far worse for the members of the Cuban exile brigade, though they would not realize it until the next morning. That evening, with the invasion ships "within sight of the Cuban shore," President Kennedy canceled most of the air strikes that were supposed to destroy Castro's air force on the ground. Hours later, before dawn on April 17, the Cuban exiles hit the beaches at the Bay of Pigs. Their hopes must have been high. They had returned home to liberate their country from Castro's dictatorship. Castro quickly moved troops to the area, and the fighting became fierce. Success depended on the exiles' controlling the sky, but with the cancellation of the last air strike, Castro's air force had survived. Bombs and bullets rained down on the outnumbered exiles. In Washington, Bissell had few options to consider, none good.[4]

The same day that Bissell's brigade was hitting the beaches at the Bay of Pigs, Leghorn received bad news from his management team. Itek's earnings per share were likely to fall far short of targets for 1961. Leghorn's senior management team was worried. They knew that strong earnings growth was essential to maintaining the company's high stock price. If earnings growth slowed, or worse, fell from the previous year's levels, the stock price would surely fall.

The news must have been a serious personal blow to Leghorn. All of his hopes, his dreams for an information revolution, rested on Itek's ever-rising stock price. Without a rising stock price, he would never be able to pay for his acquisition campaign, he would never be able to cobble together his information empire. It had all been so certain just weeks before. Now his dream was less than a faint hope. As soon as news of Itek's earnings shortfall became public, the stock would plunge, and the dream would die.

Leghorn's senior managers met to discuss the earnings problem. The focus of their conversation was product development. They believed that if the company could introduce a series of innovative commercial products before year's end, the excitement generated by the news would offset the earnings disappointment. Hopes were placed on a quick introduction of Itek's thermographic paper, a wireless transmitter, and an electronic drafting machine that Itek would dub "digigraphics." At a time when earnings were already under pressure, the program to accelerate the development of these projects would cost the company more than $400,000. Leghorn's advisers hoped that new products would "renew the sparkle on the Itek image" and "give the shareholders . . . something in lieu of improved operating performance."[5] It was a questionable strategy.

On April 18 the news from Cuba was grim. That morning, Bissell sat in the White House situation room and briefed Kennedy on the "desperate news from the beaches." When Bissell returned to CIA headquarters, the mood was bleak. The Cuban exiles were "totally outnumbered and outgunned." That night, Bissell returned to the White House. He asserted that the invasion could still succeed, but only if U.S. jets were allowed to destroy Castro's planes, and if a nearby U.S. destroyer were permitted to open its guns on Castro's tanks. Kennedy said no. The invasion collapsed, the exiles were either captured or killed, and the communists achieved another victory.[6]

The stock market shrugged off the disaster at the Bay of Pigs. The Dow Jones Industrial Average finished the week off just 8 points to close at 685. Although investors took the news in stride, the editorial staff at *Barron's* did not. "In Cuba, a small band of gallant fighters was allowed to risk the prestige of the U.S. without being granted adequate material support," the magazine's H. J. Nelson proclaimed. *Barron's* coldly concluded that the "public should start reappraising the errors that have helped to jeopardize the U.S. position in the world."[7]

Later, Kennedy called Bissell into the Oval Office for the inevitable. Kennedy told Bissell that he would have to resign as the CIA's deputy director for plans. "If this were a parliamentary government," Kennedy wryly observed, "I would have to resign and you, a civil servant, would stay on. But being the system of government it is, a presidential government, you will have to resign."[8] Bissell lingered in office for months, wrapping up unfinished business. CORONA must have been high on his agenda.

On May 5 Itek's board of directors met at the Somerset Hotel in Boston. Richard Leghorn called the meeting to order at 9:45 A.M. Shortly after the meeting began he introduced the board to Franklin Lindsay, a partner with the consulting firm of McKinsey and Company.

Inviting Lindsay to the meeting had not been Leghorn's idea. Teddy Walkowicz, along with the other board members, had grown increasingly concerned about Leghorn. Since founding Itek, Leghorn had maintained a grueling schedule, and signs of fatigue were becoming evident. The board needed to shore up Itek's shaky management team fast, but few executives had the qualifications to handle the firm's unique operating situation. Lindsay, a former commando and CIA pioneer, not to mention a longtime associate of both Nelson and David Rockefeller, was the ideal choice.

When Walkowicz approached Lindsay about serving as a consultant, it was immediately apparent that the assignment would be difficult and important. The fact that the Rockefellers put a plane at his disposal so that he could commute to Lexington from his home in Princeton underscored their sense of urgency. But Lindsay's friendship with Walkowicz, especially their experience working together for Nelson Rockefeller during Open Skies, was critical to his understanding and to his decision to take the assignment. Lindsay was not yet cleared to know about CORONA. But thanks to the oblique shared vocabulary national security insiders use to communicate when clearances are inconvenient, Walkowicz was able to convey to Lindsay the importance of Itek's work. So Lindsay agreed to step into the breach, and the board quickly resolved to retain Lindsay "for an indefinite period" as a consultant to the board of directors. The meeting adjourned at 10:15 A.M. to reconvene forty-five minutes later at Itek's research facilities in Lexington.[9]

When the board gathered at Itek Laboratories, Leghorn was missing. In his absence, Albie Pratt acted as chairman of the meeting, and the board continued with the day's agenda. Then Harper Woodward interrupted the meeting to report "on information just received." Leghorn's doctor had decided that he required immediate hospitalization for treatment of a thyroid condition. Woodward next read a statement to the directors, dictated to him by Leghorn, "requesting appropriate action in his absence." After "extended discussion," the board passed two important resolutions. First, the board granted Leghorn "a leave of absence with pay" as Itek's president. Second, the board created an executive committee to act, in effect, as Itek's chief executive officer in Leghorn's absence. The committee, which was composed of Albie Pratt, Teddy Walkowicz, and Elisha Walker, was also empowered to exercise all of the board's powers when it wasn't in session. After the resolutions were passed, Itek's top executives, including Jesse Cousins and Jack Carter, along with the board's new consultant, Franklin Lindsay, were called into the meeting. They were briefed on Leghorn's illness and the actions taken by the board. The meeting was adjourned at 4:00 P.M.

It was a stunning turn of events. Leghorn, healthy, had attended and served as chairman of the first meeting at the Somerset Hotel. In the short interval between that meeting and the second one at Itek Laboratories, Leghorn's condition had so worsened that his doctor insisted he must be hospitalized. The documentary evidence suggests that the official record of the meeting was not complete, and that there was more ailing Leghorn than a thyroid condition. An earlier draft of the meeting's minutes demonstrates that when Richard Leghorn left the board meeting that morning, he was not alone. This draft, probably edited by Harper Woodward, contains important information not in the later draft. One particular sentence is worked over repeatedly. "Mr. Woodward reported," the draft states, "that Mr. Walkowicz had just telephoned to advise that Mr. Leghorn's doctor had decided that Mr. Leghorn should be hospitalized immediately for treatment of a thyroid condition." The draft contained another important piece of information. "Mr. Woodward further read to the directors a statement dictated to him by Walkowicz over the telephone at Mr. Leghorn's."[10] When Richard Leghorn left the meeting, Teddy Walkowicz must have accompanied him. But how could they have had time to leave the Somerset Hotel, see a doctor, and return to Leghorn's home, all in time to call Harper Woodward at the board meeting? Why, if Leghorn had to be hospitalized immediately, did he first go to his home? Why was the role of Teddy Walkowicz not mentioned in later drafts?

Memories and documents provide part of the answer, but it is an incomplete one at best. On May 1, four days before the board meeting, Jesse Cousins sent the board of directors a memorandum that sheds light on the events of May 5. "At the April 26 meeting of the Board," Cousins wrote, "management was asked to advise the board of any urgent problems requiring resolution by the Chief Executive, so that the Board could determine a course of action during his absence." The facts are inescapable. By May 5 the directors already knew Leghorn would be taking a leave of absence, they knew that it would be a long one, and they were prepared to take action. But what was wrong with Leghorn?[11]

The pressure on Leghorn was intense: building the company, participating in peace conferences overseas, advising the State Department, and keeping Itek's stock price rising. It was a difficult balancing act, and it must have been taking its toll. Now that Itek's business expansion was failing, the pressure must have grown immeasurably. A lesser man, one who had not been hardened by war or faced death in the skies over Europe, might never have been able to take the constant strain. Leghorn did. But the greatest pressure of all must have come from his personal life.

Cruel, devastating, and final. Leghorn's wife had fallen in love with another man. Not any man, but Jack Carter, Leghorn's friend and hand-picked second in command. It must have felt as though his entire life was slipping through his fingers like water, maybe tears. He was mentally exhausted and was hospitalized to regain his energy. The day Leghorn was taken to the hospital, Teddy Walkowicz was by his side.[12]

On May 9 Albie Pratt sent his colleagues at Paine Webber a report on Itek. He said that a board of directors meeting had just taken place at Itek Laboratories. "This is a most impressive place," he exclaimed, "crammed" with hundreds of "professional personnel, many of them working on the forefront of knowledge." But "over-all earnings from operations will be considerably less than forecast," he warned. He placed the blame on Photostat, where a delay in introducing new products was hurting sales. Never one to focus too long on the negative, Pratt quickly shifted gears. "I am impressed with the business talent of the organization. This is no group of long-haired scientists."

Coy and subtle, Pratt next delivered the most important news. His manner was casual and his goal must have been to avoid raising the concerns of the investment community. Itek's president, he explained, "has had to take a vacation due to illness which is expected to be of short duration." In case this worried the investment community, Pratt quickly offered words of reassurance. During Leghorn's absence, he explained, "the Executive Committee of the Board, of which I am Chairman, will keep in close contact with company affairs."[13] There was no mention of a thyroid condition or an emergency hospitalization, or any hint that Leghorn's absence was expected to be a long one.

Pratt quickly returned to the subject of Itek's earnings. His words were artfully chosen. "The company's internal growth prospects are so promising that I do not feel the company is dependent on acquisitions for increased earnings over the years ahead," he deftly declared. "I still hold to the view that Itek stock should appear in the portfolio of the sophisticated long-term investor who desires to participate in the fantastic future of information technology." But in view of the company's "very high" price-to-earnings ratio, Pratt recommended that investors buy the stock only on weakness. Investors who were smart enough to buy on dips and brave enough not to be "concerned with daily market fluctuations" stood to be rewarded: "Itek's tremendous potential" made the stock an essential long-term buy. If Pratt's colleagues and friends in the investment community took him at his word, he had just created a floor for Itek's stock price. With luck, the professional investment community would follow his advice.[14]

But it didn't. Itek's stock peaked at more than $60 a share in the first week of May—just days before Leghorn went to the hospital. By the third week of May, Itek's stock had fallen below $50 a share. During the same period the Dow Jones Industrial Average was rising.[15] Why was Itek underperforming the broader market? Had word leaked that the company was in trouble?

On May 18 Itek's executive committee, chaired by Albie Pratt, held its first meeting. It now appeared that the company was facing a potential cash squeeze. Receivables—payments owed to the company by its customers—were extremely high. An apparent disagreement with the government regarding overhead costs that could be charged against government contracts was holding up payment of $250,000. Big cost overruns on the firm's largest contracts meant additional trouble. Yet the national security importance of Itek's work was so important that management was committed to proceeding, regardless of costs or lack of payment from the government. If Itek failed to deliver new cameras to Bissell's team at the CIA, President Kennedy's best source of intelligence about the Soviet Union would be interrupted, and America's national security would be endangered. In the aftermath of the failed Bay of Pigs invasion, international tensions were high and the Soviet Union might strike anywhere. The executive committee directed Jesse Cousins, as company treasurer, to negotiate an unsecured bank loan and to consider this his number one priority. If Itek needed more credit to meet its obligations to the nation, then the company would simply have to find a way to get it.[16]

On May 24 Itek's controller, Duncan Bruce, presented the board of directors with a sobering assessment of the firm's performance for the fiscal year to date. Earnings per share for 1961, before special items, had originally been forecast at $1.27. Now, with five months remaining in Itek's fiscal year, the revised forecast was eighty-four cents per share. And even that figure, which would represent a negligible increase of three cents a share over earnings in 1960, could be attained only if sales and operating profit performance for the rest of the year could be significantly improved. Bruce cautioned the board that this wouldn't be easy.[17]

The best news Bruce reported was that Itek Laboratories, the home of the firm's classified business, was performing reasonably well despite the short-term challenges created by the cash squeeze. Sales were increasing steadily and the backlog was slowly building. The rest of Itek was performing either poorly or worse. The new special equipment division, part of the old Hermes operation, was struggling to break even. Space Recovery Systems (SRS), which Leghorn had proudly purchased for a song, had already lost $80,000 on sales of $80,000. Spending two dollars for every dollar of sales was no way to run a business, but the people at SRS were trying. Itek Electro-Products, another division with links to the Hermes acquisition, forecast a 50 percent sales drop for the latter half of 1961. Yet at the same time, the division predicted a surge in profitability. In order to contribute its fair share to the second-half turnaround, Photostat would have to increase operating margins from 35.1 percent to 38.1 percent, and increase sales from $7.8 million for the first half of the year to $8.25 million in the second half. Considering that Photostat's sales were collapsing in the first months of the year, an increase in sales was a tall order. Bruce didn't assign probabilities to these outcomes; he merely reported the estimates. When Bruce presented his report to the board on May 25, he pointed out that the forecasts for the remainder of the year could not be determined "with any degree of certainty until after the end of the year." It should have been clear to anyone, either reading Bruce's memo, or listening to his presentation, that reaching the revised earnings-per-share goal of eighty-four cents was a long shot.[18]

On June 1 Itek's executive committee met at the Ritz-Carlton Hotel in Boston. In addition to Albie Pratt, who presided over the meeting and kept the official minutes, attending were his fellow committee members

Teddy Walkowicz and Elisha Walker, who had flown up from New York for the occasion. That evening they asked one other person to join them: Frank Lindsay.

At this point, Lindsay had been a consultant to Itek's board for less than four weeks. Yet that evening Itek's executive committee offered him a permanent position with the company. They wanted Lindsay to join the firm immediately as executive vice president and to assume the duties of the chief executive officer during Leghorn's absence. Leghorn had been notified that the committee was considering this step, and he called Pratt that morning to "express his reservations." Lindsay was uncomfortable with the offer and was reluctant to accept the position. But Pratt and the rest of the committee felt that "it was vital to the success of the corporation to have a single executive head without further delay." That night, Frank Lindsay became Itek's acting CEO. That same evening, Richard Leghorn's father, George, suffered a heart attack.

The next day, when the committee reconvened, Pratt and the other members "registered their deep personal shock" and expressed their "sympathy" for Richard Leghorn and his family. That day Pratt made an important, though largely symbolic, decision. Although the members of the executive committee were devoting time to the company far beyond the time required of a director, Pratt stated for the record that no members should be compensated for their work. The crisis facing the company was too serious, the national consequences too severe.[19]

13

"THEN, MR. CHAIRMAN, THERE WILL BE WAR"

On the morning of June 4, 1961, John F. Kennedy arrived at the Soviet Embassy in Vienna for the second day of his summit meeting with Nikita Khrushchev. It started amiably enough. There was small talk about Khrushchev's hometown, a little barbed banter about Laos. But the discussion quickly turned to a matter of lethal seriousness — Berlin. Since the end of World War II, Germany had been divided between East Germany, controlled by the Soviet Union, and a free West Germany. Buried deep in the Communist East Germany, like an outpost of freedom, stood lonely West Berlin. Khrushchev threatened to cut off NATO's access to the city. Kennedy said that such a restriction would be unacceptable. "If the U.S. wants to start a war over Germany let it be so," Khrushchev responded. Later that day, Khrushchev made it clear that he intended to take action by the end of the year that would deny America's access rights to Berlin. "Then, Mr. Chairman," Kennedy sternly declared, "there will be war."[1]

In a world at the brink of conflict, Frank Lindsay settled in to his new job at Itek. It was clear that America's need for intelligence about the Soviet Union was greater than ever. Itek had to survive, its staff had to be held together, and it had to keep designing and producing spy cameras to keep tabs on the Soviets.

Over the next few weeks Lindsay was a busy man. When he had jumped out of an airplane over Yugoslavia almost twenty years earlier, he had thought "You damn fool, what have you gone and done now?" The thought probably crossed his mind again. Fortunately, his experience with McKinsey gave him the tools and perspective to sort out the situation. He held meetings with the senior management and key scientists. He studied the company's organizational structure and looked for better ways to manage the company and to cut costs.[2]

Lindsay was gearing up for an extended stay at Itek. When he was hired, it was expected that Leghorn would be out of the office for months as he regained the strength and mental energy necessary to return to work. But Leghorn's recovery was swifter than expected, and his desire to return to work in late July, while understandable, was nevertheless a surprise. As Lindsay and Itek's executive committee considered how to prepare for Leghorn's return, they were probably eager to avoid any incidents that would weaken the company further. Yet at the same time management was preoccupied with these concerns, Itek's shareholders received a letter on the company's progress that was remarkably free of discouraging news. Shareholders learned that the firm's technical teams had successfully relocated to Itek's new complex in Lexington, that Frank Lindsay had been appointed as executive vice president, and that the firm's "growth prospects were excellent." They also learned that any weakness in earnings that might occur due to the costs of relocation and product development would "be more than offset by non-recurring capital gains" from the sale of the firm's investments. In short, everything was going well.

The letter was signed by Richard Leghorn. There was no discussion of Leghorn's illness or the fact that he was on a leave of absence. Leghorn merely explained that Lindsay had been a principal at McKinsey and Company. Shareholders could never be told that among Lindsay's chief qualifications for the job were his distinguished career in espionage and his strong relationships with the Rockefeller family. In fact, there was no mention that Lindsay was now serving as the firm's acting chief executive officer, or that an executive committee of the board had been overseeing the firm's operations.[3]

On July 21 Albie Pratt wrote to Leghorn and outlined the key issues that the executive committee wanted to discuss with him before he reassumed his duties as Itek's president. Although Pratt cautioned that his list was in no particular order, the first item on the agenda was Leghorn's outside activities. Other items on the agenda included Leghorn's relations with "certain other key executives," future acquisition policy, company objectives, and planning and control. Less than a week later, the board of directors, including George Kistiakowsky, met at Leghorn's summer residence in Osterville, a plush town on Cape Cod. Itek's board voted to terminate Leghorn's leave of absence, and he resumed his full duties as Itek's chief executive officer. After the vote Pratt turned the meeting over to Leghorn. He expressed his "personal gratitude" to the board for "their support and for their continued confidence in him." According to the minutes of the meeting, Lindsay was a bystander. He must have wondered how Leghorn would feel about his new executive vice president.

That day, George Kistiakowsky, President Eisenhower's former science adviser, offered Lindsay a piece of practical advice. During a private moment, he told Lindsay that Itek was finished, there was no hope the company could be saved. The best thing Lindsay could do would be to move on with his life. Lindsay was discouraged, but giving up was not his style.[4]

Leghorn, fully rested, his mind clear, realized the enormity of the task ahead of him. The company was in disarray. The 1961 fiscal year was rapidly coming to a close, and in all likelihood it would not be a good year. Itek's accounting systems, which had never received proper attention in the past, provided inadequate information about how the second half of the year was materializing. If only the company could meet Bruce's projection of eighty-four cents earnings per share. But preliminary July operating results for the company suggested that even this target could not be met.

In the meantime, Leghorn had to begin planning for the new year in the absence of solid information about the company's performance. Leghorn, whose personal philosophy was built on the promise of an information revolution, had spent so much time promoting these ideas to the outside world that he had never advanced them adequately at Itek. Without good accounting and control systems, Leghorn and the Itek management team were flying blind.[5]

Leghorn outlined his plan for 1962 in a one-page executive summary and presented it to the board at its late August meeting. His goal for Itek was a simple one. In 1962 the company would strive to achieve $50 million in sales and earnings per share of $1.25. "To accomplish this," Leghorn explained, "we are initiating programs of overhead cost reduction and tightened management and budgetary controls." Yet there was no explanation about how costs would be reduced, or what devices would be used to improve the company's controls. Nor was there any serious explanation about how sales would be increased from May's 1961 forecast of about $41 million to $50 million in 1962. The only tangible device Leghorn proposed was to resume the firm's acquisition campaign. His goal was to identify and purchase one or two companies that "would bring an improvement in [Itek's] earnings per share, plus marketing or product strengths in areas consistent with our long-range goals." But Itek's stock, which had peaked at more than $60 a share back in May, had fallen to barely $30. And there was no sign that the stock was about to stop falling. It seemed unlikely that Leghorn would be able to return to the acquisition trail in the immediate future.

Leghorn had one specific idea in his report that could readily be put into action. He wanted to create "a small, well staffed planning" group reporting directly to Frank Lindsay. Leghorn seemed poised to push Lindsay aside to a position with no operating authority and thereby remove him as a threat to his position.[6]

On August 30, the day after Itek's board meeting, the first C''' Camera was launched into space. It was a great victory for Walter Levison, Frank Madden, Dow Smith, and the rest of the technical team at Itek. When Edwin Land persuaded President Eisenhower to back Itek's complex design, he told the president that Itek's team could deliver a 100 percent improvement in camera performance. And Itek delivered on that commitment. The pictures were clear, the detail was fine, and the quality of America's intelligence was greatly improved.[7]

As Leghorn worked to shore up his position at Itek, and searched for ways to support the company's stock price, Richard Bissell worked to tie up loose ends before his departure from the CIA. It had been almost five months since the Bay of Pigs. Kennedy had never given Bissell a formal date to leave government. He probably counted on Bissell's discretion to handle the matter in a sensible fashion, one that assured an orderly transfer of Bissell's responsibilities. So Bissell moved forward. He continued to direct the CIA's anti-Castro activities and sit in on White House strategy sessions on Vietnam. But he also thought about the future.

Bissell began to plan for the day when he would no longer be around to guide the nation's overhead reconnaissance programs, especially CORONA. By early September, Bissell had put the finishing touches on a draft agreement between the Department of Defense and the CIA. It was a collaborative effort between himself and Joseph Charyk, undersecretary of the air force.

Over the years, Bissell and Charyk had developed a genuine partnership. Bissell leaned on Charyk's management abilities, while continuing to guide technical developments and handle contractor relations. Meanwhile, Charyk effectively marshaled Pentagon resources to support Bissell. They trusted each other and worked as a team. The agreement they drafted, signed on September 6 by CIA Deputy Director C. P. Cabell and Deputy Secretary of Defense Roswell Gilpatric, sought to codify their relationship so that the nation's reconnaissance programs could continue to smoothly operate after one or both were gone.

It was a historic turning point. The agreement Bissell and Charyk wrote created a new organization called the National Reconnaissance Office (NRO), which would manage all of the nation's reconnaissance programs, from the U-2 to CORONA. Because Bissell and Charyk sought to institutionalize their relationship, they specified that the NRO would be jointly managed by the undersecretary of the air force and the CIA's deputy director of plans. A small staff of CIA and Pentagon officers would be assigned to it. Although some might have been surprised by the lack of a single executive charged with running the NRO, anyone who knew how Bissell and Charyk operated would have understood the unique structure. And until Bissell's final departure from government months later, it worked. After that it would be a different story.[8]

By late September, Leghorn's goal for 1962 was already looking doubtful. Duncan Bruce, working with Itek's division managers, had developed his own forecast for the coming year. Although sales were forecast to meet Leghorn's target of $50 million, earnings per share were projected to reach a meager seventy cents. Itek Laboratories was projected to provide more than 50 percent of 1962 earnings per share. Almost all of this was related to Project CORONA. Itek's other divisions would have to turn in a stunning performance to generate the rest of the earnings forecast. "Even this reduced profit level," Bruce explained, was "dependent on the accomplishment of a number of ambitious programs at the divisional level." Photostat, for example, would have to turn back the Xerox marketing onslaught and achieve a 120 percent increase in copier sales, a 70 percent increase in offset printing sales, and a 60 percent increase in microfilm sales. If none of these gains was achieved, Bruce warned, "Photostat will be in the red."

Leghorn refused to accept Bruce's 1962 forecast. In a memorandum to the board of directors, he argued that his earnings forecast of $1.25 per share was still obtainable. He attached a copy of Bruce's forecast but dismissed it. The difference between what he called Bruce's seventy-cent program and his own $1.25 program was that his plan called for "much more selective projects designed to build for the future" and concentrated "more on immediate profits and near term products." Again, there was no discussion about how Leghorn's plan would be achieved, or why he believed he was better able than his division managers to forecast future earnings, especially after a nearly three-month leave of absence.[9]

Earnings per share had become Leghorn's mantra. It was his reason for being. If he could achieve his stated 1962 target of $1.25, Itek would be back on track as a growth company. The company's price-to-earnings ratio would expand, thanks to the premium the market places on growth, and the stock price would probably soar. Leghorn could return to the acquisition trail, and his dream of leading the information revolution would again be possible.

In late September, Duncan Bruce had more bad news for Leghorn and Itek's board of directors. It now appeared that Itek would completely miss even its revised earnings forecast for 1961. In late May, Itek's 1961 earnings per share forecast had been revised down to eighty-four cents from an original target of $1.27. Now, just days before the end of Itek's fiscal year, Bruce reported that the company would actually end fiscal 1961 in the red. The news must have been a shock. A company that seemed to be operating profitably just weeks earlier had actually been losing money all year long. And nobody had known it. The company would lose money largely due to write-offs related to the Hermes acquisition.[10]

Leghorn's acquisition spree, the foundation of his future information empire, was coming back to haunt him. His goal for 1962 now seemed all but impossible.

The financial storm that now threatened to engulf Itek had been brewing for months. Failing accounting systems, falling profit margins, and projected sales that never materialized were warning signs that deeper problems existed at the company. The gathering clouds, the growing winds had been ignored. Now the storm was hitting in full force, and Itek's executives were caught completely unprepared.

That dark September, as Itek's management team faced its moment of greatest peril, President Kennedy and his top advisers first learned about the CIA's new estimates of Soviet military strength. Kennedy had campaigned for president on a promise to close the missile gap between the United States and the Soviet Union. The CIA now confronted him with information conclusively proving that no gap had ever existed. The source was CORONA. Pictures taken by Itek's spy cameras revealed that the Soviet Union, "far from having scores of ICBMs," had six or so. The United States had nearly two hundred. The only missile gap that existed "ran very much in America's favor." Armed with better information, Kennedy was able to act with greater confidence, secure in the knowledge that he faced a weaker opponent. He began to push for a nuclear test ban and renewed his commitment to a free West Berlin. It was a moment of great triumph for America's intelligence establishment and for American technology.[11] Yet the company whose cameras made it all possible was floundering.

If Frank Lindsay was in any way discouraged by the gloomy outlook for his new employer, he kept those thoughts largely to himself. In late September, Laurance and Nelson Rockefeller sent Lindsay a present. Since 1957, when the Rockefeller Special Studies Project released its first report on national security issues, other reports on important topics had followed. Now an entire book was published, containing every report released over the years, and Nelson and Laurance sent a leather-bound copy of it to Lindsay. The inscription, signed by both brothers, read, "With grateful appreciation for your contribution toward initiating these studies and enabling us to bring them to a successful conclusion."

Lindsay's thank-you note to Laurance Rockefeller probably reflected both Lindsay's uncertainty about his future at Itek and his own evolving thoughts on the relation between business and national security. Lindsay wrote that his first reaction to receiving the book was that his "present assignment" at "Itek is far removed from the types of problems dealt with in these reports." Lindsay's choice of the word *assignment* suggested that despite his recent transition from consultant to full-time Itek executive, his sense of commitment was still in some way limited. But more important, he told Rockefeller that he realized there was a "strong connection" between the policy issues discussed in the book and Itek: "In respect to our currently major, and highly classified, military work, George Kistiakowsky has commented that he believes Itek has made as great a contribution to national security this year as any single American company." Whatever Lindsay's ambivalence about Itek, it seemed unlikely that he would abandon ship now.[12]

Meanwhile, as Itek's board of directors prepared for a late October planning meeting to address the problems plaguing the company, Duncan Bruce sent them the latest update on the firm's financial situation. It was bleak. Although Bruce was certain Itek would lose money in 1961, he didn't know how much money. "Wherever possible," he explained, "plans for 1962 have been compared with actual results for 1960 and 1961." His next sentence was astounding. "This comparison is not yet possible with respect to 1961 profit figures because certain of the audit complexities . . . have not been resolved." So throughout all of Itek's planning documents for 1962, results for 1961 (except for sales figures and corporate expenditures) were now largely blank.[13]

Itek's board of directors and the company's top executives arrived at the Andover Inn in Massachusetts on the evening of Wednesday, October 25. The two-day agenda was ambitious. Thursday morning began with Leghorn's statement of the company's goals and objectives. Briefing books prepared for the meeting indicated that Itek's goal was to build a "research based growth company in the Information Field, created by imaginative and able people operating throughout the world." But there were social objectives as well. Itek would accomplish more than a high return on equity; it would create a "climate for individual creativity and self-fulfillment," contribute to "world security through information systems" designed to stabilize the arms race, and "demonstrate that private enterprise can serve public purpose." Harper Woodward sarcastically wrote in the margins of his agenda that Leghorn's speech was "anti-sin" and "pro-motherhood."

Leghorn would leave it to Lindsay to explain Itek's 1961 results — or, rather, lack of results. When Lindsay began his presentation, and directors turned to the exhibits in their briefing books on Itek's financial performance, they found blank spaces for most of 1961. Final sales for the company were reasonably well documented, but final information on the costs of goods sold, or even the scope of needed inventory write-offs, could not be determined. As a result, almost a month after the end of Itek's fiscal year, net income for the company could not be calculated, and the final figure for earnings per share, the most important number in Leghorn's lexicon, remained unknown.

After Lindsay spoke, it was Jack Carter's turn to make a presentation. The personal tension between Leghorn and Carter must have been immense. Yet there was Carter, the man who had stolen Leghorn's wife, not only on the agenda but taking center stage to outline the future plans of Itek Laboratories, Vidya, and the lackluster Space Recovery Systems. Throughout the rest of the day, every division head would review his group's 1961 performance and propose plans for 1962. On Friday the board's finance, compensation, and research committees simultaneously met for daylong sessions on how to prepare the company for a comeback in the new fiscal year.[14]

No matter how hard Itek's management worked at Andover to prepare for the future, it couldn't change the awful reality that 1961 was nothing less than a financial meltdown. By November, Leghorn seemed to come to terms with his own responsibility for the disaster. "Much of our control problems are due to horrendous accounting and control problems in each of our acquisitions," he acknowledged to the board. "Also, my extended leave of absence this year made it difficult for controls to operate properly whatever the organizational form," he confessed. At the board of directors meeting, Leghorn announced that losses for 1961 would be far greater than preliminary estimates had suggested. The numbers were changing so quickly that management had been unable to either analyze them effectively or devise a "program to prevent their continuance." Then Leghorn reported even worse news to the board: Itek's preliminary results for October, the first month in its 1962 fiscal year, again showed losses.[15]

On December 27 Leghorn outlined his strategy for saving Itek and sent it to the board of directors. The next sixty to ninety days were "critical," Leghorn wrote. He and Frank Lindsay had agreed to divide up the company, conduct a thorough review of what had gone wrong in 1961, and develop "short-term profit improvement programs" for each subsidiary. Depending on what he and Lindsay learned, they would likely be confronted with a set of difficult choices. Unless they could develop a compelling rationale to continue Itek in its present form, they would either have to "retrench primarily to a government contract business" or merge with another company.[16] It was an ugly choice.

Less than forty-eight hours later, Richard Leghorn signed the final draft of his letter to shareholders, which would appear in the annual report for that year. "Fiscal 1961 has been a year of both advances and disappointments for Itek," he began. "Consolidated net sales rose to a new high," he proudly reported, but losses "for the 1961 fiscal year totaled $1,036,000, or 92 cents per share." Considering that just six months earlier Leghorn had believed that a profit of eighty-four cents a share was attainable, it was indeed a stunning reversal. Leghorn squarely placed the blame for the losses on his acquisition program, and on drastic inventory write-offs related to those purchases. He bluntly explained that Photostat's poor performance—namely, the unit's failure to introduce new products—also had contributed to the loss.

And as Leghorn reported bad news to his shareholders, buried in the footnotes and the financial statements of the annual report was an even darker story. Itek's consolidated balance sheet, which showed in summary form a list of the company's assets, and the liabilities incurred by the company to generate those assets, provided the first hint that Itek was in deeper trouble. The company's cash position, which had finished 1960 at nearly $1.2 million, had fallen precipitously to about $695,000. On the liability side of the balance sheet the news was even worse. Short-term debt had surged about 30 percent, while long-term debt had jumped as well. Meanwhile, shareholders' equity, the firm's capital base upon which its entire financial structure rested, had shrunk significantly. In a healthy firm shareholders' equity is supposed to grow as the company earns money and retains those earnings to make additional investments in the business. In Itek's first years of operation, retained earnings grew by $1.5 million, and shareholders' equity rose as well. As a result of the 1961 loss, retained earnings shrank by more than $1 million. Itek, which was a highly leveraged company at the end of 1960, now had an even higher debt-to-equity ratio.

Itek's income statement contained the worst news of all. Just as Leghorn's letter revealed, net income for the year indeed showed a loss of $1,036,206. But a seasoned analyst relying on the firm's consolidated income statement, even in its summary form, could uncover the grimmer truth. Itek's operating income — that is, money earned on the company's core business operations before tax credits, interest expenses, or realized gains on investments sold during the year — showed a loss of $2,175,494. That figure was more than double the loss Leghorn mentioned in his letter. So while net income may have deteriorated from a profit of $866,337 in 1960 to a loss of $1,036,206 in 1961, a swing of about $1.9 million, the decline in operating income was far worse. It plunged from a profit of $1.4 in 1960 to a jaw-dropping loss of nearly $2.2 million, or a swing of about $3.6 million. If it hadn't been for the gain Itek realized when it sold its stake in Geophysics Corporation of America, and for certain tax credits, Itek's retained earnings wouldn't just have dropped, they would have been wiped out entirely. For Itek's competitors in the spy satellite business, the message was clear — Itek was vulnerable.

Leghorn tried to put Itek's performance in a favorable light, but his words rang hollow. His attempts to offer shareholders a reason to believe that the company would enjoy a quick turnaround also seemed empty. He concluded his letter on a positive note. "I am confident that 1962 will see renewed profit," he stated without a note of reservation. Either Leghorn had conveniently forgotten that Itek was already losing money in 1962 or he was extremely confident in his abilities to turn around the company. Or he simply didn't know what else to say.

Sandwiched between Leghorn's letter and the financial statements at the back of the report was a glowing report on the scientific achievements of Itek's staff. It was the story of an exciting company, filled with energy, developing new products, entering new markets, and poised for growth. There were big pictures of Itek scientists hard at work, their Noble Prize–

winning mentors on the firm's scientific advisory board, and its chairman, George Kistiakowsky, who until recently had been Eisenhower's own science adviser. In fact, there were about seventy photographs of Itek people, products, equipment, and buildings.[17]

By the end of 1961, several weeks after the release of Itek's annual report, the bid for the company's stock in the over-the-counter market was $25 a share. The price of Itek's stock had declined in value by about 50 percent for the year. It was indeed a humbling fall. Yet for a company dangerously hemorrhaging money, with a book value well under $10 a share, the firm's stock remained richly valued.

Nevertheless, some optimistic investors, perhaps impressed by the research activities described in Itek's annual report, may have been tempted to conclude that all of the risks related to the company were already built into the stock price. But for all the pictures and all the words in Itek's annual report, there was not even a hint that the only product keeping Itek afloat was a space-age spy camera whose only purpose was to take pictures of the Soviet Union. Nor was there any way Itek shareholders could ever determine that the company's single biggest customer was the CIA, or that industrial giants like Eastman Kodak were working hard to push Itek out of the spy camera business and take it for themselves. Nor was there any suggestion that Itek's management was considering a massive retrenchment, or a merger. Shareholders would simply have to bear these business risks, whether they understood them or not.

14

"I AM TODAY FORMING A NEW CORPORATE MANAGEMENT TEAM"

On February 14, 1962, Itek's board of directors held a special meeting at 30 Rockefeller Plaza. All the usual members of the board were present, including Frank Lindsay, who was now a director. The meeting had been called on short notice to discuss proposed changes in Itek's management structure. Leghorn, who sponsored a motion on the subject, wanted immediate board action. His motion had a simple objective, to get rid of Jack Carter, president of Itek Laboratories. Soon the motion was seconded and the meeting was opened for discussion.

According to the minutes of the meeting, written by Leghorn in his role that day as corporate secretary, relations between Jack Carter and Itek's executive officers, not to mention the board, had grown strained. The minutes indicate that policy differences were the source of the tension. Indeed, they may have contributed to the problem. Key executives and scientists at the lab resented Leghorn's acquisition strategy and the drain it created on company resources. Perhaps Carter had become a spokesman for the scientists and voiced their growing opposition to Leghorn's plans. Yet it seems unlikely that a difference of opinions over acquisitions was the only topic on Leghorn's mind that day. No mention of personal matters appears in the minutes, but high above Rockefeller Center, on the fifty-sixth floor of the building known as 30 Rock, Leghorn's failed marriage could not have been far from anyone's thoughts that Valentine's Day.

Leghorn declared that all attempts to resolve his differences with Carter had been "fruitless." In fact, dealing with Carter had become a "serious drain on management time." Nothing recorded in the minutes of that meeting could have been truer. Leghorn asked the directors that day to request Carter's resignation. Looking at Leghorn, knowing what he had suffered, it would have been hard to vote against the motion. Yet one director coldly asserted that personal matters had no place in business. James Hill was the sole director to vote against Leghorn's motion. The next day, Jack Carter resigned.[1]

Carter's resignation was an important personal victory for Leghorn. Now he was ready to go on the offensive. It had been six months since he had returned from his leave of absence, and it was time to take command of the company—not just in name, but on his own terms. With Carter gone, the only real threat to Leghorn was Frank Lindsay. Getting rid of him would not be easy. Lindsay had already served as acting chief executive officer and had gained the board's respect in the process. He would only grow stronger the longer he stayed with the company.

Before dealing with Lindsay, Leghorn needed to strengthen his control over the company. In light of Itek's 1961 performance, he had to take dramatic steps to prove to the board that he was capable of turning the company around on his own. First Leghorn asked for Jesse Cousins's resignation. Someone had to take the blame for Itek's failed acquisition program and the lack of financial controls. Leghorn had already shouldered his share of the blame, and there were limits to how long he could keep saying the situation would improve without at least some change in personnel. It was time he showed the board that he was capable of taking stronger action to rectify the problem, and forcing Cousins out was how he did it.

Another lingering problem was Photostat. If a buyer could be found—and that was a big question mark—Leghorn was ready to sell the company. His brother Ken, who had been responsible for Photostat, would have to go. Photostat's company plane was put up for sale, the pilot was fired, and broader layoffs were only a step away.

In order to rid himself of Lindsay, Leghorn needed a management team in place that could not only take over Lindsay's duties but assume the roles played by Carter, Cousins, and Ken Leghorn. He found two capable candidates, Ed Campbell and Eugene Newbold. Campbell was chief financial officer of the Laboratory for Electronics (LFE), another Route 128 high-technology start-up, and Leghorn wanted him to take over Cousins's financial responsibilities as well as Photostat. David Rockefeller was a key investor in LFE, and Leghorn undoubtedly felt that Campbell's Rockefeller connection enhanced his credibility as a candidate. Eugene Newbold, another seasoned executive, was from Fairchild Stratos Corporation (a company with ties to Fairchild Camera). He was ambitious and made it very clear he wanted to be Itek's executive vice president, which no doubt pleased Leghorn. Leghorn wanted him to step into Carter's shoes to run Itek's classified business. If he could quickly recruit this pair, it would be just a matter of time before he could announce a corporate restructuring and show Lindsay the door.[2]

Then there was the matter of Itek's board of directors. Leghorn was thankful that the executive committee of the board had stepped in to run the company when he was ill. But if he was ever going to reassert his complete control over the company, he had to reduce the board's interference in the management of daily operations. He proposed that the board change its schedule: instead of meeting every month, it should begin to meet every other month. Teddy Walkowicz balked at the idea. As long as the company's financial situation was "precarious," Walkowicz insisted that the monthly meetings continue. The rest of the board agreed with him.[3] The board's decision was a setback for Leghorn, but only a minor one.

Over the next few weeks, Leghorn continued to push forward. By March, Ed Campbell was finally hired to replace Cousins, and soon Gene Newbold officially joined the firm. Leghorn also appeared finally to have a solution to his Photostat problem. After protracted negotiations with Eastman Kodak, it seemed as though Leghorn would finally be able to sell the company. Two operating problems remained. Losses at Itek Electro Products — the old Hermes crystal filter business — continued to mount. Employees at the unit were no longer showing up for work, and customers like Bendix and Raytheon were voicing their frustration with late deliveries. Yet despite these continued problems, Leghorn had performed sufficiently well to cast doubt on the need for a strong second in command like Lindsay at the firm. Lindsay would continue with the title of executive vice president through the end of the year, but his future with the company was now uncertain.[4]

On April 9 Leghorn was ready to strike. He sent a confidential letter to Itek's top managers and scientists. After briefly acknowledging Itek's poor financial results in 1961, a year described with understatement as a "financial setback," Leghorn outlined the steps he had taken to improve the company's performance in the future: "Management programs to improve financial controls" had been instituted, and "profit improvement actions" had been initiated. He reported that he had also undertaken "contingency planning in case our weak situations did not respond adequately."

"Weak situations," "profit improvement actions" — Leghorn's stilted language suggested that he was dancing around the truth. It was as if Leghorn could not bring himself to write that Itek had actually lost money, or, more accurately, that the company had suffered a near financial meltdown. Finally, Leghorn became more specific. Second-quarter earnings would soon be reported in the black, after a disappointing "red" first quarter. "In spite of our problems," he said, "Itek laboratories has continued to operate profitably and with significantly increasing sales." Leghorn was acknowledging what the scientists at the lab knew already — Itek's classified government work was carrying the company.

Next, Leghorn made a series of announcements that signaled his new confidence and his commitment to take firmer control over the company's future. All mergers and acquisitions discussions had been terminated. Leghorn would not pursue growth through acquisition again until "our operations are all clearly strong and healthy" and Itek achieved profitable internal growth. In order to manage growth better, Leghorn announced, "I am today forming a new corporate management team." From now on, he explained, Itek would "operate under strict control of divisional plans and objectives." Leghorn's new team — including Ed Campbell, who had joined the company that day — would give him the management muscle to accomplish his goal. As for Frank Lindsay, Leghorn noted that with all Itek's operating units reporting to a new management team, Lindsay would be free to concentrate on planning and business development. Lindsay had been relieved of all operating responsibilities. It was just a matter of time now, Leghorn probably believed, before Lindsay was completely forced out of the company. And Lindsay could feel Leghorn breathing down his neck. He was beginning to think that joining Itek had been a grave mistake. As for his career at the company, it seemed a lost cause.[5]

But Leghorn's victory was as brief as it was sweet. Almost immediately his plans began to unravel. At Itek's board meeting on April 26, Duncan Bruce presented a revised forecast for the company's 1962 earnings. The original forecast, which showed pretax earnings of about $1.4 million, had been revised down by almost 50 percent. The chief cause of the revision was Itek Electro Products. It seemed the more products the division sold, the more money it lost. But that wasn't Itek's only problem. Photostat was slipping again, and Kodak now appeared unwilling to buy it. Space Recovery Systems was beginning to hemorrhage money as well. To complicate matters, Itek was barely meeting the $2.2 million in working capital required by its bank loans. Leghorn may have put a new team in place, but his own disastrous decisions continued to haunt him.[6]

Leghorn must have sensed that his situation was deteriorating rapidly. Ed Campbell, Leghorn's handpicked chief financial officer, was on a cruise ship on his way to Bermuda with his wife when he received an urgent cable from Leghorn to return to Itek immediately. As soon as the boat docked in Bermuda, Campbell said goodbye to his wife and flew back to Massachusetts. He soon learned that he had taken a bigger career gamble than he realized when he joined Itek.[7]

On May 7, as part of the briefing package for that day's board of directors meeting, Leghorn sent each director a draft of a letter that he intended to mail to shareholders in four days. Leghorn asked the directors to send him their comments as soon as possible. It was classic Leghorn. Upbeat and forward looking, the letter gave no evidence that Itek's fledgling turnaround was in any way threatened. He announced Itek's new management team, proclaimed a return to profitability, and described a variety of new products under development at Itek. "Real progress has been made in these first six months," he concluded, "and I have every confidence that we shall further strengthen our position as the year proceeds."[8]

The letter was never sent. The most important topic of conversation at the board meeting that day was unrest at Itek Laboratories, where the situation was rapidly growing critical. The company's leading scientists, led by Duncan MacDonald, Walt Levison, Dow Smith, and Dick Philbrick, were not pleased with Leghorn's new management plans, and they were no longer confident that he could rebuild the company. The mounting losses at Itek Electro Products and the downward revision of 1962 earnings seemed clear enough evidence to them that they were right. They were tired of financially carrying the company. They were frustrated that the profits they generated had been invested in a series of money-losing acquisitions instead of reinvested in technology that could make the country safer. They wanted a meeting with Laurance Rockefeller to discuss their concerns.

The board instructed Leghorn to devise a better plan to reorganize the company's senior management team. On May 8 Harper Woodward called Ed Campbell and told him to make sure that Leghorn's letter not be sent under any circumstances. "I think it would be very unwise to put out any sort of letter until our current discussions have been concluded," he explained.[9]

Suddenly, Leghorn was fighting to maintain control of his company. In a lengthy and at times emotional memorandum to his board of directors, Leghorn fired his opening salvo in the battle for the future of Itek. He declared that over the past few days he had largely devoted his time to talks with members of his management team and senior scientists "on the manifestations of unrest within the company." The company's main problem and the most important responsibility of the board, Leghorn conceded, was the organization of the company's senior executive team. "When I returned July 27 from my leave of absence, we tried to share this function between two men (Frank and myself). . . . By November it was abundantly clear that this combination did not, and could not, work," he wrote. Leghorn explained that he viewed Lindsay as "miscast in the role of Executive Vice President" and that Lindsay "was not in a job suited to his talents." Then Leghorn reviewed his decision to recruit Ed Campbell and Gene Newbold and his belief that "both were potential Executive Vice Presidents." Whatever concerns the board had about his own financial and management skills, Leghorn reminded them that with the new team in place his own role would now be limited to "the leadership, planning, research, and external relations" of the company. Campbell would handle financial matters and Photostat, while Newbold would preside over Itek's classified government operations.

Then Leghorn turned his attention entirely to the subject of Frank Lindsay. "The one remaining problem revolves around Frank in the sense that many of our people are confused as to his title of Executive Vice President in relation to the executive responsibilities that Ed and Gene are in fact carrying out." Leghorn had been putting the pieces of his strategy in place for months, and now he was about to place Frank Lindsay in check, but would it be mate?

"You will recall that in order to attract Ed and Gene, I had Frank's role clarified by the Board," Leghorn reminded the directors. "This we did at our March meeting, when the Board agreed that all operating responsibilities would be assigned to Gene, Ed, and Duncan for research." The board members shared responsibility for this decision, Leghorn reminded them. "I have talked with Frank several times since last winter about a planning role in Itek, and he has indicated that he would probably leave rather than accept such a role." Now Leghorn was ready to finish him off. "I understand that Monday evening while I was not in the conference room, Frank offered his resignation if the Board felt this would help reduce the unrest in the Company. Ed, Gene, and I think it would be best for all concerned to accept his resignation now."

Next, Leghorn explained his new plan for organizing the company's senior management team. "One of the key organizational problems which you impressed on me Monday was the need to decide now which title — President or Executive Vice President — would go to Campbell or Newbold."

Although minutes from Itek's May 7 board meeting were silent on this subject, Leghorn's memorandum suggests that the board had given him a harsh set of instructions that day. He must give up his role as Itek's president and pass the job on to someone else, presumably more capable. Leghorn spent the next few days in discussions with Campbell and Newbold and arrived at an arrangement with which all three appeared to be comfortable. Leghorn would relinquish his position as president and pass that title to Newbold. Leghorn would become chairman of the board and retain his role as the company's chief executive officer. Campbell would become executive vice president and Duncan MacDonald would be appointed vice president for research.

Leghorn was apparently satisfied with this arrangement, but he did not want any management changes announced until September. He explained that "an announcement today might be misconstrued by customers, employees, and the financial community to mean another upheaval just when it is imperative to indicate stability." He also wanted Newbold and Campbell to have time to settle into their jobs and develop good working relationships with the rest of the Itek team. He had another reason. "Jack Carter is telling the key decision makers in government that we are about to fall apart, he is going into the reconnaissance business and that many of our people will come with him. Under these circumstances, I do not believe we should risk a reorganization that might be misunderstood by the customer." It was a convincing argument.

Leghorn had one last recommendation in his memorandum — a reorganization of the board of directors. His stated goal was to bring Newbold and Campbell into the board committee structure and to reduce outside board member participation on the key oversight committees. Yet his proposed reorganization seemed designed to accomplish even more. Albie Pratt, who as chairman of the executive committee effectively ran the company in Leghorn's absence, was thrown off the committee in the proposal, and Newbold and Campbell, who now owed their jobs at Itek to Leghorn, were added. If a crisis ever happened again at the company, Leghorn's team would outnumber the outside directors on that key committee — a fact that likely did not escape the notice of the rest of the board.

In the last lines of his memorandum, Leghorn dropped a bombshell: "If you would prefer a Chief Executive other than myself, I will step aside and work closely with my successor to effect a smooth phase over."[10]

That Sunday evening Leghorn sent Laurance Rockefeller a copy of his memorandum, as well as a deeply personal plea for his support. "Changes in top titles seem to be the solution of others to the unrest in the company. Maybe so." Suddenly, Leghorn seemed to be distancing himself from plans to reorganize Itek's management team. It was the "solution of others," not his own. "But, Laurance," he implored, "the gist of our problem is simple. Who is going to run the company, and frankly what support does he have."

Leghorn wanted nothing less than Rockefeller's complete, unqualified backing. But just as Leghorn needed that support to survive, he needed to assure Rockefeller that he would not fail him, that he would never again have to take a leave of absence and abandon his company. "My personal problems almost destroyed me two years ago. Itek suffered deeply as a result." Now Leghorn directly addressed the concerns he probably knew that Laurance Rockefeller was too polite ever to voice. "I am being remarried in June and these problems are finished. Yet the world has lost confidence, not knowing of the real factors behind my personal stumbling and recovery." Then Leghorn made it absolutely clear that he was willing to walk away from Itek if he could not regain Rockefeller's absolute confidence. "I know what I can do with genuine Rockefeller backing. If I don't have it now, or if I fail you in the future, please accept my enclosed, undated resignation."[11] Leghorn had played his last card. Despite his best efforts to deal with what now appeared to be a rebellion by his top scientists, it was clear that he could not control the tide of events at Itek.

Laurance Rockefeller and his staff decided that it was time to take action. Rockefeller could not allow the continued success of Project CORONA to be jeopardized by a battle for the control of Itek. It was bad enough that Itek's performance in 1961 had brought the company to the edge of financial ruin, but any further deterioration at the company, either financially or managerially, would probably destabilize it completely. Itek's custom-made spy cameras would cease to roll off the assembly lines, and America's eyes in space would go blind. At a time when the war of words between President Kennedy and Soviet Premier Khrushchev was raising the stakes in the Cold War, when the United States needed intelligence on Soviet military capabilities more than ever, this was an unacceptable outcome.

Rockefeller's staff immediately began to plan for a crucial meeting on May 16. Unless the crisis could be resolved quickly and constructively, America's national security might be severely endangered. Rockefeller would fly up from New York to meet with the Itek scientists and to listen to their concerns. Rockefeller would also hold separate meetings with Leghorn and Lindsay. Meanwhile, Itek's outside directors would simultaneously meet with Ed Campbell and Gene Newbold. When those meetings concluded, the outside directors would meet with Itek's leading scientists and managers in charge of Project CORONA — namely, MacDonald, Philbrick, Levison, and Wolfe. Finally, Rockefeller and the directors would meet for dinner with the entire group in order to reach, or announce, their conclusions. They hoped to arrive at their decision quickly and to announce it publicly as soon as possible.

The agenda for the meeting included discussion of six alternate management teams that could run the company. All six scenarios included Leghorn in some role. Depending on the scenarios, which included the status quo, Leghorn might serve as chairman of the board, as chief executive officer, or as vice chairman of the board. Campbell and Newbold were included in all of the scenarios, but so was Frank Lindsay. In most of the scenarios Lindsay was included as a senior vice president or consultant. Two scenarios stand out. In these proposals, Lindsay would serve either as chairman of the board or as Itek's president and chief executive officer. For a man who had tendered his resignation just days earlier and who was actively being pushed out of the company by its current president, Lindsay had suddenly become a dark horse candidate to take it over.[12]

On May 16 Laurance Rockefeller flew in his private plane from New York to Massachusetts to resolve the crisis at Itek. An unmarked Itek company car picked up Rockefeller at the airport and brought him to the Battlegreen Inn at Lexington.

At about 8:00 P.M., Laurance Rockefeller and members of his staff, Albert Pratt, and other Itek directors began their meeting with Itek's rebellious scientists. Rockefeller's separate meetings with Lindsay and Leghorn had never materialized. Perhaps his schedule had been too tight, perhaps he had decided that they were unnecessary. Whatever decision Rockefeller made would now rest on the outcome of the meeting this evening.

Pratt sat at the front of the room with Rockefeller quietly by his side. Still chairman of the board's executive committee, despite Leghorn's attempt to reorganize the board, Pratt was now to play a critical role in determining the besieged president's future. He had supported Leghorn during his illness; it was unclear whether he would support him now.

Not long after Pratt called the meeting to order, Rockefeller took control. His interest in the scientists' concerns was genuine. It was clear that he had come to the Battlegreen Inn with an open mind. It was equally apparent that he was searching for an immediate solution to the crisis at hand.

The tension must have been intense as Itek's top scientists and engineers, including Walter Levison, Richard Philbrick, Dow Smith, and John Wolfe, presented their argument to Rockefeller. Wolfe stood up and faced Rockefeller. Where had he been the past year? Why had he allowed the company to nearly disintegrate? Rockefeller was visibly uncomfortable as the meeting wore on, moved by the gravity of the situation.

Levison spoke up. Never one to water down his views, he declared that there had been too much change at the company, too many acquisitions, not enough focus. Now Leghorn wanted to install a new management team, Campbell and Newbold. Levison did not like it one bit. They were "unknown ringers." Their presence could only destabilize the company further.

Rockefeller listened, always respectful, even as person after person delivered the damning verdict. Leghorn must go. The mutinous scientists could no longer work with Leghorn, they said, but they trusted Frank Lindsay.[13]

Leghorn's supporters, Campbell and Newbold, waited in the hallway for their turn to speak. They watched as the mutineers filed out of the meeting. Then their turn arrived. Campbell and Newbold faced Rockefeller and the assembled board members and told them that they could work with Leghorn, that they could strengthen the company if only given a chance. Campbell sensed that by this point a decision of some kind had already been made. If Itek collapsed, they were told, it could create a national crisis. Campbell left the room and waited for an announcement that seemed all but certain.[14]

Late that night Frank Lindsay sat at home and considered his future. The crisis at the company deeply disturbed him. He had already offered to resign from Itek if his departure would help to settle the situation. Again his thoughts turned to quitting. He had been offered a job at Stanford, and he felt inclined at last to accept it.

Then his telephone rang. It was Albert Pratt. When Lindsay hung up the phone, it was clear he would never return to Stanford. He had just been made president of Itek.[15]

On May 17 Leghorn wrote one last memorandum to Itek's directors. He was clearly unaware that late the previous night Lindsay had been asked to serve as president, and that his own undated letter of resignation had been accepted. He proposed to serve at the company as chairman of the board, with Lindsay acting as his vice chairman. It was too late. Events had simply passed him by.[16]

Frank Lindsay was now in charge of Itek, and it was up to him, with Laurance Rockefeller's backing, to save it.

15

"WE ARE PROBABLY GOING TO HAVE TO BOMB THEM"

"The last few months have been a difficult time for all of us at Itek." That is how Frank Lindsay began his letter to Itek's top personnel. On June 22, when Lindsay signed his letter, he had been Itek's president for barely a month. He faced many difficult challenges in those first days, and he knew that he could succeed only with the complete support and confidence of his staff. His letter, an honest appraisal of Itek's grim situation, was part of an effort to build bridges to the people around him, letting them know that he understood their feelings and recognized the need for immediate action.

"You are now obviously, and rightly, concerned about the meaning to Itek of changes that have occurred." Although he acknowledged what had gone wrong, he did not dwell on the past. Rather, he proclaimed a more limited vision of Itek that recognized the company's inherent strength. Itek was and would continue to be a company working at the leading edge of science and engineering. But in order to succeed Itek would have to come first to market with "advanced products that are at the state of the art." Itek could not "compete in mass production with the established giants."

The one technology in which Itek enjoyed a dominant position, indeed a growing franchise, was satellite reconnaissance systems. Lindsay recognized as much when he noted that the Optical Systems Division, the heart of Itek's classified operations, was on track to show "the finest performance in its history." But Leghorn's acquisitions had nearly brought down the company despite the success of Itek's government business. Lindsay made it clear that he would take rapid action to correct the situation. Any products or ventures that Itek could not realistically support on its own, or that did not fit with the company's core strategy, would probably be sold. These must have been soothing words to the rebellious scientists and engineers who had overthrown Leghorn.[1]

So Lindsay spent his first weeks putting out fires. Not only did he have to bolster morale, but he had to quickly take steps that would stabilize the company's financial position. Bank loans had to be renegotiated, subsidiaries had to be reorganized or put up for sale. And employees who were considering defecting to the competition had to be persuaded to stay. Jack Carter, who was now employed by Allied Research Associates, was beginning to poach Itek's personnel roster. That had to be stopped immediately. By fall Lindsay was determined to pare down Itek aggressively, concentrating the firm's limited resources on a "smaller number of opportunities with the highest potential."[2]

The pressure on Lindsay must have been intense. To compound matters, Itek's stock price, which had been hovering near $20 a share when Leghorn resigned, had plummeted to less than $10.

In late September, Lindsay and his new management team gave the board an update on their progress. Although a few employees had indeed defected to Jack Carter, the trickle never developed into a flood. The company's internal audit system was now working, the problems had been identified, and Lindsay was prepared to aggressively tighten the belt further in fiscal 1963. Most important, Itek continued to have a near lock on satellite reconnaissance systems. Notes from the board meeting reveal that management believed that Itek had an "almost complete monopoly." It would be the only supplier to the government through at least 1964.

And Lindsay intended to secure Itek's lead. Under Leghorn's reign, Itek's profitable reconnaissance business had been used as a cash cow to fund a variety of commercial initiatives that never bore fruit. Instead of reinvesting the profits from CORONA in the firm's classified operations, Leghorn had squandered the funds. Lindsay's budget for 1963 changed all that. The research and development budget for Itek's reconnaissance operation was more than doubled, funding for commercial products was sharply cut back. If Kodak, Fairchild, or Perkin-Elmer intended to challenge Itek's position in space reconnaissance, Lindsay was prepared to fight back.[3]

On Tuesday morning, October 16, McGeorge Bundy walked into President Kennedy's bedroom. The photographs under his arm probably attracted Kennedy's curiosity. Bundy, the president's national security adviser, wasted no time in delivering his news. "Mr. President, there is now hard photographic evidence, which you will see, that the Russians have offensive missiles in Cuba." Kennedy looked at photographs of the missiles taken from a U-2 spy plane. "We are probably going to have to bomb them," Kennedy said. The Cuban missile crisis had begun.[4]

Over the following days, U-2 flights over Cuba took place at a quickening pace. Most U-2 missions, previously flown by CIA pilots, were now flown by air force pilots. On Friday the CIA's Art Lundahl briefed the president's top advisers about the Cuban situation while Kennedy made a campaign trip to Chicago in order to keep up normal appearances. Lundahl revealed new details about "the magnitude of the Soviet threat." He explained that based on the latest photography his analysts now considered two of the missiles to be operational. According to Lundahl, the group became "nervous and jittery." It wasn't a good sign. That day Kennedy's advisers, dubbed the Ex Comm, short for executive committee, had begun to lean toward an air strike to destroy the Soviet missiles on the ground. Bundy, speaking to his Ex Comm colleagues, stated that he now supported "decisive action with its advantages of surprise and confronting the world with a fait accompli." Dean Acheson, the former secretary of state, supported Bundy's view. Maxwell Taylor, the president's trusted military adviser, said that it was "now or never for an air strike."[5]

On the basis of photographs taken from a plane, Kennedy and his advisers were contemplating action that would take the world to the brink of nuclear war. Yet as one CIA analyst recalled in his history of the crisis, the "relatively small scale of the U-2 photography presented problems to the policy planners." Although the photography was more than adequate for CIA analysts to identify the missiles, "it was evident that the president, Bobby, and others were still having difficulty fully understanding the detailed information that was being derived from the photography."[6]

Top CIA officials became deeply concerned that the air force would order its pilots to fly U-2 missions at lower altitudes to improve the resolution of the photography. Flying at a lower altitude would increase the odds of being shot down and raise the probability that the Cold War would turn into a hot one.[7]

CIA Director John McCone wanted to take any step that would minimize the chance of war. He turned to John Parangosky, a protégé of Bissell's who had worked on the U-2 and CORONA programs. McCone told him to get a better camera flying in the U-2, one that would allow the pilots to stay at high altitudes and avoid unnecessary risks. There was little time to spare. Parangosky immediately thought of Itek and its space camera. "We wanted high resolution data," he recalled, and the Itek camera was the best tool in America's intelligence arsenal. Not only did he respect Itek's technology and its personnel, but, especially important during a time of crisis, he trusted the security at the company.[8]

There were security reasons why Itek's camera had never flown in a U-2. Before the crisis, the CIA had kept cameras in the spy satellite program secret and apart from the U-2 program. Not only did this reduce the number of people who would be aware of the technology, and of the CORONA program itself, but as Gary Powers's flight had already demonstrated, the U-2 was vulnerable. Itek's spy camera could not be allowed to fall into Soviet hands. But in a world poised at the edge of the nuclear precipice, compromises had to be made.[9]

Selecting Itek's camera was a natural decision for Parangosky, and not only because of its power. Itek products had already played an important role in the early days of the crisis. In the previous two years, clear, highly detailed photographs of the Soviet Union taken by Itek cameras had allowed CIA analysts to develop a comprehensive catalogue of the kinds of buildings, roads, and missile-defense systems used by the Soviets to support and protect their nuclear missile force. These structures often had unusual architectural features, or were arranged in recognizable patterns. The CIA analysts who looked for missiles called these patterns "signatures." Analysts used the signatures to identify with confidence the location of a Soviet nuclear missile installation. On October 17, using knowledge about signatures developed from CORONA photography, CIA analysts were able to determine that the Soviets were constructing a storage bunker for nuclear weapons.[10] Nuclear warheads had to be close by. Time was running out.

Rick Manent and Gary Nelson, two of Itek's top technicians on CORONA, received the urgent call from the CIA. There was a national emergency. Could Manent and Nelson install Itek's CORONA camera in a U-2 spy plane? Immediately? Manent and Nelson were instructed that their mission was highly classified, and that they could inform only their immediate supervisor, Tom Hobin, of the request. Hobin, Manent, and Nelson were all instructed that no one else at Itek could know about their whereabouts, or their task. That included Walt Levison, Frank Madden (Itek's chief engineer for Project CORONA), and even Itek's president—Frank Lindsay.[11]

In a national emergency, abiding by Itek's corporate chain of command probably seemed an unnecessary courtesy. Little more than two years later, CIA executives again attempted to give Itek employees direct instructions without regard for the company's hierarchy. That time there was no national emergency, and the CIA's actions led to disaster for Itek.

Itek's C''' camera for the CORONA program had been designed to fly in a space capsule, not in a U-2. Nelson and Manent, with Hobin's support, worked covertly within their own company to obtain a camera from the test lab. They were now a classified operation within a classified operation. No one asked questions about what they were doing, no discussions took place. After years of working within a classified environment, the entire workforce was conditioned to look the other way. Short of both time and information, Nelson and Manent did their best to build a mock-up of the U-2's Q-bay, the part of the plane where the cameras were mounted. Then they reconfigured the camera to operate in the Q-bay. They quickly realized that although the camera would fit in the U-2, it was too big to get through the hatch of the Q-bay in one piece. They could redesign the key parts and adapt the camera and its mount so that it would fit, but that would take about six months. Or they could get out a box of tools and use their mechanical skills to come up with a faster, perhaps less tidy, solution. They chose the second course of action.

The camera hung on a honeycomb aluminum frame designed to meet the space requirements of a satellite. The main plate was thirty-six inches in diameter, circular to fit a circular spacecraft. But the shape did not fit the U-2. So they had to reshape the plate. Nelson and Manent developed a low-tech solution to the problem — they took a hacksaw and cut the frame down to size — while the camera was still attached. They had to accomplish this without distorting the plate. If the plate became distorted, it could unbalance the entire camera system, put the focal plane in the wrong place, and result in an unfocused picture. Satisfied that they could get the camera into a U-2, they headed to Lockheed in California to test what they had done.

Lockheed mounted the camera in a real U-2 and flew it over the Golden State. To complete the test the photographs would have to be developed and evaluated. Nelson and Manent, now assisted by Itek's Harold Alpaugh, set up a darkroom in a dingy motel room not far from Lockheed. Lockheed was flying the camera, but for security reasons only Itek personnel were allowed to handle and develop the film. It might have been a national emergency, but as Nelson recalled, their accommodations were "like the Bates Motel. We weren't going first-class anywhere." So the film was developed in the bathtub and dried in front of an air conditioner. The pictures were clear and beautiful, and the camera was ready to be used over Cuba.[12]

As U-2 missions continued over Cuba, armed at least part of the time with an Itek camera, pictures taken from space by yet more Itek cameras "steeled the nerves of the Kennedy administration." Itek's eyes in space allowed Kennedy and his advisers to "judge not only whether missile sites in the Soviet Union were making launch preparations, but also whether other types of Soviet forces were moving into position for offensive operations." Kennedy's intelligence advisers confidently told him that the Soviets were not getting ready for an attack; as a result, Kennedy had the confidence that time was on his side to reach "a negotiated settlement."[13]

Although the Cuban missile crisis was peacefully resolved by the end of October, it was indeed a close call. It dramatically demonstrated to the public and policy makers alike the importance of reconnaissance and intelligence in the atomic age. President Kennedy, an avid consumer of intelligence before the crisis, had an even deeper appreciation for its value afterward.

In the aftermath of the crisis, Itek's government systems division began to gear up for an increased level of business. On October 1, just days before the missiles were discovered in Cuba, Itek began its 1963 fiscal year with a sales backlog of $8 million. By the end of November the sales backlog had leaped to $23 million. New orders for reconnaissance systems, cameras for CORONA, and other projects were soaring.

Richard Philbrick, who now served as head of Itek's government systems division, realized that Itek needed more scientists, bigger test facilities, and more advanced equipment to support this sudden growth. In a memorandum that was to be distributed to Itek's board of directors, Philbrick outlined the urgent need for additional capital investment in Itek's classified operations. The cost was in the millions.

Yet for all of Philbrick's balanced reasoning, and the clear evidence of market research to support his request, board approval would again require the kind of leap of faith that had long ago become customary at Itek. "For security reasons," Philbrick explained, "we are not able to identify the specific details of the programs." Philbrick quickly assuaged any concerns, however, by noting that "since making the projections" he had "tested their validity by reviewing them with our customers." Although the products were unnamed and the customers were officially unknown to Philbrick's readers, by late 1962 many of Itek's directors, including those who did not hold high-level security clearances, like James Hill and Elisha Walker, likely understood that Itek built reconnaissance cameras that somehow took pictures of the Soviet Union.

One paragraph in Philbrick's memorandum must have been particularly reassuring. He said that discussions with "high level personnel" in the "customer's organization" revealed that Itek's camera system was "the work horse of the community." Furthermore, "all other competitive programs have [been] aborted." Unsigned notes on a copy of Philbrick's memorandum found in Laurance Rockefeller's Itek papers, perhaps written by Peter Crisp, are revealing of the state of mind of Rockefeller's staff. Philbrick's request for additional capital is deemed a "Hobson's Choice. . . . Want to diversify, but there is a real opportunity here."[14]

On the last day of November, Lindsay signed his first letter to stockholders as president of Itek. It appeared in the company's 1962 annual report. He reported that Itek's sales had climbed 9 percent to $40 million, and most important, the company had returned to profitability. Lindsay explained, "Itek's efforts have been concentrated in profitable" fields—namely, "optical systems and reconnaissance, office reproduction equipment and supplies, and advanced information processing systems." He reported that operations of Space Recovery Systems, the company that Leghorn had so proudly purchased for a song, had been discontinued. Itek Electro-Products, the old Hermes crystal filter outfit, had been sold. Lindsay was especially candid about the future of Itek's Business Products Division, the old Photostat Corporation. Although the market for copiers was growing fast, it was "extremely competitive"—corporate shorthand for "Xerox is unbeatable." But Lindsay could note with pride that Photostat, which had lost money in 1961, was now breaking even. And although Itek would cede many segments of the photocopying market to the competition, new product developments were under way and defensible niches had been identified. Lindsay even saw opportunities for Itek to apply its optical skills for NASA, perhaps building a lunar mapping camera that could take pictures of the moon from an orbiting satellite. Lindsay concluded his letter with optimism: "All of us associated with Itek look to the future with confidence."[15]

For many shareholders, Lindsay's letter was their first opportunity to appraise Itek's new president. The first impression was of an executive taking charge, shaking up the company, and refocusing it for growth. And Itek's stock, which had been bouncing around near $10 a share for months, trying to find a bottom, had at last begun to rise again. Slowly, steadily, Itek's stock climbed past $13 a share by year's end. At last, it seemed, the worst was over.

16

WASHINGTON TROUBLES

Although fiscal 1963 had begun on a promising note, revenues and profits for the first five months were far below the original projections. Lindsay's monthly progress report to the board of directors wasted few words in getting to the heart of the matter. "The delay in additional contracts in the reconnaissance field," he explained, was due to "organizational problems in Washington."[1]

It was a vexing phrase. "Organizational problems in Washington" could mean many things. For Lindsay it had a very definite meaning, one that he could not share with his board of directors. Since the Cuban missile crisis, when President Kennedy decided to put Air Force Strategic Air Command pilots in CIA U-2's over Cuba, the Agency had become increasingly sensitive about its territorial rights in reconnaissance matters. Many at the CIA were convinced that the air force had "usurped" the CIA's reconnaissance mission; the National Reconnaissance Office (NRO), which many Agency officials viewed as little more than an air force Trojan horse, was seen to be encroaching on the CIA's turf in the CORONA program.

Joseph Charyk, director of the NRO, understood that the CIA resented his young organization. It was a sad turn of events. The CIA, under Bissell's leadership, had helped to give birth to the NRO. Hoping that some aspect of what he and Bissell had accomplished could be saved, Charyk spent the first months of 1963 working on a new agreement that would strengthen their original understanding. When Bissell had been at the

CIA, there had been little need for an extensive accord. Bissell and Charyk respected each other, appreciated the importance of their mission, and focused on achieving it. Turf battles were for other people. Now, with Bissell gone and Charyk himself on the verge of leaving the NRO, it was essential to resolve the differences that were beginning to slow development of the nation's satellite reconnaissance capability.

By the middle of March 1963, a new agreement had been drafted and approved by CIA Director John McCone, Joseph Charyk, and Roswell Gilpatric, deputy secretary of defense. Charyk negotiated an agreement that significantly strengthened the NRO's authority while at the same time institutionalizing a cooperative role for the CIA in its management. The 1962 agreement had given the CIA "supervisory authority in engineering analysis" for satellite reconnaissance systems, but now the NRO was given that responsibility.

McCone's willingness to make concessions to the NRO, including certain budgetary authority, was at least in part due to his own experience as an undersecretary of the air force. McCone was sympathetic to air force ambitions in space. Because the NRO was a creature of both the CIA and the air force, it seemed reasonable to concede some authority to the new organization. Although the NRO's new powers had the potential to threaten the CIA's role in defining and managing future reconnaissance systems, a role that the Agency now viewed as its birthright, it also called for a CIA executive to fill the position of NRO deputy director. It seemed a fair compromise.[2]

The agreement was approved but never implemented. There was no guarantee that CIA personnel would accept their new station in life, or that all of Itek's Washington troubles were over.

Pete Scoville was the CIA leader chosen to be the new NRO deputy director. Brockway McMillan, who had recently been appointed Charyk's successor as director of the NRO, sought to overcome the differences that had in the past separated the two agencies from building a good working relationship. Scoville, mindful of the CIA's territorial rights, responded by refusing to take up his new office in the Pentagon near McMillan. Instead, Scoville remained at the CIA, "continued to use his CIA staff for immediate support," and appeared to refuse to acknowledge the NRO's existence. It probably seemed to McMillan that Scoville's purpose was to torpedo the NRO, not help manage it.[3]

The bureaucratic logjam in Washington continued, Itek's new orders failed to materialize, and the company remained saddled with a cost structure geared to a higher level of business. In a letter to Itek's board of directors, Lindsay warned, "If the expected reconnaissance business is further delayed, profit forecasts for the second half will be reduced and further cuts in indirect expenses will be made promptly."[4]

As the bureaucratic gridlock continued, Itek's CORONA team pushed forward on a variety of fronts to improve the effectiveness of the program. One of those areas was photointerpretation. In the short time since the first successful CORONA mission, the Soviet Union had already developed major countermeasures to evade CORONA's peering eyes. One obvious countermeasure was to limit certain key activities to the night. Itek proposed an "analysis of light patterns" that would "significantly contribute" to the fight against nighttime countermeasures. Itek proposed taking photographs of a study area both during the day and the night for an extended period. The daytime photographs would provide a map of the actual changes that occurred, for example, in missile deployments. The nighttime photographs would reveal a series of light patterns related to the work that occurred under darkness. Over time, study of these light patterns, and the subsequent changes that occurred on the ground, would provide keys that could be used to reveal the purpose behind nighttime activities. The CIA's John Parangosky, an old Bissell protégé, approved the study before the end of the month.[5]

In the meantime, as Itek's scientists and engineers worked on these new proposals, a steady stream of enhancements continued on the camera system itself. Itek's Mural camera system, essentially two C''' cameras mated to provide stereo photography, had been a great leap forward. It provided CIA analysts, particularly photointerpreters, with an enhanced level of detail. This allowed them to make more precise measurements of objects on the ground and improved their ability to distinguish one weapon system from another.

Yet even Mural (M) had its limitations. Sending capsules and cameras into space was a costly proposition, not to mention a risky one. If

CORONA missions could be extended, the program's cost efficiency and productivity would be improved. Itek was already developing a successor called the J camera that would accomplish those goals.

Essentially, the J camera provided the same coverage as two CORONA M missions, but at the "cost of one booster." This was accomplished by developing the capability to send "two buckets of film" back to Earth at different times. In all previous Itek camera models, the mission ended when the film was ejected from the capsule and sent back to Earth in the satellite recovery vehicle (SRV). Certainly the mission could be extended by sending a camera in space with a larger roll of film. But a bigger roll of film also meant that it would take longer to get the results back to Earth. For times when extended coverage over the Soviet Union and a quick return of information were needed, there had to be a better solution than sending a steady stream of rockets into space.

To accomplish this technical feat, Itek's engineers and scientists redesigned the camera system so that it could load a roll of film, cut the film on command when certain mission objectives were accomplished, and load that roll into an SRV bucket for transport back to Earth. Then the camera would reload itself with more film to continue the mission. All these steps were controlled by signals from Earth. CORONA missions, which originally lasted just hours, could now provide up to three weeks of coverage over the Soviet Union. But the camera's subsystems and wiring needed to be modified to conserve power and allow for weight reduction if these enhancements were to occur. If this could be done, then the size and weight of the battery carried into space could be reduced, making room for more film.[6]

By late May, Peter Crisp, who was actively monitoring the Itek situation for Harper Woodward and Teddy Walkowicz, was guardedly optimistic. Although revenues continued to fall behind target, profits had surged. In fact, for the first seven months of Itek's fiscal year, profits were 120 percent of budget, even though gross revenues remained at little more than 80 percent of original projections. Crisp was now confident that Itek would achieve its minimum profit forecast of fifty-two cents per share. Itek Business Products was continuing to show signs of improvement, with higher margins on sales of photocopy supplies and booming sales of Project-a-Lith, a new inexpensive copying process, which was now running at a rate of more than 300 percent of original forecasts.[7]

In spite of signs that Itek was picking up momentum and likely to achieve strong results for 1963, Lindsay continued to look for ways to trim costs and improve profitability. The Digigraphics Project (DGP), a high-technology holdover from the Leghorn era, was a white elephant whose time for disposition had arrived. DGP was a technological breakthrough for the early 1960s. It allowed a person to draw an image on a computer screen with a special pen. The image could be printed, or stored for later reference. Although DGP's promise for a wide variety of applications appeared genuine, Itek had yet to complete all the needed programming required for commercial applications, nor had a reliable display console been built. Meanwhile, the project had now run out of budgeted funds for the year. It was time to sink more money in the project, sell it, or close it down. Lindsay negotiated a sale of the DGP assets to Control Data and persuaded the board to approve the action. Now Lindsay could focus his attention on strengthening Itek's position in the reconnaissance market, "building greater marketing strength" in Itek Business Products (IBP) and developing a new film technology called the RS System.[8]

Lindsay's restructuring efforts were beginning to capture the attention of the national press. *Forbes,* in an article headlined "Itek's Fix-It Man," cast Lindsay in the role of a Cinderella consultant invited to advise the company, who had unexpectedly ended up as its president. Itek was called a "sprightly little technology outfit with a barrel of trouble," and Lindsay was the "coldly efficient" consultant whose "biting criticism" and "repeated clashes" with Richard Leghorn had forced the company's founder to resign. *Forbes* praised many of Lindsay's actions to restructure the company but questioned whether he was prematurely closing the door on new business opportunities. Lindsay defended his actions. "We can't afford to stay in anything unless we can do it well," he explained. "We haven't got financial strength," he admitted, "or a tremendous marketing organization." He concluded that a company "as small as Itek hasn't a prayer unless it is technologically a leader." *Forbes* jokingly explained the problems at Itek's Photostat unit by noting the company's reproduction products "had been Xeroxed." *Forbes* praised Lindsay's achievements, but the endorsement fell short of a complete vote of confidence in his abilities. "So far," the magazine observed, "Lindsay has merely done a topnotch consultant's job of cutting loss operations." *Forbes* concluded that Lindsay now faced "the challenge that confronts all consultants who turn administrators: Can he lead the company in new directions?"[9]

Forbes was not alone in putting pressure on Lindsay to perform. Itek's board of directors, signaling that the period of restructuring was over, also pushed Lindsay to demonstrate that he could grow the company. The board instructed Lindsay to develop a long-range growth plan. Certainly internal growth was acceptable, but if Itek was unable to gain market share and build its own business, then mergers and acquisitions should be considered. Less than eighteen months after Leghorn's own acquisition strategy had nearly ruined the company, the board was now pushing Lindsay onto the same questionable path to prosperity. And if Lindsay was not up to the task, several directors had already hinted to him that they knew "certain large corporations" willing to acquire Itek. One piece of news probably cheered Lindsay's spirits. By the end of June 1963, Pete Scoville had left the CIA. Perhaps relations between the NRO and the CIA would at last improve, easing business conditions for Itek. It was possible, but much would depend on the attitude of the CIA's Albert (Bud) Wheelon, the Agency executive now in charge of its satellite reconnaissance efforts.[10]

By the end of the summer Itek was picking up momentum, and profits were at last soaring. And, especially impressive, all of its divisions were profitable — even the Photostat operation. But there were "soft spots" in the company's performance. "Photostat, the company's only true commercial business, accounted for 37% of sales" but only "4.8% of operating income." And if it hadn't been for Project-a-Lith, the division would have lost money. Itek's classified government operations, on the other hand, continued to carry the company, providing "57% of Itek's sales and 75% of its operating income." If Lindsay and his team could keep up the trend for just one more month, Itek would have a record year in sales and profits, and the company's resurrection would be complete.[11]

Meanwhile, relations between the NRO and the CIA had continued to deteriorate despite a new agreement. CIA Director John McCone began to actively challenge the NRO's authority, as well as the March 1963 agreement that had formalized the agencies' respective roles—an agreement McCone himself had supported. McCone's change of heart was the work of Bud Wheelon. Behind the scenes at the CIA headquarters, Wheelon had convinced McCone that covert reconnaissance programs, particularly spying from satellites, were essential to national security—and that only the CIA, long the leader in the field, could properly manage such programs. Following Wheelon's argument to its conclusions meant that a reduced role for the CIA in CORONA's management, not to mention the design of future systems, threatened to undermine national security.

But there was more to Wheelon's crusade. He also believed that competition between government agencies promoted creativity. Unless the CIA put up a stiff fight against the NRO's expansion, the younger organization would probably become the government's single voice on satellite reconnaissance matters, and the nation would lose the benefits of competition. Wheelon's prophetic argument strengthened McCone's desire to fight.[12]

As the battle between the CIA and the NRO intensified, Itek's camera performance continued to be plagued by a problem dubbed CORONA discharge. This was an ungainly phrase for a technical problem that threatened the program's existence. Since the first successful satellite launch in 1961, CORONA photography had periodically been marred, even ruined, by a mysterious fog that covered parts of a given photograph. At times the film returned from space faded, or "marked with spectacular branch-like patterns." And in spite of advances in the camera technology and the spacecraft, CORONA discharge seemed to be getting worse.[13]

The fogging had serious national security implications. In the aftermath of the Cuban missile crisis, it was clear that overhead reconnaissance was essential to maintaining America's security. Although the Soviet Union had pulled its missiles out of Cuba, deployments were likely to continue at an accelerating pace within the U.S.S.R. itself. CORONA photographs were the United States' only hope for maintaining close tabs on Soviet activity. But if the photographs were fogged, CIA analysts could never be certain whether the area photographed was free of missiles.

Itek's scientists suspected that the source of the problem was static electricity. They knew from their experience with aerial cameras that when film becomes dry and moves through the various wheels and cogs of a camera system, the friction that occurs can cause an electrostatic discharge that produces a flash of light. That flash, however brief, exposes part of the film and ruins it. When the film is later developed, the sections exposed to these flashes appear to be fogged.[14]

But did the experience gathered from flying cameras in planes apply to space? On a typical mission, the CORONA camera used hundreds of feet of film. This film, moist when placed in the capsule and launched into space, "might sit exposed to the very low space pressure from one to several hours." This exposure to the low-pressure environment of the capsule "gave the moisture in the emulsion and base time to evaporate." The film became dry and vulnerable to a static charge. Dry film, running through the transport mechanism of the camera system at a high speed, "with intimate contact between the film and the rollers," provided an ideal condition for electrostatic discharge. In early missions, which had been short, CORONA discharge had been present but not significant. As the system improved, and the missions became longer, the film was exposed for longer periods of time to the capsule's low-pressure environment. This, Itek's Frank Madden theorized, had allowed even more moisture to evaporate, and worsened the problem. Before they could develop a solution, Madden and his team first had to prove that the theory for the discharge was correct. Two cameras, all ready to be launched into space, were now diverted by the CIA to Itek's laboratories for a round of tests.[15]

On August 24 Itek's new J camera was at last launched into space. It was destined to become the workhorse of the CORONA program. Between its first launch in 1963 and its last launch in 1969, it flew fifty-two missions, or more than half of the missions flown over the life of the program. The quantity and quality of information captured by Itek's J cameras "revolutionized the field of intelligence in general and photo-interpretation in particular."[16]

In spite of all the progress, CORONA discharge remained a major technical problem that continued to threaten the quality of intelligence gathered by the program. By the beginning of September, rigorous testing at Itek's facilities confirmed Madden's theory about the cause of the discharge. The culprit was indeed the friction that resulted as dry film rubbed against the rollers on its voyage through the camera system. Lockheed, in its role as the lead contractor, issued a technical directive to Itek, instructing the company to focus its research efforts on the rollers. Ideally, Itek would be able to identify how the rollers contributed to CORONA discharge and then set new "standards for the production of future rollers."[17]

Meanwhile, the CIA's Albert Wheelon was growing impatient with progress at Itek. Yet there were few steps Wheelon could take on his own to solve the problem. In part, it was a legacy of the Bissell era. From the earliest days of the U-2 program, the CIA had relied almost entirely on private-sector expertise to develop technical solutions for national security problems. Bissell built partnerships with corporate America, liberated scientists and engineers from the red tape that strangled initiative, and set them free to achieve the CIA's goals. Because his staff was small, Bissell relied entirely on contractors like Lockheed's Kelly Johnson. Bissell acknowledged years later that "more of the decision making in the U-2 project was made by the contractor than would have been made in an air force, or other military program." His method worked, and it was a style he continued to employ in the early days of CORONA as well.[18]

But to Bud Wheelon, Bissell's approach was a luxury that the CIA could no longer afford. As Wheelon waited for Itek to find a solution to Corona discharge, he began to build a bigger staff. He wanted more scientists and engineers. He wanted technicians who could better oversee developments in the private sector. He wanted problems solved, faster and more effectively. If he assembled the right team, he would be able to seize the initiative on technical developments. The CIA would now drive system improvements, not the contractor community. And Wheelon would lead by example — working long hours, taking the initiative, pushing the contractor community when necessary. If Wheelon was successful, the CIA might gain an edge in its competition with the NRO. The CIA's role in the spy satellite business would be saved, and Wheelon's vision of creative competition between government agencies would be secured.[19]

But swift progress at Itek was hampered by security requirements. Only a limited number of scientists in the country were cleared to know about the CORONA program. Madden and the Itek team had to rely largely on themselves. And they began to run out of ideas. In desperation, they even tried rubbing the film with rabbit fur, hoping to eliminate the static charge when the film made contact with the rollers. It didn't work.

Wheelon was not happy. He and his new staff began to put pressure on the firm to improve its performance. Suddenly, the CIA was following developments at Itek more closely than ever before, monitoring progress, making technical suggestions, intervening to get the best product possible. It was a new approach, and it must have been unsettling for Itek veterans.

But Madden's team remained focused. They regularly worked around the clock to find a solution. Staying away from their families for long stretches of time created difficulties at home, especially because they could not explain why they had to work so hard. But they knew that the stakes were high, that the safety of their own families and communities depended on them. So they persevered, "trying dozens of possibilities that required hundreds of hours of testing." Because Madden's team was certain that the charge was caused by the loss of moisture in the low-pressure environment, they began to consider the possibility of pressurizing the capsule. But every ounce of weight was already accounted for in the program. If a "pressure makeup system" were included in the capsule, then many other aspects of the program would have to be redesigned to compensate for the new weight. There was only so much weight that Lockheed's Agena rocket could carry into space. This was not the solution. There had to be a better way.[20]

Then the moment of truth arrived. Great heroes are often anonymous. They are ordinary people who dutifully go to work every day and rise to the occasion when history demands it. They make their contribution, the moment passes, and they quietly go on with their lives. And so it was at Itek. Although the exact identity of the man is uncertain, one day a member of Madden's team made a strikingly simple suggestion. Perhaps the film transport rollers were in some small way contaminated and they should be cleaned in a pressure cooker. For a team willing to try rabbit fur, surely a pressure cooker was a reasonable suggestion.

It worked. Madden and his team were exhilarated. America's eyes in space would not go blind, vital intelligence about Soviet military activity would flow to the president in ever greater quantity, and the country would be safer. Now rollers were being steamed at Itek for hours throughout the day. After steaming, the rollers were mounted in a camera and tested in the company's vacuum chamber. If they worked, they would be sent into space. If not, they would be steamed again. As Madden recalled years later, "all this testing consumed hundreds of around-the-clock hours, and we estimate that about 200 rollers were in the loop at any one time and the yield was about 10 percent."[21]

Madden's team had eliminated the CORONA discharge, but that wasn't the only problem that Itek's scientists and technicians were working on. Itek's project on night photography light pattern analysis continued. Arthur Lundhal, director of the CIA's National Photographic Interpretation Center, was sufficiently convinced of the importance of Itek's work that he decided to fund continued research on the project in 1964. The company also worked to simplify and improve the circuitry of the camera system. CORONA may have been up and flying on a regular basis now, and the problem of CORONA discharge solved, but Itek was steadily working to improve the performance and reliability of the system.[22]

On September 30 Lindsay finished his first full fiscal year as Itek's president. In his letter to shareholders, signed a month later, Lindsay noted that many important business accomplishments had been achieved in 1963. Itek's net income, which reached $904,000, or seventy-five cents a share, was more than triple 1962 earnings and exceeded Itek's previous record high of $705,000 in 1960. Considering that Itek's revenues for the year, $37.7 million, were 7 percent lower than the year before, this achievement was all the more impressive. Itek was working leaner, more efficiently, and profit margins were expanding. Lindsay was even able to boast that the company's long-term debt had been reduced by 6 percent.[23]

Investors, who had refused to consider buying Itek stock since 1961, had a reason to take a fresh look at the company. Itek's 1963 annual report was filled with exciting news about promising Itek research initiatives. At a time when President Kennedy's commitment to send a man to the moon loomed large in the public mind, Itek's annual report stressed that the company was developing the photoreconnaissance technology that NASA could use to survey the moon "for suitable landing places for manned spacecraft." Itek was applying its photo-optical skills to "automatic language translation" products and graphic data equipment that could "automatically read, interpret, and store large volumes of photographic data." Investors who wanted to understand better how Itek's current business related to these products were instructed that "much of the company's research work cannot be disclosed because of government security or proprietary reasons."[24]

The story of Itek's miraculous turnaround, and Lindsay's role in it, was again the subject of national press attention when *Time* magazine profiled the company after the release of the 1963 report. The punsters at *Time* whimsically titled the article "Itek Refocused." The article noted that "during the high-flying days of the scientific glamour stocks, few soared farther or faster than Itek Corp., a secretive Massachusetts maker of aerial photo gear." Although CORONA was still a carefully guarded secret, the magazine's reporter knew enough about the company to explain that although Itek was "primarily a defense contractor," the company was "not bothered by talk of disarmament. Two thirds of its sales come from aerial reconnaissance cameras and systems that are useful in gathering military intelligence and would be valuable for policing disarmament." Americans love a comeback kid, and *Time* made it clear that Itek was coming back.[25]

And so was Itek's stock. After trading in a tight range near $15 a share for the first half of 1963, Itek stock made an impressive breakout in the summer. After *Forbes* profiled Itek in June, it began to climb toward $20 a share. Then by the fall, as the broader stock market began to soar, Itek surged again toward $30. All the glamour stocks from the late 1950s had come roaring back to life — Polaroid, Xerox, and Texas Instruments, just to name a few. And, it seemed, Itek had rejoined them, regaining the favor of growth stock investors and reclaiming its place in the capital markets firmament.

Yet what the American people never knew was that just days before the *Time* article appeared, Brockway McMillan, head of the NRO, had ordered the cancellation of the top secret Lanyard Project. It was a smart decision. Technical evaluations suggested that Lanyard, for all its cost, would do no better than CORONA at providing the intelligence community with the information it needed. But Lanyard was a major satellite contract for Itek, and an important source of the company's expected revenues for the coming year. Now all work on Lanyard was immediately halted, and Itek was suddenly in trouble again.[26] It seemed that Itek's CORONA team, "walled off" from the Lanyard team for security reasons, had done too good a job of improving its capabilities.

Two months into Itek's new fiscal year, the company's revenue and earnings were suddenly in a steep nosedive. Itek's secretive government operations had been hit hard by the Lanyard cancellation. New government contracts failed to materialize to replace the lost revenues. To compound matters, Itek's Project-a-Lith sales, booming just weeks earlier, abruptly began to tumble. For November total company revenues had slumped to 56 percent of budget, while the earnings picture was even worse. Suddenly, Itek was losing money.[27]

Meanwhile, McCone's campaign against the NRO's authority was picking up momentum. In a series of meetings with Deputy Secretary of Defense Roswell Gilpatric, Secretary of Defense Robert McNamara, and National Security Adviser McGeorge Bundy, McCone pressed for strengthening the CIA's role in the program. McMillan, convinced that Wheelon was indeed behind McCone's offensive, let it be known that "he would no longer deal with Wheelon in matters affecting NRO." Their relationship, McMillan conceded years later, was becoming a personal feud. Wheelon remembered that he probably never did respond to McMillan's letters. But that was because he was too busy getting things done. Either way, communications between the two men had broken down, and the nation's overhead reconnaissance program was mired in conflict.

On September 11 Gilpatric stepped into the role of "peacemaker" and met with both McMillan and McCone to resolve the conflict. McCone was briefly pacified, but on November 8 he made a decision that revealed his commitment to battle. On that day he appointed Albert Wheelon as the CIA's deputy director for science and technology. Wheelon, his authority enhanced and his backing by McCone secure, continued his campaign to protect and expand the CIA's role in overhead reconnaissance. The escalating battles between the NRO and the CIA for control over satellite reconnaissance "hampered" the NRO's own "decision making process" and harmed the CIA's ability to make progress in the area. It also hurt Itek.[28]

That fall an American-supported coup in South Vietnam, the murder of its president, Ngo Dinh Diem, and the overall escalation of tensions in Southeast Asia underscored the dangerous state of world affairs. But the assassination of John F. Kennedy and Lyndon Johnson's hasty swearing in as president aboard Air Force One was the bloody exclamation point to a season of killing. In late November, President Johnson looked out at a world that must have seemed unpredictable and hostile. The need for a steady stream of intelligence into the Oval Office was greater than ever.

In January 1964 Itek submitted an ambitious proposal to the CIA's Wheelon to conduct a five-month study designed to define the performance characteristics for "the next generation search system." Itek believed the next system, a follow-on to CORONA, should provide "maximum" assurance that the United States would "maintain an *efficient* and *effective* and *secure*" satellite reconnaissance capability over the Soviet Union. Itek was especially concerned that the next system have the capability to withstand any physical countermeasures the Soviets might develop. But that was just a beginning.

There had been a debate in the intelligence community for some time about what functions the next system should be able to perform. CORONA had done a great job of piercing the Iron Curtain and discovering military installations on the ground. Now that many of these facilities had been located, thanks to CORONA's search capabilities, it was important that the next system be able not only to search but to take close-up photographs of key areas of concern. Itek would work at developing a system that could accomplish these intelligence community objectives. Wheelon liked the plan. The proposal that evolved from it was given the top secret code name FULCRUM. It soon became central to Wheelon's plan to reassert CIA domination of satellite reconnaissance and thwart the ambitions of the NRO.[29]

Meanwhile, CIA adviser and Polaroid President Edwin Land asked scientist Ed Purcell to serve as chairman of a panel that would evaluate the ideas that would shape the follow-on system to CORONA. The panel determined that one of the critical issues that needed to be resolved if both high-resolution and broad-area coverage were to be achieved was the need for a fast-moving film transport mechanism. The Purcell panel went before CIA Director McCone and urged him to move forward with a system that combined CORONA's search capabilities with close-up "spotting" capabilities. As a result, McCone approved funding for an Itek study on the subject and for development of a working model, with an emphasis on addressing the film-transport issues related to the system. In addition to members of the Purcell panel, the NRO's Brockway McMillan was present, as well as the CIA's John McMahon.[30]

McMillan was probably invited grudgingly. In the conflict between the CIA and the NRO, CIA executives saw McMillan as the enemy. But he was still director of the NRO, the agency responsible for coordinating satellite reconnaissance policy, and it was inescapable that at some point he would be briefed on the CIA's progress. At this meeting, McMahon remembered, McMillan received a briefing book filled with charts that described the purpose and technical objectives of FULCRUM. McMahon recalled that McMillan left the meeting, book in hand, and shortly thereafter initiated an NRO program using air force resources that would accomplish the same objectives.

McMillan's program was called the S2. At the heart of the S2 mission, as well as FULCRUM's, was a camera. McMillan contacted both Eastman Kodak and Itek to begin competitive camera design studies for the program. Itek set up a special S2 design team, "walled off" from the FULCRUM team for security purposes, and began work.[31]

McMillan recalled events differently. Years later he acknowledged having turned to both Itek and Kodak for camera design studies for a follow-on system to CORONA. He also recalled that he wanted to build a spy satellite with the same objectives as FULCRUM. But according to McMillan, he arrived at the idea on his own. The CIA, McMillan argued, had tried to conceal FULCRUM from him — even though he was charged with running the nation's overhead reconnaissance programs. In fact, according to McMillan, he was not briefed on FULCRUM until a mock-up of the system had already been built. Only then was it unveiled to him in a surprise briefing at the CIA.[32]

It is possible that the differences between McMillan's and McMahon's recollections will never be resolved. FULCRUM remains classified, and even if declassification occurs, it may not provide the documents needed to properly reconstruct events. Yet several critical points are clear. By 1964 a consensus had emerged within the intelligence community that a new kind of spy satellite needed to be built, one that combined search with spotting capabilities. The CIA's Bud Wheelon and the NRO's Brockway McMillan, competing for control of the nation's overhead reconnaissance program, began work that year on satellite projects that would accomplish the same goal: FULCRUM and S2.[33]

It was natural that the CIA and the NRO would both turn to Itek for a proposal. But it was not inevitable that Itek would accept work on both proposals. Although in defense and intelligence contracting circles it is not unusual to set up competitive teams within the same corporation, in the context of Washington politics circa 1964 it was an act fraught with unforeseen consequences. Once Itek made that decision, and accepted both jobs, it would be drawn deeper and deeper into the middle of the struggle. The outcome of this conflict was to be determined within the intelligence community by a high-level scientific panel. Whichever Itek design was judged best, the result might very well determine the balance of power between the CIA and the NRO.

Meanwhile, as the conflict deepened, Itek was taking important steps to strengthen its relations with the broader intelligence community. It announced plans to open a data-analysis center in Alexandria, Virginia. Close to the Pentagon and the CIA, Itek's new office would do more than manage customer relations; it would also provide support services to the people at the CIA's photointerpretation center who analyzed CORONA photography looking for clues on the military capabilities and intentions of the Soviet Union. In fact, one of the main purposes of the data-analysis center was to develop new "interpretation aids and keys," the kinds of tools the CIA's photointerpreters used to identify Soviet military equipment on the ground. In order to make sure that Itek's new facility would best meet the needs of its customers, the company even solicited input from intelligence community executives. Itek was not taking its customer relations for granted.[34]

On February 4 CIA Deputy Director Wheelon traveled to Itek headquarters to discuss the FULCRUM proposal with Frank Lindsay, Walt Levison, and Duncan MacDonald. By the end of the meeting Itek had been authorized to begin its study immediately. Wheelon gave Itek three months to complete the first phase of the program, which focused on the research to define the follow-on system. If all went well, Itek would begin a second three-month research project to devise "a feasibility engineering and design study for the search system."

On February 10 Bud Wheelon wrote Lindsay a thank-you letter. In the tense, competitive atmosphere within the intelligence community that year, it was a courtesy whose graciousness was probably not lost on Lindsay. "I am personally encouraged," Wheelon wrote, "by the conversations between our two organizations during our recent visit." Wheelon was optimistic that "the concept we are settling on has real promise of furnishing some badly needed information." If Lindsay was in any way concerned about relations with Itek's single most important customer, Wheelon's letter must have been a great relief. It seemed that Itek's partnership with the CIA was as secure as ever.[35]

When the CIA's John McMahon met with Itek's representatives two months later, he reported that work had "proceeded according to schedule"; there were "no particular trouble areas . . . at the moment." By early May, John McMahon was sufficiently impressed with the progress at Itek that he advised Wheelon to consider the next steps needed to gear the CIA up for the developmental phase of the program. The only disconcerting note in McMahon's progress report was a small one. He noted that "Itek has pretty much concluded what characteristics the next generation system should look like, *at least from their point of view*."[36]

Perhaps Itek's confidence about the correctness of "their point of view" in reconnaissance matters was beginning to wear a little thin on their CIA counterparts. Now that Bud Wheelon's assembly of his own technical staff at the CIA was well under way, the Agency would soon be in a position to articulate its own point of view, not to mention more closely supervise Itek.

And Bud Wheelon was checking up on Itek. A. B. Meinel, director of the Steward Observatory at the University of Arizona, met with Itek's FULCRUM team at Wheelon's request. Meinel reported, "My brief exposure to the proposed Itek system impressed me that the group working on this job appear to have all the potential problem areas that I expressed to you quite well in hand." Meinel's report must have been good news to Wheelon.[37]

By spring, as Itek's scientists were hard at work on FULCRUM, President Johnson's Foreign Intelligence Advisory Board (PFIAB), a kind of board of directors for the intelligence community, focused its attention on the deepening conflict between the CIA and the NRO. A small panel of the PFIAB was assigned to examine the problem and prescribe a solution. The CIA hoped that the panel would endorse its bid for complete control of the CORONA program and responsibility for the next satellite system. The NRO sought PFIAB support for the complete implementation of the 1963 agreement that enhanced its powers. After carefully examining the matter, the members of the PFIAB panel concluded that the nation's reconnaissance program was in trouble. "In our opinion," the panel recommended, "action must be directed from the Presidential level" in order to "assure that this vital national asset is preserved and strengthened."

In May 1964 the PFIAB sent its report to the White House, and McGeorge Bundy, President Johnson's national security adviser, began the time-tested process of crafting a consensus solution. He invited commentary on the report from two key antagonists in the conflict, Secretary of Defense McNamara and CIA Director McCone.[38]

Despite Bundy's initial effort to follow up on the PFIAB's recommendations, President Johnson never directed his attention to that matter, nor would any orders be issued to resolve it. Events in Vietnam, in all likelihood, made sure of that. On August 2 the U.S. Navy destroyer *Maddox* was cruising off the coast of North Vietnam. It was chased into the Gulf of Tonkin and attacked by North Vietnamese patrol boats. Tensions mounted and Johnson ordered another destroyer to the scene. On the night of August 4 the *Maddox* and the *Turner Joy,* their commanders believing themselves under torpedo attack from North Vietnamese naval vessels, fired their guns through the night in self-defense. Although the historical record remains in dispute about the facts surrounding that second attack—including whether it occurred at all—the historical consequences were grave. President Johnson sent to Congress what would become known as the Gulf of Tonkin resolution, authorizing military escalation without a declaration of war. The resolution resoundingly passed and America's war in Vietnam had truly begun. The PFIAB's call for presidential intervention in the CIA-NRO battle was forgotten, drowned out by the growing din over Vietnam. The battle of the government agencies intensified, and Itek was caught in the middle.[39]

But Itek was fighting its way back from winter's dismal financial performance to a stellar summer. Revenues and profits, $30 million and $750,000, respectively, were now running more than 20 percent ahead of the previous year's levels, and the company was still picking up momentum.

Lindsay had more good news to report. He told Itek's directors that the firm had just "received a go-ahead on a sole source contract of approximately $3 million." Lindsay was talking about FULCRUM. "This is for the first phase of a new system," he explained, "which ultimately could amount to $50–$100 million in business for Itek." But Lindsay ended his report on an ominous note. Itek's success in this new venture was dependent on "the successful resolution of conflicting views in Washington in respect to responsibility for the employment of the system."[40]

Unknown to Lindsay, other potential problems loomed in Washington that might prove harmful to Itek. Albert Wheelon's assistant, John McMahon, was growing concerned about the CIA's ability to continue funding certain projects at Itek. Evidently the limited research funds that CIA Director John McCone had approved for work on a fast film-transport system and a new camera design had been spent on a variety of projects, not all of which he had actually approved. McMahon warned Wheelon that "by mid-September we will have used up all of our" funds "which we have earmarked for Itek." McMahon was worried about the prospects: "I for one am going to be slightly embarrassed come mid-September" when the money was spent and "instead of a fast film transport system, we have many pieces to many things." One of the projects McMahon decided to spend money on was a competitive FULCRUM design study by Perkin-Elmer. When Perkin-Elmer finished its work, Itek's design remained the best.[41]

Itek, now with undivided support from the CIA's Bud Wheelon and John McMahon, was racing ahead on its design for FULCRUM. Executives like Walter Levison and his team had some growing technical differences with Wheelon's staff about the design, but they were moving forward rapidly anyway. In part, Itek was willing to proceed, despite the ongoing technical debate, because the CIA allowed the firm to continue to develop alternative design studies related to FULCRUM. Meanwhile, Brockway McMillan's S2 project, the NRO's competitive answer to FULCRUM, remained on Itek's blackboard, little more than a study contract.[42]

At the end of September 1964 Itek's board of directors met to discuss corporate strategy for 1965. Walter Levison, vice president and general manager of government systems, was optimistic for the year ahead. He emphasized that Itek was hard at work to broaden its customer base away from one customer. Although all of the directors would have appreciated this as a reference to the government, and in all likelihood the Pentagon, many would still have lacked the complete knowledge that the customer was the CIA, though they probably knew the product was a camera that spied on the Soviet Union. Levison explained that he had hired two hundred employees in the past two months to work on a study that could very well lead to a three-year $60 million contract. He was talking about FULCRUM. Levison noted that his main challenge was finding enough scientists and technicians with the right security clearances. Although he was confident about the future, he added an important warning. Performance alone would not determine success. The politics in Washington surrounding the program was intense. Nothing else Levison said that day could have been truer.[43]

The strain on Itek, evident in Levison's staffing problems, was beginning to show. Itek had limited resources. It was much smaller than competitors like Eastman Kodak and Perkin-Elmer. Yet in addition to its work on CORONA, it had in the past year taken on work for two new projects, FULCRUM and S2. And as Levison explained, Itek could not hire enough people to staff up for FULCRUM. It would be difficult to follow through on the design work for S2, let alone any other new opportunities. If work on McMillan's S2 began to accelerate, Itek would have a big problem. Simply put, the firm was stretched thin.

At the end of October, when Lindsay released Itek's report for fiscal 1964, he was able to announce that both revenues and profits had reached record levels. With sales of $43 million and earnings of more than $1.2 million, Itek had indeed surged well beyond 1963 sales and earnings of $37.7 and $994,000, respectively. And there was more good news. Thanks to the recent introduction of Itek's offset platemaking equipment — namely products like Project-a-Lith and Platemaster — the firm's commercial sales had "increased from 35 percent to 44 percent of total company sales during the year." In his letter to shareholders, included in the report, Lindsay proudly noted that a "growing and profitable government business is now balanced by a growing and profitable commercial business."

The company had even continued to pay down its outstanding debt. As a result, its debt-to-equity levels had dropped to the lowest point in years.

Lindsay's letter was more than a confident review of the year's accomplishments; it was a reflection of how the former commando had managed to apply his own ideas about civic duty and national security to his business pursuits. Lindsay understood the danger of war and the importance of early warning of attack. No one knew better than Lindsay that satellites, not spies, were the only realistic option for learning what the Soviet military was doing. When Lindsay explained to shareholders that "aerial reconnaissance is now an essential element in national security," it was a fusion of his business interests and his beliefs. When he pointed out that the technology was "an area where government spending had been steadily increasing," he was proclaiming a trend that he believed to be good for Itek and for the country. He assured investors that "no matter what happens in the international political climate, we expect to see further increases in the years ahead." Certainly investors understood the role of reconnaissance in a world at the brink of war. But Lindsay also explained that "if the world moves toward arms reduction and control, reconnaissance will certainly play a major role in the inspection system." And Itek would be a major player in that as well.[44]

In the last days of 1964 Frank Madden was worried. So far work on the FULCRUM research proposal had gone well enough, but the project had stalled. The documentary evidence is unclear, but it appears that funding for the project had somehow been delayed. Perhaps this funding roadblock was in some way related to McMahon's concerns in the summer — namely, that the CIA had spent money on a series of unauthorized projects at Itek instead of a chosen few. It is impossible to say with certainty. Nevertheless, we do know that Madden was exceedingly concerned that unless FULCRUM moved forward again, he was going to have to fire a significant part of the team that had taken him months to assemble. That would set the project back for months when the go-ahead signal was finally given. But as the next several weeks demonstrated, that was the least of Madden's concerns.[45]

17

FULCRUM

On January 11, 1965, Bud Wheelon sent CIA Deputy Director Marshall Carter a brief update on the status of negotiations with the NRO's Brockway McMillan over the future management of CORONA. The brevity of Wheelon's cover note was more than balanced by the attached "Memorandum of Agreement" hammered out over an extended period of time between CIA and NRO executives. Past agreements, revised as the relationship between the two agencies deteriorated, had grown longer and more complex. And they did little to improve the situation. It was unlikely this agreement would, either.

In this draft, CORONA was defined as a "joint endeavor" of the U.S. Air Force and the CIA, "within the purview" of the NRO. Although an air force general, reporting to the NRO director, was now the "single authoritative program manager" for the program, a "senior CIA CORONA representative" was in charge of "technical direction for the payload" — the camera and all of the ancillary systems needed to support it. Thus the CIA's representative was "the single point of contact" in the government for all CORONA payload contractors, including Lockheed, G.E., and Itek.[1] Although the CIA was holding on to its special position in the program, it was no longer in charge of the program; an air force officer working for the NRO was in command. The balance of power was tilting toward the NRO.

The next day, Walter Levison had a top-level meeting with key CIA representatives. The meeting is nearly lost to history. Two summaries of it, written the same day, have survived. Obtained through the Freedom of Information Act, the documents are cryptic, in part because they were written in a manner designed to hide the true identities of key meeting participants, and in part because certain names remain classified.

Levison was angry. Evidently the CIA had excluded the Itek team from an important briefing of the NRO's Brockway McMillan. "Why weren't we there?" he demanded. "Would you give us the briefing?" Levison probably harbored dark suspicions regarding the reasons for Itek's exclusion from the briefing. Was it to ensure that McMillan never had the chance to directly question the company about its own growing technical concerns about the best design for FULCRUM? It was a thought that no doubt crossed Levison's mind.

Before Levison left the CIA that day he made a startling announcement. Although "he could not speak for all Itek management he felt that he could decide now as to whether he wanted in" on the program. It seemed clear to the CIA's anonymous record keeper that Levison was ready to turn his back on the project.[2]

Levison's frustration had been building gradually. Since Richard Bissell's departure in 1962, Levison's working relationship with his CIA counterparts had deteriorated. Levison felt that Bissell had always dealt with him openly as a partner, giving him wide latitude to pursue the best technical course of action. Now, with Wheelon in charge, he felt like little more than a hired hand.

Perhaps this change was inevitable. In the early days of CORONA, Bissell had neither the staff nor the time to track developments closely at Itek. In addition to his other CORONA responsibilities he was in charge of the U-2 program and the SR-71 program. Thanks to his role as CIA deputy director for plans, a position he had been given in 1959, Bissell was also head of all covert operations, not to mention the CIA's global network of spies. Bissell's personal philosophy predisposed him to give contractors great freedom, and the increasing demands on his time required it. And Itek thrived in this atmosphere, initiating a series of technical enhancements to the CORONA camera system that greatly improved the program's capabilities.

But Wheelon had built a staff rich in scientific and administrative talent. Close oversight that had been impractical in Bissell's era was now possible. Technical and administrative prodding from the CIA steadily increased under Wheelon's command. It was a changed relationship, and it was hard for Itek executives like Lindsay, Levison, or Philbrick to accept.

Yet it was a dangerous time for Levison's attitude toward the CIA to darken. If Levison turned against the agency, Wheelon and his team had good reason to fear what he might say. A key issue critical to the success of FULCRUM was in dispute. Although the subject matter — the scan angle of the camera coverage — was arcane, it was central to the system's design and purpose. The scan angle, ultimately an engineering issue, determines how much land each picture will cover. The more the camera swings back and forth, or the greater the scan angle, the more land in each picture. The CIA wanted Itek to design a camera system that would cover a scan of 120 degrees. In other words, as the satellite flew around Earth, the camera should be able to take photographs not only while facing straight down but when it swung 60 degrees to the left or right of center.

After months of research, Itek's engineers had concluded that the CIA's requirement for a 120 degree scan angle was unnecessary. Although Itek worked hard on developing a camera to satisfy the CIA's requirement, on its own initiative it had simultaneously been working on other technical solutions that would meet the agency's intelligence objectives equally well or better. Lindsay had briefed Wheelon on Itek's decision to develop an alternative approach and had even secured his approval and funding for the effort. As a result, Itek's John Watson was put in charge of this alternative study, and his research, almost completed, suggested that there were indeed better design solutions than the Agency's 120 degree scan requirement.[3]

The CIA's deteriorating relationship with Itek, the nation's premier manufacturer of satellite spy cameras, was bad news for Agency executives like Wheelon. It was tough enough that the Agency was losing ground in its war of attrition with the NRO, but Itek's increasingly independent attitude created a new set of challenges. The CIA's case for a major role in overhead reconnaissance rested squarely on its reputation as an innovative contract manager. As the January draft agreement between the NRO and the CIA demonstrated, Agency control over the CORONA payload contractors was central to its future mission in the field. If Itek's views and behavior became broadly known within the government, some might conclude that the CIA's reputation was little more than a historical artifact of the Bissell era, and that its vaunted competitive advantage as a contract manager had been frittered away.

The next time McMillan was scheduled to be briefed on FULCRUM, along with other top intelligence community leaders, the location would be at Itek headquarters. Nobody knew with certainty just how the growing impasse between Itek and the CIA would be resolved, or what Levison and the other Itek executives would say.[4]

That January, Frank Lindsay briefed Itek's shareholders about two technological breakthroughs at the company's research labs. First, Lindsay announced that the company's scientists had invented a new substance called RS, which stood for "recording system." *Business Week* reported that RS "may revolutionize the printing and reproduction industry and have a major impact on information retrieval systems." Lindsay also unveiled a "new optical memory system computer" that would "use the RS material to record and retrieve massive amounts of information at speeds far in excess of any now available."

Lindsay's announcements were startling. Little more than three years earlier, Itek had been on the verge of a financial collapse. Now, with Lindsay at the helm, Itek was back on track to lead a real information revolution. And this time it would be achieved the right way, not by cobbling together a confederation of aging brand names like Dictaphone, but by developing technology at Itek's own labs and swiftly bringing it to the marketplace.

Gilbert King, Itek's new director of research, gave Lindsay's announcements added credibility. Before joining Itek, King had been head of research at IBM. King confidently explained to *Business Week* that Itek was not going to fight the major computer makers for market share. "We're going to enter a new area of data processing," he boldly stated. "There are enough words to process in the world; we're not too interested in numbers."

Itek's course was clearly charted. The future was in word processing, and Itek was going to get there first with language translation machines and memory-centered computers. There would even be a new kind of film based on RS technology, cheaper and better than regular film. Time, Inc., parent company of *Time* magazine and a well-known user of words and pictures, was sufficiently impressed that the media giant announced plans to take a stake in Itek.[5]

And Itek's stock, stuck in a narrow trading range for much of 1964, began to soar. The initial breakout had begun not long after the firm released its 1964 report. But the rally accelerated after Lindsay's announcements in January. By the end of the month, the bid on Itek's stock was $47 a share, up more than 30 percent since the start of 1965. Not only was Itek far ahead of the Dow Jones Industrial Average, which at 902 was up barely 3 percent for the year, but it had impressively outpaced fellow CORONA contractors like Eastman Kodak, General Electric, and Lockheed. It was an auspicious start for the new year.

Over the coming weeks, as Lindsay considered how to safely guide Itek though the growing CIA-NRO conflict, the firm's rising earnings, buoyant stock price, and shining prospects gave him confidence. If tough decisions were going to have to be made about Itek's relations with either government agency, Lindsay could rest assured that the firm's strengthening commercial operations would carry the company though any difficulties that might lie ahead.[6]

On February 11, 1965, with Itek's stock climbing toward $50 a share, Frank Lindsay, Ed Campbell, and Walt Levison arrived at Chicago's O'Hare Airport on their way to a business meeting at Chicago Aerial. With Itek's stock rising, Lindsay and the rest of Itek's management had returned to the acquisition trail. Chicago Aerial, a respected manufacturer of tactical reconnaissance cameras, was at the top of the list of potential targets. Now Itek was deep in negotiations to acquire the company. But that day, instead of heading directly to their hotel rooms or preparing for their meeting, they went to the Ambassador's Club, a lounge for first-class passengers at the airport. They sat there and waited for a call from one of Itek's top scientists, John Wolfe.

At that moment, Wolfe was in Washington to perform a dry run of Itek's FULCRUM presentation. The presentation itself was scheduled to be days later at Itek's headquarters in Lexington. The stakes were high and nothing was left to chance. At the final presentation not only would CIA Director John McCone be present, along with Bud Wheelon, Les Dirks, and Jack Maxie, but so would the NRO's Brockway McMillan, luminaries like Polaroid's Edwin Land and some of the best scientific minds in the country. If the presentation went well, FULCRUM would probably be anointed as the next major satellite system and the CIA's chance to retain control of future satellite development efforts would be strengthened. If it went poorly, FULCRUM's future would be less certain, and the CIA's grip on power would be weakened.[7]

John Watson, who had been asked to work on the alternate FULCRUM design studies, had just given his results to Wolfe. Watson had concluded that if the system was redesigned with a 105 degree camera scan, the technical difficulties of the original requirement could be avoided and the intelligence objectives of the system could still be met. When Wolfe reported the results of the Watson study to his CIA counterparts, they were not pleased.

Wolfe had other bad news to report. Unless it was redesigned, the FULCRUM system would be inherently unstable. This was in part due to the huge film spools needed to carry the film. Wolfe declared that if the FULCRUM film spools moved as little as one hundredth of an inch, it could cause enough vibration in the system to "seriously impact [the] resolutions of the system." One hundredth of an inch may seem an extremely small margin for error, but the huge film spools required a lot of energy to start and stop them. In short, if the film spools wiggled just the slightest bit off their programmed course, the pictures would fail to meet the CIA's requirements. All of these technical matters were complicated by the 120 degree area coverage required by the CIA.

When Wolfe finished his presentation, Bud Wheelon immediately queried each member of his staff to find out who was responsible for insisting on the 120 degree requirement. Les Dirks, Jack Maxie, and the rest all denied any role in the decision. At that point, John McMahon, who was the contracting officer on FULCRUM, walked into the meeting. Wheelon asked him the same question. It was a requirement of the contract, he simply replied. Although no one admitted to having introduced the requirement, it was apparently written in black and white.[8]

The forces of history were pulling control of the nation's satellite reconnaissance program away from the CIA — and the men in the room could feel it. Wheelon's assistant, Jack Maxie, told Wolfe that "to a large extent this whole thing was a game and that the agency intended to win. If we change designs at [this] point the agency would lose control and maybe lose the whole game." Jack Maxie now demanded that Wolfe and Itek publicly defend the 120 degree requirement at the upcoming presentation at Itek.[9]

Wolfe refused. Now it was Wheelon's turn to apply the pressure. He told Wolfe that when Itek received the FULCRUM contract, it would be so large that the CIA would effectively own 90 percent of Itek. The size of the FULCRUM project, Wheelon stressed to Wolfe, would essentially require that Itek create a separate division to manage it. The CIA would want its own man to be in charge of the FULCRUM division—naturally, a high-level vice president's position—and John Wolfe would be that man. All Wolfe had to do was to defend the 120 degree FULCRUM design at the upcoming meeting.[10]

When the phone rang for Lindsay, Levison, and Campbell in the Ambassador's Lounge, they knew that it was Wolfe and that the news might be bad. Levison took the receiver and listened intently to Wolfe as he relayed what had happened in Washington. It probably seemed to Levison that not only the design of a satellite system but the future of Itek was at stake. Wolfe told him that he wanted to become a vice president of Itek one day, but not this way. After hanging up the phone, Levison took a cab with Lindsay and Campbell to their hotel. They quickly agreed to meet with Wolfe and Richard Philbrick when they returned to Lexington to make a final decision about how to proceed.[11]

Meanwhile, Philbrick recalled years later, Wheelon had located him and explained that he wanted Philbrick to brief the Land panel, along with the rest of the audience, along Agency lines. Wheelon insisted that Philbrick defend the 120 degree scan angle requirement at the Itek briefing. He wanted him to tell the panel that a camera that covered a scan of 120 degrees was just as good as one that covered 60 degrees, or 90 degrees.

But the larger the scan angle, according to Philbrick, the more problematic the system became. Obtaining clear photographs from space was a matter complicated not only by distance and the motion of the satellite, but by the amount of cloud cover and haze that separated the camera from its target. When a camera took photographs of Earth from space, the distance between the camera and the target on the ground was shortest when the camera was facing straight down. As the camera is positioned at an angle to take pictures of an object farther away, it inevitably has to shoot through more cloud cover and haze. The FULCRUM proposal, with a much wider scan angle than Itek's CORONA cameras, promised a significant degradation of the image as the camera moved off-axis. If Philbrick followed Wheelon's instructions, he would betray his own judgment and jeopardize his own reputation for honesty with men like Edwin Land, whom he had known for years. Philbrick rebuffed Wheelon's instructions. And Philbrick resented Wheelon's attempt to order Itek executives around. As far as Philbrick was concerned, Wheelon was interfering in the management of a publicly owned corporation. Maybe he could exercise that kind of authority at his own shop, Philbrick told Wheelon, but not at Itek.[12]

Yet Wheelon still had an important card to play. He controlled the money. His next move was to order Itek to cancel John Watson's alternative design study. Itek's conclusions about a better design were preliminary. Wheelon's decision to cut the funding for the project seemed an attempt to silence Itek's growing concerns. Days later, a furious Frank Lindsay flew to Washington to protest Wheelon's decision. Wheelon refused to reverse his decision and was brutally candid about his reason. If it ever became known that the CIA had not backed the best design, Lindsay recalled Wheelon saying, the NRO would finally win complete control of the nation's satellite reconnaissance programs.[13]

After Lindsay, Levison, and Campbell returned to Itek, they made a fateful decision. Supported by Philbrick and Wolfe, they decided that as a company they could not publicly defend a technical requirement that they did not believe was the best. They had worked with men like Edwin Land and James Killian for years. They could not look them in the face and tell them that FULCRUM's scan angle requirement was the best possible technical choice, when in their view it was not. Nor could they continue to tolerate the CIA's attempts to tell Itek executives how to manage the company. They decided that unless the CIA was willing to redesign the system based on Itek's recommendations, the company would voluntarily give up a contract worth as much as $80 million in revenue. Perhaps hopeful that a compromise could still be worked out, that the CIA would see the light and allow Itek to revise the scan angle requirement, the executives decided to keep their decision to themselves. In the hours before the presentation, Itek reached a cold peace with the agency. The CIA's Les Dirks would make the part of the presentation that had to do with the 120 degree angle of coverage requirement. Itek's scientists would make presentations about other aspects of the system, ranging from lens to camera design.[14]

Bud Wheelon recalled events differently. Thirty-five years later, he admitted that his assistant, Jack Maxie, could be heavy-handed and difficult. So could Itek's John Wolfe, he recalled. But he was certain that neither he nor Maxie had interfered in Itek's management. He was equally adamant that the issue of the best scan angle, critical from the perspective of Itek's executives, was not a matter he or his subordinates would declare war over. It is a historical disagreement not easily resolved.[15]

Recently declassified documents, particularly minutes of conversations between top Itek and CIA executives, shed some light on the matter:

On February 18, 1965, Frank Lindsay placed a telephone call to Bud Wheelon to discuss the upcoming presentation at Itek. The tone was cordial. Lindsay teased Wheelon and asked, "Is this a convention you are holding up here?" Wheelon joked that they had tried to keep the number of "straphangers down," but it turned out that the final headcount was expected to be forty-three. Trying to be a gracious host, Lindsay attended to details. "Would you like us to have cocktails for the group at the end of the first day?" Lindsay inquired. "Or," he offered, he could "arrange a buffet supper." Under trying circumstances, Lindsay was doing his best to maintain good relations with his client. Wheelon was appreciative of Lindsay's offer but felt it best to keep the meeting focused on business. "Well," Lindsay said, "we would be delighted to do it in any way that seems best."

With these pleasantries out of the way, Lindsay raised the issue of technical matters. Evidently, Itek understood one of the requirements for FULCRUM was to obtain the program's intelligence objectives within a mission of no more than four days. This time constraint, Lindsay explained, had a direct bearing on Itek's own technical concerns. The shorter the satellite's mission, the fewer passes it would make over a target area. In order for the camera to collect the maximum possible information during a shorter mission, it was important for it to capture the widest possible swath of land in every photograph. This meant a wide scan angle.

While Itek recognized the importance of a wide scan angle, Lindsay explained that the CIA's 120 degree requirement was too wide. Lindsay read Wheelon an Itek memorandum outlining the firm's concerns. Wheelon asked for time to think about the memorandum, and Lindsay closed the conversation by saying that he had to focus on legal issues related to Itek's pending acquisition of Chicago Aerial.[16]

The next day, Itek's John Wolfe was preparing for the big meeting at Itek, and he was feeling "pretty cruddy." A memorandum of a conversation between Wolfe and an intelligence community executive, probably from the CIA, reveals the nervous atmosphere at the time.

"We got king-size troubles," the CIA executive explained. "We're a long way from having a briefing and we've discovered lots of technical problems that we have to have answered before we make the charts."

Wolfe made it clear that as far as the presentation was concerned, he wanted to avoid the question-and-answer session. The key issue that both Wolfe and the CIA executive recognized was central to the system was the scan angle.[17]

That day Frank Lindsay and Bud Wheelon again spoke by telephone. There was no more talk about cocktails, no discussion of dinner plans, no jokes. "Frank," Wheelon began, "I took up the matter that you raised with me and find that there is a very serious misunderstanding and lack of understanding about what the constraints really are and really are not." Less than ninety-six hours before the presentation at Itek, Wheelon and Lindsay were suddenly debating the requirements of the system. "There is in fact no firm requirement for four days," Wheelon declared. "There are," Wheelon concluded, "some persuasive arguments for large scan angles." The conclusion is unmistakable. Whatever Itek's confusion about FULCRUM's mission length, the size of the camera's scan angle was important. The larger the angle, from Wheelon's perspective, the better.

Wheelon was anxious. "The reason I am concerned about this," he told Lindsay, "and the reason that I talked to Levison is because Levison has" publicly made statements to the CIA's John McCone and Air Force Secretary Cyrus Vance. The exact nature of Levison's discussions with McCone and Vance is unclear from the minutes of the conversation. But it is evident that Levison's comments bothered Wheelon and that Wheelon had spoken to him about it. Worried about what Itek might say at the meeting, Wheelon told Lindsay that he was taking steps to orchestrate the presentation, to downplay any differences that might exist between the Agency and Itek. "We will lead John Wolfe thoroughly through this whole business," Wheelon said. "And we are not going to call on Itek to defend the original task."

Lindsay interjected, "We don't want to be put in the position of having to defend the requirements," he said, "or the constraints."

"There should be no gratuitous statements from the floor," Wheelon instructed Lindsay. The call soon ended.[18]

February 23, the day of the presentation, arrived. Less than a week earlier, Itek's stock had leaped to a new high for the year at $59 a share. The stock market was blissfully ignorant of the classified controversy swirling about the firm. The risks to the firm kept rising, but so did the stock price.

Frank Madden, Itek's engineer in charge of developing the mechanical aspects of the FULCRUM camera, was surprisingly optimistic that day. He kept his focus on the mechanical challenges of actually building the system and sidestepped the technical and political issues that had absorbed Lindsay, Levison, and Philbrick. He knew about the controversy over the scan angle requirement but was unaware that his superiors had already made a fateful decision. He remained hopeful that a solution could be found.

Madden and his team had just completed a working prototype of the camera system that he would unveil at the presentation. It was huge, ten times as big as the CORONA camera system. And it required almost eight feet of film for every picture. One of the most complicated aspects of the camera, which Madden would explain, was that the film never stopped moving. Picture after picture was taken as the film moved through the camera at high speeds. FULCRUM was Madden's masterpiece, a nonstop, clicking, whirring giant of a space camera that could search wide swathes of land for missiles or take close-up photographs of military installations of particular concern. It might not have been the perfect system, the scan angle might not have been the best one possible, but Madden could build it.

In fact, Madden was not the only Itek executive who believed that the system could be built. Dow Smith, in charge of the optics for the system, recognized that technical challenges remained, but he felt that they could be overcome.[19] But Levison and Philbrick insisted that better design options should be considered, and along with Lindsay and Campbell they were adamant that Wheelon could not boss Itek's management team around any longer.

The CIA's John McMahon had arrived early at Itek's headquarters to help with the preparations for the meeting. One of his tasks was to pick up CIA Director McCone at a nearby military airport and accompany him to Itek. McMahon was not alone that day as he waited at the airport for McCone; with him was Itek's president, Frank Lindsay. McCone got in the back seat of the car with Lindsay. Lindsay mentioned to McCone that Itek had begun work on a design study for the NRO for a satellite that would accomplish the same goals as FULCRUM. Lindsay's briefing was a courtesy to McCone, but given the strained relations between the CIA and the NRO, it could not have been warmly received.[20]

Little time could have elapsed between McCone's arrival at Itek and the beginning of the briefing. One of the last people to walk into the room was NRO Director Brockway McMillan. He "recognized perhaps a dozen people among the roughly 50 in attendance." He saw Edwin Land, chairman of the CIA's scientific advisory board, and many of the best minds of the scientific community present. McMillan sat quietly in the audience as speaker after speaker described various aspects of the proposed FULCRUM system, including Madden's presentation of the mechanics of the camera. The design review added nothing to what McMillan knew already. It was without quantitative data or any real analysis of the crucial issue—the technical challenges of the scan angle. Finally, the CIA's Les Dirks rose to speak. His job was to defend the 120 degree scan angle requirement. As McMillan listened to Dirks, it quickly became apparent that he had padded his talk with charts and minute detail, most of it irrelevant or elementary. Dirks never made a direct justification for the requirement.

As Lindsay and Levison sat quietly in the audience, they hoped that someone from the gathered scientific community would raise a question. Perhaps a probing question about the scan angle would persuade the CIA executives to change their requirement for the 120 degree scan angle, a compromise with Itek's management could be negotiated, and the firm could keep the contract without compromising its technical views. The audience was silent. No one raised any objections, and no one from Itek voiced their own concerns.[21]

Few remain alive who attended the briefing that day at Itek. Their memories are fragmented, and they seldom overlap. In the patchwork quilt of recollections that have survived, one important fragment belongs to John McMahon. McMahon, who observed so much in those early days of overhead reconnaissance, recalled that the CIA's gruff director, John McCone, asked a question. He directed it to Walt Levison.

"Is this the best design Itek has come up with?" McCone demanded.

If McMahon's recollection is correct — and he is the only survivor who remembers this exchange — it must have been a horrible moment for Levison. In his heart Levison believed that FULCRUM was a flawed system and that Itek had better solutions to achieve the CIA's objectives. But in an attempt to maintain a cold peace with Wheelon's team, Itek's objections had not been raised publicly at the meeting. And as McCone already knew, Itek was also hard at work on another design study for the NRO to achieve the same mission — the S2. It was an awkward situation.

Staring out at an audience that had traveled from across the country for the meeting, looking at some of the most important figures in the nation's intelligence community, Levison, it seems, was at a loss for words. Slowly he began to speak. But he tried to put McCone off as he searched for the right words.

"It was a yes or no question!" McCone declared.

McCone was right. It was a yes or no question. But it was also a trap. If Levison's answer was yes, he would undermine the NRO's confidence in Itek's design for the S2, and his own reputation for integrity would be harmed. If he said no, the entire audience would wonder why they had been asked to travel to Itek in order to hear about a flawed system.

At that moment it must have become apparent to Levison and the other members of Itek's management team that it had been a horrible mistake to chase both CIA and NRO design studies. It must have been equally clear to Itek's management team that it had been a major miscalculation to allow the FULCRUM presentation to occur. Once Itek decided that it could no longer work with Wheelon's team on FULCRUM, it should have walked away from the contract immediately. Instead, Levison was now left twisting in the wind. McMahon remembered that after much agonizing, Levison's answer was yes — FULCRUM was Itek's best design. As the sound of Levison's answer filled the room, he must have been a very unhappy man.[22]

As the presentation neared its conclusion, Levison, who was now sitting near Brockway McMillan, snorted under his breath, "That tears it!" Levison got up and left the meeting. He prepared for what he years later called "our suicide punch." Levison abruptly rushed to Lindsay's office, where he, Lindsay, and the rest of the Itek management team decided to publicly announce that they would no longer work for the CIA on FULCRUM. The presentation had put them in an ugly situation. It was time to do what they should have done before — get out of the program.[23]

When the presentation ended, Frank Madden was unaware that Levison had already angrily left the room. As far as Madden could tell, the presentation had gone as well as it possibly could. Itek may not have explicitly endorsed the CIA's technical requirement for the camera's 120 degree scan angle, but it had backed the program, and Madden had demonstrated a mechanical prototype that showed a working system. Wheelon came up to Madden at the end of the presentation. "I didn't think you guys would come through," he said with a mixture of astonishment and relief. For a brief moment, it seemed that it would all work out.[24]

The next day, February 24, Itek's executives decided to communicate their decision to turn down the FULCRUM contract to the CIA, the NRO, and the cleared scientific community. Lindsay, Levison, and Philbrick felt pressured to act fast. They knew that at that same moment various high-level government committees were getting ready to endorse FULCRUM, on the assumption that Itek was completely behind the program. Top presidential science advisers like Land and Killian would feel betrayed if they endorsed the system only to find out later that Itek did not.

Lindsay, Levison, and Philbrick decided to make their announcement in stages. First, they would tell Land and Killian. Then they would tell their customer, the CIA. It seemed an unlikely approach. Yet operating in a crisis atmosphere, they concluded that if they told the CIA first, before they told the scientific community about their reasoning, the Agency would abruptly announce that Itek had been fired. Then, they reasoned,

Itek's explanations would seem little more than the carping of a losing contractor.

Walter Levison and John Wolfe hurried to Edwin Land's Cambridge office to announce Itek's decision. Unexpectedly, Land was not alone. Meeting with him at the same time were Brockway McMillan and Bud Wheelon, the prime antagonists in the struggle over the future of satellite reconnaissance. Uncomfortable but committed to his decision, Levison flatly announced that Itek would not pursue the contract and would co-operate with whatever vendor was selected to build the design.[25]

At the same time that Levison and Wolfe were on their way to their meeting with Land, Frank Lindsay called James Killian. Lindsay reached Killian at his apartment in Cambridge and told him Itek had decided to withdraw from the program. After listening to Lindsay's explanation for the decision, Killian was silent. He asked no questions. He simply thanked Lindsay for calling and hung up the phone. Killian's response left Lindsay with a bad feeling.[26]

Lindsay's next move was to go immediately to Washington to meet with CIA Director McCone. Lindsay asked Richard Philbrick to accompany him on the trip. After taking off from Boston's Logan Airport, they sat uncomfortably next to each other. They were about to tell their best customer that they refused to accept the biggest order in Itek's history. Lindsay had another reason to feel uncomfortable. He turned to Philbrick and announced that he had just received a call from the White House. He had been told that he was under consideration to be the next director of the CIA. Philbrick was stunned. Although the thought was unspoken, they both must have recognized that Lindsay's appointment would soon be in jeopardy. The plane landed, and Lindsay and Philbrick went to meet with McCone.

Lindsay's meeting with McCone was a disaster. Almost immediately he was on the defensive. If Itek had so many problems working with the CIA, McCone demanded, why hadn't Lindsay ever talked to him about it? It was a difficult question to answer. Then McCone accused Lindsay of selling out to the air force component at the NRO and undermining the CIA's credibility for the promise of future contracts. In the context of the CIA's struggle with the NRO, seen by the agency as little more than an air force Trojan horse, Itek's decision was viewed as a bald attempt to curry favor with another benefactor. By the time Lindsay left McCone's office, he was dazed and exhausted. McCone's accusations were not entirely unfounded. Itek, after all, was working on an alternate design study for the NRO, the S2. Afterward, Lindsay received a call from the White House. President Johnson had decided to appoint Adm. William Raborn as the next CIA director. Years later Lindsay acknowledged that McCone had probably been right. Lindsay should have spoken with him long before events had come to a head.[27]

About a week after the "Boston Tea Party," as the Itek presentation and its aftermath became known in intelligence circles, Frank Madden traveled to CIA headquarters. For Madden it was a truly sad mission. All his career he had worked on developing technical solutions to national security problems. He believed that FULCRUM, despite its flaws, could make a positive contribution to national security and advance the state of the art in the field. Instead, on March 2 he went to agree on a plan for turning over the FULCRUM designs to Perkin-Elmer, the company chosen to take Itek's place. The meeting began on a sour note. Asked by a CIA executive whether it was true that six Itek officials had threatened to resign if the company did not "terminate its associations" with the program, Madden denied that such a threat had been made. But he conceded that he had "asked to be relieved from the program, because he felt that he was not up to it."

John McMahon, observer of Itek and frequent writer of CIA minutes, commented that "with these amenities out of the way, the meeting proceeded into a review" of what Itek had already accomplished on the program. It must have felt like an eternity for Madden as the meeting ground forward. Madden and his CIA counterparts identified "what had been accomplished," determined "whether or not work should cease immediately" on various aspects of the project, and established the steps that needed to be "taken to prepare a finished report." The next day the CIA sent Itek a cable with the final instructions to wrap up the firm's participation in the program. Over the next few weeks, Itek would have to box up all its plans and paperwork and ship it to the agency. Surplus personnel who had worked on the program would be debriefed and fired. All of Itek's FULCRUM papers, including Madden's working prototype, would be sent to Perkin-Elmer.[28] But Itek still had a chance to win a satellite contract. The S2 design for the NRO could accomplish many of the same objectives as FULCRUM. Although the S2 was in a much earlier stage of development than FULCRUM, there was still a possibility that Edwin Land's scientific panel would recognize Itek's concerns about FULCRUM and select the S2 as the best choice.

On March 8 John McMahon met Richard Garwin, one of the members of Land's panel, at the Old Executive Office Building. He brought Garwin to CIA headquarters to discuss the NRO's organizational structure. When their car pulled up to the Agency and Garwin stepped out, McMahon explained "that the working level of troops at Itek were extremely dismayed" at the loss of the FULCRUM contract. They were "obviously in low spirits having spent a good deal of the last six months bringing this program to fruition only to see Itek management kick it away." Garwin expressed his "utter amazement at the Itek handling of the matter." Garwin believed that Itek had "miscalculated," that the company had tried to use the Land panel "as pawns." He suspected the company of having engineered the crisis to demonstrate the CIA's inability to work with the firm, "leaving the obvious conclusion for the Panel to suggest that this marvelous system be continued under Air Force management."[29]

Although it seemed Itek's relationship with the CIA couldn't get any worse, it did. Itek's withdrawal from the program had shaken the confidence of the CIA. The Agency's credibility was weakened, its management was confused, and precious energy was focused on a campaign to force Itek to apologize, to embarrass the company, or simply to punish it. By the end of March the CIA's chief of special projects staff in the Directorate of Science and Technology informed the Agency's deputy director that Itek's senior management had "alleged" that "unnamed officers of this Agency are exerting improper pressure on other Government agencies and other contractors." Now the situation was getting ugly. "Considered in the light of other affronts from this company against the Agency," the special projects chief suggested, "it seems to me mandatory that we take steps to surface these allegations and to force Itek to withdraw them."[30]

That March, Brockway McMillan, director of NRO, decided that the time was ripe to settle the issue of which government agency controlled CORONA, especially the critical issue of payload responsibility—the CIA's historic turf. In the middle of the month, McMillan sent Gen. Marshall

Carter, deputy director of the CIA, a new proposal on CORONA management that strengthened the position of the NRO. Carter's response, written on March 16, must have surprised McMillan. Not only did Carter's
response reveal a new commitment at the CIA to "retain complete responsibility" for "those aspects of CORONA that 'historically' had been in the
Agency's custody," but it "had the tone of a proclamation." The CIA
would not recognize the NRO's "authority to control any important aspect
of CORONA."[31]

Like a wounded lion, cornered, weakened, but not bowed, the CIA had
defiantly roared. Now the CIA's counterattack began in force. It "recommended dissolution of the NRO," with the CIA assuming "total responsibility" for the key aspects of any satellite reconnaissance program, not
just CORONA. According to the CIA plan, the NRO's Satellite Operation
Center would now fall under Agency control, and Pentagon agencies
would be involved in the program only to the extent that they provided
support services, "such as launching, commanding, tracking, and recov-
ering."[32]

Caught in a crossfire between dueling government agencies, Itek's besieged CEO tried to regain the CIA's confidence. Lindsay believed that a
genuine apology and an honest review of the facts would clear the air. On
April 5, 1965, in an attempt to repair Itek's tattered relationship with the
CIA, Lindsay wrote to John McCone and apologized for causing any em-
barrassment to the agency. He admitted that Itek had made mistakes, but
he attributed "this situation basically to the exercise of too close supervision
of Itek's work, in [a] manner which we had not experienced in years of
harmonious and productive work for the agency." Although Lindsay was
respectful, he nevertheless left no doubt that the ultimate fault rested with
the CIA. He also conceded no ground on the correctness of Itek's technical
appraisal of the program. "In the absence of a firm requirement for the
120 degree scan angle," he explained, "Itek could not endorse the FULCRUM
design as the one best adapted to satisfying the Agency's needs whether
from the standpoint of performance, reliability or delivery schedule." Itek
had a moral obligation to act decisively to bring attention to a design that
"would have poorly served the national interest." Lindsay closed his letter
on a note that was forward-looking and melancholy at the same time. "We
earnestly hope," he declared, "that Itek's special skills will be used with

maximum effectiveness, and that our procedural mistakes and matters of personal friction will not stand in the way." Finally, Lindsay said, "I am ready to do everything possible to repair our damaged relations."[33] But it was too late. The damage was done.

Itek and the CIA were like partners trapped in a failed marriage. Although they may have been bitter and resentful toward each other, they were stuck in the relationship — CORONA made sure of that. As long as CORONA was the nation's space reconnaissance workhorse, Itek's cameras would continue to fly into orbit. But when it was time to negotiate new CORONA contracts, the talks were lengthy and difficult. In late April the CIA's contracting officer reported that several offers had been made to Itek, "each time at an increase," but that the company "has not found these acceptable and has not chosen to make a reasonable counter offer." In at least one meeting, Itek's negotiators "violently objected" to the CIA's offer of a 10 percent profit margin. The Agency also proposed that in the case of either cost overruns, or underruns, the CIA would split the expenses and the spoils, in a ratio of 75 percent for the CIA and 25 percent for Itek. Itek wanted a 10.3 percent profit, which the CIA termed "unacceptable." In addition to a higher profit margin, Itek wanted to reduce the company's financial exposure to cost overruns. Finally, the CIA gave Itek an April 30 deadline to either accept or reject the last offer, but the date passed by without an agreement. By early May, Itek still found the CIA offer unacceptable. If the CIA wanted Itek's high-quality, highly reliable product, it would have to pay.

On May 11 John McMahon reported that "at long last the Itek negotiations have concluded." Itek would earn a 10.2 percent profit margin on the order for nineteen camera systems, assorted ancillary equipment, and supporting field services through February 1966. In the case of either cost overruns or underruns, the CIA agreed to a ratio of 80 percent to 20 percent. By holding firm, despite the intense pressures of the time, Itek's management succeeded in both expanding the firm's profit margin and better protecting the company from an unforeseen rise in expenses. And there were other incentives for Itek to earn "additional profit through cost savings." Over the years, the CIA continued to renew CORONA contracts with Itek. In fact, Itek built cameras for the CORONA program until its end in 1972.[34]

But CORONA proved to be Itek's grand and final masterpiece. When the scientists who advised the CIA and the NRO gathered once more to give the final go-ahead for the follow-on system to CORONA, they considered Itek's S2 design but chose that of Perkin-Elmer, a revision of Itek's original FULCRUM proposal. Never again would Itek win a contract for a new spy satellite camera system—the political fall-out from FULCRUM was simply too great.[35]

The CIA continued to be suspicious of Itek's motives, and John McMahon closely tracked every move at Itek's headquarters to keep his boss, Bud Wheelon, fully informed of any mischief that the contractor might be about to create. When McMahon learned that the NRO's McMillan was visiting Itek headquarters in June, he reported speculation about his possible agenda. When Itek's acquisition of Chicago Aerial fell apart, and Itek sued the company, McMahon could not "dismiss the suspicion that Itek would be most pleased with the opportunity to publicly air their accomplishments and undertakings vis-à-vis black contracts." McMahon even suspected that Itek's lawsuit was a Trojan horse, a trick to get back into the CIA's good graces. He argued that Itek was "going through the motions, knowing that we will prevent" them from discussing classified systems, "and, hence, we 'owe' them one." When McMahon learned that Itek's work on the Apollo program was moving forward, he advised the CIA's security staff to "remain alert to activities at Itek and, in general, be aware that any NASA camera program is a potential threat to the security of the satellite photographic technology."[36]

It was a poisonous atmosphere. The CIA's top-level executives saw Itek's actions as "a betrayal by a contractor from whom complete loyalty was expected." Itek's decision to walk away from FULCRUM resulted in the CIA's being "humiliated" within the cleared scientific community, and "questioned as to its scientific integrity." As Lindsay's meeting with McCone demonstrated, Itek was "suspected of the worst of motives," including having sold out to the air force and the NRO for generous contracts. Thirty-five years later, veteran CIA executives from the period still remained bitter and suspicious about Itek's motives. They continued to believe that Itek had indeed sold out.[37]

Itek's senior executives, meanwhile, recalled their decision as a principled stand. When he was approaching eighty years old, Walter Levison reflected on Itek's blow-up with the CIA. "We were spitting in the eye of our best customer. Did we really do it on a matter of principle? The answer is: Yeah, we did. We did." It was a dark epiphany for Levison. "We thought people would appreciate our intellectual integrity," he sighed. "They didn't."[38]

Ruminating on the FULCRUM fiasco more than thirty-five years after the fact, Philbrick echoed Levison's sentiments. He wistfully concluded, "Somehow, in some crazy way, we felt that integrity would carry us through. It didn't." FULCRUM could have been a huge contract for Itek, if management had accepted the Agency's terms. Instead, it was "the beginning of the end."[39]

"I often wonder," reflected the NRO's Brockway McMillan, "how Frank Lindsay broke the news to his Board of Directors that he had just turned down" a huge contract. "I think you now see the basis for my great respect for Lindsay and Levison. You also see that the only thing Itek management could have done to pick up the successor to CORONA was to compromise their principles." McMillan explained that a company could build what Itek was asked to build, but only with great difficulty, and at risk of its corporate reputation for competence and engineering judgment. Itek's management simply was not willing to take the risk or to compromise its principles. Thirty-five year later, McMillan's admiration for Itek's decision was unwavering. "I was then, and still am, impressed."[40]

CIA Deputy Director Wheelon reflected on Itek's decision and reached a different conclusion. He recalled Itek's technical capabilities with great esteem and concluded that Itek's decision was indeed a "corporate tragedy." But he declined to credit Itek management with a principled stand. In the development of cutting-edge technology, Wheelon explained, everyone gets along well when progress is made. But when difficulties arise, clients and contractors can have a parting of the ways. Personality differences, hidden by the mask of success when all is well, suddenly come to the fore when progress grinds to a halt. Wheelon was under pressure in 1965 to maintain the CIA's presence in satellite reconnaissance, and Itek was deeply concerned about its ability to meet FULCRUM's requirement for a 120 degree scan angle. Perhaps Itek's decision to walk away from FULCRUM was less an act of principle, Wheelon argued, than an admission it could not accomplish the goal. After all, he concluded, Perkin-Elmer did build the system.[41] Until all the documents related to FUL-CRUM are declassified, it is a matter that will remain unresolved.

Wheelon's conclusion, that FULCRUM was a "corporate tragedy," is inescapable. The profits on the contract would have been in the millions, and afterward Itek's classified operations began a steep and long decline. But it was also a national security tragedy. In the months leading up to the debacle, it seems that the CIA's John McMahon asked Jack Ledford to review Itek's performance history. Ledford wrote that Itek had perhaps the "best technical competence" of any camera contractor, and that its "response to direction and cooperation" with the CIA's contracting and technical personnel had been excellent. After FULCRUM, however, the firm was tainted. Few within the intelligence community wanted to award the renegades at Itek a major contract.[42] As a result, the full power of the company's creative talent was lost to the nation.

In the aftermath of FULCRUM, the success of Itek's commercial operations was more important than ever to the company's future. If Itek's new RS technology and its memory-centered computers fulfilled their promise, the company's future would still be bright.

18

BRAINS INTO GOLD

In 1965, when Itek's management walked away from FULCRUM, Frank Lindsay and the others still had reason to be optimistic. CORONA remained central to America's intelligence efforts and continued to be the nation's reconnaissance workhorse until 1972. But there were to be no big follow-on systems for Itek, no new contracts for spy satellite cameras.

At first it seemed that everything would somehow work out. Although Itek's stock suffered a steep correction in the second half of 1965, falling back below $40 a share, it resumed its upward climb in 1966. Speculation over Itek's promising RS technology fueled the rally, along with continued confidence in Lindsay's management abilities. After all, with Lindsay at the helm, Itek's sales and earnings had moved steadily upward. If the new products under development at Itek's research labs could successfully be brought to market, there was no limit to how high the stock could climb.

And as the stock rose again, Lindsay led an aggressive acquisition campaign. After FULCRUM it must have been obvious to Lindsay that Itek had to diversify its sources of revenues. If Itek's scientists could develop the technology to see Soviet missiles from space, then they should certainly be able to improve the quality of everyday eyeglasses. So Lindsay bought an eyeglass company, Pennsylvania Optical Company. And when Lindsay briefed the New York Society of Security Analysts in late 1966, he confidently predicted that Itek would close the year with record profits. In late September, when Itek's shares were listed on the New York Stock Exchange, Itek's stock price rocketed toward $90 a share.

The only disconcerting note was a brief but sharp drop in Itek's stock price in October. Perkin-Elmer announced that it had won a major contract, though it refused to provide details, including the name of the customer. Simultaneously, Itek announced that one if its government contracts had been canceled. When *The Wall Street Journal* asked Itek whether the cancellation was related to Perkin-Elmer's new contract, the company spokesman simply replied, "no comment," prompting the paper to confidently report that the contracts were the same. More than a year after the Boston Tea Party at Itek's headquarters, that was all the public was to learn about FULCRUM — a hint of trouble at Itek, nothing more.[1]

Itek's stock resumed its rally, and Lindsay continued to aggressively diversify through acquisitions. Where Leghorn had failed on the acquisition trail, it seemed that Lindsay would succeed. In 1967 Lindsay bought Applied Technology (A.T.), which made a variety of electronic countermeasures to protect U.S. military planes from being shot down. Although the acquisition now made Itek a genuine player in the defense industry, another aspect to the A.T. acquisition was particularly appealing. It also made systems for electronic reconnaissance. Now Itek was the only company with a major presence in photo-optics and electronic reconnaissance. Not even Eastman Kodak or Perkin-Elmer could make that claim.

Meanwhile, excitement on Wall Street continued to build over Itek's RS technology. Rumors "swept the investment community" as Wall Street analysts envisioned all the money Itek would earn when it introduced its new line of RS film and other products based on the RS technology. While Itek officials cautioned the press that new products were still far down the road, the frenzied speculation forced the New York Stock Exchange to temporarily halt trading in the firm's stock. The buzz around Itek seemed justified. Not only did its stock price soar to new highs, so did its earnings.[2]

By 1969 Itek was running out of steam. Gilbert King, former director of research at IBM, had joined Itek with great fanfare in the mid-1960s, but now he was gone. His visionary new products, announced to the world in the weeks before the FULCRUM fiasco, never materialized. The translation device failed to work as advertised, and the futuristic photo-optical memory system computer never computed. To make matters worse, earnings at Applied Technology collapsed in 1968, and Itek's own earnings suffered along with it. Itek's stock, which peaked at $172 a share in 1967, was down to $55 by the summer. Although Lindsay was still promoting the promise of its RS film technology, Wall Street was growing skeptical.[3]

Yet Itek's technical virtuosity in designing highly customized optical solutions for clients, the source of its great achievements in the past, was undiminished. Although CORONA remained the firm's sole spy satellite contract, it won important new contracts from NASA. When Neil Armstrong landed on the moon in 1969, Itek's expertise and products were present — from the planning for the experiments he conducted, to the window finishing for the command vehicle, *Columbia,* to "the protective quartz coverings for the tracking lights on the lunar module *Eagle.*" Later Apollo command modules carried Itek cameras for mapping the moon, and *Skylab* carried Itek cameras. When NASA's *Viking Lander* settled onto Martian soil, Itek cameras were on board to take photographs of the red planet. But special projects like these, despite their prestige, did not carry big enough price tags, or long enough production runs, to carry all of Itek's scientists and engineers, let alone an entire company.

In 1970 more than a thousand employees were fired in an attempt to restructure the company. In a desperate effort to maintain financial support for the scientists and engineers at the heart of its reconnaissance operations, Itek began to aggressively peddle its spy cameras to foreign governments. Itek's top executives traveled to the far reaches of the world to drum up business. The shah of Iran became an active customer. So did South Korea, Israel, and Egypt, not to mention a variety of countries in Africa and Latin America. Although the U.S. government never allowed Itek to sell its best cameras abroad, it encouraged other sales. It was a retail version of Open Skies, promoting stability in troubled regions by marketing Itek cameras to potential enemies. But the sales, impressive in scope, did not generate much in terms of revenues or profits.

Hopes that Itek's RS technology would save the company were fading fast. By the early 1970s sales of products based on the technology were less than $2 million. The RS camera film itself was never marketed, and the much-hyped competitive threat to Kodak never materialized.

In 1972 President Richard Nixon signed the Strategic Arms Limitation Treaty (SALT) with the Soviet Union. Itek's cameras had demonstrated that compliance with the treaty could be monitored from space. Nixon's knowledge of this technology was critical to his willingness to sign the treaty. Détente had begun—a historic moment made possible, in part, by Itek. Yet for all of Itek's contributions to national security and world security, when the CORONA program was over that same year, Lindsay was regrettably forced to let go many of the scientists and engineers who had made CORONA possible.[4]

By the mid-1970s Itek was sinking. The company was losing money and its stock was trading at just $7 a share. The Rockefellers, who once had controlled the company, now owned only 4 percent of it. Wall Street analysts who once had avidly tracked Itek, promoting it as the next great growth story, stopped following it. And Lindsay, championed as the company's savior in the 1960s, was increasingly coming under fire for the company's ill fortune. "The hardest thing in the world is to move technology from the lab into successful products," Lindsay told *Forbes*. "We haven't done as well as we should have." *Forbes* coldly observed that Lindsay's "eyes light up" when he talks about Itek's cameras for NASA's Voyager program. But "technical savvy has not yet taught [Itek] how to turn brains into gold." Weeks later, in "a surprise move," Lindsay stepped down as Itek's president and chief executive officer and relinquished all operating responsibilities. He was promoted to chairman of the board, a position he quietly occupied until his retirement.[5]

When Litton Industries acquired Itek in the early 1980s, the company finally lost its independence. It was an anticlimactic end to a company that had made so many important contributions to America's national security.[6]

But for many of Itek's executives, the end of their involvement with the company was just another beginning. For them, Itek had been a cause. Now they moved on to other causes and companies, or found new ways to make a contribution to the world around them.

When Richard Leghorn left Itek, he remained involved in Pugwash and continued an active business career. He became president of DASA, a telecommunications company that took on AT&T, and then he moved into cable television, building a local cable company on his beloved Cape Cod. After selling his holdings to TCI, he founded CableLabs, an industry research and development consortium, and worked to promote television standards to protect children from inappropriate entertainment.[7]

When the Soviet Union collapsed, Franklin Lindsay could claim justifiable pride in knowing that he had contributed to America's victory in the Cold War. At more than seventy years old, it must have been tempting for Lindsay to take a rest and watch history unfold from the comfort of the sidelines.

But Lindsay, the old commando, the former head of the CIA's covert operations in Eastern Europe, heard the trumpets call him again. Fearful that the newly liberated countries might not survive as free nations, and that a new Iron Curtain would again divide the continent, he packed up his bags and moved to Ukraine with his wife, Margot. His mission—to secure the independence of the largest of the newly independent states. For the next several years Frank Lindsay and his wife spent much of each year in Kiev. There, he developed a working relationship with top Ukrainian officials, and with the assistance of Harvard's John F. Kennedy School of Government engaged them in an ongoing dialogue about issues ranging from defense reconversion to constructing an effective national security apparatus.[8]

The NRO's Brockway McMillan, tired from his struggles with the CIA, returned to Bell Laboratories in late 1965.

Bud Wheelon stayed at the CIA for a little longer, waiting until 1966 to leave the Agency for a position in the private sector. Wheelon joined Hughes Aircraft Company, where he was a vice president for engineering in charge of satellites. Under his direction, Hughes built more than half of the world's commercial communications satellites, not to mention satellites for the military. By the time he left Hughes in 1988, Wheelon was chairman of the board.

John McMahon stayed at the CIA long after the code name FULCRUM had been forgotten. By the 1980s McMahon was deputy director of the Agency, chief operating officer with responsibility for managing the organization's global activities. He played a key role in obtaining congressional support for the CIA's secret war against the Soviet Union in Afghanistan, a pivotal episode in the history of the Cold War. In 1986 he joined Lockheed Missiles and Space Company, and by the time he retired in 1994, he was the company's president.

As for Laurance Rockefeller, Itek was just one of many important companies his venture capital operations funded. But over the years, his stake in Itek was steadily reduced, and his own active involvement in venture capital declined. Instead, Rockefeller devoted his energies increasingly to conservation. As the noted historian Robin Winks observed, "One cannot drive the Palisades Parkway in New York, stroll through Woodstock, Vermont, swim in the Virgin Islands, or hike the trails of the Tetons without seeing and benefiting from his work."[9]

EPILOGUE

In the aftermath of Sputnik, during a time of national crisis, when America's need for intelligence about the Soviet Union was greater than ever, Pentagon budget cuts threatened the existence of a group of scientists at Boston University—Duncan MacDonald's team of spy camera experts. Although their skills were essential to the nation's intelligence efforts, the demise of MacDonald's group seemed inevitable.

Yet they survived. An entrepreneur with vision and connections, Richard Leghorn sensed the gravity of the government's error and seized the opportunity it created. Teddy Walkowicz risked his reputation with his boss, Laurance Rockefeller, and asked him to support Leghorn's acquisition of the lab. Rockefeller, confident that an opportunity of some kind existed, decided to put his own capital at risk to close the deal.

Yet Leghorn, for all his energy and entrepreneurial vision, was only able to throw the Boston University lab a lifeline. It took the CIA's Richard Bissell, another kind of entrepreneur, to guarantee the laboratory's complete rescue—with contracts.

By 1957, when Bissell first became involved with CORONA, he was already developing new ways to leverage the best brains and technologies in America. Scientific Engineering Institute, a CIA front company, was one example. Betting on small companies, even start-ups, was another Bissell technique. Bissell's counterparts at the Pentagon were loath to risk their careers on unproven designs, or unknown companies. But Bissell saw these risks as opportunities.

Bissell's innovations in program management earned the CIA a reputation for project development prowess and fostered an entrepreneurial spirit in the Agency that flowered under his leadership. His techniques, developed to harness the wonders of a vibrant free-market economy, had no counterpart in the Soviet Union.

In culture, disposition, and character, Bissell's CIA was less a bureaucracy than a venture capital fund. Under his leadership, the Agency developed an entrepreneurial prowess that emboldened it to engage America's private sector in a vigorous exchange of ideas, and contract orders. This dialogue of dollars and designs sharpened America's competitive edge in the Cold War and quantifiably strengthened U.S. national security.

For all of Bissell's historic accomplishments, Itek's story suggests that his innovations could have unintended consequences. When a corporation entered Bissell's secret world, American capitalism was transformed. The result was spy capitalism, the intersection of business and espionage.

Itek's relationship with the CIA and its work on CORONA were highly classified. And maintaining these secrets successfully was an essential part of conducting business. Imperceptibly, as Itek's business grew, a culture of secrecy came to permeate the company's decision-making process. As Itek worked to overcome a series of technical, financial, and managerial problems in order to grow and survive in a world of industrial giants, it probably became progressively easier for Itek's management to rationalize questionable acquisitions and hide poor decisions, or any bad news, from the public in the name of national security.

Leghorn's failed acquisition campaign, and his quest to lead an information technology revolution, epitomized one aspect of this operating condition. Leghorn could charm the financial press and the markets with his talk of an information revolution when Itek's revenues and profits were steadily rising. Because he could never disclose the nature of Itek's classified contracts with the government, Leghorn could leave the impression that genuine synergies existed between the firm's classified "information technology" contracts and its acquisitions.

Although Leghorn may have believed this story himself, it was a strategy that failed to hold together under the competitive pressures of the marketplace. Leghorn's dream about an information revolution was prophetic, but impossible to achieve with the technologies available in his time. The companies he cobbled together were a flammable mixture of patents, possibilities, and products still in development. The marketplace demanded products that could be sold, not dreams.

When Franklin Lindsay, Walter Levison, and Richard Philbrick decided to walk away from the FULCRUM contract, they illustrated another side of spy capitalism. Although management may have believed that the firm's integrity was at stake, the decision cost the company millions of dollars in lost revenues. Itek's top executives could make this decision with the certainty that shareholders and the financial press would never fully know about it.

Yet for all of Itek's problems, deceptions, and mistakes, it is clear that when America was in danger, the company's scientists and engineers crafted a product that made the country more secure. Their accomplishment was possible because a businessman, Richard Leghorn, envisioned Itek; a venture capitalist, Laurance Rockefeller, financed it; and a management consultant, Frank Lindsay, saved it. In retrospect, we can say that these men did not always make the best business decisions. Dealing with the daily uncertainties that characterize the marketplace, no executive ever can. But they were all men driven by a shared vision of American national security transformed by technology.

At the dawn of the twenty-first century, the CIA has launched a new initiative to reach out to young technology companies like Itek. It is called In-Q-Tel, and it is a CIA-owned venture capital fund. It was created because the CIA, once a technology leader, had increasingly fallen behind the private sector in an area critical to its core mission — information management. In-Q-Tel's job is to revolutionize the CIA's information technology capabilities by investing in the kinds of start-up companies in which promising, cutting-edge technologies are likely to be developed.

Almost fifty years after the birth of Itek, In-Q-Tel's incorporation is an ironic turn of events that is at once promising and problematic. In the 1950s Laurance Rockefeller's venture capital operation funded Itek — just one of many investments Rockefeller made to advance technologies that might prove important to America's national security. He made these investments because he thought that they would be profitable, and because at a time when America was in danger, he thought that these technologies might make the country more secure.

Today there is no Laurance Rockefeller stepping into the breach with his own capital. Nor is there a Teddy Walkowicz using his connections to bridge the gap between national security requirements and the marketplace. Instead, the CIA has created its own venture capital fund. Now it will attempt to achieve on its own what was accomplished in partnership with the capitalists and executives of another age.

Staffed by a small group of dealmakers, analysts, and technologists, In-Q-Tel has the checkbook and independence to pursue its mission. Just as Bissell's U-2 project office was stripped from the CIA's bureaucracy and set up as a special-purpose procurement office, so has In-Q-Tel been freed. With offices near the CIA and in Silicon Valley, In-Q-Tel is well positioned to serve as a bridge between the Agency and the most creative area of American industry. By developing relations with these companies when they are young and their products still on the drawing board, In-Q-Tel has the potential to gain important insights that can help the CIA better design its own information technology strategy. And because In-Q-Tel is making deals outside of the CIA's regular channels, it should be able to move faster and more effectively.

In many ways In-Q-Tel faces a more difficult task than either Laurance Rockefeller's venture capital operation or Richard Bissell's development projects staff. When Bissell developed the U-2 and CORONA, he was charged with creating the technology the CIA needed *and* forging a considerable part of the staff and structure that could effectively exploit the new flow of intelligence. In-Q-Tel must work with the CIA's staff and structure as they exist today.

When Laurance Rockefeller invested in a start-up company, he often became the dominant shareholder. This gave his investment team great influence over a company's management. In-Q-Tel, whose investment capital is small by the standards of today's venture capital industry, is unlikely to have similar clout.

If In-Q-Tel lacks many of the advantages that either Rockefeller or Bissell enjoyed, it also is likely to avoid at least one problem—classification. All of In-Q-Tel's investments are openly posted on its own website. This high degree of openness means that many of the unintended consequences of spy capitalism that characterized Itek's early history are likely to be avoided in In-Q-Tel's relations with corporate America—at least initially.

Identifying new technologies and cutting deals are just one part of In-

Q-Tel's challenge. In order for In-Q-Tel's work to have an impact on how the CIA operates, the new tools it identifies must be rapidly deployed within the CIA and quickly integrated into the agency's operations. More than traditional measures of financial performance, In-Q-Tel must ultimately be judged on its ability to promote change within the CIA. If In-Q-Tel makes a fortune for the U.S. government but the CIA continues to fall behind the technology curve, the experiment will have failed.

But calculated risks can have big payoffs. When Bissell bet on Itek, the company was less than a year old. Three-axis stabilization, the concept at the heart of Itek's spy satellite proposal, was nothing more than an untested idea. Yet Bissell selected Itek, and the rest is history.

As Itek's story demonstrates, capitalism in defense of liberty can be a messy affair. But it worked. Itek delivered its cameras, and America was safer. Nothing could be clearer. Except, perhaps, a photograph of the Soviet Union taken by an Itek camera.

NOTES

1. The Battlegreen Inn

1. Walter Levison and Harold Sprague, interview with author, Concord, Mass., 27 February 1998; Ed Campbell, interview with author, Dartmouth, Mass., 20 September 1997.

2. Peter Crisp, interview with author, New York, 2 July 1997; Peter Crisp, telephone conversation with author, 29 January 1998; Najeeb Halaby, *Crosswinds: An Airman's Memoir* (Garden City, N.Y.: Doubleday, 1978), 59–62; Najeeb Halaby, telephone conversation with author, 6 March 1998; Peter Collier and David Horowitz, *The Rockefellers: An American Dynasty* (New York: Holt, Rinehart, and Winston, 1976), 294–295; Alvin Moscow, *The Rockefeller Inheritance* (Garden City, N.Y.: Doubleday, 1977), 178.

3. Richard P. Cook, "Laurance Rockefeller Finds Risky New Uses for Old Millions; Nelson's Brother Invests in Ideas, Turns Tiny Firms into Scientific Pacemakers; The Case of Fabulous Itek," *Wall Street Journal*, 13 July 1959, pp. 1, 6; "Prodigy with a Flair for Profit," *Business Week*, 18 July 1959, pp. 78–84; Charles M. Macko, "Venture Capitalist: Laurance Rockefeller Has Put His Fortune to Work Creating New Wealth," *Barron's*, 14 August 1961, pp. 9, 25; Walter Levison, telephone conversation with author, 13 May 1997; Frank J. Madden, "The CORONA Camera System: Itek's Contribution to World Stability," Hughes Danbury Optical Systems, Inc. Lexington, Mass., 1997, photocopy, pp. 6–7, 10; Ernest R. May, "Strategic Intelligence and U.S. Security: The Contributions of CORONA," in *Eye in the Sky: The Story of the CO-RONA Spy Satellite*, ed. Dwayne A. Day, John M. Logsdon, and Brian Latell (Washington: Smithsonian Institution Press, 1998), 21–28; Kenneth E. Greer, "CORONA," in *CORONA: America's First Satellite Program*, ed. by Kevin C. Ruffner (Washington: Central Intelligence Agency, 1995), 37–39.

4. Campbell interview, 20 September 1997; Walter Levison, interview with author, Harvard, Mass., 21 August 1998; Richard Philbrick, interview with author, Orleans, Mass., 19 August 1997; Crisp interview, 2 July 1997.

5. Dow Smith, interview with author, Harvard, Mass., 21 August 1998; Levison interview, 21 August 1998; Philbrick interview, 19 August 1997; Walter Levison and Franklin Lindsay, interview with author, Cambridge, Mass., 7 June 1997; Levison and Sprague interview, 27 February 1998.

6. Franklin Lindsay, interview with author, Cambridge, Mass., 6 June 1997; Levison and Lindsay interview, 7 June 1997. Lindsay's memoir of his years in the OSS provides important background on his early years; see Franklin Lindsay, *Beacons in the Night: With the OSS and Tito's Partisans in Wartime Yugoslavia* (Stanford: Stanford University Press, 1993).

2. "You damned fool, now look what you've gone and done"

1. Franklin Lindsay, *Beacons in the Night: With the OSS and Tito's Partisans in Wartime Yugoslavia* (Stanford: Stanford University Press, 1993), 1–7, 87; Franklin Lindsay, telephone conversation with author, 27 August 2000. For a fuller discussion of the origins and early days of the OSS see Burton Hersh, *The Old Boys: The American Elite and the Origins of the CIA* (New York: Scribner's, 1992); Thomas F. Troy, *Wild Bill and Intrepid: Donovan, Stephenson, and the Origin of CIA* (New Haven: Yale University Press, 1996); Robin Winks, *Cloak and Gown: Scholars in the Secret War, 1939–1961* (New Haven: Yale University Press, 1987).

2. Franklin Lindsay, telephone conversations with author, 9 November 1998, 27 August 2000.

3. Lindsay telephone conversation, 9 November 1998.

4. Franklin Lindsay, interview with author, Cambridge, Mass., 13 March 1999; Franklin Lindsay, telephone conversations with author, 19 May 1997, 21 May 1997.

5. Franklin Lindsay, *Beacons in the Night: With the OSS and Tito's Partisans in Wartime Yugoslavia* (Stanford: Stanford University Press, 1993), 15.

6. Ibid., 7–8, 51–52.

7. Ibid., 52–56; Lindsay telephone conversation, 27 August 2000.

8. Lindsay, *Beacons in the Night,* 70–83, 87.

9. Ibid., 181–183, 194–197, 209, 239, 253; Lindsay telephone conversation, 27 August 2000.

10. Robert Joyce to Director, OSS/Washington & Chief, SI/Washington, 30 August 1945, Personal Papers of Franklin Lindsay.

11. Lindsay telephone conversation, 21 May 1997; Franklin Lindsay, telephone conversation with author, 30 July 1998; Jordan A. Schwarz, *The Speculator: Bernard M. Baruch in Washington, 1917–1965* (Chapel Hill: University of North Carolina Press, 1981), 490–492.

12. Schwarz, *The Speculator,* 490–492; Joyce to Director, 30 August 1945; James Grant, *Bernard M. Baruch: The Adventures of a Wall Street Legend* (New York: Simon and Schuster, 1983), 305.

13. Grant, *Baruch,* 309–312. In his memoirs, Baruch explains his thinking behind his revision to the Acheson-Lilienthal report: "If I had learned anything out of my

experiences in international affairs, it was that world peace is impossible without the force to sustain it." Bernard M. Baruch, *Baruch: The Public Years* (New York: Holt, Rinehart and Winston, 1960), 367, 369–370.

14. Schwarz, *The Speculator,* 500.

15. Lindsay recalled discussing with Gromyko an article on U.S.-Soviet talks that appeared in the *New York Times.* According to Lindsay, Gromyko commented that the article was "half right, half wrong, but I guess that's what you in America call balanced reporting." Lindsay telephone conversation, 30 July 1998; United States Department of State, *Foreign Relations of the United States,* 1946, 1:955–960. Over the next few weeks Lindsay participated in a variety of meetings with senior U.S. foreign policy makers, like George Kennan, and with other members of the Soviet government. United States Department of State, *Foreign Relations of the United States,* 1946, 1:1011, 1016–1019, 1021–1025.

16. Franklin Lindsay, telephone conversations with author, 12 May 1997, 30 July 1998, 27 August 2000.

17. Lindsay telephone conversation, 12 May 1997; Robert Marjolin, *Europe and the United States in the World Economy* (Durham: Duke University Press, 1953), 3–4; Stanley Hoffman, *The Marshall Plan: A Retrospective* (London: Westview, 1984), 101–102.

18. Lindsay telephone conversation, 12 May 1997; Lindsay, *Beacons in the Night,* 295–297, 330–331; Peter Grose, *Gentleman Spy: The Life of Allen Dulles* (Boston: Houghton Mifflin, 1994), 280.

19. Lindsay telephone conversation, 12 May 1997; Richard M. Bissell Jr., with Jonathan E. Lewis and Frances T. Pudlo, *Reflections of a Cold Warrior: From Yalta to the Bay of Pigs* (New Haven: Yale University Press), 34–35.

20. Bissell, *Reflections of a Cold Warrior,* 39–40, 67–68; Lindsay telephone conversation, 12 May 1997; Lindsay interview, 13 March 1999.

21. Bissell, *Reflections of a Cold Warrior,* 68; Hersh, *The Old Boys,* 236; Lindsay telephone conversation, 27 August 2000.

22. Lindsay and many of his colleagues had assumed that their World War II experiences were directly relevant to fighting the Soviet Union. He later recognized that their education, measured in human life, was costly. Franklin Lindsay, interview with author, Cambridge, Mass., 27 February 1999; Lindsay telephone conversation, 30 July 1998; Hersh, *The Old Boys,* 237, 242.

23. Franklin Lindsay, "A Program for the Development of New Cold War Instruments," 22 October 1952, Private Papers of Franklin Lindsay.

24. Franklin Lindsay, "National Research in Cold War Weapons and Strategies," 12 May 1954, Private Papers of Franklin Lindsay. Lindsay continued to develop these themes throughout 1954. Franklin Lindsay, "Recommendation for Continuation of Project Gossard Activities," 14 July 1954, Private Papers of Franklin Lindsay; Allen Dulles to Rowan Gaither, 11 September 1954, Private Papers of Franklin Lindsay.

25. Cary Reich, *The Life of Nelson A. Rockefeller: Worlds to Conquer, 1908–1958* (New York: Doubleday, 1996), 551–552, 558–559, 622–624, 627–631; Stephen E. Ambrose, *Eisenhower: The President* (New York: Simon and Schuster, 1984), 257–259, 264–267;

Michael R. Beschloss, *May-Day: Eisenhower, Khrushchev, and the U-2 Affair* (New York: Harper and Row, 1986), 98–100, 103; Franklin Lindsay, interview with author, Cambridge, Mass., 8 November 1997; Lindsay telephone conversations, 27 February 1999, 27 August 2000.

26. Lindsay telephone conversation, 27 August 2000; Franklin Lindsay to Nelson Rockefeller, 12 June 1956, folder 320, box 29, subpanel 4, V4D, Special Studies Project, RAC.

27. Franklin Lindsay, notes on evening panel meeting, 20 November 1956, 7 December 1956, folder 174, box 15, subpanel 2, V4D, Special Studies Project, RAC; Townsend Hoopes, minutes of first meeting, 29–30 November 1956, undated, folder 174, box 15, subpanel 2, V4D, Special Studies Project, RAC; Townsend Hoopes, minutes of second meeting, 20 December 1956, undated, folder 174, box 15, subpanel 2, V4D, Special Studies Project, RAC; Townsend Hoopes, minutes of third meeting, 24–25 January 1957, undated, folder 174, box 15, subpanel 2, V4D, Special Studies Project, RAC.

28. Lindsay interview, 8 November 1997; Ambrose, *Eisenhower*, 434–435; McGeorge Bundy, *Danger and Survival: Choices About the Bomb in the First Fifty Years* (New York: Random House, 1988), 335–337.

3. Corporation X

1. Eisenhower's military experience gave him important insights into the role of intelligence in preserving national security. His support of the U-2 reflected his insistence that "the U.S. Government keep itself at the cutting edge of technology." He "saw to it that his nation's best scientists were working for the government on matters of national security." Stephen Ambrose, *Ike's Spies: Eisenhower and the Espionage Establishment* (Garden City: Doubleday, 1981), 267–278. See also Richard M. Bissell Jr. with Jonathan E. Lewis and Frances T. Pudlo, *Reflections of a Cold Warrior: From Yalta to the Bay of Pigs* (New Haven: Yale University Press, 1996), 115.

2. When the SAGE early-warning system was first deployed in early 1958, it used two IBM-FSQ-7 digital computers. "Each of these computers weighed 275 tons, housed two million memory cores, 50,000 vacuum tubes, 600,000 resisters, 170,000 diodes, 1,042 miles of internal and external wiring and cables." Robert Buderi, *The Invention That Changed the World: How a Small Group of Radar Pioneers Won the Second World War and Launched a Technical Revolution* (New York: Simon and Schuster, 1996), 381–406.

3. Important new details about early U-2 missions can be found in the CIA's own internal history of the program, which was recently declassified. Eisenhower was a strong believer in fully utilizing the most advanced technologies to enhance national security and intelligence collection. In 1954 he recruited James Killian to chair a Technological Capabilities Panel that would investigate these areas. The work of the panel contributed directly to Eisenhower's support of the U-2 and the intelligence community's initial emphasis on planes, rather than satellites, as the nation's top priority intelli-

gence collection platform. Funding slowly shifted to satellites, and by late 1957 funding for satellites was increasing sharply. Gregory W. Pedlow and Donald E. Welzenbach, *The CIA and the U-2 Spy Program, 1954–1974* (Washington: Central Intelligence Agency, 1998), 26–33; Michael Beschloss, *Mayday* (New York: Harper and Row, 1986), 74–75; James Killian Jr., *Sputnik, Scientists, and Eisenhower: A Memoir of the First Special Assistant to the President for Science and Technology* (Cambridge: MIT Press, 1977), 68–71. Killian's report asserted, "We must find ways to increase the number of hard facts upon which our intelligence estimates are based, to provide better strategic warning" in order to minimize surprise attack. "To this end," it concluded, "we recommend adoption of a vigorous program of extensive use, in many intelligence procedures, of the most advanced knowledge in science and technology." Merton E. Davies and William R. Harris, *RAND's Role in the Evolution of Balloon and Satellite Observation Systems and Related U.S. Space Technology* (Santa Monica, Calif.: RAND, 1988), 61, 73–74, 94–95; William E. Burrow, *Deep Black: Space Espionage and National Security* (New York: Random House, 1986), 86–87.

4. Richard Leghorn, telephone conversation with author, 14 April 1997; Richard Leghorn, interview with author, Hyannis, Mass., 17 August 1997.

5. Richard Leghorn, interviews with author, Hyannis, Mass., 15 August 1997, 17 August 1997.

6. Theodore von Karman with Lee Edson, *The Wind and Beyond: Pioneer in Aviation and Pathfinder in Space* (Boston: Little, Brown, 1967), 267–268.

7. Bernard A. Schriever, "Military Space Activities: Recollections and Observations," in *The U.S. Air Force in Space: 1945 to the 21st Century,* ed. R. Cargill Hall and Jacob Neufeld (Washington: U.S. Government Printing Office, 1998), 12–13; Gen. Bernard A. Schriever, telephone conversation with author, 9 March 1998; von Karman, *The Wind and Beyond,* 269.

8. Schriever, "Military Space Activities," 11. Schriever had known Arnold since before World War II; in fact, Schriever had been married in Arnold's house. Schriever telephone conversation, 9 March 1998.

9. Schriever, "Military Space Activities," 11–12; Schriever telephone conversation, 9 March 1998.

10. Schriever telephone conversation, 9 March 1998; Davies and Harris, *RAND's Role,* 3–10.

11. Gen. Bernard A. Schriever, telephone conversations with author, 9 March 1998, 4 April 1998.

12. Schriever telephone conversation, 4 April 1998.

13. Ibid.

14. Richard Leghorn, telephone conversation with author, 11 July 1997; Leghorn interviews, 15 August 1997, 17 August 1997.

15. Even then it was clear to Schriever that Leghorn was an entrepreneur. Gen. Bernard A. Schriever, telephone conversations with author, 1 April 1998, 4 April 1998. Leghorn worked directly for Schriever for two years. Schriever telephone conversation, 9 March 1998.

16. Courtland Perkins, telephone conversation with author, 31 July 1998.

17. Schriever telephone conversation, 9 March 1998.

18. Schriever, "Military Space Activities," 15–16. For a detailed description of Schriever's role in the ICBM program, and insight into the web of government-business relations developed during the period, see Thomas P. Hughes, *Rescuing Prometheus* (New York: Pantheon, 1998), 69–139.

19. According to Schriever, Walkowicz was familiar with all the key air force developments of the time. Schriever telephone conversation, 9 March 1998.

20. Alvin Mosco, *The Rockefeller Inheritance* (Garden City, N.Y.: Doubleday, 1977), 178–180; Peter Collier and David Horowitz, *The Rockefellers: An American Dynasty* (New York: Holt, Rinehart, and Winston, 1976), 217–218; Peter Crisp, interview with author, New York, 2 July 1997.

21. Collier and Horowitz, *The Rockefellers,* 218.

22. Ibid., 294–295.

23. Mosco, *The Rockefeller Inheritance,* 178; Crisp interview, 2 July 1997.

24. Rockefeller's investments in "Marquardt Aviation, which built ramjets . . . Wallace Aviation, which built jet engine blades," Flight Refueling, Airborne Instrument Laboratory, and Aircraft Radio all took place in this period. Collier and Horowitz, *The Rockefellers,* 295–296.

25. Ibid., 299–300. According to Najeeb Halaby, Strauss used his connections to obtain information from the government for investment purposes. Najeeb Halaby, telephone conversation with author, 6 March 1998.

26. Halaby also worked on Rockefeller's investments in Reaction Motors, an early manufacturer of rocket engines. Halaby, who worked for Rockefeller in the 1950s, was later appointed by President Kennedy to be the country's first federal aviation administrator. Following his tour of duty in government, he served as chairman of Pan American World Airways. Years later, Halaby's daughter became a queen by marrying King Hussein of Jordan. Najeeb Halaby, *Crosswinds: An Airman's Memoir* (Garden City, N.Y.: Doubleday, 1978), ix–x, 39–41, 43, 49, 53.

27. Halaby telephone conversation, 6 March 1998.

28. Halaby and Walkowicz worked together on other assignments as well, like going together to meetings at the Council on Foreign Relations to make connections and to obtain investment ideas. Ibid. Laurance Rockefeller communicated his concerns about civil aviation to Eisenhower through his brother Nelson, who was working for the president at that time. Halaby, *Crosswinds,* 59–62; Robert Wood, "The Awakening to Safety," *Aviation Week,* 13 March 1953, p. 78; Philip Klass, "New GCA Gives Precision at Low Cost," *Aviation Week,* 3 May 1954, pp. 54–61; Ed Campbell, interview with author, Dartmouth, Mass., 20 September 1997.

29. Leghorn was already setting up meetings with Rockefeller's senior advisers to educate them on the future company's technology and to introduce them to its inventor, Art Tyler. Randolph Marston to Harper Woodward and Theodore Walkowicz, "Proposal for an Information Processing Company" [labeled with the handwritten note "LEGHORN & CO. 5/27/58"], general 1957–1958, no. 1, box 42, Itek Corporation,

investments, Rockefeller Family Archives, RAC; Leghorn interview, 17 August 1997. Leghorn's belief in an information revolution was prophetic, but his military experience gave him key insights that allowed him to grasp the future. In the military he had seen the impact of intelligence on the battlefield. He felt information could revolutionize commercial life in the same way. Merton Davies, telephone conversation with author, 10 November 1998.

30. Theodore Walkowicz to Randolph Marston and Harper Woodward, 17 June 1957, general 1957–1958, no. 1, box 42, Itek Corporation, investments, Rockefeller Family Archives, RAC. Marston confirmed the arrangements discussed in the interoffice memo in a letter to Leghorn. Leghorn was retained as a consultant to the Rockefeller office at a monthly rate of $2,500. "It is understood that this in no way commits either you or us to any further arrangement but that you will give us an opportunity to consider participating in any program that is evolved through the study work mentioned above." Randolph Marston to Richard Leghorn, 18 June 1957, general 1957–1958, no. 1, box 42, Itek Corporation, investments, Rockefeller Family Archives, RAC.

31. "Proposal to Form Corporation X," 4 September 1957, original financing phase one, box 257, Itek Corporation, investments, Rockefeller Family Archives, RAC.

32. The company's business plan also said that the company would conduct research and development, systems engineering, and custom building of information-processing equipment. Most of these contracts were a special category of classified cost-plus-fixed-fee (CPFF) programs in intelligence and reconnaissance. In these kinds of contracts the government covered all the costs a company incurred in developing a product. For a start-up company with limited resources, this was an attractive business arrangement. There was a trade-off, however: in exchange for guaranteeing that costs would be covered, the government limited the profit margin a company could obtain — usually to about 5 percent. "Proposal to Form Corporation X," 4 September 1957; Leghorn telephone conversation, 14 April 1997.

33. "Proposal to Form Corporation X," 4 September 1957; A. W. Tyler and W. L. Myers, "A Minicard System for Documentary Information," paper presented at the Symposium on Systems Information Retrieval at Western Reserve University, April 1957, general 1957–1958, no. 1, box 42, Itek Corporation, investments, Rockefeller Family Archives, RAC; Leghorn telephone conversation, 14 April 1997.

34. Richard Leghorn, "Notes About Work Plan," 2 July 1957, general 1957–1958, no. 1, box 42, Itek Corporation, investments, Rockefeller Family Archives, RAC; Randolph Marston to Charles Borman, 31 July 1957, general 1957–1958, no. 1, box 42, Itek Corporation, investments, Rockefeller Family Archives, RAC; Leghorn telephone conversation, 14 April 1997. Carter's credibility with Lockheed made him an extremely attractive asset for the fledgling company. Walter Levison, telephone conversation with author, 28 January 1998.

35. "Proposal to Form Corporation X," 9 August 1957, general 1957–1958, no. 1, box 42, Itek Corporation, investments, Rockefeller Family Archives, RAC.

36. Leghorn also explained that security clearances would take time. Richard Leghorn to Theodore Walkowicz, 13 August 1957, general 1957–1958, no. 1, box 42, Itek

Corporation, investments, Rockefeller Family Archives, RAC. Perhaps Leghorn was starting to have second thoughts about how much control he was losing. An unsigned "Suggested Financing Plan," probably written by Leghorn, once again suggests that the sponsoring investor should pledge $1 million to finance the company. One hundred thousand dollars would be the initial investment. The investor and founders would each appoint four board members; a ninth member would be jointly appointed. "Suggested Financing Plan," 23 August 1957, general 1957–1958, no. 1, box 42, Itek Corporation, investments, Rockefeller Family Archives, RAC.

37. "Proposal to Form Corporation X," 4 September 1957.

38. Harper Woodward to Laurance Rockefeller, 6 September 1957, general 1957–1958, no. 1, box 42, Itek Corporation, investments, Rockefeller Family Archives, RAC.

39. Stuart Scott to Richard Leghorn, 6 September 1957, general 1957–1958, no. 1, box 42, Itek Corporation, investments, Rockefeller Family Archives, RAC.

40. Leghorn and partners like Arthur Tyler would invest their own capital as well, for a total of an additional $10,000. Allied Research Associates, a Boston firm whose largest shareholder was Laurance Rockefeller, would also be given the opportunity to invest. This was in exchange for the office space and administrative support the firm was expected to provide to the new company. "Corporation X: Projected Sales and Profits," original financing phase one, box 257, Itek Corporation, investments, Rockefeller Family Archives, RAC; "Summary: Leghorn Project (Corporation X)," original financing phase one, box 257, Itek Corporation, investments, Rockefeller Family Archives, RAC.

41. Theodore Walkowicz to Laurance Rockefeller, "Status Report—Leghorn Project," 23 September 1957, original financing phase one, box 257, Itek Corporation, investments, Rockefeller Family Archives, RAC. On October 3 Leghorn sent Walkowicz a quick note summarizing a recent conversation. At this point Jack Carter was still in on the deal and was putting up money for shares. The four founding officers were Leghorn, Tyler, MacDonald, and Cousins. One of the last points on the document was an abbreviated note—"Scientific Engineering Institute Contract—short duration." Leghorn to Walkowicz, 3 October 1957, general 1957–1958, no. 1, box 42, Itek Corporation, investments, Rockefeller Family Archives, RAC. Another undated handwritten note from the period simply says "consulting services arrangement with Scientific Engineering Institute." Undated, unsigned note, general 1957–1958, no. 1, nox 42, Itek Corporation, investments, Rockefeller Family Archives, RAC; Randolph Marston to Harper Woodward, undated memo with list of potential names, general 1957–1958, no. 1, box 42, Itek Corporation, investments, Rockefeller Family Archives, RAC; George Valley, telephone conversation with author, 22 August 1998.

42. Theodore Walkowicz to Nelson and David Rockefeller, "Proposal to Form a Document Processing Company," 16 September 1957, general 1957–1958, no. 1, box 42, Itek Corporation, investments, Rockefeller Family Archives, RAC.

43. Stuart Scott to Theodore Walkowicz, 23 September 1957, original financing phase one, box 257, Itek Corporation, investments, Rockefeller Family Archives, RAC.

44. Theodore Walkowicz to Harper Woodward, 7 October 1957, general 1957–1958,

no. 1, box 42, Itek Corporation, investments, Rockefeller Family Archives, RAC. Walkowicz noted that Leghorn was still trying to reach Chapman at Kodak and would let them know as soon as he had "paved the way" for their call.

45. Leghorn to Gen. Gordon Saville, 7 October 1957, general 1957–1958, no. 1, box 42, Itek Corporation, investments, Rockefeller Family Archives, RAC.

46. Walter Levison, telephone conversation with author, 22 July 1997; Randolph Marston to Theodore Walkowicz and Harper Woodward, 17 June 1957, general 1957–1958, no. 1, box 42, Itek Corporation, investments, Rockefeller Family Archives, RAC.

4. Sputnik

1. Cary Reich, *The Life of Nelson A. Rockefeller: Worlds to Conquer, 1908–1958* (New York: Doubleday, 1996), 664.

2. "Abreast of the Market," *Wall Street Journal,* 8 October 1957, p. 25.

3. Malcolm D. Perkins to Stuart N. Scott, 7 October 1957, original financing phase one, box 257, Itek Corporation, investments, Rockefeller Family Archives, RAC.

4. Malcolm D. Perkins, "Itek CORPORATION — Action to be taken at the meeting of the Board of Directors to be held October 10, 1957," 7 October 1957, original financing phase one, box 257, Itek Corporation, investments, Rockefeller Family Archives, RAC; Richard Leghorn, telephone conversation with author, 14 April 1997. Leghorn believed that Walkowicz may have helped Bissell set up SEI. Richard Leghorn, telephone conversation with author, 28 July 1997. George Valley recalled that at least twenty scientists in the Cambridge area did work for SEI, many of whom had worked with him at Lincoln Labs. According to Valley there were at least three other companies on Route 128 sponsored by the CIA. George Valley, telephone conversation with author, 22 August 1998.

5. Richard Leghorn, "U.S. Can Photograph Russia from the Air Now: Planes Available, Equipment on Hand, Techniques Set," *U.S. News and World Report,* 5 August 1955, 71; Leghorn telephone conversation, 14 April 1997.

6. Richard Leghorn, telephone conversations with author, 14 April 1997, 2 November 1998.

7. Richard Leghorn to Gen. Gordon Saville, 7 October 1957, general 1957–1958, box 42, Itek Corporation, investments, Rockefeller Family Archives, RAC.

8. "Review and Outlook," *Wall Street Journal,* 8 October 1957, p. 14; "Abreast of the Market," ibid., 25.

9. Theodore Walkowicz to Harper Woodward, "Itek Closing," 8 October 1957, original financing phase one, box 257, Itek Corporation, investments, Rockefeller Family Archives, RAC.

10. Randolph B. Marston to Mr. Munro, "Itek Closing," 8 October 1957, original financing phase one, Box 257, Itek Corporation, investments, Rockefeller Family Archives, RAC; Malcolm Perkins to Jesse Cousins, 8 October 1957; Perkins to Stuart Scott, 8 October 1957, original financing phase one, box 257, Itek Corporation, investments, Rockefeller Family Archives, RAC.

11. "What's News," *Wall Street Journal,* 9 October 1957, p. 1.

12. "Itek Corporation: Special Meeting of the Board of Directors," 10 October 1957, Bylaws/Certificate of Incorporation, box 256, Itek Corporation, investments, Rockefeller Family Archives, RAC; Laurance Rockefeller to Richard Leghorn, 10 October 1957, original financing phase one, box 257, Itek Corporation, investments, Rockefeller Family Archives, RAC.

13. Richard S. Leghorn, telephone conversation with author, 12 April 1999.

14. H. J. Nelson, "The Trader Gives His Views of the Market," *Barron's,* 14 October 1957, 2–4.

15. Harper Woodward to Laurance Rockefeller, 14 October 1957, general 1957–1958, box 42, Itek Corporation, investments, Rockefeller Family Archives, RAC.

16. H. J. Nelson, "The Trader Gives His Views of the Market," *Barron's,* 14 October 1957, 2–4.

17. Reich, *Nelson Rockefeller,* 664–665.

18. Henry Kissinger to Franklin Lindsay, Subpanel 4, box 29, folder 320, record group V4B, Special Studies Project, RAC. As early as summer 1956 Kissinger was pushing Walkowicz to turn in his paper. Originally Kissinger wanted it by October 1, 1956; then he extended the deadline to October 30. The deadline continued to slip for many months. Henry Kissinger to Theodore Walkowicz, 2 August 1956, Subpanel 2, box 13, folder 153, record group V4B, Special Studies Project, RAC; Henry Kissinger to Theodore Walkowicz, 27 August 1956, Subpanel 2, box 13, folder 153, record group V4B, Special Studies Project, RAC.

19. Press Release, 17 October 1957, general 1957–1958, box 42, Itek Corporation, Rockefeller Family Archive, RAC.

20. H. J. Nelson, "The Trader Gives His Views of the Market," *Barron's,* 21 October 1957, 2.

21. H. J. Nelson, "The Trader Gives His Views of the Market," *Barron's,* 28 October 1957, 2

22. Theodore Walkowicz to Laurance Rockefeller, 23 October 1957, general 1957–1958, box 42, Itek Corporation, Rockefeller Family Archive, RAC.

23. Walter Levison, telephone conversation with author, 29 May 1997. Marston's concerns are handwritten on a letter from Richard Leghorn to Theodore Walkowicz. Leghorn's letter, sent the day Walkowicz wrote his note outlining Case's proposal to Rockefeller, included a brochure on the laboratory. Richard Leghorn to Theodore Walkowicz, 23 October 1957, general 1957–1958, box 42, Itek Corporation, Rockefeller Family Archive, RAC.

24. At that time a spin-stabilized design was being developed at Fairchild Camera and Instrument Corporation. Leghorn and Duncan MacDonald, through their contacts and their own involvement in the air force science advisory board, knew the technical limitations of Fairchild's concept. They knew Amrom Katz and Mert Davies at RAND and were familiar with RAND's own classified research on satellite reconnaissance. The problem with spin stabilization is that it does not compensate for image motion when the weight of the camera shifts. But spin stabilization, though problem-

atic, was a proven concept. John "Jack" Herther, telephone conversation with author, 26 August 1998; Merton Davies, telephone conversation with author, 6 October 1998.

25. Kimberly Yaman, "High Resolution," *NC State: The Alumni Magazine of North Carolina State University,* Winter 1996, p. 13.

26. Herther telephone conversation, 26 August 1998; Yaman, "High Resolution," 13; Curtis Peebles, *High Frontier: The U.S. Air Force and the Military Space Program* (Air Force History and Museums Program, 1997), 6.

27. Herther telephone conversation, 26 August 1998. "We knew our concept far outpaced that of the competition," said Herther. Yaman, "High Resolution," 13.

28. Richard Leghorn to Harold Case, draft letter, 28 October 1957, general 1957–1958, Itek Corporation, Rockefeller Family Archive, RAC; Richard Leghorn to Harold Case, 4 November 1957, Correspondence between President Case, Itek Officials, and the U.S. Air Force, Special Collections, Boston University Archives.

29. Theodore Walkowicz, "Survival in an Age of Technological Contest," 4 November 1957, box 13, folder 154, record group V4B, Special Studies Project, RAC. Homer Stewart, who was a member of the Air Force SAB and was deeply involved in the early days of America's satellite efforts, knew Walkowicz well. Stewart remembered him as an early believer in the importance of technology to national security. According to him, Walkowicz gained an invaluable appreciation of key technologies supported by the U.S. government during those days. Homer Stewart, telephone conversation with author, 10 August 1998. According to Walter Levison, all of Walkowicz's investments were motivated by his interest in defeating the Soviets in the Cold War. Walter Levison, telephone conversation with author, 11 July 1997.

30. Theodore Walkowicz to Harper Woodward, 11 November 1957; Theodore Walkowicz to John H. Carter, 14 November 1957, general 1957–1958, box 42, Itek Corporation, Rockefeller Family Archive, RAC.

31. Before Case responded to Leghorn's proposal, it appears that J. Wendall Yeo, vice president of Boston University, accompanied by Dow Smith, director of the lab, met with Itek's Duncan MacDonald for preliminary discussions. Harold Case to Richard Leghorn, 15 November 1957, Correspondence between President Case, Itek Officials, and the U.S. Air Force, Special Collections, Boston University Archives.

32. Harold Case to Lt. Gen. Donald Putt, 18 November 1957, Correspondence between President Case, Itek Officials, and the U.S. Air Force, Special Collections, Boston University Archives.

33. Harold Case to Lt. Gen. Donald Putt, draft telegram, 22 November 1957, Correspondence between President Case, Itek Officials, and the U.S. Air Force, Special Collections, Boston University Archives.

34. Colonel Surles to Harold Case, draft telegram from Lt. Gen. Donald Putt to Harold Case, 29 November 1957, Correspondence between President Case, Itek Officials, and the U.S. Air Force, Special Collections, Boston University Archives. Putt finally sent his message on 3 December 1957. Harold Case to Lt. Gen. Donald Putt, 13 December 1957, Correspondence between President Case, Itek Officials, and the U.S. Air Force, Special Collections, Boston University Archives; Richard Leghorn to

Harold Case, 4 December 1957, 6 December 1957, Correspondence between President Case, Itek Officials, and the U.S. Air Force, Special Collections, Boston University Archives.

35. Leghorn felt that MacDonald's relationship with Boston University was key to getting the lab. Leghorn telephone conversation, 14 April 1997; Jesse Cousins to Theodore Walkowicz, 5 December 1957, general 1957–1958, box 42, Itek Corporation, Rockefeller Family Archive, RAC.

36. Cousins to Walkowicz, 5 December 1957; Harold Case to Lt. Gen. Donald Putt, 13 December 1957, Correspondence between President Case, Itek Officials, and the U.S. Air Force, Special Collections, Boston University Archives.

37. Boston University Press Release no. 550-57, 24 December 1957, Correspondence between President Case, Itek Officials, and the U.S. Air Force, Special Collections, Boston University Archives.

38. Proposed Financing of Itek Corporation, undated, box 257, original financing phase one, Itek Corporation, investments, Rockefeller Family Archive, RAC. Leghorn recalled that after the lab was acquired, he went to speak with the scientists. The mood was dark at first, but John Wolfe transformed it when he stood up and stated, "I think this is the greatest thing that ever happened to us. We can now get some money. We can do the things we want. It's time for us to get out of the academic environment." Richard Leghorn, interview with author, Hyannis, Mass., 17 August 1997.

5. The Coffee Slurpers and the Front-Office Pros

1. *700 News,* 19 January 1954, vol. 1, no. 6, pp. 1–2, Papers of William C. Britton; *700 News,* 22 December 1953, vol. 1, no. 4, p. 1, Papers of William C. Britton; *700 News,* 2 February 1954, vol. 1, no. 8, p. 3, Papers of William C. Britton; John Watson, telephone conversation with author, 13 July 1998; *700 News,* 10 March 1954, vol. 2, no. 3, p. 1, Papers of William C. Britton; *700 News,* 1 November 1955, vol. 4, no. 4, p. 1, Papers of William C. Britton.

2. Certainly, other leaders in the field had built an important foundation for Mac-Donald's breakthrough. George W. Goddard was the father of aerial photoreconnaissance. He was a prophet whose resolute and at times lonely voice convinced America's military leadership of the tactical importance of spying from planes. During the years between World War I and World War II, Goddard campaigned for his cause and slowly built a professional photoreconnaissance capability in the military. During World War II his disciples included Richard Leghorn and Walt Levison. James G. Baker, another pioneer in the field, was an astronomer who answered the call of duty when Major Goddard asked him for help in late 1939. German lenses, the best in the world, were unavailable, and Goddard needed a new source if his work was to continue and if the military was to have an uninterrupted source of good photointelligence in the event of war. Baker responded like a patriot and turned his attention from making telescopes to making camera lenses strong enough to photograph enemy activity on the ground. He built a team of scientists at Harvard University to develop new lens

systems for the war effort. He repeatedly made new advances in lens technology that increased the power of the nation's spy cameras. His deputy and protégé was a young man named Duncan MacDonald. R. Cargill Hall, "Strategic Reconnaissance in the Cold War," *Prologue,* Summer 1996, p. 108. See George Goddard's memoir for an insider's account of the early years of reconnaissance. George W. Goddard, *Overview* (New York: Doubleday, 1969). Bill Attaya recalled that MacDonald was a prophet, a man concerned with all aspects of aerial reconnaissance. Bill Attaya, telephone conversation with author, 23 October 1998.

3. "Dynamic Decade," undated promotional brochure for BUPRL published in 1957, Papers of William C. Britton.

4. *700 News,* 22 November 1955, vol. 10, no. 10, p. 2, Papers of William C. Britton; Duncan E. MacDonald, "Technical Note no. 72: Criteria for Detection and Recognition of Photographic Detail," October, 1950, Boston University Physical Research Laboratories, Papers of William C. Britton. Other subjects covered by technical notes included mounts and stabilization, illumination, atmospheric optics, filters, focusing, processing equipment, printing, and photo interpretation. "BUPRL Technical Notes: Subject Classification," undated, Papers of William C. Britton.

5. MacDonald, "Technical Note no. 72"; "BUPRL Technical Notes: Subject Classification."

6. *700 News,* 21 April 1954, vol. 2, no. 9, p. 2, Papers of William C. Britton.

7. *700 News,* 28 April 1954, vol. 2, no. 10, p. 2, Papers of William C. Britton.

8. *700 News,* 5 May 1954, vol. 3, no. 1, pp. 2–3, Papers of William C. Britton. Smith had received his B.A. and M.A. in physics from Queens University in 1947 and 1948. He received his Ph.D. in optics from the University of Rochester. He became a U.S. citizen in 1949. *700 News,* 25 October 1955, vol. 10, no. 10, p. 2, Papers of William C. Britton.

9. If Smith's letter to the editor worried his colleagues at the lab, there's no evidence in the subsequent editions of the *700 News. 700 News,* 19 May 1954, vol. 3, no. 3, p. 1, Papers of William C. Britton; *700 News,* 19 August 1954, vol. 4, p. 2, Papers of William C. Britton.

10. *700 News,* 2 September 1954, vol. 4, p. 2, Papers of William C. Britton.

11. *700 News,* 16 September 1954, vol. 4, pp. 1–2, Papers of William C. Britton. In 1956 Levison testified before the Subcommittee on Disarmament of the Senate Committee on Foreign Relations. He was a frequent participant in National Planning Association panels and was a contributor to *Inspection for Disarmament.* Seymour Melman, editor, *Inspection for Disarmament* (New York: Columbia University Press, 1958), 59–74.

12. R. Cargill Hall, "Strategic Reconnaissance in the Cold War," *Prologue,* Summer 1996, pp. 108–109; Richard Leghorn, interviews with author, Hyannis, Mass., 15 August 1997, 17 August 1997.

13. Levison remembered that much of the time on the island was filled with worry. "Nobody really knew what would happen." Walter Levison, telephone conversation with author, 11 April 1997.

14. Hall, "Strategic Reconnaissance"; Leghorn interview, 15 August 1997; Richard Leghorn, telephone conversation with author, 28 July 1997. When Walter Levison returned to the United States, he was assigned the task of creating an index and catalogue for every roll of film from the tests. His work directly contributed to more effective study of military tactics and nuclear weapons. He left Bikini with the belief that nuclear war had to be avoided. Levison telephone conversation, 11 April 1997.

15. Richard S. Leghorn, "Objectives for Research and Development in Military Aerial Reconnaissance," 13 December 1946, in "Technical Note no. 44," Boston University Optical Research Laboratory, 30 September 1948, pp. 40–43, Papers of William C. Britton; Hall, "Strategic Reconnaissance."

16. Leghorn, "Objectives"; Hall, "Strategic Reconnaissance."

17. R. Cargill Hall, "The Truth About Overflight," *Quarterly Journal of Military History,* Spring 1997, pp. 27–33.

18. Untitled, undated memo found in the Papers of William C. Britton. Britton believes that this memo was written sometime in 1957, as it became clear that defense cuts might endanger the lab. The memo highlights the lab's many accomplishments and its industrial relations. The memo may have been used when senior members of the lab sought a new home. Many of the accomplishments of the lab are related to its support of various air force programs. "Dynamic Decade," undated promotional brochure for the lab published in 1957, Papers of William C. Britton.

19. Untitled, undated memo found in the Papers of William C. Britton.

20. Dwayne A. Day, John M. Logsdon, and Brian Latell, *Eye in the Sky: The Story of the CORONA Spy Satellites* (Washington, D.C.: Smithsonian Institution Press, 1998), 192–196. "You could ask the question of why we used panoramic photography," Levison explained at a 1995 conference sponsored by the CIA's Center for the Study of Intelligence. "It's very difficult to get wide-angle coverage from a lens and still get high resolution. But with a panoramic camera you just have to cover a very narrow angle and sweep the rest of the picture mechanically." The team at BUPRL designed a twelve-inch f/5 triplet lens for the camera. F. Dow Smith, "The Design and Engineering of Corona's Optics," in *CORONA — Between the Sun and the Earth: The First NRO Reconnaissance Eye in Space,* ed. Robert A. McDonald (Bethesda, Md.: American Society for Photogrammetry and Remote Sensing, 1997), 111–114; Curtis Peebles, *The CORONA Project: America's First Spy Satellites* (Annapolis: Naval Institute Press, 1997), 29–30; Merton E. Davies and William R. Harris, *RAND'S Role in the Evolution of Balloon and Satellite Observation Systems and Related U.S. Space Technology* (Santa Monica, Calif.: RAND, 1988), 78–83.

21. Richard S. Leghorn, "Warfare, Stalemate, and Security," transcript of speech to the Franklin Institute, Philadelphia, 19 December 1957, pp. 1–10, Papers of Richard S. Leghorn.

22. Leghorn telephone conversations, 14 April 1997, 2 November 1998; Leghorn interview, 15 August 1997. Thanks to his contacts, Leghorn had learned that the video and television technology behind the SAMOS spy satellite was unworkable in the short term. His friend Maj. Gen. Bernard Schriever, for whom Leghorn had worked during

the Korean War, had kept him up to date on progress related to WS-117L. Although the concepts were promising in the long term, offering the possibility of real-time intelligence, deployment of such a satellite in the near future was clearly impossible. Schriever, along with his deputy, Gen. Osmond Ritland (who had previously worked as Bissell's deputy on the U-2 program), consulted Leghorn about how to proceed with the program. The old friends quickly agreed. If the program was to be successful, "it would require presidential approval and the highest of national priorities." Most important, to move the project forward quickly they must cloak it in the deepest of secrecy and manage it covertly like the U-2. Schriever knew how to sell his ideas, and by late 1957 the plan had reached Eisenhower's new science adviser (and Richard Leghorn's old fraternity brother), James Killian, for review. Killian's White House meeting, which included Edwin Land, the CIA's Richard Bissell, and General Schriever, was inconclusive. Yet although no final decision was made, a consensus was building for a covertly managed film recovery satellite as the nation's highest priority intelligence project. And Richard Leghorn was getting ready for business. R. Cargill Hall, "Postwar Strategic Reconnaissance and the Genesis of CORONA," in Day, Logsdon, and Latell, *Eye in the Sky*, 110–111.

6. Into the Black

1. Cary Reich, *The Life of Nelson A. Rockefeller: Worlds to Conquer, 1908–1958* (New York: Doubleday, 1996), 664–665.

2. Ibid., 665; "3 Congressman Urge Close Study of Report," *New York Times*, 6 January 1958.

3. *Prospect for America: The Rockefeller Panel Reports* (Garden City, N.Y.: Doubleday, 1961), 96.

4. Ibid., 93, 100–102.

5. Philip Benjamin, "Arms Rise Urged Lest Reds Seize Lead in 2 Years," *New York Times*, 6 January 1958.

6. Jack Raymond, "Burke Backs Joint Chiefs; Warns of One Man Rule," *New York Times*, 7 January 1958; "Review and Outlook: Realities and the Role of Force," *Wall Street Journal*, 7 January 1958, p. 14; Reich, *Nelson Rockefeller*, 665–667.

7. James Reston, "The Rockefeller Report: An Evaluation of Contributions Made by Private Citizens to Foreign Policy," *New York Times*, 6 January 1958.

8. Laurance Rockefeller to David Rockefeller, 17 January 1958, 1958 financing phase two, box 257, Itek Corporation, investments, Rockefeller Family Archives, RAC; Richard Leghorn to Laurance Rockefeller, 13 January 1958, 1958 financing phase two, box 257, Itek Corporation, investments, Rockefeller Family Archives, RAC.

9. Richard Leghorn to Laurance Rockefeller, 16 January 1958, 1958 financing phase two, box 257, Itek Corporation, investments, Rockefeller Family Archives, RAC; William J. Masson to Theodore Walkowicz, 10 January 1958, 1958 financing phase two, box 257, Itek Corporation, investments, Rockefeller Family Archives, RAC.

10. Laurance Rockefeller to David Rockefeller, 17 January 1958, 1958 financing phase

two, box 257, Itek Corporation, investments, Rockefeller Family Archives, RAC; Laurance Rockefeller to Nelson Rockefeller, 17 January 1958, 1958 financing phase two, box 257, Itek Corporation, investments, Rockefeller Family Archives, RAC; David Rockefeller to Theodore Walkowicz, 29 January 1958, 1958 financing phase two, box 257, Itek Corporation, investments, Rockefeller Family Archives, RAC.

11. Walter Levison, telephone conversations with author, 17 April 1997, 22 July 1997. According to James Reber, who worked with Bissell at the CIA and was later a top official of the National Reconnaissance Office, Bissell nurtured companies in their relationship with the CIA. James Reber, telephone conversation with author, 27 February 1997.

12. Harper Woodward to Files, 17 January 1958, 1958 financing phase two, box 257, Itek Corporation, investments, Rockefeller Family Archives, RAC; Louis E. Walker to William J. Masson, 31 January 1958, 1958 financing phase two, box 257, Itek Corporation, investments, Rockefeller Family Archives, RAC; William J. Masson to Raymond H. Wilkens, 31 January 1958, 1958 financing phase two, box 257, Itek Corporation, investments, Rockefeller Family Archives, RAC; Jesse Cousins to The Several Purchasers of Common Stock and Debentures of Itek Corporation, 30 January 1958, 1958 financing phase two, box 257, Itek Corporation, investments, Rockefeller Family Archives, RAC; Randolph B. Marston to Harper Woodward, 28 January 1958, general 1957–1958, no. 1, box 42, Itek Corporation, investments, Rockefeller Family Archives, RAC.

13. William J. Masson to Raymond H. Wilkens, 1 May 1958, 1958 financing phase two, box 257, Itek Corporation, investments, Rockefeller Family Archives, RAC; Albert Pratt, interview with author, Osterville, Mass., 14 July 1998; Albert Pratt to Harper Woodward, 31 January 1958, 1958 financing phase two, box 257, Itek Corporation, investments, Rockefeller Family Archives, RAC.

14. R. Cargill Hall, "Post War Strategic Reconnaissance and the Genesis of Project Corona," in *CORONA: Between the Sun and the Earth,* ed. Robert A. McDonald (Bethesda, Md.: American Society for Photogrammetry and Remote Sensing, 1997), 26; Richard Leghorn to James Killian, 3 February 1958, LEF-LEV, box 32, White House Office of Science and Technology, DDE.

15. Albert Pratt to Harper Woodward, 10 February 1958, general 1957–1958, no. 1, box 42, Itek Corporation, investments, Rockefeller Family Archives, RAC.

16. Harper Woodward to Laurance Rockefeller, 6 February 1958, 1958 financing phase two, box 257, Itek Corporation, investments, Rockefeller Family Archives, RAC; Harper Woodward to David Rockefeller, 17 February 1958, 1958 financing phase two, box 257, Itek Corporation, investments, Rockefeller Family Archives, RAC; William J. Masson to Leslie Q. Miller, 24 February 1958, 1958 financing phase two, box 257, Itek Corporation, investments, Rockefeller Family Archives, RAC.

17. R. Cargill Hall, "Postwar Strategic Reconnaissance and the Genesis of CORONA," in *Eye in the Sky: The Story of the Corona Spy Satellites,* ed. Dwayne A. Day, John M. Logsdon, and Brian Latell (Washington, D.C.: Smithsonian Institution Press, 1998), 111–112; Kenneth E. Greer, "CORONA," Studies in Intelligence, Supple-

ment, 17 (1973), in *CORONA: America's First Satellite Program,* ed. Kevin C. Ruffner (Washington: Center for the Study of Intelligence, 1995), 4–5.

18. Hall, "Postwar Strategic Reconnaissance," 111–113; Dwayne A. Day, "A Strategy for Reconnaissance: Dwight D. Eisenhower and Freedom of Space," in Day, Logsdon, and Latell, *Eye in the Sky,* 138; Jerome Everett Katz, *Presidential Politics and Science Policy* (New York: Praeger, 1978), 101.

19. Hall, "Postwar Strategic Reconnaissance," 113; John Parangosky, telephone conversations with author, 25 March 1997, 16 May 1997.

20. Hall, "Postwar Strategic Reconnaissance," 115.

21. Bernie Marcus, telephone conversation with author, 17 August 1998.

22. Hall, "Postwar Strategic Reconnaissance," 113.

23. Ibid., 113–114; Greer, "CORONA," 6.

24. Curtis Peebles, *The CORONA Project: America's First Spy Satellites* (Annapolis: Naval Institute Press, 1997), 45–46.

25. Hall, "Postwar Strategic Reconnaissance," 116. There is some disagreement about the location of the meeting. According to an earlier history published by the National Reconnaissance Office, the meeting took place in Cambridge, Massachusetts. Frederic C. E. Oder, James C. Fitzpatrick, and Paul E. Worthman, *The CORONA Story* (Chantilly, Va.: National Reconnaissance Office, 1988), 25.

26. Hall, "Postwar Strategic Reconnaissance," 116.

27. Over the years, MacDonald served on many intelligence community advisory boards. As a result, he had a deep understanding of the needs of the intelligence community and of the CIA's photo interpreters in particular. He had many important contacts within the community, and that gave him great credibility with Bissell. Jack Herther, telephone conversation with author, 19 October 1998; Hall, "Postwar Strategic Reconnaissance," 116–117; Oder et al., *The CORONA Story,* 27.

28. Hall, "Postwar Strategic Reconnaissance," 116–117; Greer, "CORONA," 7.

29. [Classified] to Project Security Officer, "Report on CORONA Meeting, 26 March 1958," 27 March 1958, NRO; Hall, "Postwar Strategic Reconnaissance," 116–117; Greer, "CORONA," 7.

30. Acquisition of the lab had enabled Itek to maintain the contract for building spy cameras for the CIA's balloon program. Itek received the order directly from Bissell. Levison telephone conversation, 17 April 1997; Theodore Walkowicz to Laurance Rockefeller, 31 March 1958, Itek Corporation — Review of Operations, box 42, Itek Corporation, investments, Rockefeller Family Archives, RAC; Press release, 9 April 1958, Itek Corporation general 1957–1958, no. 1, box 42, Itek Corporation, investments, Rockefeller Family Archives, RAC.

7. Pugwash

1. Joseph Rotblat, *Pugwash: The First Ten Years* (London: Heinemann Educational, 1967), 11–12, 14–17, 77–79.

2. Ibid., 14–16, 18–19; Richard Leghorn, interview with author, 17 August 1997. By

this time Leghorn had written numerous articles on the arms race and arms control. Although he believed that nuclear war had to be avoided, he was equally adamant that nuclear weapons could play a role in building a secure world balance of power. Richard Leghorn, "No Need to Bomb Cities to Win War," *U.S. News and World Report,* 28 January 1955, 79–94. A nuclear balance of power was only an interim solution, Leghorn wrote. He explained that "although a balance of mutual terror has been urged as the basis for world security, mutual terror in reality is no security reliance at all, but a reliance on fear and insecurity." Leghorn believed that fear could be overcome by freedom of information about the superpowers' nuclear stockpiles and deployment strategies. "The crux of the entire security issue is internationally available information about arms matters." He argued that the United Nations should be central to a "universal" approach to arms control. Richard Leghorn, "Controlling the Nuclear Threat in the Second Atomic Decade," *Bulletin of the Atomic Scientists,* vol. 12, no. 6, June 1956, 189–195.

3. Stephen E. Ambrose, *Eisenhower: The President* (New York: Simon and Schuster, 1984), 451–452.

4. "Minutes of the Second Meeting of the Second Pugwash Conference," *Documents of Second Pugwash Conference of Nuclear Scientists, 3/31–4/11/58,* Papers of Richard Leghorn; McGeorge Bundy, *Danger and Survival: Choices About the Bomb in the First Fifty Years* (New York: Random House, 1988), 33–37, 95; Richard Leghorn, interview with author, Hyannis, Mass., 15 August 1997.

5. Jerome B. Wiesner, Untitled working paper, *Documents of Second Pugwash Conference,* Papers of Richard Leghorn.

6. Richard Leghorn, "Science, Arms Control, and the U.S.: A Proposal for a U.N. Arms Research and Information Agency," *Documents of Second Pugwash Conference,* Papers of Richard Leghorn.

7. "Minutes of the Fourth Meeting of the Second Pugwash Conference," *Documents of Second Pugwash Conference,* Papers of Richard Leghorn.

8. Richard Leghorn, "Design of a World Security System," *Documents of Second Pugwash Conference,* Papers of Richard Leghorn; Leghorn interview, 15 August 1997.

8. Bissell for Vice President

1. Richard Leghorn to Harper Woodward, 9 April 1958, Itek Corporation general 1957–1958, no. 1, box 42, Itek Corporation, investments, Rockefeller Family Archives, RAC; Theodore Walkowicz to Harper Woodward, 23 April 1958, general 1957–1958, no. 1, box 42, Itek Corporation, investments, Rockefeller Family Archives, RAC.

2. *Itek Intelligence,* vol. 1, no. 1, April 1958, p. 2, Papers of William C. Britton.

3. R. Cargill Hall, "Postwar Strategic Reconnaissance and the Genesis of Corona," in *Eye in the Sky: The Story of the Corona Spy Satellites,* ed. Dwayne A. Day, John M. Logsdon, and Brian Latell (Washington, D.C.: Smithsonian Institution Press, 1998), 117; Kenneth E. Greer, "CORONA," Studies in Intelligence, Supplement, 17 (Spring 1973), in *CORONA: America's First Satellite Program,* ed. Kevin C. Ruffner (Washing-

ton: Center for the Study of Intelligence, 1995), 7; Frederic C. E. Oder, James C. Fitzpatrick, and Paul E. Worthman, *The CORONA Story* (Chantilly, Va.: National Reconnaissance Office, 1988), 27.

4. Bissell's decision was to have historic ramifications. From that point on every satellite program used three-axis stabilization. Hall, "Postwar Strategic Reconnaissance," 117; Oder, Fitzpatrick, and Worthman, *The CORONA Story,* 27; Greer, "CORONA," 7–8.

5. Oder, Fitzpatrick, and Worthman, *The CORONA Story,* 28.

6. Ibid.

7. Greer, "CORONA," 8–9.

8. Elisha Walker Jr. to Randolph Marston, 10 June 1958, directors meetings, box 46, Itek Corporation, investments, Rockefeller Family Archives, RAC; John "Jack" Herther, telephone conversation with author, 26 August 1998.

9. *Itek Intelligence,* vol. 1, no. 3, June 1958, p. 1, Papers of William C. Britton.

10. *Itek Intelligence,* vol. 1, no. 4, July–August 1958, p. 1, Papers of William C. Britton; "Dun and Bradstreet, Inc., Analytical Report—Itek Corporation," 3 July 1958, Itek Corporation general 1959–1960, no. 2, box 42, Itek Corporation, investments, Rockefeller Family Archives, RAC; Jesse Cousins, interview with author, New Bedford, Mass., 7 June 1997.

11. [Classified] to Richard Bissell, Special Assistant to the Director for Planning and Development, "Visit to Itek, Boston, Massachusetts, 10–11 June 1958," 24 June 1958, NRO. The identity of the writer of the memo, an air force lieutenant colonel on assignment to Bissell's staff, is unknown. NRO.

12. Offering Circular—Itek Corporation, 10 October 1958, Prospectus, box 44, Itek Corporation, investments, Rockefeller Family Archives, RAC; Itek Annual Report—1958, 9 January 1959, p. 6, Papers of William Britton.

13. Jesse Cousins to William Mason, 4 September 1958, 1958 financing phase two, box 257, Itek Corporation, investments, Rockefeller Family Archives, RAC; Frank Madden, interviews with author, Brewster, Mass., 20 August 1997, Quincy, Mass., 8 November 1997.

14. Cornelius H. Borman Jr. to Theodore Walkowicz, 8 September 1958, 1958 financing phase two, box 257, Itek Corporation, investments, Rockefeller Family Archives, RAC.

15. Raymond H. Wilkens to Randolph B. Marston, 8 September 1958, 1958 financing phase two, box 257, Itek Corporation, investments, Rockefeller Family Archives, RAC.

16. Leghorn to Holders of Common Stock, 10 October 1958, Rights Offering 1958, box 257, Itek Corporation, investments, Rockefeller Family Archives, RAC.

17. Offering Circular—Itek Corporation, 10 October 1958; Itek Annual Report—1958, 9 January 1959, p. 6.

18. Notice—Itek Board of Directors Meeting, 15 October 1958, directors meetings, box 46, Itek Corporation, investments, Rockefeller Family Archives, RAC; Draft Minutes—20 October 1958 Board of Directors' Meeting, undated, directors meetings, box 46, Itek Corporation, investments, Rockefeller Family Archives, RAC.

19. Richard E. Murray to Harper Woodward, 21 October 1958, general 1957–1958, no. 1, box 42, Itek Corporation, investments, Rockefeller Family Archives, RAC.

20. Itek Corporation — Sales Analysis, 31 October 1958, directors meetings, box 46, Itek Corporation, investments, Rockefeller Family Archives, RAC.

21. R. S. Leghorn to Board of Directors, "Summary of Merger and Acquisitions Possibilities," 8 December 1958, directors meetings, box 46, Itek Corporation, investments, Rockefeller Family Archives, RAC.

22. J. X. Cousins to R. S. Leghorn, 5 December 1958, directors meetings, box 46, Itek Corporation, investments, Rockefeller Family Archives, RAC.

23. R. S. Leghorn, Memorandum to the Board, 9 December 1958, directors meetings, box 46, Itek Corporation, investments, Rockefeller Family Archives, RAC.

24. Itek Corporation, Meeting of the Board of Directors, 17 December 1958, directors meetings, box 46, Itek Corporation, investments, Rockefeller Family Archives, RAC.

9. Going Public

1. Richard Leghorn to Stockholders, 9 January 1959, Itek stockholders meetings 1958–1959, box 259, Itek Corporation, investments, Rockefeller Family Archives, RAC; "Notice of Special Meeting in Lieu of Annual Meeting of Stockholders," 9 January 1959, Itek stockholders meetings 1958–1959, box 259, Itek Corporation, investments, Rockefeller Family Archives, RAC; Richard Leghorn, interview with author, Hyannis, Mass., 15 August 1997.

2. Malcolm D. Perkins to the Directors of Itek Corporation, 17 January 1959, directors meetings, box 46, Itek Corporation, investments, Rockefeller Family Archives, RAC; "Itek Corporation: Meeting of the Board of Directors," 25 February 1959, Itek — April 21, box 46, Itek Corporation, investments, Rockefeller Family Archives, RAC; "Draft Agreement for the Promotion and Financing of Vidya," 17 January 1959, directors meetings, box 46, Itek Corporation, investments, Rockefeller Family Archives, RAC.

3. Richard Leghorn to Stockholders, 9 January 1959; "Notice of Special Meeting in Lieu of Annual Meeting of Stockholders"; "Special Meeting of Stockholders in Lieu of Annual Meeting," 28 January 1959, Itek stockholders meetings 1958–1959, box 259, Itek Corporation, investments, Rockefeller Family Archives, RAC; Harper Woodward to Laurance Rockefeller, 22 January 1959, general 1959–1960, no. 2, box 42, Itek Corporation, investments, Rockefeller Family Archives, RAC.

4. "Preliminary Prospectus: Itek Corporation," 6 March 1959, financing 1959, box 257, Itek Corporation, investments, Rockefeller Family Archives, RAC; "Prospectus: Itek Corporation," 11 March 1959, financing 1959, box 257, Itek Corporation, investments, Rockefeller Family Archives, RAC.

5. Years later, Leghorn reviewed the prospectus and acknowledged that no investor could ever appreciate all the risks involved with the company. Leghorn interview, 15 August 1997.

6. Richard Leghorn to Board of Directors, 10 March 1959, directors meetings, box 46, Itek Corporation, investments, Rockefeller Family Archives, RAC; Arthur Young and Company to Richard Leghorn, 17 February 1959, box 46, Itek Corporation, investments, Rockefeller Family Archives, RAC; Richard Leghorn to Harper Woodward (including attached memorandum, Itek profit control plan, 16 March 1959), 17 March 1959, budgetary control systems, box 42, Itek Corporation, investments, Rockefeller Family Archives, RAC.

7. Thomas Hobin, interview with author, Harvard, Mass., 21 August 1998.

8. Walter Levison and Franklin Lindsay, interview with author, Cambridge, Mass., 7 June 1997.

9. Richard Leghorn to Board of Directors, "Summary of Merger or Acquisition Possibilities," 21 April 1959, mergers: general 1958–1960, box 42, Itek Corporation, investments, Rockefeller Family Archives, RAC.

10. Richard Leghorn to Board of Directors, "Remington Rand," 21 April 1959, mergers: general 1958–1960, box 42, Itek Corporation, investments, Rockefeller Family Archives, RAC.

11. Richard Leghorn to Board of Directors, "Kalvar Corporation," 21 April 1959, mergers: general 1958–1960, box 42, Itek Corporation, investments, Rockefeller Family Archives, RAC.

12. At some point Randolph Marston obtained a copy of Pratt's bulletin. He forwarded it to Harper Woodward with the following notation at the bottom: "It's nice to have an enthusiastic director but I agree that any circularization should be cleared by the board." Albert Pratt to Partners, Managers, and Registered Representatives, 28 April 1959, general 1959–1960, no. 2, box 42, Itek Corporation, investments, Rockefeller Family Archives, RAC. An internal Itek document, "Analysis of Operating Profit and Net Profit" dated 15 April 1959, forecast operating profit at $675,000. "Analysis of Operating Profit and Net Profit," Itek — April 21, box 46, Itek Corporation, investments, Rockefeller Family Archives, RAC.

13. Philip Donham to Richard Leghorn, 12 June 1959; Arthur D. Little, "Itek Corporation — Report of Progress," 12 June 1959, pp. 1–2, progress reports, box 44, Itek Corporation, investments, Rockefeller Family Archives, RAC.

14. Little, "Itek Corporation."

15. Richard Leghorn to Harper Woodward, 14 July 1959, general 1959–1960, no. 2, box 42, Itek Corporation, investments, Rockefeller Family Archives, RAC; Harper Woodward, handwritten notes, undated, general 1959–1960, no. 2, box 42, Itek Corporation, investments, Rockefeller Family Archives, RAC.

16. Harper Woodward to Laurance Rockefeller, "Itek — Affiliation with Bell & Howell," 25 February 1958; Randolph Marston to Woodward and Walkowicz, "Bell & Howell," 2 April 1959; Harper Woodward to Laurance Rockefeller, "Itek — Bell & Howell," 23 July 1959, mergers: general 1958–1960, box 42, Itek Corporation, investments, Rockefeller Family Archives, RAC.

17. Leghorn sent Woodward a short summary of their discussions. Woodward filed what appears to be his own handwritten minutes along with Leghorn's memo. Richard

Leghorn to Harper Woodward, 14 July 1959, general 1959–1960, no. 2, box 42, Itek Corporation, investments, Rockefeller Family Archives, RAC; Harper Woodward, handwritten notes, undated, general 1959–1960, no. 2, box 42, Itek Corporation, investments, Rockefeller Family Archives, RAC.

18. Richard P. Cooke, "Laurance Rockefeller Finds Risky New Uses for Old Millions: Nelson's Brother Invests in Ideas, Turns Tiny Firms into Scientific Pacemakers — The Case of Fabulous Itek," *Wall Street Journal,* 13 July 1959, pp. 1, 6.

19. "Prodigy with a Flair for Profit," *Business Week,* 18 July 1959, pp. 78–84.

20. Albert Pratt, Bulletin on Itek, telegram, 21 July 1959, general 1959–1960, no. 2, box 42, Itek Corporation, investments, Rockefeller Family Archives, RAC.

21. Harper Woodward to Randolph Marston, 7 August 1959, general 1959–1960, no. 2, box 42, Itek Corporation, investments, Rockefeller Family Archives, RAC.

22. Richard Leghorn to James Hill, Elisha Walker, Theodore Walkowicz, and Harper Woodward, 17 July 1959, general 1959–1960, no. 2, box 42, Itek Corporation, investments, Rockefeller Family Archives, RAC.

23. Leghorn to Board of Directors, "General Report," 26 July 1959, pp. 1–7, directors meeting, 28 July 1959, box 46, Itek Corporation, investments, Rockefeller Family Archives, RAC.

24. Richard Leghorn to Board of Directors, "Flofilm Division — Diebold, Inc.," 24 July 1959, directors meeting, 28 July 1959, box 46, Itek Corporation, investments, Rockefeller Family Archives, RAC.

25. Memorandum, "Itek CORPORATION," undated, Photostat Corporation 1959–1962, box 43, Itek Corporation, investments, Rockefeller Family Archives, RAC; "Introducing Kenneth M. Leghorn," *Itek Intelligence,* vol. 2, no. 4, June 1959, p. 3.

10. "An excuse to sell"

1. Stephen Ambrose, *Eisenhower: The President* (New York: Simon and Schuster, 1984), 532–535; Oliver J. Gingold, "Abreast of the Market," *Wall Street Journal,* 6 August 1959, p. 18; "Over-the-Counter Markets," ibid., 14; Oliver J. Gingold, "Abreast of the Market," *Wall Street Journal,* 7 August 1959, p. 19; "Over-the-Counter Markets," ibid., 16; "Over-the-Counter Markets," *Wall Street Journal,* 10 August 1959, p. 18. H. J. Nelson, "The Trader," *Barron's,* 10 August 1959, p. 2; Oliver J. Gingold, "Abreast of the Market," *Wall Street Journal,* 10 August 1959, p. 21.

2. Oliver J. Gingold, "Abreast of the Market," *Wall Street Journal,* 11 August 1959, p. 23.

3. Ibid.; "The Market's Big Spill: Sharpest in Four Years," *Business Week,* 15 August 1959, 25.

4. Oliver J. Gingold, "Abreast of the Market," *Wall Street Journal,* 14 August 1959, p. 19.

5. H. J. Nelson, "The Trader," *Barron's,* 17 August 1959, 2.

6. Oliver J. Gingold, "Abreast of the Market," *Wall Street Journal,* 19 August 1959, 23.

7. Louis Kraar, "Weapons Shakeout," *Wall Street Journal,* 20 August 1959, p. 1; H. J. Nelson, "The Trader," *Barron's,* 24 August 1959, p. 2.

8. Louis Kraar, "Air Force Secretary Says He May Be Able to Keep Major Projects Despite Economies," *Wall Street Journal,* 27 August 1959, p. 2; Oliver J. Gingold, "Abreast of the Market," *Wall Street Journal,* 28 August 1959, p. 17.

9. "Highlights of the Acquisition Program," general 1959–1960, no. 2, box 42, Itek Corporation, investments, Rockefeller Family Archives, RAC. The memorandum is undated, but Harper Woodward's notes in the margins reveal that it was written before an Itek board meeting on October 14.

10. Daniel E. Hogan Jr. to Richard Leghorn, 29 September 1959, general 1959–1960, no. 2, box 42, Itek Corporation, investments, Rockefeller Family Archives, RAC; "Report on the Printing Industry," 2 October 1959, general 1959–1960, no. 2, box 42, Itek Corporation, investments, Rockefeller Family Archives, RAC; "Highlights of the Acquisition Program," general 1959–1960, no. 2, box 42, Itek Corporation, investments, Rockefeller Family Archives, RAC.

11. Richard Leghorn to Board of Directors, 22 October 1959, general 1959–1960, no. 2, box 42, Itek Corporation, investments, Rockefeller Family Archives, RAC; Richard Leghorn to James Killian, 22 October 1959, general 1959–1960, no. 2, box 42, Itek Corporation, investments, Rockefeller Family Archives, RAC. Years later Leghorn recalled that Rockefeller had asked him whether he had learned to delegate responsibility. At the time, Leghorn believed that he was effective at delegation and that this allowed him to pursue his public policy agenda while running the company. In retrospect, he realized that he had delegated too much responsibility and had not been as involved in company operations as he should have been. Richard Leghorn, interview with author, Hyannis, Mass., 15 August 1997. Leghorn also believed that his continued commitment to disarmament during this period may have been a turning point in his personal relationship with Teddy Walkowicz, who was a hard-line anticommunist. Richard Leghorn, telephone conversation with author, 11 July 1997.

12. Harper Woodward to Richard Leghorn, 28 October 1959, general 1959–1960, no. 2, box 42, Itek Corporation, investments, Rockefeller Family Archives, RAC.

13. Harper Woodward to Laurance Rockefeller, 29 October 1959, general 1959–1960, no. 2, box 42, Itek Corporation, investments, Rockefeller Family Archives, RAC.

14. Albert Pratt to Richard Leghorn, 28 October 1959, general 1959–1960, no. 2, box 42, Itek Corporation, investments, Rockefeller Family Archives, RAC.

15. Albert Pratt to Underwriters, 28 October 1959, general 1959–1960, no. 2, box 42, Itek Corporation, investments, Rockefeller Family Archives, RAC.

16. "Rockefeller Brothers Visit Itek," *Itek Intelligence,* December 1959, vol. 2, no. 12, pp. 1, 4, Papers of William C. Britton; F. Dow Smith, interview with author, Romney, N.H., 12 August 1997; Walter Levison, telephone conversation with author, 20 May 1997; Frank Lindsay, interview with author, Cambridge, Mass., 29 January 2000; Harper Woodward to David Rockefeller, 4 November 1959, general 1959–1960, no. 2, box 42, Itek Corporation, investments, Rockefeller Family Archives, RAC.

17. Richard Leghorn to Laurance Rockefeller, 4 November 1959, general 1959–1960,

no. 2, box 42, Itek Corporation, investments, Rockefeller Family Archives, RAC; Laurance Rockefeller to Richard Leghorn, 13 November 1959, general 1959–1960, no. 2, box 42, Itek Corporation, investments, Rockefeller Family Archives, RAC.

18. Richard Leghorn to Board of Directors, November ? 1959 (date handwritten on margin of memorandum), Hermes Electronics, box 43, Itek Corporation, investments, Rockefeller Family Archives, RAC; "Hermes Electronics Co.," undated marketing brochure, Hermes Electronics, box 43, Itek Corporation, investments, Rockefeller Family Archives, RAC; "Financial Data — Hermes — Itek," 15 November 1959, Hermes Electronics, box 43, Itek Corporation, investments, Rockefeller Family Archives, RAC.

19. William H. Gregory, "Data Systems May Supplement Weapons," *Aviation Week,* 7 December 1959, rpt., general 1959–1960, no. 2, box 42, Itek Corporation, investments, Rockefeller Family Archives, RAC; Richard Leghorn to Board of Directors, 29 December 1959, general 1959–1960, no. 2, box 42, Itek Corporation, investments, Rockefeller Family Archives, RAC.

20. Carl M. Loeb, Rhoades and Co., "Research Department Notes," 18 December 1959, general 1959–1960, no. 2, box 42, Itek Corporation, investments, Rockefeller Family Archives, RAC.

21. Itek, *Annual Report 1959,* 8 January 1960, Papers of William C. Britton.

11. "Friendly in the extreme"

1. Michael R. Beschloss, *May-Day: Eisenhower, Khrushchev, and the U-2 Affair* (New York: Harper and Row, 1986), 226.

2. Harper Woodward to Richard Leghorn, 20 January 1960, 8 February board of directors meeting, box 46, Itek Corporation, investments, Rockefeller Family Archives, RAC.

3. Ken Leghorn to Richard Leghorn, 27 January 1960, Photostat Corporation 1959–1960, box 43, Itek Corporation, investments, Rockefeller Family Archives, RAC.

4. Stephen E. Ambrose, *Eisenhower: The President* (New York: Simon and Schuster, 1984), 558–564; Richard M. Bissell Jr., with Jonathan E. Lewis and Frances T. Pudlo, *Reflections of a Cold Warrior: From Yalta to the Bay of Pigs* (New Haven: Yale University Press, 1996), 130–131.

5. "Schedule of Meetings: February 8 & 9, 1960," undated, 8 February board of directors meeting, box 46, Itek Corporation, investments, Rockefeller Family Archives, RAC; Handwritten notes, 8 February 1960, 8 February board of directors meeting, box 46, Itek Corporation, investments, Rockefeller Family Archives, RAC. Although the author of the notes is not identified, it was probably either Harper Woodward or Teddy Walkowicz.

6. Robin W. Winks, *Laurance S. Rockefeller: Catalyst for Conservation* (Washington: Island, 1997), 121–122.

7. Laurance S. Rockefeller, Speech before the Interior and Related Agencies Sub-

committee of the Committee on Appropriations, United States Senate, 11 February 1960, Laurance S. Rockefeller speeches, box 1 (97-29), Rockefeller Family Archives, RAC.

8. Norman Taylor to Distribution, "Meeting with Hermes Electronics Company, February 10, 1960," 12 February 1960, Hermes Electronics, box 43, Itek Corporation, investments, Rockefeller Family Archives, RAC.

9. Harper Woodward to Jesse Cousins, 23 February 1960; Jesse Cousins to Harper Woodward, 26 February 1960; Richard Leghorn to Harper Woodward, 1 March 1960, Hermes Electronics, box 43, Itek Corporation, investments, Rockefeller Family Archives, RAC.

10. Harper Woodward to Richard Leghorn and Jesse Cousins, 18 March 1960, Hermes Electronics, box 43, Itek Corporation, investments, Rockefeller Family Archives, RAC.

11. Richard Leghorn to Board of Directors, 29 February 1960, Board Meetings 12 April 1960, box 46, Itek Corporation, investments, Rockefeller Family Archives, RAC.

12. Bissell, *Reflections of a Cold Warrior,* 121; Dwayne A. Day, "The Development and Improvement of the CORONA Satellite," in *Eye in the Sky: The Story of the CORONA Spy Satellites,* ed. Dwayne A. Day, John M. Logsdon, and Brian Latell (Washington, D.C.: Smithsonian Institution Press, 1998), 57; Curtis Peebles, *The CORONA Project: America's First Spy Satellites* (Annapolis: Naval Institute Press, 1997), 75–76.

13. Ambrose, *Eisenhower,* 564.

14. Richard Leghorn to Harper Woodward, 31 March 1960, Hermes Electronics, box 43, Itek Corporation, investments, Rockefeller Family Archives, RAC.

15. Bissell, *Reflections of a Cold Warrior,* 123–124; Gregory W. Pedlow and Donald E. Welzenbach, *The CIA and the U-2 Program, 1954–1974* (Washington, D.C.: Center for the Study of Intelligence, 1998), 167.

16. Day, "Development and Improvement," 58; Peebles, *The CORONA Project,* 76–77; Bissell, *Reflections of a Cold Warrior,* 125.

17. Bissell, *Reflections of a Cold Warrior,* 125–127; Ambrose, *Eisenhower,* 572, 579–580.

18. Richard Leghorn to Board of Directors, 9 May 1960; "Itek and Hermes Corporations Plan Merger," 12 May 1960, Hermes Electronics, box 43, Itek Corporation, investments, Rockefeller Family Archives, RAC. Leghorn recalled the acquisition was facilitated by Weisner, who "wanted to do it very much." Richard Leghorn, interview with author, Hyannis, Mass., 17 August 1997.

19. Day, "Development and Improvement," 59.

20. Richard Leghorn to Shareholders, 24 June 1960; "Hermes Electronics Co.—Itek Corporation: Explanatory Statement for Special Meetings of Stockholders July 20, 1960," advance proof, 23 June 1960, pp. 2–4, Itek stockholders meetings 1958–1962, box 259, Itek Corporation, investments, Rockefeller Family Archives, RAC.

21. Jesse Cousins to Harper Woodward, 25 June 1960, mergers: general 1958–1960, box 42, Itek Corporation, investments, Rockefeller Family Archives, RAC; Preliminary Report and Analysis of Seeburg Corporation, 25 June 1960, mergers: general 1958–1960, box 42, Itek Corporation, investments, Rockefeller Family Archives, RAC.

298 NOTES TO PAGES 167-173

22. Richard Leghorn to Board of Directors, 3 August 1960, Ditto Inc., box 42, Itek Corporation, investments, Rockefeller Family Archives, RAC.

23. Jesse Cousins to Harper Woodward, 20 April 1960, Dictaphone Corporation, box 42, Itek Corporation, investments, Rockefeller Family Archives, RAC.

24. "Dictaphone Corporation," internal undated and unsigned Itek memorandum, Dictaphone Corporation, box 42, Itek Corporation, investments, Rockefeller Family Archives, RAC. Charles Borman forwarded the memorandum to Harper Woodward. Handwriting on the document suggests that it was written in August 1960. In 1963 the possibility of a Dictaphone merger surfaced again, and the facts of the 1960 attempt and its failure were reviewed. Duncan Bruce to File, 24 September 1963, Dictaphone Corporation, box 42, Itek Corporation, investments, Rockefeller Family Archives, RAC.

25. C. K. Woodbridge to Richard Leghorn, 28 July 1960; Richard Leghorn to Theodore Walkowicz, 1 August 1960; Anice Berthier to Theodore Walkowicz, 4 August 1960, Dictaphone Corporation, box 42, Itek Corporation, investments, Rockefeller Family Archives, RAC; Duncan Bruce to File, 24 September 1963, Dictaphone Corporation, box 42, Itek Corporation, investments, Rockefeller Family Archives, RAC.

26. Day, "Development and Improvement," 59.

27. Ibid., 60–61; Peebles, *The CORONA Project,* 88–89, 91–94.

28. Frederic C. E. Oder, James C. Fitzpatrick, and Paul E. Worthman, *The CORONA Story* (Chantilly, Va.: National Reconnaissance Office, 1988), 77–78.

29. Michael R. Beschloss, *The Crisis Years: Kennedy and Khrushchev 1960–1963* (New York: HarperCollins, 1991), 28; Peebles, *The CORONA Project,* 97; Joseph Charyk, interview with author, Falmouth, Mass., 16 July 1998.

30. Bissell, *Reflections of a Cold Warrior,* 153–156, 160.

31. Richard Leghorn to Board of Directors, 26 September 1960; "Commerical and Financial Analysis of Dialaphone," 15 November 1960, Dialaphone Inc., box 42, Itek Corporation, investments, Rockefeller Family Archives, RAC.

32. Richard Leghorn to Board of Directors, 20 November 1960; "Report on Space Recovery Systems, Inc.," undated and unsigned analysis of the company; "Itek Corporation Purchases Space Recovery Systems, Inc.," 7 December 1960, Space Recovery Systems, box 44, Itek Corporation, investments, Rockefeller Family Archives, RAC.

33. "Itek Corporation Purchases Space Recovery Systems, Inc.," 7 December 1960, Space Recovery Systems, box 44, Itek Corporation, investments, Rockefeller Family Archives, RAC.

34. William A. Sheppard to Theodore Walkowicz, 27 December 1960, Space Recovery Systems, box 44, Itek Corporation, investments, Rockefeller Family Archives, RAC.

35. "Itek Corporation and Subsidiaries Consolidated Preliminary Summary Statement of Income for the Fiscal Year Ended September 30, 1960, and Comparison with Budget Dated February 1, 1960," undated; "Operating Budget for Fiscal Year October 1, 1960, Through September 30, 1961," 23 September 1960, Itek directors meetings 1960, box 46, Itek Corporation, investments, Rockefeller Family Archives, RAC.

36. "Negotiating Position," undated and unsigned summary of negotiating history between Itek and Ditto, Ditto Inc., box 42, Itek Corporation, investments, Rockefeller Family Archives, RAC.

37. Harper Woodward to Richard Leghorn, 13 October 1960, general 1959–1960, no. 2, box 42, Itek Corporation, investments, Rockefeller Family Archives, RAC.

38. Board of Directors Meeting Agenda, 29 December 1960, directors meetings, January–September 1961, box 47, Itek Corporation, investments, Rockefeller Family Archives, RAC. Although the handwritten notes on the agenda are unsigned, they appear to be in Woodward's handwriting and are attached to typewritten notes from another meeting labeled as Woodward's.

39. "We did not pay attention to acquisitions. We didn't even know it was happening. . . . We had enough problems to keep our attention." Frank Madden, interview with author, Brewster, Mass., 20 August 1997; F. Dow Smith, "The Design and Engineering of Corona's Optics," in *CORONA: Between Earth and the Sun,* ed. Robert A. McDonald (Bethesda: American Society for Photogrammetry and Remote Sensing, 1997), 117–118; Frank Madden, *The CORONA Camera System: Itek's Contribution to World Stability* (Lexington, Mass.: Hughes Danbury Optical Systems, 1997), mimeo, 16–17.

12. "This is no group of long-haired scientists"

1. Richard Leghorn, "Information Technology: Basis of the Emerging Information Industry," 9 March 1961, Itek Corporation general, 1960–1967, box 129, Itek Corporation, investments, Rockefeller Family Archives, RAC.

2. Richard M. Bissell Jr., with Jonathan E. Lewis and Frances T. Pudlo, *Reflections of a Cold Warrior: From Yalta to the Bay of Pigs* (New Haven: Yale University Press, 1996), 168–171.

3. Ibid., 182–183; Richard Reeves, *President Kennedy: Profile of Power* (New York: Simon and Schuster, 1993), 85–86.

4. Bissell, *Reflections of a Cold Warrior,* 184, 187; Peter Wyden, *Bay of Pigs: The Untold Story* (New York: Simon and Schuster, 1979), 228–232.

5. Board of Directors Meeting Agenda plus Harper Woodward's attached typewritten notes, 26 January 1961, directors meetings, January–September 1961, box 47, Itek Corporation, investments, Rockefeller Family Archives, RAC; Itek Corporation—Annual Meeting of Stockholders, 26 January 1961, Itek stockholders meetings, 1958–1962, box 259, Itek Corporation, investments, Rockefeller Family Archives, RAC; John E. Johnson to Richard Leghorn, 17 April 1961, proposed new product program, box 44, Itek Corporation general, 1960–1967, box 129, Itek Corporation, investments, Rockefeller Family Archives, RAC.

6. Bissell, *Reflections of a Cold Warrior,* 188–189; Reeves, *President Kennedy,* 92–93.

7. H. J. Nelson, "The Trader," *Barron's,* 24 April 1962, p. 4; "The World at Work," ibid., 7.

8. Bissell, *Reflections of a Cold Warrior,* 191.

9. Richard Leghorn, telephone conversation with author, 2 November 1998; "Minutes — Itek Corporation: Meeting of the Board of Directors," May 5, 1961, directors meetings, January–September 1961, box 47, Itek Corporation, investments, Rockefeller Family Archives, RAC; Franklin Lindsay, interview with author, Cambridge, Mass., 27 February 1999; Franklin Lindsay, telephone conversation with author, 27 August 2000.

10. "Draft Minutes — Itek Corporation: Meeting of the Board of Directors," May 5, 1961, directors meetings, January–September 1961, box 47, Itek Corporation, investments, Rockefeller Family Archives, RAC.

11. Cousins's memorandum also addressed many of the same business issues discussed in John Johnson's memorandum of 17 April 1961. Cousins stressed the likelihood that earnings would be disappointing in 1961. "This is an unfortunate situation in any company, but for us these results, standing by themselves, might deal a serious blow to the future of the company," he wrote. He explained that bad earnings would result in a sharp decline in the company's stock price and that this would have "an adverse effect" on Itek's ability to acquire other companies. Cousins emphasized the need to roll out new products in 1961, like Thermographic Paper. "Doubts now [exist] in the minds of sophisticated investors and security analysts that Itek does not know how to convert technology into products," he said. Introducing new products to the market, he asserted, would allay those concerns. Cousins also noted that there were "strongly divergent views" within management on the importance of these programs. Jesse Cousins to Board of Directors, 1 May 1961, directors meetings, January–September 1961, box 47, Itek Corporation, investments, Rockefeller Family Archives, RAC.

12. Sheila Perkins, telephone conversation with author, 5 August 1998. Carter confided the details to Marcus, who joined Itek not long after its incorporation. Bernard Marcus, telephone conversation with author, 18 August 1998; Albert Pratt, interview with author, Osterville, Mass., 14 July 1998; Richard Philbrick, interview with author, Orleans, Mass., 27 August 2000; Ed Campbell, telephone conversation with author, 22 May 1997.

13. Albert Pratt to Paine Webber Partners and Registered Representatives, "Current Report on Itek Corporation," 9 May 1961; Albert Pratt to Certain Investment Bankers, "Itek Corporation," 9 May 1961, prospectus, box 44, Itek Corporation, investments, Rockefeller Family Archives, RAC.

14. Pratt to Paine Webber Partners, "Current Report," 9 May 1961.

15. Stock price history from *Barron's*.

16. The committee postponed any further consideration of the acquisition program. "Itek Corporation: Draft Minutes of Executive Committee Meeting," 18–19 May 1961, directors meetings, January–September 1961, box 47, Itek Corporation, investments, Rockefeller Family Archives, RAC. In Cousins's May 18 memorandum to the executive committee, he explained the financial challenges that Itek had to overcome to secure additional credit from its bank, the First National of Boston. At that time, Itek had a "V" loan with the bank that had a $2.5 million credit ceiling. This loan limit was

driven by a complex formula that related to the size of Itek's outstanding receivables and reimbursable costs related to government contracts. The problem for Itek was that its most important government program was so highly classified that the company could not provide the bank with any information about it. Thus Itek's receivables and reimbursable expenses from CORONA could not be discussed with the bank or included in the formula that determined Itek's borrowing limits. In order to obtain additional financing from the bank, Cousins would have to persuade the CIA to allow Itek to disclose at least some information about its CORONA contract. Cousins told the board that he had met with the bank and "our customer to devise a method that will satisfy legal requirements without breaching security." The customer, never mentioned by name, was of course the CIA. After discussions with Cousins the CIA agreed to allow "assignment" of the receivables to the bank by Itek "if and when requested." Cousins explained that a loan agreement was being drafted and that it would probably have a tight working-capital restriction. Chase Manhattan, where David Rockefeller worked, would also probably participate in the loan. Jesse Cousins to Executive Committee, "Status of Loan Agreement," 18 May 1961, loan agreements, box 42, Itek Corporation, investments, Rockefeller Family Archives, RAC. Cousins had additional hurdles to leap before he could obtain a larger loan. Although the CIA would allow Itek to disclose to the bank basic financial data about the company's contract, a certified public accountant needed to verify the financial details in order to meet the bank's underwriting criteria. Cousins persuaded the CIA to give a high-level security clearance to John March of Arthur Anderson to furnish the necessary data to the banks. Cousins told the executive committee, "March will furnish a statement to the banks in a form satisfactory to them without disclosing classified information." During the negotiations with the bank it was decided to repackage the loan on a "non-V basis." Jesse Cousins to Executive Committee of the Board of Directors, "Status of Loan Agreement," 24 May 1961; Richard D. Hill to Jesse Cousins, 24 May 1961, draft copy of proposed basic terms for unsecured revolving credit agreement, 18 May 1961, loan agreements, box 42, Itek Corporation, investments, Rockefeller Family Archives, RAC.

17. Duncan Bruce to Board of Directors, 24 May 1961, directors meetings, January–September 1961, box 47, Itek Corporation, investments, Rockefeller Family Archives, RAC.

18. Ibid.; Itek Corporation: Meeting of the Board of Directors, 25 May 1961, directors meetings, January–September 1961, box 47, Itek Corporation, investments, Rockefeller Family Archives, RAC.

19. Itek Corporation: Meeting of the Executive Committee of the Board of Directors, 1–2 June 1961, directors meetings, 1961–1962, box 157, Itek Corporation, investments, Rockefeller Family Archives, RAC. On June 19 the executive committee met again at the Ritz Carlton at 4:00 P.M. They discussed how to announce to the public Frank Lindsay's appointment as executive vice president. At 6:30 P.M. Richard Leghorn and his brother, Kenneth, president of Photostat, arrived at the meeting. According to the minutes, a "discussion of various corporate matters" followed. Itek Corporation: Meeting of the Executive Committee of the Board of Directors, 19–

20 June 1961, directors meetings, 1961–1962, box 157, Itek Corporation, investments, Rockefeller Family Archives, RAC. On June 23 Pratt had lunch with Leghorn and gave him a copy of the resolutions passed at the May 5 board meeting. Albert Pratt to Theodore Walkowicz, 26 June 1961, directors meetings, 1961–1962, box 157, Itek Corporation, investments, Rockefeller Family Archives, RAC. "I knew it had to work," Pratt said years later. "We had to make it go." Pratt interview, 14 July 1998.

13. "Then, Mr. Chairman, there will be war"

1. Richard Reeves, *President Kennedy: Profile of Power* (New York: Simon and Schuster, 1993), 167–171; Michael R. Beschloss, *The Crisis Years: Kennedy and Khrushchev, 1960–1963* (New York: HarperCollins, 1991), 223–224.

2. Meeting of the Executive Committee of the Board of Directors, 28 June 1961, directors meetings, 1961–1962, box 157, Itek Corporation, investments, Rockefeller Family Archives, RAC; Meeting of the Executive Committee of the Board of Directors, 21 July 1961, directors meetings, 1961–1962, box 157, Itek Corporation, investments, Rockefeller Family Archives, RAC.

3. Richard Leghorn to Itek Shareholders, 18 July 1961, Itek Laboratories, box 43, Itek Corporation, investments, Rockefeller Family Archives, RAC.

4. Albert Pratt to Richard Leghorn, 21 July 1961, directors meetings, January–September 1961, box 47, Itek Corporation, investments, Rockefeller Family Archives, RAC; Meeting of the Board of Directors, 27 July 1961, directors meetings, January–September 1961, box 47, Itek Corporation, investments, Rockefeller Family Archives, RAC; Franklin Lindsay, interview with author, Cambridge, Mass., 27 February 1999.

5. Richard Leghorn to Board of Directors, 11 August 1961, directors meetings, January–September 1961, box 47, Itek Corporation, investments, Rockefeller Family Archives, RAC.

6. Richard Leghorn to Board of Directors, 29 August 1961, directors meetings, January–September 1961, box 47, Itek Corporation, investments, Rockefeller Family Archives, RAC; Meeting of the Executive Committee of the Board of Directors, 29 August 1961, directors meetings, 1961–1962, box 157, Itek Corporation, investments, Rockefeller Family Archives, RAC.

7. Dwayne A. Day, "Development and Improvement of the CORONA Satellite," in *Eye in the Sky: The Story of the CORONA Spy Satellites*, ed. Dwayne A. Day, John M. Logsdon, and Brian Latell (Washington, D.C.: Smithsonian Institution Press, 1998), 65.

8. Years later, Charyk recalled he had a "very good relationship with Bissell." "We spoke to each other quite frequently," he explained, "and whenever he would have some problems with the air force aspect of it, I would try to work those out." Conversely, when Charyk needed help dealing with the CIA, Bissell was always ready to assist him. Joseph Charyk, interview with author, Falmouth, Mass., 16 July 1998; Frederic C. E. Oder, James C. Fitzpatrick, and Paul E. Worthman, *The CORONA Story* (Chantilly, Va.: Government Printing Office, 1988), 69–70; Robert L. Perry, *Manage-*

ment of the National Reconnaissance Program (Chantilly, Va.: NRO History Office, 1969), 26–27; Gerald Haines, "The National Reconnaissance Office: Its Origins, Creation, and Early Years," in Day, Logsdon, and Latell, *Eye in the Sky,* 148–149.

9. Richard Leghorn to Board of Directors, 27 September 1961, directors meetings, January–September 1961, box 47, Itek Corporation, investments, Rockefeller Family Archives, RAC.

10. Meeting of the Board of Directors, 28 September 1961, directors meetings, October 1961, box 47, Itek Corporation, investments, Rockefeller Family Archives, RAC.

11. Ernest R. May, "Strategic Intelligence and U.S. Security: The Contributions of CORONA" in Day, Logsdon, and Latell, *Eye in the Sky,* 25; Reeves, *President Kennedy,* 228–229, 335.

12. Nancy Hanks to Franklin Lindsay, 22 September 1961, subpanel 4, box 29, folder 320, record group V4B, special studies project, RAC; Franklin Lindsay to Laurance Rockefeller, 2 October 1961, subpanel 4, box 29, folder 320, record group V4B, special studies project, RAC.

13. Duncan Bruce to Board of Directors, 20 October 1961, financial forecasts, box 259, Itek Corporation, investments, Rockefeller Family Archives, RAC.

14. Board of Directors Meeting Agenda, 26–27 October 1961, directors meetings, October 1961, box 47, Itek Corporation, investments, Rockefeller Family Archives, RAC; Presentation to Itek Board of Directors, 26 October 1961, directors meetings, October 1961, box 47, Itek Corporation, investments, Rockefeller Family Archives, RAC.

15. Richard Leghorn to Board of Directors, 17 November 1961, management survey, Ralph Hunt report, box 42, Itek Corporation, investments, Rockefeller Family Archives, RAC; Itek Corporation Meeting of the Board of Directors, 29 November 1961, directors meetings, November–December 1961, box 47, Itek Corporation, investments, Rockefeller Family Archives, RAC. Internal company financial documents from the middle of December reveal that additional inventory write-offs at Itek Electro-Products and Photostat were almost entirely responsible for the increased losses. Itek Corporation Comparison of Final Pretax Income with Preliminary Results dated 26 October 1961, 12 December 1961, directors meetings, November–December 1961, box 47, Itek Corporation, investments, Rockefeller Family Archives, RAC.

16. Richard Leghorn to Board of Directors, 27 December 1961, directors meetings, November–December 1961, box 47, Itek Corporation, investments, Rockefeller Family Archives, RAC.

17. Annual Report to Shareholders of Itek Corporation for the Year Ending September 30, 1961, Papers of William C. Britton, 1–3, 5–8, 14–19; Franklin Lindsay, telephone conversation with author, 27 August 2000.

14. "I am today forming a new corporate management team"

1. Handwritten comments in the margins of Harper Woodward's copy read, "Not what happened." Woodward also noted that the wording needed to be checked with

Hill. Itek Corporation Special Meeting of the Board of Directors, 14 February 1962, directors meetings, January–July 1962, box 47, Itek Corporation, investments, Rockefeller Family Archives, RAC; Minutes of Itek Corporation Meeting of the Board of Directors, 21 February 1962, directors meetings, January–July 1962, box 47, Itek Corporation, investments, Rockefeller Family Archives, RAC; Franklin Lindsay and Walter Levison, interview with author, Cambridge, Mass., 7 June 1997.

2. In January, Leghorn outlined his plans for 1962 to *Forbes*. Itek would again be profitable, he predicted, thanks to a greater reliance on internal expansion. "Dreams Delayed," *Forbes*, 15 January 1962, p. 16. Handwritten notes from Itek's February 21, 1962, meeting provide great detail about Leghorn's prospective plans. Although the notes are unsigned, they were probably written by Peter Crisp, a new assistant in Laurance Rockefeller's office who years later rose to head the operation. Itek Corporation Meeting of the Board of Directors, 2/21/62, Directors Meetings January to July 1962, Box 47, Itek Corporation, Investments, Rockefeller Family Archives, RAC.

3. Itek Corporation Meeting of the Board of Directors, 21 February 1962, directors meetings, January–July 1962, box 47, Itek Corporation, investments, Rockefeller Family Archives, RAC.

4. Itek Corporation Meeting of the Board of Directors, 29 March 1962, directors meetings, January–July 1962, box 47, Itek Corporation, investments, Rockefeller Family Archives, RAC; Peter Crisp, handwritten notes from Itek Corporation Meeting of the Board of Directors, 29 March 1962; Peter Crisp to Theodore Walkowicz, 2 April 1962, directors meetings, January–July 1962, box 47, Itek Corporation, investments, Rockefeller Family Archives, RAC.

5. Richard Leghorn to Itek Supervisors and Senior Staff, 9 April 1962, management survey, Ralph Hunt report, box 42, Itek Corporation, investments, Rockefeller Family Archives, RAC; Franklin Lindsay, interview with author, Cambridge, Mass., 27 February 1999.

6. Itek Corporation Meeting of the Board of Directors, 26 April 1962, directors meetings, January–July 1962, box 47, Itek Corporation, investments, Rockefeller Family Archives, RAC; handwritten notes on meeting agenda for Itek's 26 April 1962 meeting, undated and unsigned, though probably written by Peter Crisp, directors meetings, January–July 1962, box 47, Itek Corporation, investments, Rockefeller Family Archives, RAC.

7. Ed Campbell, interview with author, Dartmouth, Mass., 20 September 1997.

8. Richard Leghorn to Board of Directors, 7 May 1962, directors meetings, January–July 1962, box 47, Itek Corporation, investments, Rockefeller Family Archives, RAC.

9. Harper Woodward to Files, 8 May 1962, directors meetings, January–July 1962, box 47, Itek Corporation, investments, Rockefeller Family Archives, RAC; Richard Leghorn to Board of Directors, 13 May 1962, management survey, Ralph Hunt report, box 42, Itek Corporation, investments, Rockefeller Family Archives, RAC.

10. Leghorn to Board of Directors, 13 May 1962.

11. Richard Leghorn to Laurance Rockefeller, 13 May 1962, management survey, Ralph Hunt report, box 42, Itek Corporation, investments, Rockefeller Family Archives, RAC.

12. Joseph Charyk, interview with author, Falmouth, Mass., 16 July 1998; Agenda Meeting of Non-Management Directors of Itek Corporation, 16 May 1962, undated and unsigned, management survey, Ralph Hunt report, box 42, Itek Corporation, investments, Rockefeller Family Archives, RAC.

13. Lindsay interview, 27 February 1999; Dow Smith, interview with author, Romney, N.H., 12 August 1997; Walter Levison, interview with author, Harvard, Mass., 21 August 1998; Richard Philbrick, interviews with author, Orleans, Mass., 19 August 1997, 15 July 1998; Lindsay and Levison interview, 7 June 1997. Albert Pratt remembered Levison as "sort of the leader" of the mutineers. Albert Pratt, interview with author, Osterville, Mass., 14 July 1998.

14. Campbell interview, 20 September 1997.

15. Franklin Lindsay, interview with author, Cambridge, Mass., 6 June 1997; Lindsay and Levison interview, 7 June 1997.

16. Richard Leghorn to Board of Directors, 17 May 1962, directors meetings, January–July 1962, box 47, Itek Corporation, investments, Rockefeller Family Archives, RAC.

15. "We are probably going to have to bomb them"

1. Franklin Lindsay, "Letter to Executive, Professional, and Supervisory Personnel," 22 June 1962, directors meetings, box 47, Itek Corporation, investments, Rockefeller Family Archives, RAC.

2. Revised Agenda, Itek Board of Directors Meeting, 28 June 1962, directors meetings, box 47, Itek Corporation, investments, Rockefeller Family Archives, RAC; Ed Campbell to Board of Directors, 26 June 1962, directors meetings, box 47, Itek Corporation, investments, Rockefeller Family Archives, RAC; Ed Campbell to Files, "Jack Carter," 25 June 1962, directors meetings, box 47, Itek Corporation, investments, Rockefeller Family Archives, RAC. To the best of Ed Campbell's knowledge, the CIA never understood the depth of Itek's financial problems during this period. Ed Campbell, interview with author, Dartmouth, Mass., 20 September 1997. Allied wanted to become a force in satellite payloads. Malcolm Malcolmson, telephone conversation with author, 4 March 1999; Bernie Marcus, telephone conversation with author, 17 August 1998; Ed Campbell to Files, "Itek Electro-Products," 21 September 1962, directors meetings, box 47, Itek Corporation, investments, Rockefeller Family Archives, RAC; Franklin Lindsay to Board of Directors, 1963 Itek management objectives, 26 September 1962, directors meetings, box 47, Itek Corporation, investments, Rockefeller Family Archives, RAC.

3. Itek Corporation: Board of Directors Meeting Agenda plus unsigned handwritten notes, 26 September 1962, directors meetings, box 47, Itek Corporation, investments, Rockefeller Family Archives, RAC; Presentation to the Board of Directors, 26 Septem-

ber 1962, directors meetings, box 47, Itek Corporation, investments, Rockefeller Family Archives, RAC.

4. Richard Reeves, *President Kennedy: Profile of Power* (New York: Simon and Schuster, 1993), 368, 370.

5. Dino A. Brugioni, *Eyeball to Eyeball: The Inside Story of the Cuban Missile Crisis* (New York: Random House, 1991), 181, 246, 303–304; Michael R. Beschloss, *The Crisis Years: Kennedy and Khrushchev, 1960–1963* (New York: HarperCollins, 1991), 459–460.

6. Brugioni, *Eyeball to Eyeball,* 305.

7. Rick Manent and Gary Nelson, interview with author, Hudson, Mass., 19 September 1998.

8. John Parangosky, telephone conversation with author, 20 October 1998.

9. Ibid.

10. Curtis Peebles, *The CORONA Project: America's First Spy Satellites* (Annapolis: Naval Institute Press, 1997), 219.

11. Rick Manent, telephone conversation with author, 25 August 1998; Manent and Nelson interview, 19 September 1998.

12. Manent telephone conversation, 25 August 1998; Manent and Nelson interview, 19 September 1998; Tom Hobin, interview with author, Waltham, Mass., 19 September 1998.

13. Ernest R. May, "Strategic Intelligence and U.S. Security: The Contributions of CORONA," in *Eye in the Sky: The Story of the Corona Spy Satellites,* ed. Dwayne A. Day, John M. Logsdon, and Brian Latell (Washington, D.C.: Smithsonian Institution Press, 1998), 26.

14. Itek Corporation: Board of Directors Meeting Agenda plus unsigned handwritten notes, 30 November 1962, directors meetings, box 47, Itek Corporation, investments, Rockefeller Family Archives, RAC; Richard Philbrick to Franklin Lindsay, 29 November 1962, directors meetings, box 47, Itek Corporation, investments, Rockefeller Family Archives, RAC; Richard Philbrick, interview with author, Orleans, Mass., 27 August 2000.

15. Earnings from operations were $280,000, or twenty-four cents a share. After a tax adjustment for prior-year losses, earnings were $439,000, or thirty-eight cents a share. Itek 1962 Annual Report, Private Papers of Franklin Lindsay.

16. Washington Troubles

1. Actual gross revenues were only 79 percent of budget. Net income was even lower. Franklin A. Lindsay to Board of Directors, 19 March 1963, progress reports, 1963, box 45, Itek Corporation, investments, Rockefeller Family Archives, RAC; "Itek Corporation: Progress Report—February 1963," 19 March 1963, progress reports, 1963, box 45, Itek Corporation, investments, Rockefeller Family Archives, RAC.

2. Franklin Lindsay, interview with author, Cambridge, Mass., 29 January 2000; Joseph Charyk, interview with author, Falmouth, Mass., 16 July 1998. The new agree-

ment defined the NRO as "a separate operating agency of the Department of Defense." No longer was it under the authority of the secretary of the air force. Now the secretary of defense was the "executive agent" of the nation's reconnaissance programs, and the NRO was under his "direction, authority, and control." The agreement also included language that gave the director of the NRO increased influence over the CIA's technical and management personnel. Robert L. Perry, *Management of the National Reconnaissance Program, 1960 to 1965* (Chantilly, Va.: National Reconnaissance Office, 1999), 52–55; John McMahon, telephone conversation with author, 13 November 2000. "Despite the new agreement, the Air Force continued to press for complete control of the overhead reconnaissance programs." Gerald Haines, "The National Reconnaissance Office: Its Origins, Creation, and Early Years," in *Eye in the Sky: The Story of the CORONA Spy Satellites,* ed. Dwayne A. Day, John M. Logsdon, and Brian Latell (Washington, D.C.: Smithsonian Institution Press, 1998), 152–153.

3. Perry, *Management of the National Reconnaissance Program,* 56; Charyk interview, 16 July 1998.

4. Franklin A. Lindsay to Board of Directors, 19 March 1963, progress reports, 1963, box 45, Itek Corporation, investments, Rockefeller Family Archives, RAC; "Itek Corporation: Progress Report—February 1963," 19 March 1963, progress reports, 1963, box 45, Itek Corporation, investments, Rockefeller Family Archives, RAC.

5. Eugene P. Kiefer, "Memorandum for the Record Re: M-2 Committee," 8 April 1963, NRO; Itek Corporation, "Statement of Work for Photographic Light Pattern Analysis," 5 April 1963, NRO; John Parangosky, "Activity Program," 16 April 1963, NRO.

6. Curtis Peebles, *The CORONA Project: America's First Spy Satellites* (Annapolis: Naval Institute Press, 1997), 156–157; Frederic C. E. Oder, James C. Fitzpatrick, and Paul E. Worthman, *The CORONA Story* (Chantilly, Va.: National Reconnaissance Office, 1988), 93; F. Dow Smith, "The Design and Engineering of CORONA's Optics," in *CORONA: Between the Sun and the Earth,* ed. Robert A. McDonald (Bethesda, Md.: American Society for Photogrammetry and Remote Sensing, 1997), 117; Dwayne A. Day, "The Development and Improvement of the CORONA Satellite," in Day, Logsdon, and Latell, *Eye in the Sky,* 75–77; A. Johnson, "Technical Directive Authorization Sheet," 22 April 1963, NRO; Unsigned, "Lockheed Missiles and Space Company: Proposed Technical Directive," 22 April 1963, NRO; Unsigned, "Classified Message," 5 June 1963, NRO.

7. Peter Crisp to Harper Woodward and Theodore Walkowicz, Itek April progress report, 24 May 1963, progress reports, 1963, box 45, Itek Corporation, investments, Rockefeller Family Archives, RAC. Unknown to Crisp, Itek's impressive performance on CORONA also contributed to the profit turnaround. Although the documentary evidence is ambiguous on this point, it seems likely that the performance incentives often built in to Itek's contracts with the government led to the higher than expected profitability. Itek Corporation: Progress Report—April 1963, 17 May 1963, box 45, Itek Corporation, investments, Rockefeller Family Archives, RAC.

8. Franklin Lindsay to Board of Directors, disposition of DGP project, 28 May 1963,

directors meetings, 1963, box 47, Itek Corporation, investments, Rockefeller Family Archives, RAC.

9. "Itek's Fix-It Man," *Forbes,* 15 June 1963, p. 45.

10. Franklin Lindsay, draft memorandum, 25 June 1963, box 47, Itek Corporation, investments, Rockefeller Family Archives, RAC; Perry, *Management of the National Reconnaissance Program,* 58–59.

11. Peter Crisp to Harper Woodward and Theodore Walkowicz, Itek August progress report, 25 September 1963, box 45, progress reports, 1963, Itek Corporation, investments, Rockefeller Family Archives, RAC; "Itek Corporation: Progress Report—August 1963," 19 September 1963, box 45, progress reports, 1963, Itek Corporation, investments, Rockefeller Family Archives, RAC.

12. Perry, *Management of the National Reconnaissance Program,* 65, 69–72, 74; Haines, "National Reconnaissance Office," 152–153; Albert D. Wheelon, "CORONA: Triumph of American Technology," in Day, Logsdon, and Latell, *Eye in the Sky,* 42.

13. Name redacted, "CORONA Discharge Testing," 5 August 1963, NRO; Undated and unsigned memorandum, "CORONA Discharge," NRO; Day, "Development and Improvement," 69–70; Frank Madden, *The CORONA Camera System: Itek's Contribution to World Stability* (Lexington, Mass.: Hughes Danbury Optical Systems, 1996), 15.

14. Name redacted, "CORONA Discharge Testing"; Undated and unsigned memorandum, "CORONA Discharge"; Madden, *The CORONA Camera System,* 15.

15. Experience with recent flights suggested that "CORONA discharge may be aggravated by extended periods of time" in the vacuum of space. Name redacted, "CORONA Discharge Testing"; Undated and unsigned memorandum, "CORONA Discharge"; Madden, *The CORONA Camera System,* 15.

16. Day, "Development and Improvement," 75–77.

17. Name of author redacted, Lockheed Aircraft Corp.—Missiles and Space Division, "Technical Directive Authorization Sheet—CORONA Discharge Test," 5 September 1963, NRO.

18. Jonathan E. Lewis, "Tension and Triumph: Civilian and Military Relations and the Birth of the U-2 Program," in McDonald, *CORONA,* 14–15.

19. Albert Wheelon, telephone conversations with author, 15 November 2000, 19 November 2000; McMahon telephone conversation, 13 November 2000; Roland Inlow, telephone conversation with author, 26 March 1997.

20. Madden, *The CORONA Camera System,* 15; Wheelon telephone conversation, 15 November 2000; John McMahon, telephone conversations with author, 8 November 2000, 13 November 2000.

21. Madden, *The CORONA Camera System,* 15–16; Day, "Development and Improvement," 69–70.

22. Name redacted, Lockheed Aircraft Corp.—Missiles and Space Division, "Proposed Technical Directive—J Camera Exposure Modification for Night Use," 11 September 1963, NRO; Name redacted, Lockheed Aircraft Corp.—Missiles and Space Division, "Technical Directive Authorization Sheet—J Camera Exposure Modification for Night Use," 11 September 1963, NRO; Arthur Lundahl, "Research and Devel-

opment Project Approval Request for Photographic Light Pattern Analysis," approved 3 April 1964, NRO; Name redacted, Lockheed Aircraft Corp.—Missiles and Space Division, "Proposed Technical Directive—Interrogate Circuit," 18 September 1963, NRO; Name redacted, Lockheed Aircraft Corp.—Missiles and Space Division, "Technical Directive Authorization Sheet—Interrogate Circuit," 18 September 1963, NRO; Name redacted, Lockheed Aircraft Corp.—Missiles and Space Division, "Proposed Technical Directive—Dust Covers over Subassemblies," 21 October 1963, NRO; Name redacted, Lockheed Aircraft Corp.—Missiles and Space Division, "Technical Directive Authorization Sheet—Dust Covers over Subassemblies," 21 October 1963, NRO.

23. Itek Annual Report, 1963, Private Papers of Franklin Lindsay.

24. Ibid.

25. "Itek Refocused," *Time,* 8 November 1963, pp. 85–86.

26. Brockway McMillan to General Greer, "Lanyard," 23 October 1963, NRO. The effective date of the stop work order to Itek was October 25. Name redacted to name redacted, "Termination of Lanyard Program," 27 November 1963, NRO.

27. Franklin Lindsay to Board of Directors, 13 December 1963, box 45, progress reports, 1963, Itek Corporation, investments, Rockefeller Family Archives, RAC; "Itek Corporation: Progress Report—November 1963," 14 December 1963, box 45, progress reports, 1963, Itek Corporation, investments, Rockefeller Family Archives, RAC.

28. Perry, *Management of the National Reconnaissance Program,* 65, 69–72, 74; Haines, "National Reconnaissance Office," 152–153; Brockway McMillan, telephone conversation with author, 14 November 2000; Wheelon telephone conversation, 19 November 2000; Wheelon, "CORONA," 42.

29. Name redacted to Albert Wheelon, Itek proposal for follow-on system, 16 January 1964, NRO; Name redacted to Albert Wheelon, Itek proposal, 22 January 1964, NRO; Perry, *Management of the National Reconnaissance Program,* 76–78; Inlow telephone conversation, 26 March 1997; Frank Madden, interview with author, Brewster, Mass., 1 September 2000.

30. McMahon telephone conversation, 13 November 2000. Brockway McMillan does not recall being at CIA briefings in the early stages of FULCRUM's development. The CIA, he recalled, tried to hide the project from him. McMillan telephone conversation, 14 November 2000.

31. McMahon telephone conversations, 8 November 2000, 13 November 2000; Roy Burks, telephone conversation with author, 17 November 2000.

32. McMillan telephone conversation, 14 November 2000. Perry, a historian for the NRO, wrote a history that supports McMillan's view. Perry, *Management of the National Reconnaissance Program,* 96.

33. Burks telephone conversation, 17 November 2000; McMillan telephone conversation, 14 November 2000; Inlow telephone conversation, 26 March 1997.

34. Burks telephone conversation, 17 November 2000; Name redacted to name redacted, 30 January 1964, NRO.

35. Albert D. Wheelon to Franklin A. Lindsay, 10 February 1964, NRO.

36. Unsigned, Memorandum for the Record—Itek Proposals, 5 February 1964, NRO (italics added); John N. McMahon, Memorandum for the Record—Meeting with Itek on 17 April 1964, 5 May 1964, NRO; John N. McMahon to Albert Wheelon, 5 May, 1964, NRO.

37. Although the letter does not specifically mention FULCRUM (the letter was unclassified, and the system was classified), based on the events at the time it seems reasonable that the system Meinel refers to is indeed the follow-on to CORONA. A. B. Meinel to Albert D. Wheelon, 8 June 1964, NRO.

38. Perry, *Management of the National Reconnaissance Program,* 82–83.

39. Ibid., 82–83, 89; Marilyn B. Young, *The Vietnam Wars: 1945–1990* (New York: HarperCollins, 1991), 117–119; Michael H. Hunt, *Lyndon Johnson's War: America's Cold War Crusade in Vietnam, 1945–1968* (New York: Hill and Wang, 1996), 84.

40. Peter Crisp to Harper Woodward and Theodore Walkowicz, 4 May 1964, box 45, 1964: January–December, Itek Corporation, investments, Rockefeller Family Archives, RAC; Peter Crisp to Harper Woodward and Theodore Walkowicz, 25 May 1964, box 45, 1964: January–December, Itek Corporation, investments, Rockefeller Family Archives, RAC; Peter Crisp to Harper Woodward and Theodore Walkowicz, 23 July 1964, box 45, 1964: January–December, Itek Corporation, investments, Rockefeller Family Archives, RAC; Franklin Lindsay to Board of Directors, 17 July 1964, box 45, 1964: January–December, Itek Corporation, investments, Rockefeller Family Archives, RAC; Lindsay interview, 29 January 2000; Franklin Lindsay, telephone conversation with author, 26 August 2000; Madden interview, 1 September 2000.

41. John N. McMahon, "Status of 'Head Above Water,' 6 August 1964," NRO; McMahon telephone conversation, 13 November 2000.

42. Richard Philbrick, unpublished and undated paper, "Summary of the Events Leading to the Termination of Project 9204," Papers of Richard Philbrick.

43. Unsigned handwritten minutes of Itek Board of Directors Meeting, 29–30 September 1964, directors meetings, 1964, box 47, Itek Corporation, investments, Rockefeller Family Archives, RAC; Peter Crisp to Harper Woodward and Theodore Walkowicz, 28 October 1964, box 45, 1964, Itek Corporation, investments, Rockefeller Family Archives, RAC; Richard Philbrick, interview with author, Orleans, Mass., 27 August 2000; Madden interview, 1 September 2000.

44. Itek Annual Report, 1964, Private Papers of Franklin A. Lindsay.

45. Frank J. Madden to name redacted, 21 December 1964, NRO; Madden interview, 1 September 2000.

17. FULCRUM

1. Albert Wheelon to Gen. Marshall Carter, 11 January 1965, NRO; Gen. Marshall Carter and Brockway McMillan, "Memorandum of Agreement," undated, NRO.

2. The same day, either Levison or another Itek executive with him at the meeting stated that as a matter of "corporate policy that any briefing given at Itek would be

made by Itek." The memorandum writer concluded that Itek's management would take CIA direction only "as long as it suited" the company. Unsigned, "Highlights of Conversation Itek Management/CIA," 12 January 1965, NRO; Unsigned, "Events in [deleted]'s Office," 12 January 1965, NRO.

3. Walter Levison, interview with author, Harvard, Mass., 6 June 1997. Richard Philbrick recalled that the CIA tried to restrain Itek from having discussions with McMillan about the FULCRUM proposal. Richard Philbrick, interview with author, Orleans, Mass., 15 July 1998. John McMahon recalled Wheelon's efforts to strengthen the CIA's scientific staff. John McMahon, telephone conversation with author, 13 November 2000; Richard Philbrick, telephone conversation with author, 12 November 2000; F. Dow Smith, telephone conversation with author, 11 November 2000.

4. Levison interview, 6 June 1997; Walter Levison, unpublished paper, "The FULCRUM Story," 12 February 1988, Papers of Walter Levison; Franklin Lindsay to John McCone, 5 April 1965, Papers of Richard Philbrick; Brockway McMillan, letter to author, 18 September 1998; Richard Philbrick, unpublished and undated paper, "Summary of the Events Leading to the Termination of Project 9204," Papers of Richard Philbrick.

5. "Many Tricks in Itek's New Bag," *Business Week,* 30 January 1965, pp. 60–62; Franklin Lindsay, telephone conversation with author, 12 November 2000.

6. "Many Tricks," pp. 60–62; Lindsay telephone conversation, 12 November 2000. Ed Campbell, Itek's chief financial officer, recalled this as a period of great optimism for Itek's future. Itek's senior management team was unanimous in its belief that the company's commercial operations were at last on the verge of a major success. Ed Campbell, telephone conversation with author, 18 November 2000.

7. Levison, "The FULCRUM Story"; Levison interview, 6 June 1997; Philbrick, "Summary of the Events"; Richard Philbrick, interview with author, Orleans, Mass., 27 August 2000.

8. Levison, "The FULCRUM Story"; Philbrick, "Summary of the Events."

9. Levison, "The FULCRUM Story"; Philbrick, "Summary of the Events." Frank Lindsay later recalled that in a private meeting with Wheelon he was told that if the CIA ever admitted that its design for FULCRUM was less than perfect, the air force would gain control of the spy satellite program. Franklin Lindsay and Walter Levison, interview with author, Cambridge, Mass., 7 June 1997.

10. Levison, "The FULCRUM Story." The CIA owned a number of companies in those days. Levison interview, 6 June 1997. Years later Frank Lindsay recalled that at this point the CIA "wanted to run our business as though it was their private business." Lindsay and Levison interview, 7 June 1997; Frank Madden, interview with author, Brewster, Mass., 1 September 2000.

11. Levison, "The FULCRUM Story."

12. Richard Philbrick, interviews with author, Orleans, Mass., 19 August 1997, 27 August 2000; Levison interview, 6 June 1997; Robert L. Perry, *Management of the National Reconnaissance Program, 1960–1965* (Chantilly, Va.: NRO, 1969), 96; Frank Madden, telephone conversation with author, 11 November 2000.

13. Franklin Lindsay, interview with author, Cambridge, Mass., 29 January 2000. Lindsay found Wheelon to be arrogant and demanding. Franklin Lindsay, interview with author, Cambridge, Mass., 13 March 1999.

14. Levison, "The FULCRUM Story"; Lindsay and Levison interview, 7 June 1997; Lindsay interview, 29 January 2000; Philbrick interview, 27 August 2000; Smith telephone conversation, 11 November 2000; Madden interview, 1 September 2000.

15. Albert Wheelon, telephone conversation with author, 15 November 2000. Wheelon admitted that he could be forceful with contractors when necessary. Albert Wheelon, telephone conversation with author, 19 November 2000; Levison, "The FULCRUM Story."

16. Minutes of telephone conversation with Frank Lindsay, 18 February 1965, NRO; Wheelon telephone conversation, 19 November 2000.

17. Unsigned Memorandum of Conversation, 19 February 1965, NRO. Although Wolfe's partner in the discussion is not formally identified as a CIA executive, references in the conversation made this identification seem appropriate.

18. Minutes of Telephone Conversation with Frank Lindsay, 19 February 1965, NRO.

19. Levison, "The FULCRUM Story"; Madden interview, 1 September 2000; Smith telephone conversation, 11 November 2000.

20. John McMahon, telephone conversation with author, 8 November 2000. Lindsay did not recall the encounter. Lindsay telephone conversation, 12 November 2000.

21. McMillan letter, 18 September 1998; Levison, "The FULCRUM Story"; Lindsay and Levison interview, 7 June 1997. McMillan's feelings about Dirks changed from suspicion to respect. He had shown himself an honest and courageous man. Brockway McMillan, telephone conversation with author, 30 June 1998; Levison interview, 6 June 1997.

22. McMahon telephone conversations, 8 November 2000, 13 November 2000.

23. McMillan letter, 18 September 1998; Levison, "The FULCRUM Story"; Lindsay and Levison interview, 7 June 1997; Franklin Lindsay, telephone conversation with author, 18 November 2000.

24. Madden interview, 1 September 2000.

25. Levison, "The FULCRUM Story"; Philbrick, "Summary of the Events"; Lindsay and Levison interview, 7 June 1997; Philbrick interview, 27 August 2000; Madden interview, 1 September 2000; McMillan letter, 18 September 1998; Perry, *Management of the National Reconnaissance Program,* 95; Levison interview, 6 June 1997.

26. Lindsay and Levison interview, 7 June 1997.

27. Philbrick interview, 27 August 2000; Franklin Lindsay, interview with author, Cambridge, Mass., 8 November 1997; Lindsay telephone conversation, 12 November 2000; Levison, "The FULCRUM Story." Lindsay told Campbell that he had never been chewed out by anyone as much as by McCone—almost as though he had been unpatriotic. Ed Campbell, interview with author, Dartmouth, Mass., 20 September 1997.

28. John N. McMahon, Meeting with Itek Representatives in Headquarters on 2 March 1965, 8 March 1965, NRO; Unsigned Memorandum for Chief, Security Staff, OSA, "Program Termination Procedures (Itek/Burlington)," 9 March 1965, NRO; Madden interview, 1 September 2000. Madden later recalled McMahon as a "straight shooter," always fair even during difficult times. Madden telephone conversation, 11 November 2000; McMahon telephone conversation, 13 November 2000.

29. John N. McMahon, Discussions on Itek/NRO problems with Dr. Richard Garwin, 8 March 1965, NRO.

30. Chief, Special Projects Staff, Directorate of Science and Technology to Deputy Director of Central Intelligence, 20 March 1965, NRO.

31. Perry, *Management of the National Reconnaissance Program,* 94.

32. Ibid.

33. Franklin Lindsay to John McCone, 5 April 1965, Papers of Richard Philbrick.

34. James McDonald, Classified Message, 27 April 1965, NRO; Unidentified Itek Executive, Classified Message, 5 May 1965, NRO; James McDonald, Precontract Approval Record, 27 May 1965, NRO; John McMahon, Memorandum, 11 May 1965, NRO.

35. McMahon telephone conversation, 13 November 2000; Roy Burks, telephone conversation with author, 17 November 2000; Lindsay telephone conversation, 18 November 2000.

36. John McMahon to Albert Wheelon, "NRO Staff Visit to Itek," 4 June 1965, NRO; John McMahon, "Itek vs. Chicago Aerial Law Suit," 16 July 1965, NRO; John McMahon, "Apollo Lunar Photographic System Effort Carried on at Itek Corporation," 18 August 1965, NRO.

37. Philbrick, "Summary of the Events"; Perry, *Management of the National Reconnaissance Program,* 96–97; McMahon telephone conversations, 8 November 2000, 13 November 2000; Wheelon telephone conversation, 15 November 2000.

38. Levison interview, 6 June 1997.

39. Philbrick interview, 27 August 2000.

40. McMillan letter, 18 September 1998.

41. Wheelon telephone conversations, 15 November 2000, 19 November 2000.

42. Itek's history of cost overruns was better than competitors', and, when given the proper financial incentives, the company had "an excellent record of cost savings and control." Itek was, after all, "exceedingly profit conscious." Jack C. Ledford to Deputy Director for Science and Technology, "Itek Contract Performance History," Date Deleted, NRO. Based on the contracts described in the memorandum, it was probably written in either 1964 or early 1965. And the CIA received "outstanding service" from Itek. The people at Itek were "dedicated" and "concerned" about performance. They "looked for ways to get the absolute best for the size and weight" limitation provided for the camera. In short, Itek performed. Roy Burks, telephone conversations with author, 31 March 1998, 17 November 2000.

18. Brains into Gold

1. Franklin Lindsay, interview with author, Cambridge, Mass., 29 January 2000; "Itek Plans to Acquire Pennsylvania Optical," *Wall Street Journal,* 21 January 1966, p. 22. "Recent strength in Itek is attributed by Franklin A. Lindsay . . . partly to the company's current business outlook and partly to its application for listing on the New York Stock Exchange." "Abreast of the Market," *Wall Street Journal,* 7 July 1966, p. 31. "Mr. Lindsay says Itek's volume has doubled over the past 3.5 years, while operating profit has increased tenfold." "Itek Predicts Gains in 1966 Sales, Profits," *Wall Street Journal,* 27 September 1966, p. 27; "Perkin-Elmer Receives Optical Work Contract But Gives No Details," *Wall Street Journal,* 13 October 1966, p. 6; Itek Annual Report, 1966.

2. Alan Adelson, "Itek Has Rudimentary Photographic System for Reproducing Pictures Without Silver," *Wall Street Journal,* 10 November 1967, p. 8; "Poor Luck? Or Poor Management," *Forbes,* 1 April 1969, pp. 15–16; Ed Campbell, interview with author, Dartmouth, Mass., 20 September 1997.

3. Lindsay interview, 29 January 2000; "Poor Luck?" pp. 15–16; Dan Dorfman, "Heard on the Street," *Wall Street Journal,* 20 August 1969, p. 31.

4. *Itek News,* September 1969, pp. 1, 12; *Itek News,* December 1969, pp. 1, 12; *Itek News,* August 1970, pp. 1, 2; *Itek News,* May 1973, pp. 1, 4; Ron Ondrejka, telephone conversation with author, 2 March 1998; "Itek Says It Cut Work Force by 1,000 During the Past Year," *Wall Street Journal,* 20 November 1970, p. 22; Jeffrey T. Richelson, *A Century of Spies: Intelligence in the Twentieth Century* (New York: Oxford University Press, 1995), 331. Richard Helms recalled that Nixon told him, "If you can't verify an arms control treaty, we're not going to hold any arms control negotiations." CORONA's capabilities were critical to Nixon's willingness to negotiate and sign the treaty. Dwayne A. Day, John M. Logsdon, and Brian Latell, *Eye in the Sky: The Story of the CORONA Spy Satellites* (Washington, D.C.: Smithsonian Institution Press, 1998), 180.

5. "EGBAR on Its Face?," *FORBES,* 15 November 1974, p. 130; "Itek's Lindsay to Quit as President and Chief to Take Chairmanship," *Wall Street Journal,* 7 January 1975, p. 32.

6. "Litton Industries to Acquire Itek for $240 Million," *Wall Street Journal,* 17 January 1983, p. 7.

7. Richard Leghorn, telephone conversation with author, 30 October 2000; Robert Wells, "CableLabs Turns 10," *Communications Technology,* June 1998.

8. Lindsay interview, 29 January 2000.

9. Robin W. Winks, *Laurance S. Rockefeller: Catalyst for Conservation* (Washington: Island, 1997), 204.

ACKNOWLEDGMENTS

Two people deserve a special word of thanks, though they both died before work on this book began — McGeorge Bundy and Richard Bissell. Bundy was my history professor at New York University. Without his casual suggestion that I call Bissell to learn more about the Marshall Plan, I would not have met Bissell, or cowritten his memoirs. Of course, I owe a deep personal debt to Richard Bissell. He gave me the chance to work with him. It was an education for which I will always be thankful. My work with Bissell led directly to this book.

Among the many Itek veterans who made this book possible, I owe special thanks to William C. Britton. Fortunately, Bill was Itek's self-appointed archivist, and he preserved Itek's history in the basement of his home. Bill and his wife, Jean, allowed me to interrupt the peace of their home on many occasions. Without Bill's efforts, important parts of Itek's story could not have been told.

Walter Levison's help was invaluable. In addition to the many Itek alumni he introduced to me, he patiently spent hours talking with me on the telephone and at his home. In many ways, this book would not have been possible without his help. Sadly, he died in early 2000.

I was extremely fortunate to be able to interview at length both of Itek's first two presidents. Richard Leghorn's Itek legacy is a triumph tinged with sadness. Yet in our conversations, both on the telephone and in person, he faced his past courageously, recalling proud achievements and moments of personal disappointment with candor and charm. Dick and Nancy Leghorn were always gracious hosts.

Over the years, Franklin Lindsay was unfailingly courteous and patient with my questions. Beyond the hours he spent talking with me on the telephone and meeting with me in person, he generously opened his home and his personal papers to me. Frank and his wife, Margot, made me feel extremely welcome.

In fact, all the Itek executives, engineers, and scientists I contacted thoughtfully answered my questions over the phone, invited me into their homes, and accommodated my work schedule. One, Frank Madden, even opened his camper to me when he was vacationing on Cape Cod. Among the Itek alumni who were kind enough to talk with me, I would also like to thank Harold Alpaugh, Bill Attaya, Ray Babcock, Bill Barnes, Duncan Bruce, Ed Campbell, Jesse Cousins, Wally Davis, Pete Gilson, Geoff Harvey, Dave Healy, Jack Herther, Tom Hoban, Hut Howell, Don Kelliher, Malcolm Malcolmson, Rick Manent, Bernie Marcus, Gary Nelson, Ron Ondrejka, Richard Philbrick, Albert Pratt, Dow Smith, Howard Sprague, Paul Sullivan, John Watson, and Dick Wollensak.

CIA veterans of the period were also extremely helpful. I am grateful to the following former agency officers for their willingness to talk with me: Stan Beerli, Dino Brugioni, Roy Burks, Roland Inlow, Dan Kelly, Carol Lucas, James MacDonald, Chris Mares, John McMahon, John Parangosky, Don Schloesler, and Albert Wheelon.

I was extremely fortunate that both of the first two heads of the NRO, Joseph Charyk and Brockway McMillan, allowed me to interview them. RAND's Merton Davies was also helpful. Gen. Leo Geary and Gen. Andrew Goodpaster gave me advice and direction in the early stages of my research.

Katherine Kominis, an archivist at Boston University's Department of Special Collections, located valuable papers in the collection of President Harold Case that were essential to re-creating Itek's early history.

Barbara Freimann, Chief of the NRO's Information Access and Release Center, was extremely supportive of this project. Thanks to her efforts, important documents were located and declassified in a timely manner that greatly assisted my research.

The history of Itek is best understood in the context of the early history of overhead reconnaissance. Don Welzenbach shared with me an early draft of his unpublished study on overhead reconnaissance. It was Welzenbach who suggested that I contact Richard Leghorn. Cargill Hall, historian for the NRO, has written extensively on the early history of overhead reconnaissance. His pioneering work is essential reading for anyone concerned with this period.

I owe the greatest debt to the Rockefeller family, particularly Laurance and David Rockefeller. Although there are elements of a spy yarn in Itek's story, and the threatening thunder of the Cold War is ever present, this book is ultimately a management study. As the endnotes readily demonstrate, the management decisions made by Itek's executives, and the business climate they operated in, could never have been reconstructed without access to Laurance S. Rockefeller's Itek papers, located at the Rockefeller Archive Center (RAC).

Ellen R. C. Pomeroy, a member of Laurance Rockefeller's staff as well as his attorney, was especially helpful in arranging my access to Rockefeller's papers. Darwin Stapleton, director of the RAC, and Tom Rosenbaum, a senior RAC archivist, were always supportive and took the initiative to facilitate my research. Tom's help was simply priceless.

In order to re-create the world of Laurance Rockefeller's venture capital operation, I was also fortunate to be able to speak with veterans like Peter Crisp, Najeeb Halaby, and Ken Rind. Teddy Walkowicz, who played such a critical role in Itek's story, died long before work on this book began. Gen. Bernard Schriever, a close friend of Walkowicz, and of Leghorn and Carter, was of great assistance in helping me to understand Walkowicz. He also gave me important leads to pursue. Thanks to General Schriever, I also interviewed Ivan Getting, Reuben Mettler, Simon Ramo, Ivan Sutherland, Edward Teller, and Jasper Welch. Courtland Perkins also provided me with important details about Walkowicz, as did George Valley.

Gerry Haines, the CIA's chief historian, was extremely supportive. At the beginning of my research his comments helped me to better define the scope of my work, and as I finished the manuscript, his suggestions about the draft greatly improved it. Robin Winks, the Randolph W. Townsend, Jr., Professor of History at Yale University, offered valuable encouragement and advice when this work was in its earliest stages and read the manuscript when it was finally completed. Bradford Westerfield, a professor of political science at Yale University, and Jeffrey Landau, a managing director at the Bank of New York, both read the manuscript and offered important criticism and comments.

I am grateful to Chuck Grench, executive editor at Yale University Press when I began this book, for his early confidence in the project. Lara Heimert, who stepped into Chuck's shoes later in the game, offered me support and understanding, especially when I wrote a book that was longer than originally expected. Dan Heaton, my manuscript editor, reviewed the book with a careful eye.

My wife, Laura, deserves a special word of thanks. On weekends I often worked on this book, traveling to interview former Itek executives or writing at home. Her support never wavered, and her love and patience were invaluable. My son Steven was less than a year old when I began my research for *Spy Capitalism*. Now he is five. In many ways he has grown up with this book. On many weekends, when I worked on this manuscript in the evening, he would gently walk up to me, give me a hug for encouragement, and renew my energy. My beautiful daughter Hannah was born as this book neared completion. The wonder of her birth and the warmth of her smile are treasures I will always cherish. My father, Robert, and my mother, Nancy, now well into their eighties and seventies, respectively, have given me the same love and support as an adult as they did when I was Steven's age. Their encouragement was priceless.

INDEX

181; executive committee of, 181, 185,
186; receives earnings update, 185;
goals for fiscal *1962*, 194, 195; Leghorn proposes reorganization of,
206; pressures Lindsay for acquisitions, 224
—CORONA and: cameras for, 3, 165,
169, 170, 174, 215, 221, 222, 226; film
recovery creates opportunities for
firm, 88; unsolicited bid for, 90;
proposed camera design for, 93, 94;
film transport system, 111, 112; corona discharge and, 225, 226
—Finances of, 112, 117, 120, 125, 134,
229, 232, 236, 237, 238, 239; initial
projections, 41, 42; initial financing,
49, 50; liquidity crisis, 82, 83, 184;
phase two financing, 83, 84, 85, 86;
turns profitable, 95; annual report
of, 119, 123, 156, 229, 230; lack of
controls, 126, 127, 148, 149, 189; *1960*
earnings revisions, 160; earnings
problems, 174, 179; projections for
1962 and crisis related to, 191, 192,
193, 194, 195, 196, 197; profit surge,
222, 223, 224; V-loans, 300–301n16
—FULCRUM and, 232, 233, 234, 237,
239, 244, 245, 246, 256, 259, 260;
management gives up contract for,
247, 248, 253; scan angle for, 248,
249; presentation at headquarters,
251, 252, 253; impact on relations
with CIA, 259
—stock and shareholder issues: risks
to investors, 2, 3, 118, 119, 120, 121,
125, 126, 137, 150, 151, 155, 156, 198;
stock performance, 2, 83, 84, 115,
121, 125, 134, 135, 143, 145, 184, 190,
198, 212, 218, 230, 244, 250, 262,
263, 264, 265; development of over-
the-counter market in shares, 113;
stock offering and preparations for,
113, 114, 117, 118; prospectus for offer-

ing, 124, 125, 126; stock recommended
by Carl M. Loeb, Rhoades and Co.,
156; shares listed on NYSE, 263

Jaffe, Irving, 128
Johnson, Lyndon, 231, 232, 236
Joyce, Robert, 12

Katz, Amrom, 71, 92
Keelan, Harry, 67, 68, 69
Kennedy, John F., 158, 190, 193, 207,
219; missile gap and, 170; briefed by
Bissell, 171, 177, 178; Bay of Pigs
and, 180; dependence on Itek
technology, 184; summit with
Khrushchev, 187; Cuban Missile
Crisis and, 213, 216; assassination of,
231
Kennedy, Robert, 213
Khrushchev, Nikita, 99, 142, 143, 158,
159, 207; Open Skies and, 21, 22;
prepares for Eisenhower's visit, 157;
response to test ban proposal, 163;
Paris Summit and, 164; meeting
with Kennedy, 187
Killian, James, 87, 88, 89, 92, 253, 254;
offered position on Itek board, 147;
technological capabilities panel and,
276–277n3
King, Gilbert, 243, 263
Kissinger, Henry, Rockefeller Brothers
study project and, 23, 53, 54, 58, 79,
80
Kistiakowsky, George, 189, 198; on
Itek's historic role, 194
Kucera, George, 94, 95

Laboratory for Electronics, 37, 43
Land, Edwin, 88, 89, 92, 104, 169,
174, 190, 232, 244, 247, 253, 254,
256; Rockefeller Special Studies and,
23; asks Eisenhower to support Itek,
169, 170